Printed and bound by GZH Zagreb, Yugoslavia.

10 9 8 7 6 5 4 3 2 1

Library of Congress Catalog Card Number: 86-61531

ISBN: 0-88176-340-3

On the front cover: Cold Yogurt Soup

On the back cover (clockwise, from top left): Wine-Roasted
Chicken with Rice Dressing; Jicama Salad; Coconut
Strawberry Freeze; Pear Nut Bread; Blueberry Cheese Tart

CONTENTS

America Cooks!

What fun to explore this great country by getting acquainted with the foods enjoyed from shore to shore, in rural kitchens and on city dinner tables. This cookbook-guidebook celebrates American cooking with more than 650 recipes representing the productivity of the land and the various peoples who have come to settle in the United States.

This collection of appetizers, soups, sandwiches, main dishes, salads, vegetable and side dishes, breads and all kinds of desserts and snacks really demonstrates how **America Cooks** today. Certainly, this cooking includes such well-known "all-American" favorites as apple pie, fried chicken, roast turkey, grilled steak and corn on the cob. But present-day American cooking is also a rich mixture of the culinary heritages of the ever-growing number of nationalities who have migrated to this country.

The influences of ethnic food combinations and methods of preparation have affected cooking in America ever since the first colonists arrived and, of course, continue to do so today. In turn, the availability of ingredients and cooking utensils and materials also produces changes in the content and techniques of the cooking brought here by the many ethnic groups who have come from all parts of the world.

What is American cooking today? It is hot dogs and hamburgers, pizza and pasta, scrapple and bratwurst, tacos and guacamole, gingered pork and sweet-sour shrimp, kolaches and Stollen, roast beef and boiled potatoes, souffles and cream puffs, gumbo and candied yams. What kinds of ingredients are used in American cooking? Anything and everything, from chilies to cranberries, from corn to kiwi fruit, from rice to ripe olives, from red cabbage to coconuts. How are American foods cooked? In skillets, soup kettles, steamers, casserole dishes, woks, saucepans and Dutch ovens; on griddles and grills; in ovens and broilers.

America Cooks foods of infinite variety, both traditional and innovative at the same time. It is cooking that is not just one "style," but an ever-evolving combination of classic recipes and newly created dishes, adapting and integrating ideas from a myriad of sources.

For convenience, the book is divided into five regional chapters. Boundaries are intentionally sketchy because recipes, like people, travel across county and state lines. Each chapter brings together unique regional favorites, a selection of ethnic specialties and versatile dishes that are at home anywhere. Recipes reflect locally produced foods, the cooking heritage of the region's long-time inhabitants and the continuing culinary additions brought by newcomers.

Whether you just enjoy browsing through a cookbook or immediately check the kitchen cupboard for the ingredients to make a new recipe, you'll appreciate the hundreds of color photos and the diversity of recipes, all presented with easy-to-follow step-by-step directions. In addition, many of the recipes begin with comments that contain helpful or interesting information or suggestions. There is also an extensive Index at the end of the book to help you find just the right recipe for any occasion or for those times when you have particular ingredients on hand and want to find a great recipe in which to use them.

Start your travels through American cooking in the Yankee kitchens of the Northeast, wend your way South of the Mason-Dixon line, move up the Mississippi to the farmland of Middle America, journey West to the mountains and canyons, and cross the Continental Divide to head toward the bountiful Pacific coasts. It's a great trip!

Lobster Pot to Melting Pot

THE NORTHEAST

Great recipes have been coming to America since the first settlers landed on the rocky New England coast. The delicious trend continues, but with a difference. Those early colonists had no food markets, no convenient sources of familiar ingredients or seasonings. Modern cities are dotted with ethnic neighborhoods where newcomers can find people and foods from home and area residents can sample items from almost anywhere in the world.

Some of the recipes in this chapter have been prepared in virtually the same way since Colonial times, but most reflect the influence of the many nationalities who have come to live in the United States and the creative touches added by succeeding generations of good cooks.

Crops and game found in the New World—cranberries, turkey, pumpkins and corn, for example—determined for the most part what New England settlers ate. They simmered cranberry sauces, added the tart red berries to meat dishes and baked special pies. You'll want to prepare a tantalizing Cranberry Chuck Roast and serve a Cape Cod Cranberry Velvet Pie. Roast Turkey with Oyster Dressing is a tradition carried on today. Though Pumpkin Pie with Sour Cream Topping is a splendid dessert for Thanksgiving dinner, you can use pumpkin any time of year to make a moist and flavorful Banana Pumpkin Bread or blend it in a cheesecake mixture for a spectacular Pumpkin Cream Cheese Tart.

Cornmeal was a staple used for breads and for desserts. Indian Pudding is a homey molasses-sweetened dessert, even better served warm with a scoop of vanilla ice cream. The Pennsylvania Dutch fried slices of cornmeal mixed with pork; Old-Fashioned Scrapple is still delicious with sausage for a Sunday brunch. The Dutch in New Amsterdam, later renamed New York, introduced vinegar-dressed chopped cabbage, which is still popular today. The crunchy combination called Colorful Coleslaw adds carrots and green pepper for an easy salad.

Later immigrants who poured through the port of New York have influenced the variety of foods enjoyed by following generations. Jewish families brought special foods, including Cheese Blintzes and their Sabbath bread, Challah. They also introduced the chewy doughnut-shaped Egg Bagels, which are now universally popular. Irish Corned Beef and Cabbage is mighty welcome on a cold winter night. Add potatoes, onions and carrots to the pot and you have what Yankees call a New England boiled dinner.

New recipes come to us in other ways, too. Americans who travel abroad return with an interest in the foods of countries visited. You don't have to come from Italy to serve Pasta Antipasto as an appetizer or Zabaglione as a dessert. Cooks of many backgrounds rave about Hot and Sour Soup or Almond Chicken. They welcome the spiciness of Festive Greek Beef Cubes and admire the subtle seasonings of Chicken Portuguaise.

The entire region is noted for its fish and seafood. You'll want to try creamy New England Clam Chowder thickened with potatoes and crackers, or Boston Bouillabaise, which is a marvelous meal of fish and shellfish in saffron-flavored broth. An up-to-date Manhattan Fish Stew boasts tomatoes with thyme and white fish in a base of potato soup.

In addition to chowders and stews, look for Oven-Poached Scallops, Whiting with Polenta, Chatham Scrod à la King and Cod Fillets Kiev, golden brown on the outside with parsley butter inside. You'll also savor Diamond Jim Flounder cooked the way the flamboyant Mr. Brady liked it.

Meat choices offer the same delectable variety. Don't pass up a Crusty Rack of Lamb roasted to perfection or Lamb Chops with Maple Fruit Sauce, which features apricots and raisins simmered in maple syrup. Pinwheel Loaf Wellington is baked in a pastry crust, and Ham Steak Viennese rests on a bed of well-seasoned sauerkraut.

Kitchen gardens and truck farms add seasonal fruits and vegetables to the choices shipped in from around the country. In this northern climate, root vegetables, beans and squash grow and store particularly well. New England Baked Beans made with salt pork and molasses are particularly famous, especially when served with steamed Boston Brown Bread. Potatoes can be baked or boiled simply—or blended elegantly with caviar in a North Sea Potato Salad. Blushing Beet Salad Ring shows off the beautiful red color of another root vegetable. You'll certainly want to try a Winter Vegetable Melange of matchstick strips of cooked rutabaga, carrot and turnip.

Regional desserts also parallel the tastes and backgrounds of the residents. Try an elegant Viennese Almond Torte, a sinfully rich New York Cheesecake or chocolate Pots de Creme for a special occasion. Simpler delights such as Sour Cream Gingerbread, Maple Syrup Doughnuts and Blueberry Grunt are great family desserts to serve any day of the week.

PASTA ANTIPASTO

As a first course for festive occasions, an Italian appetizer platter of cheese, salami and marinated vegetables is a work of art for eye and appetite.

Makes about 8 servings

½ **pound rotelle or ziti macaroni**
1 **cup bottled classic herbal Italian dressing**
1 **cup sliced mushrooms**
1 **cup pitted ripe olives**
½ **cup sliced roasted red bell pepper**
  Lettuce leaves
3 **medium tomatoes, sliced**
3 **hard-cooked eggs, sliced**
1 **cup cooked or canned artichoke hearts, cut into halves**
¼ **pound thinly sliced salami or pepperoni**
¼ **pound provolone or mozzarella cheese, cut into thin strips**

1. Cook macaroni according to package directions; rinse under cold water until completely cool. Drain well.

2. Combine ⅔ cup of the dressing, the mushrooms, olives and red pepper in large bowl. Add macaroni; toss to mix well.

3. On large lettuce-lined platter, arrange macaroni mixture, tomatoes, eggs, artichokes, salami and cheese; refrigerate, covered.

4. Just before serving, drizzle with the remaining ⅓ cup dressing.

HOT AND SOUR SOUP

Highly spiced Szechuan cooking has an avid following among New Yorkers who not only enjoy Chinese restaurants but also want to prepare this favorite soup at home.

Makes 6 to 8 servings

1 **ounce dried Chinese mushrooms**
  Boiling water
6 **ounces uncooked boneless lean pork**
4 **ounces cooked ham**
2 **quarts chicken stock**
½ **cup dry white wine**
4 **teaspoons soy sauce**
½ **teaspoon Chinese chili sauce**
2½ **tablespoons cornstarch**
5 **tablespoons water**
1 **small red bell pepper, cut into slivers**
½ **cup water chestnuts, sliced**
2 **teaspoons vinegar**
1 **teaspoon sesame oil**
1 **large egg**
8 **green onions, finely chopped**
8 **ounces bean curd, diced (½-inch)**
8 **ounces shrimp, shelled, deveined**

1. Place mushrooms in bowl with boiling water to cover; let stand 30 minutes. Drain. Remove and discard stems; cut caps into thin slices.

2. Cut pork and ham into "match-stick" thin strips.

3. Mix stock, wine, soy sauce and chili sauce in Dutch oven; heat mixture to boiling. Reduce heat; simmer, uncovered, 5 minutes.

(Continued)

4. Mix cornstarch and 4 tablespoons of the water in small bowl; slowly stir into soup. Cook and stir until soup boils. Add mushrooms, pork, ham, red bell pepper and water chestnuts. Simmer, uncovered, 5 minutes. Stir in vinegar and oil.

5. Beat egg and remaining 1 tablespoon water in small bowl; gradually drizzle into soup while stirring vigorously. Add onions, bean curd and shrimp; cook until shrimp are opaque, 1 to 2 minutes.

CURRIED CAULIFLOWER HORS D'OEUVRE

Makes 8 to 12 servings

1 **medium cauliflower, trimmed**
1 **teaspoon salt**
2 **cups mayonnaise**
1 **tablespoon grated onion**
2 **teaspoons curry powder**
1 **teaspoon garlic powder**
  Assorted crackers

1. Place cauliflower in large saucepan; add cold water to cover. Add salt; heat to boiling. Reduce heat; simmer, covered, until fork pierces stem easily, about 20 minutes. Drain well; let cool.

2. Mix mayonnaise, onion, curry powder and garlic powder in medium bowl. Spread on cauliflower to cover completely; refrigerate, covered, 24 hours.

3. Serve with crackers and a small knife for cutting cauliflower.

CHEESE CHUTNEY SQUARES

Delicious puffed-up hot canapes with the spiciness of chutney and mellowness of Cheddar.

Makes 20 squares

¾ **cup shredded Cheddar cheese**
2 **tablespoons chutney**
½ **teaspoon Worcestershire sauce**
1 **large egg white**
5 **slices bread, toasted, crusts trimmed**
2 **tablespoons butter, room temperature**
  Cherry tomato wedges and parsley sprigs for garnish

1. Mix cheese, chutney and Worcestershire sauce in small bowl.

2. Beat egg white in small mixer bowl until soft peaks form. Fold in cheese mixture.

3. Spread toast with butter; cut each piece into 4 squares. Spread squares evenly with cheese mixture; place on baking sheet.

4. Broil 5 to 6 inches from heat source just until puffy and brown, 1 to 2 minutes. Garnish with tomatoes and parsley.

Kielbasa Vegetable Soup

KIELBASA VEGETABLE SOUP

Makes 6 to 8 servings

2 medium onions, chopped
2 medium leeks (white part only), thinly sliced
1 large clove garlic, minced
3 tablespoons butter or margarine
4 carrots, cut into julienne strips
5 cups chicken stock
⅓ cup instant rice
8 ounces kielbasa or other Polish sausage, sliced
6 ounces fresh spinach, cut into 3-inch pieces
2 small zucchini, sliced
1 cup frozen green beans, thawed
    Salt and pepper to taste
    Grated Parmesan cheese, if desired

1. Saute onions, leeks and garlic in 2 tablespoons of the butter in Dutch oven over medium heat until soft, about 5 minutes. Add carrots; saute 3 minutes longer.

2. Add stock; heat to boiling. Stir in rice; reduce heat. Simmer, covered, 10 minutes.

3. Meanwhile, saute kielbasa in remaining 1 tablespoon butter in medium skillet over medium heat until brown, about 5 minutes; drain and pat dry with paper toweling.

4. Add spinach, zucchini, green beans, salt and pepper to soup; mix well. Simmer, covered, 5 minutes. Stir in kielbasa. Serve with Parmesan cheese.

BUTTERNUT SQUASH BISQUE

You'll recognize a winter butternut squash by its buff to dark yellow color and its banjo shape with long neck and bulbous bottom.

Makes 6 to 8 servings

1 cup diced onion
1 cup diced celery
2 tablespoons butter or margarine
9 cups cubed, seeded, pared butternut squash
    (about 3½ pounds)
3 cans (13¾ ounces each) chicken broth
¾ cup milk
½ teaspoon salt
⅛ teaspoon hot red pepper sauce
    Ground nutmeg to taste
1 tablespoon chopped parsley

1. Saute onion and celery in butter in 4-quart saucepan over medium heat until the vegetables are soft, about 5 minutes.

2. Stir in squash and broth; heat to boiling. Reduce heat; simmer, covered, stirring occasionally, until squash is tender, 15 to 20 minutes. Let cool slightly, uncovered.

3. Process ⅓ of the soup at a time in blender until smooth; return to saucepan. Stir in milk, salt, red pepper sauce and nutmeg. Heat over medium heat just until hot.

4. To serve, ladle into soup bowls; sprinkle with parsley.

SPINACH SOUP WITH TINY MEATBALLS

Makes 6 servings

   4 pounds beef soup bones
   2 quarts water
   1 can (6 ounces) tomato paste
2½ teaspoons salt
   ¼ teaspoon pepper
   ¾ pound ground beef
   1 cup fresh breadcrumbs
   1 large egg
   ¼ cup grated Parmesan cheese
   3 tablespoons chopped parsley
   1 clove garlic, minced
   ¼ teaspoon dried basil, crumbled
   1 pound fresh spinach, chopped
   ¾ cup uncooked soup pasta

1. Combine bones, water, tomato paste, 2 teaspoons of the salt and ⅛ teaspoon of the pepper in large saucepan. Heat to boiling; reduce heat. Simmer, covered, 1 hour; remove and discard bones.

2. Combine beef, breadcrumbs, egg, cheese, parsley, garlic, basil, remaining ½ teaspoon salt and remaining ⅛ teaspoon pepper in large bowl; mix well. Shape into ¾-inch balls.

3. Add meatballs to hot stock; simmer, covered, stirring occasionally, 15 minutes. Stir in spinach and pasta; cook, uncovered, until pasta is tender, about 10 minutes.

NEW ENGLAND CLAM CHOWDER

Crackers soaked in milk and diced white potatoes thicken this marvelous seafood soup relished from Colonial days.

Makes 6 servings

   2 dozen fresh clams, scrubbed*
   Water
   ¼ pound salt pork or bacon, minced
   ½ cup finely chopped onion
   5 cups diced potatoes
   2 cups milk
   8 saltine crackers
   2 cups half-and-half
   2 tablespoons margarine or butter
   Chopped parsley for garnish

1. Combine clams and 1 cup water in large pot; heat to boiling. Reduce heat; simmer until clams open, 5 to 8 minutes. Mince clams; discard shells and any unopened clams. Strain and measure cooking liquid; add water if needed to make 1½ cups.

2. Cook salt pork in large saucepan until brown and crisp; remove salt pork from pan, reserving 2 tablespoons drippings.

3. Saute onion in reserved drippings over medium heat until soft, about 4 minutes. Stir in reserved cooking liquid and the potatoes. Heat to boiling; reduce heat. Simmer until potatoes are tender, about 10 minutes.

4. Pour milk over saltines in medium bowl; let stand until soft. Stir milk and saltines, the half-and-half, salt pork and margarine into saucepan. Cook over medium-low heat, stirring occasionally, just until hot. Garnish with parsley.

Note: *2 cans (8 ounces each) minced clams can be substituted for fresh. Omit Step 1. Drain clams, reserving liquid; add enough water to liquid to make 1½ cups.*

CLAM FRITTERS

Makes 8 to 12 servings

   1 cup all-purpose flour
1½ teaspoons baking powder
   1 teaspoon salt
   ¼ teaspoon ground black pepper
   ¼ teaspoon onion powder
   2 cans (6½ ounces each) minced clams, drained,
      liquid reserved
   ¼ cup milk
   2 large eggs, separated
   1 tablespoon vegetable oil
   3 cups cooked rice, cool
   ¼ cup minced green bell pepper
   Vegetable oil for frying
   Devil Sauce (recipe follows)

1. Sift flour, baking powder, salt, ground pepper and onion powder into large bowl. Whisk ½ cup of the reserved clam liquid, the milk, egg yolks and 1 tablespoon oil in small bowl until blended. Add to flour mixture; beat until smooth. Stir in clams, rice and green bell pepper.

2. Heat 3 inches oil in large deep saucepan to 370°F. Beat egg whites in small mixer bowl until stiff but not dry; fold into rice mixture.

3. Carefully drop batter by heaping tablespoons into oil; fry, turning once, until golden, about 2½ minutes per side. Drain on paper toweling; serve with Devil Sauce.

DEVIL SAUCE

   1 can (10¾ ounces) condensed tomato soup
   ¼ cup clam juice
   2 teaspoons prepared mustard
   3 to 6 drops hot red pepper sauce

Mix all ingredients in small saucepan; heat over medium heat until hot.

MANHATTAN FISH STEW

Residents of Manhattan are not alone in liking tomatoes in their clam chowders and delicious fish stews.

Makes 4 servings

1½ cups sliced carrots
   1 cup water
   1 can (10 to 12 ounces) condensed cream of
      potato soup
   1 can (10 ounces) tomatoes, undrained, chopped
   1 package (9 ounces) frozen cut green beans,
      thawed
   1 can (5 ounces) evaporated milk
   1 teaspoon onion salt
   ¼ teaspoon dried thyme, crumbled
   1 pound fresh or thawed frozen fish fillets, cut
      into 1-inch pieces
   Crusty bread or crackers

1. Combine carrots and water in large saucepan; simmer, covered, until carrots are almost tender, about 15 minutes.

2. Stir in potato soup, tomatoes, beans, milk, onion salt and thyme; heat to boiling. Stir in fish; reduce heat. Simmer, covered, until fish flakes with fork, 10 minutes. Serve with bread.

BOSTON BOUILLABAISSE

Pronounce it boo-yuh-base, *but call it delicious as you savor the mixed fish and shellfish stew in its saffron-yellow broth.*

Makes 8 servings

 ¾ **cup chopped onion**
 ¾ **cup sliced celery**
 1 **clove garlic, minced**
 ⅓ **cup butter**
 2 **cans (16 ounces each) tomatoes, undrained, chopped**
 2 **cups fish stock or bottled clam juice**
 1 **cup water**
 ½ **teaspoon dried thyme, crumbled**
 1 **bay leaf, finely crumbled**
 1 **pound cod fillets**
 1 **pound pollock fillets**
 1 **pound flounder fillets**
 1 **pound sea scallops**
   Salt and pepper to taste
 ½ **teaspoon saffron threads, if desired, crushed**
 2 **small lobsters, if desired, cooked**
   French bread

1. Saute onion, celery and garlic in butter in large saucepan until soft, about 5 minutes. Stir in tomatoes, stock, water,

(Continued)

thyme and bay leaf; heat to boiling. Reduce heat; simmer 10 minutes.

2. Cut fillets into 2-inch pieces. Add fillets and scallops to soup; simmer 10 minutes longer. Stir in salt, pepper, and saffron.

3. Remove meat from lobster tails; dice. Crack lobster claws and remove meat. Add lobster to soup; serve with bread.

MARINATED HERRING

Crumbled blue cheese harmonizes elegantly with wine and herring in a dilled sour cream sauce.

Makes 8 servings

 ½ **cup sour cream**
 1 **tablespoon lemon juice**
 1 **tablespoon chopped green onion or chives**
 1 **teaspoon dill weed**
 1 **teaspoon sugar**
 ½ **teaspoon salt**
 ¼ **cup crumbled Danish blue cheese**
 1 **jar (12 ounces) wine herring snacks**

Combine all ingredients except herring in medium bowl; mix well. Gently fold in herring; refrigerate, covered, at least 2 hours to allow flavors to blend.

Boston Bouillabaisse

CURRIED APPLE SOUP

Curry powder releases its full flavor and color in heated butter or oil. That's why it is often stirred into sauteed mixtures at the beginning of a recipe.

Makes 8 servings

- 2 large sweet onions, coarsely chopped
- ¼ cup butter or margarine
- 2 tablespoons curry powder
- 1 quart apple juice, hot
- 4 envelopes instant chicken broth powder
- 2 tablespoons cornstarch
- ¼ cup cold water
- 4 large egg yolks, lightly beaten
- 1 cup whipping cream
- 2 apples, pared, cored, finely chopped
  Juice of 1 lemon
  Salt and freshly ground pepper to taste
  Unpared red apple slices for garnish

1. Saute onions in butter in large saucepan over medium heat until soft, about 5 minutes; stir in curry powder. Stir in apple juice and broth powder.

2. Mix cornstarch with cold water in small bowl; whisk into saucepan. Cook and stir over medium-low heat until mixture thickens and boils for 1 minute.

3. Gradually whisk 1 cup of the hot mixture into egg yolks in small bowl; gradually whisk egg yolks into remaining hot mixture in pan. Cook and stir 1 minute; do not boil. Remove from heat.

4. Add cream to pan; mix well. Stir in chopped apples. Process soup in blender until smooth. Add lemon juice, salt and pepper.

5. Reheat soup until hot or refrigerate until cold. Serve garnished with apple slices.

Garden Vegetable Soup

HALE AND HEARTY BEEF CHOWDER

Sprinkling flour over the cooked vegetables is an easy way to add the thickening and keep the milk broth smooth.

Makes 8 to 10 servings

- ¼ cup butter
- 3 to 4 medium potatoes, pared, shredded
- 1 stalk celery, shredded
- 1 small onion, minced
- 1¼ cups water
- 1 tablespoon all-purpose flour
- 3 cups milk
- 1 can (7 ounces) vacuum-packed whole kernel corn
- 1 package (3 ounces) smoked sliced beef, chopped
- 1 teaspoon beef stock base
- ¾ teaspoon salt
  Pinch pepper
- 1 cup sour cream

1. Melt butter in large saucepan; stir in potatoes, celery and onion. Add water; heat to boiling. Reduce heat; simmer, covered, until potatoes are tender, about 10 minutes.

2. Sprinkle flour over potatoes; mix well. Cook and stir over medium heat 1 minute. Gradually stir in milk; cook and stir over low heat 3 minutes.

3. Add corn, beef, stock base, salt and pepper; mix well. Stir in sour cream; cook just until hot. Do not boil.

GARDEN VEGETABLE SOUP

Makes 4 servings

- 1 cup chopped onion
- 1 clove garlic, minced
- 2 tablespoons corn oil
- 3 cups beef broth
- 2 tomatoes, coarsely chopped
- 1 cup sliced carrots
- ¼ pound green beans, cut in 1¼-inch pieces
- 1 small zucchini, sliced
- ¼ teaspoon dried thyme, crumbled
- ¼ teaspoon pepper
- ⅛ teaspoon celery seed
- 2 tablespoons cornstarch
- ¼ cup cold water

1. Saute onion and garlic in oil over medium heat in Dutch oven until soft, about 4 minutes.

2. Stir in broth, tomatoes, carrots, beans, zucchini, thyme, pepper and celery seed. Heat to boiling; reduce heat. Simmer, covered, until the vegetables are tender, about 20 minutes.

3. Mix cornstarch with water in small bowl until smooth; stir into soup. Cook and stir over medium heat until soup thickens and bubbles for 3 minutes.

Hoagie

HOAGIES

Makes 6 to 9 servings

1 jar (6 ounces) mild pickled Italian peppers
   (peperoncini), undrained
1 medium onion, thinly sliced
3 submarine or Italian rolls (8 inches long), split
⅓ cup butter or margarine, room temperature
3 tablespoons spicy coarse-grain mustard
12 slices German bologna
6 slices Muenster cheese, cut diagonally into
   halves
3 teaspoons fines herbes*
12 slices beerwurst
6 slices mild Cheddar cheese, cut diagonally into
   halves

1. Combine pickled peppers and onion in medium bowl; toss to mix.

2. Spread cut sides of rolls with butter, then with mustard.

3. For each sandwich, layer 4 bologna slices and 4 pieces of Muenster cheese on bottoms of rolls. Sprinkle with fines herbes; top with 4 beerwurst slices.

4. Drain peppers and onions; pat dry with paper toweling. Arrange on top of beerwurst; top each with 4 pieces of Cheddar cheese. Cover with tops of rolls; cut sandwiches crosswise into halves or thirds to serve.

Note: A mixture of equal parts chives, parsley and tarragon can be substituted for fines herbes.

CORNED BEEF AND CABBAGE

Makes about 12 servings

1 corned beef brisket (3 to 4 pounds)
6 whole peppercorns
1 bay leaf
2 tablespoons packed brown sugar
1 tablespoon all-purpose flour
3 tablespoons catsup
½ teaspoon dried oregano, crumbled
¼ teaspoon grated orange rind
⅛ teaspoon cracked pepper
1 head green cabbage, cut into 12 wedges
2 green bell peppers, cut into rings

1. Combine corned beef, peppercorns and bay leaf in Dutch oven; add water to cover. Heat to boiling; reduce heat. Simmer, covered, until meat is tender, 3 to 4 hours.

2. Remove meat from cooking liquid; place, fat side up, on rack in roasting pan. Mix sugar and flour in small bowl; stir in catsup, oregano, orange rind and cracked pepper. Spread mixture on top of brisket.

3. Bake in preheated 350°F oven until topping is set, 15 to 20 minutes.

4. Meanwhile, heat cooking liquid to boiling. Add cabbage; boil until crisp-tender, 10 to 15 minutes. Add green pepper; boil 3 minutes.

5. Drain cabbage and green pepper; arrange on platter with corned beef. Cut corned beef across the grain into thin slices.

DELI BRISKET BAKE

Slow cooking gives foil-wrapped beef brisket ample time to take on the enticing flavors of mustard and mixed pickling spices.

Makes 4 to 6 servings

　1 beef brisket (2½ pounds)
½ cup prepared mustard
¼ cup mixed whole pickling spices
　1 can (27 ounces) sauerkraut, rinsed, drained
¼ pound Swiss cheese, shredded
　　Prepared mustard

1. Place brisket on large piece of aluminum foil; spread all sides of brisket with ½ cup mustard and pickling spices. Wrap securely in foil; place in 10× 8-inch baking pan.

2. Bake in preheated 225°F oven until very tender, about 3½ hours.

3. Remove brisket from foil. Scrape off pickling spices; trim and discard excess fat. Cut brisket crosswise into 4 to 6 equal pieces; return to baking pan.

4. Place sauerkraut on top of brisket; sprinkle with cheese. Broil until cheese is melted and light brown, 8 to 10 minutes; serve with mustard.

CRUNCHY CORNED BEEF SANDWICHES

Makes 6 sandwiches

　1 small green bell pepper, cut into thin strips
　1 small red bell pepper, cut into thin strips
　2 tablespoons red wine vinegar
　3 tablespoons butter, room temperature
½ teaspoon celery salt
12 slices rye bread
12 slices (4 × 4 inches) Swiss cheese
　1 pound thinly sliced cooked corned beef

1. Add green and red peppers to large saucepan of boiling water; cook 2 minutes. Drain well; toss with vinegar in medium bowl. Refrigerate, covered, 30 minutes.

2. Mix butter and celery salt in small bowl; spread bread with seasoned butter.

3. Place 1 cheese slice on each of 6 slices of bread; top with 2 strips each green and red pepper. Top each with ⅙ of the corned beef, then with 2 more strips each green and red pepper. Top with remaining cheese slices; cover with remaining bread.

4. Wrap each sandwich securely in double thickness of heavy-duty aluminum foil; place on grill rack over medium-hot coals. Grill, turning occasionally, 15 minutes.

Crunchy Corned Beef Sandwiches

GREEK BROILED LAMB CHOPS

Poking holes in the meat lets mint and lemon juice flavor the inside as well as the surface of the lamb.

Makes 4 servings

4 lean loin lamb chops, ¾ inch thick
2 tablespoons lemon juice
2 tablespoons chopped fresh mint or 2 teaspoons dried mint, crumbled
⅛ teaspoon ground cinnamon
⅛ teaspoon ground nutmeg
⅛ teaspoon garlic powder
   Salt and pepper to taste
   Fluted lemon slices, cut into halves, and fresh mint sprig for garnish

1. Sprinkle lamb with lemon juice, chopped mint, cinnamon, nutmeg, garlic, salt and pepper; pierce all over with fork. Refrigerate, covered, 4 to 8 hours.

2. Broil or charcoal-grill, turning once, until brown and crisp outside and cooked to desired degree of doneness in center. Garnish with lemon slices and mint sprig.

LAMB CHOPS WITH MAPLE FRUIT SAUCE

Makes 8 servings

8 loin lamb chops
1 tablespoon bacon drippings or vegetable oil
1½ cups beef stock
1½ tablespoons cornstarch
⅔ cup packed brown sugar
½ cup pure maple syrup
⅓ cup halved dried apricots
¼ cup raisins
1 tablespoon minced onion
½ teaspoon ground ginger

1. Cook lamb chops in bacon drippings in large skillet over medium heat, turning once, until brown. Remove chops; keep warm. Pour off and discard fat.

2. Mix stock and cornstarch in skillet until smooth; stir in remaining ingredients. Cook, stirring constantly, over medium heat to boiling. Return lamb chops to skillet; reduce heat. Simmer, covered, until lamb is tender, 12 to 15 minutes. Serve with sauce.

Greek Broiled Lamb Chops

Ham Steak Viennese

HAM STEAK VIENNESE

*For a milder sauerkraut flavor, rinse the kraut quickly in
cold running water. Drain well and proceed with the recipe.*

Makes 4 servings

    1 ham steak (1 pound), patted dry
    1 tablespoon butter
  ½ teaspoon ground black pepper
    1 can (27 ounces) sauerkraut, rinsed, drained
    1 can (16 ounces) tomatoes, undrained, chopped
    1 green bell pepper, cut into 1-inch strips
2½ tablespoons instant minced onion
  ¼ teaspoon dried thyme, crumbled

1. Cook ham in butter in large skillet over medium heat,
turning once, until brown, about 8 minutes. Sprinkle with
¼ teaspoon of the ground pepper.

2. Combine remaining ¼ teaspoon ground pepper and remaining ingredients in large bowl; mix well. Spread in
greased shallow 2-quart baking dish; top with ham steak.

3. Bake, covered, in preheated 325°F oven 30 minutes. Uncover dish; continue baking 20 minutes.

BUFFET BEEF AU JUS SANDWICHES

Makes 6 to 8 servings

  2 large sweet onions, sliced
  2 cups water
¼ cup soy sauce
  2 cloves garlic, minced
½ package (1¼ ounces) dry onion soup mix
  1 boneless beef tip or top round roast (2 to 3
      pounds)
    French rolls, split, toasted
  1 cup shredded Swiss cheese

1. Place 1 of the onions, the water, soy sauce, garlic and
soup mix in bottom of 2-quart baking dish. Place beef, fat
side down, in dish; top with remaining onion.

(Continued)

2. Bake, covered, in preheated 325°F oven until beef is
tender, 2 to 3 hours. Remove beef from dish; let stand 20
minutes. Strain and degrease pan juices.

3. Cut beef across the grain into thin slices. Combine slices
and pan juices in large saucepan; heat until hot.

4. Place hot beef slices on rolls, open-faced; sprinkle with
cheese. Broil until cheese is melted; serve with pan juices.

DUTCH RAREBIT WITH BACON CURLS

*When making bacon curls, partially cook bacon just long
enough so that you can wind it around the tines of a fork.
Fasten with a wooden pick and finish cooking the bacon.*

Makes 6 servings

12 slices bacon
  2 tablespoons butter
  4 cups shredded Gouda cheese (1 pound)
  1 tablespoon Worcestershire sauce
½ teaspoon dry mustard
⅛ teaspoon ground red pepper
  2 large eggs, lightly beaten
½ cup half-and-half
12 thin tomato slices
12 slices buttered toast

1. Cook bacon in large skillet over medium heat until light
brown but still soft; remove to paper toweling. Roll up
bacon slices; secure with wooden picks. Drain fat from
skillet. Cook bacon curls in skillet until crisp. Drain on
paper toweling; remove picks.

2. Melt butter in heavy 2-quart saucepan over medium-low
heat. Add cheese; cook, stirring constantly, until cheese is
melted. Stir in Worcestershire sauce, mustard and red pepper; remove from heat.

3. Mix eggs and half-and-half in small bowl; stir into cheese
mixture until blended. Cook over medium-low heat, stirring constantly, until thickened; do not boil.

4. Arrange tomato slices and bacon curls on top of toast;
top with cheese sauce.

OLD-FASHIONED SCRAPPLE

Makes 10 to 12 servings

1 pound cooked boneless pork, chopped
1 can (14½ ounces) chicken broth
1 cup yellow cornmeal
¼ teaspoon dried thyme, crumbled
¼ teaspoon salt
½ cup all-purpose flour
¼ teaspoon pepper
3 to 6 tablespoons vegetable oil
　Hot cooked breakfast sausage patties and fresh
　　fruit slices, if desired
　Fresh herbs for garnish

1. Combine pork, broth, cornmeal, thyme and salt in large saucepan; heat, stirring frequently, to boiling. Reduce heat; simmer, stirring constantly, until mixture is very thick, about 2 minutes. Remove from heat.

2. Line 8×8×2-inch baking pan or 9×5×3-inch loaf pan with waxed paper, allowing 3- to 4-inch overhang at ends of pan. Spoon pork mixture into pan; press firmly with back of spoon. Refrigerate, covered, 4 hours or overnight.

3. Unmold scrapple; cut into ½-inch thick squares. Mix flour and pepper in shallow bowl; dip scrapple into flour mixture to coat lightly.

4. Fry scrapple in oil in large skillet over medium heat, turning once, until light brown. Serve with sausage and fruit; garnish with herbs.

RED WINE ROUND ROAST

Makes 8 to 10 servings

1 beef bottom round roast, boned and tied (3½
　　pounds)
2 tablespoons vegetable oil
½ teaspoon poultry seasoning
½ teaspoon pumpkin pie spice
　Pinch garlic powder
　Salt and pepper to taste
½ cup dry red wine
½ cup water
1 bay leaf
2 cups small white onions
2 cups sliced mushrooms
2 tablespoons all-purpose flour
¼ cup cold water

1. Cook beef in oil in Dutch oven over medium heat, turning occasionally, until brown on all sides, 15 to 20 minutes. Sprinkle with poultry seasoning, pumpkin pie spice, garlic powder, salt and pepper.

2. Add wine, ½ cup water and bay leaf to Dutch oven; heat to boiling. Reduce heat; simmer, covered, until beef is almost tender, about 2½ hours. Add onions and mushrooms; continue cooking until onions are tender and beef is very tender, about 30 minutes longer. Remove and discard bay leaf; remove beef and vegetables with slotted spoon to platter.

3. Mix flour with cold water in small cup; gradually whisk into cooking liquid. Cook and stir over medium-low heat until sauce thickens and bubbles for 1 minute; serve with beef and vegetables.

Old-Fashioned Scrapple

SAVORY BEEF ROLL

Tender braised round steak contains a luscious cache of ham, hard-cooked egg slices, raisins, olives and seasonings to enjoy with tomato-rich pan juices.

Makes 6 servings

1 boneless beef round steak or flank steak (2
　　pounds)
¼ cup fresh lemon juice
2 tablespoons soy sauce
2 cloves garlic, minced
½ teaspoon pepper
½ pound cooked smoked ham, cut into thin strips
2 hard-cooked eggs, sliced
2 tablespoons raisins
6 green olives, chopped
2 cups water
1 can (8 ounces) tomato sauce
1 medium onion, sliced
¼ cup cider vinegar

1. Pound beef with flat meat mallet to ¼-inch thickness; sprinkle with lemon juice, soy sauce, garlic and pepper. Top beef with ham and eggs; sprinkle with raisins and olives.

2. Starting at narrow end, roll up beef, jelly-roll style; tuck in ends. Tie beef securely in several places with kitchen string; place in deep skillet or Dutch oven.

3. Add water, tomato sauce, onion and vinegar to pan; heat to boiling. Reduce heat; simmer, covered, until beef is fork-tender, about 1¼ hours.

4. Remove beef to deep serving platter; remove string. Pour sauce and onions over beef; cut beef crosswise into thin slices.

Savory Beef Roll

WARM-UP WINTER SUPPER

Here's a meal-in-one stewpot with beef cubes and vegetables simmered in a caraway-flavored beer and onion gravy.

Makes 4 to 6 servings

- 1½ pounds boneless beef chuck, cut into 1-inch cubes
- 2 tablespoons all-purpose flour
- 2 tablespoons vegetable oil
- 1½ cups beer
- ½ cup water
- 1 envelope beefy-onion or onion soup mix
- ½ teaspoon caraway seeds
- 4 medium potatoes, pared, cut into 2 × 1-inch pieces
- 4 carrots, cut into 2-inch lengths
- 1 package (10 ounces) frozen cut green beans

1. Toss beef with flour in medium bowl to coat evenly. Cook beef in oil in large skillet over medium heat, turning frequently, until brown, about 10 minutes.

2. Mix beer, water, soup mix and caraway seeds in small bowl. Add to beef; mix well. Heat to boiling; reduce heat. Simmer, covered, 30 minutes.

3. Stir in potatoes and carrots; simmer, covered, 30 minutes longer. Stir in beans; continue cooking until beef and vegetables are tender, about 10 minutes longer.

FESTIVE GREEK BEEF CUBES

Makes 6 to 8 servings

- 3 pounds boneless beef chuck, cut into 1-inch cubes
- ½ cup butter, melted
- ½ teaspoon salt
- ⅛ teaspoon pepper
- 1 package (16 ounces) frozen pearl onions
- 1 can (6 ounces) tomato paste
- 2 tablespoons dry red wine
- 2 tablespoons raisins
- 1 tablespoon packed brown sugar
- 1 large clove garlic, minced
- ½ teaspoon ground cumin
- ¼ teaspoon ground cloves
- 1 stick cinnamon (about 2 inches)
- 2 bay leaves
- Hot cooked rice or crusty bread

1. Combine beef, butter, salt and pepper in 3 to 4 quart baking dish; mix well. Top with onions.

2. Mix tomato paste, wine, raisins, sugar, garlic, cumin and cloves in medium bowl. Mixture will be stiff. Spread over onions; do not stir. Insert cinnamon stick in center of beef; tuck in bay leaves.

3. Bake, covered, in preheated 300°F oven 3 hours. Remove and discard cinnamon stick and bay leaves. Stir stew gently; serve over rice or with bread.

Warm-Up Winter Supper

Crusty Rack of Lamb

CRUSTY RACK OF LAMB

Serve a rack, or standing rib, of lamb prepared in the French style—pink and rare in the center.

Makes 2 servings

  1 rack of lamb (1¾ to 2 pounds; 6 to 8 ribs)
    Salt
    White pepper
  1 tablespoon Dijon-style mustard
  1 tablespoon minced parsley
  2 teaspoons olive oil
  1 teaspoon dry vermouth
  1 clove garlic, minced
  ½ teaspoon dried oregano, crumbled
  ¼ teaspoon dried thyme, crumbled
  ½ cup soft breadcrumbs
    Watercress for garnish

1. Trim and discard surface fat from lamb; sprinkle lamb with salt and pepper. Place lamb, rounded side up, on rack in roasting pan. Insert meat thermometer into thickest part of meat away from bone.

2. Roast in preheated 450°F oven 15 minutes. While lamb is roasting, combine mustard, parsley, oil, vermouth, garlic, oregano and thyme in small bowl; mix well. Stir in breadcrumbs.

3. Press breadcrumb mixture firmly on top of lamb. Roast until thermometer registers 145°F, 10 to 15 minutes longer. Transfer to serving platter; garnish with watercress.

BEEF SHORT RIBS WITH HORSERADISH

The grill-easy way to do short ribs outdoors. Foil wrapping cooks them tender; basting with nippy horseradish seasons them with authority.

Makes 5 to 6 servings

  3 pounds beef short ribs
  2 tablespoons dry white wine
  2 tablespoons prepared horseradish
  1 tablespoon vegetable oil
  ½ teaspoon dry mustard
  ½ teaspoon salt
  ¼ teaspoon pepper

1. Place ribs in center of double-thick rectangle of heavy-duty aluminum foil (length of rectangle should be twice the circumference of the ribs plus 8 inches). To form packet, bring 2 opposite ends of foil together over top of meat. Fold edges over 3 or 4 times, creasing each fold tightly. (Allow some air space.) Flatten foil at one open side; fold to form triangle and crease tightly. Fold end of triangle over several times toward package, pressing tightly to seal. Repeat procedure at other open side.

2. Place packet on grill rack over low to medium coals; cook 1 hour. Turn packet over; cook 1 hour longer.

3. Meanwhile, mix wine, horseradish, oil, mustard, salt and pepper in small bowl.

4. Remove ribs from foil packet; place ribs on grill rack. Grill, turning and brushing occasionally with sauce, 30 minutes.

Pinwheel Loaf Wellington

PINWHEEL LOAF WELLINGTON

A tasty ham-and-cheese-filled takeoff on the pastry-wrapped beef of classic cooking fame.

Makes 8 servings

  2 pounds lean ground beef
  ¾ cup soft breadcrumbs
  3 large eggs
  ½ cup catsup
  1 envelope onion or beefy onion soup mix
  1 teaspoon dried oregano, crumbled
  6 slices cooked ham
  2 cups shredded mozzarella cheese
    Pastry dough for 1 double-crust 9-inch pie
    Watercress and tomato roses for garnish

1. Combine beef, breadcrumbs, 2 of the eggs, the catsup, soup mix and oregano in large bowl; mix well. Place mixture on piece of waxed paper; pat into 12 × 10-inch rectangle.

2. Arrange ham on beef mixture, leaving 1-inch border uncovered; sprinkle ham evenly with cheese. Starting at 10-inch end, roll up jelly-roll style, removing waxed paper as you roll; pinch bottom seam to seal.

3. Roll out pastry dough on floured surface into 14 × 12-inch rectangle.

4. Wrap meat roll completely in pastry. Trim excess pastry; pinch bottom and end seams firmly to seal. Place loaf on rack in baking pan.

5. Beat remaining egg in small bowl. Brush pastry with egg. Decorate top with cutouts made from dough trimmings; brush with egg. Pierce pastry in several places with fork.

6. Bake in preheated 350°F oven 1 hour. Carefully transfer loaf to platter; garnish with watercress and tomato roses.

CRANBERRY CHUCK ROAST

Makes 6 servings

  3 tablespoons all-purpose flour
  1 teaspoon salt
  ¼ teaspoon pepper
  2 pounds boneless beef chuck roast, cut into
      2-inch cubes
  3 tablespoons vegetable oil
  2 medium onions, cut into quarters
  1 can (10½ ounces) beef bouillon
  ½ cup water
  1 teaspoon parsley flakes
  1 teaspoon dried oregano, crumbled
  ½ teaspoon ground ginger
  ½ teaspoon prepared mustard
  1 cup fresh cranberries
  ¼ cup dry sherry
  2 tablespoons packed brown sugar
  ⅔ cup pitted ripe olives

1. Mix flour, salt and pepper in large bowl. Add beef; toss to coat evenly.

2. Cook beef in oil in Dutch oven over medium heat, turning occasionally, until brown on all sides, about 12 minutes.

3. Add onions, bouillon, water, parsley, oregano, ginger and mustard to Dutch oven; mix well. Heat to boiling; reduce heat. Simmer, covered, 1 hour.

4. Meanwhile, heat cranberries and sherry in small saucepan to boiling. Add sugar; boil until cranberries are tender, about 1 minute.

5. Stir olives into beef mixture; continue cooking, covered, until beef is tender, about 30 minutes longer. Stir in cranberry mixture; cook 1 minute.

QUICHE LORRAINE

This is the quiche, the creamy onion and Swiss cheese pie with bacon, that has launched a thousand variations.

Makes 6 to 8 servings

 1 unbaked pie shell (9-inch)
 8 slices bacon, cut into 1-inch pieces
 1 medium onion, chopped
 2 tablespoons all-purpose flour
 4 large eggs
 1 teaspoon salt
 ¼ teaspoon dry mustard
  Pinch ground nutmeg
 2 cups milk or half-and-half
 6 ounces Swiss, Cheddar or Monterey Jack cheese, shredded

1. Bake pie shell in preheated 425°F oven 10 minutes; cool on wire rack.

2. Cook bacon in medium skillet over medium heat until crisp; drain on paper toweling. Discard all but 2 tablespoons bacon drippings.

3. Saute onion in drippings over medium heat until soft, about 4 minutes. Sprinkle with flour; cook and stir for 1 minute.

4. Whisk eggs, salt, mustard and nutmeg in medium bowl; stir in milk and onion mixture.

5. Sprinkle cheese in even layer in pie shell. Pour egg mixture over cheese; sprinkle with bacon.

6. Bake in preheated 350°F oven until knife inserted near center is withdrawn clean, 35 to 45 minutes. Cool on wire rack at least 10 minutes before serving; serve warm.

BRAISED LAMB CHOPS WITH DILL

Lamb shoulder chops simmer gently to a succulent tenderness in a dill-seasoned broth that is then transformed into a tangy sauce with the addition of sour cream.

Makes 4 servings

 8 frozen imported lamb shoulder chops, thawed
  Salt and pepper to taste
 1 tablespoon vegetable oil
 1 cup chicken stock
 1 cup sliced onion
 ¾ cup sliced celery
 ¾ teaspoon dried dill weed
 1 bay leaf
 ½ cup sour cream

1. Sprinkle lamb chops with salt and pepper; cook in oil in large skillet over medium heat, turning once, until brown, about 6 minutes. Remove chops to plate; pour off and discard fat.

2. Add stock to skillet; cook over medium heat, scraping up brown bits from bottom. Add onion, celery, ½ teaspoon of the dill and the bay leaf; mix well.

3. Return lamb chops to skillet; heat to boiling. Reduce heat; simmer, covered, until lamb is tender, about 35 minutes. Remove to platter; keep warm. Remove and discard bay leaf.

4. Cook vegetables and cooking juices over high heat until liquid is reduced by half; reduce heat. Stir in sour cream and remaining ¼ teaspoon dill; cook and stir just until hot. Do not boil. Pour sauce over lamb.

SLIM-BUT-SAUCY POT ROAST

Boiled potatoes with their skins on would be a calorie-wise accompaniment to take advantage of the marvelous cheesy tomato sauce.

Makes 6 to 8 servings

 1 beef arm pot roast (3 pounds)
 2 teaspoons salt
 ⅛ teaspoon pepper
 2 medium onions, sliced
 ½ can (10¾-ounce size) condensed cheddar cheese soup
 1 can (8 ounces) tomato sauce
 1 can (4 ounces) mushroom stems and pieces, undrained
 ¼ teaspoon dried oregano, crumbled
 ¼ teaspoon dried basil, crumbled

1. Place pot roast in nonstick roasting pan; roast, uncovered, in preheated 475°F oven just until beef is brown. Pour off pan drippings; reduce oven setting to 325°F.

2. Sprinkle beef with salt and pepper. Add remaining ingredients; cover pan tightly.

3. Roast at 325°F, turning beef occasionally, until tender, about 2½ hours.

Slim-but-Saucy Pot Roast

TURKEY SOUFFLE

When serving a delicate souffle, work quickly using two forks to gently tear apart and lift out individual portions.
Makes 4 to 5 servings

¼ cup olive oil
3 tablespoons all-purpose flour
1 cup hot milk
¾ cup turkey or chicken stock
½ teaspoon salt
½ teaspoon dried thyme, crumbled
⅛ teaspoon white pepper
1½ cups minced cooked turkey
¼ cup plus 2 tablespoons dried breadcrumbs
1 teaspoon grated lemon rind
4 large egg yolks, beaten
3 tablespoons dry sherry
2 tablespoons butter
6 large egg whites

1. Heat oil in medium skillet over medium heat until hot; stir in flour until smooth. Cook and stir 5 minutes. Whisk in milk until smooth; whisk in stock, salt, thyme and pepper. Cook, stirring constantly, until sauce thickens and bubbles for 1 minute; remove from heat.

2. Add turkey, ¼ cup of the breadcrumbs and the lemon rind to skillet; mix well. Remove from heat; stir in egg yolks and sherry; transfer to large bowl.

3. Butter 6-cup freezer-to-oven souffle dish; coat with remaining 2 tablespoons breadcrumbs. Place in freezer to chill well, about 30 minutes. *(Continued)*

4. Beat egg whites until stiff but not dry. Stir ⅓ of the egg whites into turkey mixture; fold in remaining egg whites. Pour into souffle dish.

5. Bake on center rack in preheated 400°F oven until puffed and golden brown, 25 to 35 minutes. Serve immediately.

CHICKEN CACCIATORE

Serve this satisfying Italian "hunter-style" chicken with crusty slices of garlic bread and a dry red wine.
Makes 4 to 6 servings

1 large green bell pepper, cut into ½-inch-wide strips
1 clove garlic, minced
2 tablespoons olive oil
1 broiler-fryer chicken, cut up (3 to 3½ pounds)
2 jars (16 ounces each) Italian cooking sauce
1 teaspoon dried basil, crumbled
½ teaspoon salt
⅛ teaspoon ground black pepper

1. Saute green bell pepper and garlic in oil in large skillet over medium heat 3 minutes; remove pepper and garlic to plate.

2. Add chicken to skillet; cook until brown on all sides, about 8 minutes. Drain and discard fat.

3. Add cooking sauce, basil, salt and ground pepper to skillet; stir in green peppers and garlic. Heat to boiling; reduce heat. Simmer, covered, until chicken is tender, 45 to 50 minutes.

Chicken Cacciatore

Glazed Cornish Hens

ALMOND CHICKEN

The Chinese round-bottomed wok evolved in a country where kitchen fuel was scarce. Its extended cooking surface makes a wok ideal for stir-frying small pieces of chicken and vegetables quickly on all sides.

Makes 4 servings

1½ cups water
 4 tablespoons dry sherry
2½ tablespoons cornstarch
 4 teaspoons soy sauce
 1 teaspoon instant chicken bouillon granules
 1 large egg white, beaten
 ½ teaspoon salt
 4 whole chicken breasts, skinned, boned, cut into
   1-inch pieces
 3 cups vegetable oil
 ½ cup whole blanched almonds
 1 large carrot, diced
 1 teaspoon grated, pared fresh ginger root
 8 mushrooms, sliced
 6 green onions, cut into 1-inch pieces
 3 stalks celery, sliced
 ½ cup sliced bamboo shoots

1. Mix water, 2 tablespoons of the sherry, 1½ tablespoons of the cornstarch, the soy sauce and bouillon granules in small saucepan. Cook and stir over medium heat until sauce thickens and bubbles for 3 minutes.

2. Mix remaining 2 tablespoons sherry, 1 tablespoon cornstarch, the egg white and salt in medium bowl; stir in chicken.

3. Heat oil in wok over high heat to 375°F. Add ⅓ of the chicken pieces, one at a time, to oil; cook until light brown, 3 to 5 minutes. Remove with slotted spoon to paper toweling. Repeat until all chicken has been fried.

(Continued)

4. Remove all but 2 tablespoons oil from wok. Stir-fry almonds in oil until golden, about 2 minutes. Remove from wok with slotted spoon; drain.

5. Add carrot and ginger to wok; stir-fry 1 minute. Add mushrooms, onions, celery, and bamboo shoots; stir-fry until crisp-tender, about 3 minutes. Stir in chicken, almonds and sauce; stir-fry until hot.

GLAZED CORNISH HENS

Makes 4 servings

1¼ cups cider or apple juice
 1 envelope onion soup mix
 2 cups unseasoned cube-style stuffing mix
 ⅓ cup raisins
 ⅓ cup coarsely chopped walnuts
 4 Cornish hens (1 to 1½ pounds each)
 2 large apples, cored, sliced
 ¼ cup packed brown sugar
 ½ teaspoon ground cinnamon
   Curly endive

1. Mix cider and soup mix in small bowl.

2. Combine stuffing mix, raisins and walnuts in medium bowl. Add ½ of the cider mixture; toss to moisten evenly.

3. Spoon stuffing mixture into hens; close openings with wooden picks. Place hens and apples in roasting pan.

4. For glaze, combine remaining cider mixture, the sugar and cinnamon in small bowl; mix well.

5. Brush hens and apples with ½ of the glaze. Roast in preheated 350°F oven, basting occasionally with remaining glaze, until juices run clear when inner thigh is pierced, 1 to 1¼ hours.

6. Remove hens to platter lined with endive. Place apples around hens.

TURKEY MARENGO

Makes 6 servings

3 pounds turkey wings
2 tablespoons vegetable oil
1 can (16 ounces) tomatoes, undrained, chopped
2 cups water
1 large onion, sliced
1 can (4 ounces) chopped mushrooms, undrained
½ cup dry white wine
1 teaspoon salt
1 teaspoon dried oregano, crumbled
½ teaspoon pepper

1. Remove and discard turkey wing tips; separate wings into 2 sections. Cook wings in oil in Dutch oven over medium heat, turning occasionally, until brown on all sides, about 10 minutes.

2. Add remaining ingredients to Dutch oven; mix well. Heat to boiling; reduce heat. Simmer, partially covered, until turkey is tender, about 2 hours.

3. Cook, uncovered, over medium heat until liquid is reduced by about ½.

CHINESE SWEET AND SOUR CHICKEN

Makes 4 servings

1¼ pounds chicken thighs (about 5), boned
1 large egg, separated
2 tablespoons soy sauce
¼ cup plus ½ teaspoon sugar
¾ teaspoon salt
  Pinch ground black pepper
½ cup plus 2 tablespoons cornstarch
½ cup chicken stock or broth
3 tablespoons distilled white vinegar
2 tablespoons rice wine
½ cup water
½ cup all-purpose flour
4 cups vegetable oil
3 tablespoons peanut oil
2 large green bell peppers, cut into 1¼-inch
  pieces
1 small clove garlic, cut in half
1½ cups fresh or drained canned pineapple chunks
  (about 1 × ⅜-inch)
1 tablespoon sesame oil

1. Cut chicken into ¾-inch pieces. Mix with egg yolk, 1 tablespoon of the soy sauce, ½ teaspoon each of the sugar and salt and the ground pepper in medium bowl. Sprinkle with 1 tablespoon of the cornstarch; mix well. Let stand at room temperature 30 minutes.

2. Mix remaining ¼ cup sugar and ¼ teaspoon salt with 1 tablespoon of the cornstarch in small bowl. Stir in stock, vinegar, rice wine and remaining 1 tablespoon soy sauce.

3. Whisk egg white in medium bowl until foamy; whisk in water. Whisk in remaining ½ cup cornstarch until smooth; whisk in flour until smooth. Reserve batter.

4. Heat wok over high heat 20 seconds; add vegetable oil and heat to 350°F. Using ⅓ of the chicken pieces at a time, dip each piece in reserved batter and add to wok; stir gently. Fry until crisp, golden and cooked through, 4 to 5 minutes. Remove chicken with strainer; drain on paper toweling. Repeat with remaining chicken. Remove oil from wok; wipe clean.   *(Continued)*

5. Heat wok over high heat 15 seconds; add 2 tablespoons of the peanut oil and heat until hot, about 30 seconds. Add green peppers and garlic; stir-fry 2 minutes. Remove with slotted spoon to plate; discard garlic.

6. Add remaining 1 tablespoon peanut oil to wok; reduce heat to medium. Add pineapple; stir-fry 30 seconds. Stir stock mixture; add to wok. Increase heat to high; cook and stir until sauce thickens and bubbles for 1 minute. Drizzle with sesame oil; stir 2 or 3 times. Return green peppers and chicken to wok; stir just until coated with sauce. Serve immediately.

ROAST TURKEY WITH OYSTER DRESSING

Makes 12 to 15 servings

1 turkey (12 pounds), liver reserved for Oyster
  Dressing
Oyster Dressing (recipe follows)
Melted butter
Turkey or chicken stock
⅓ cup all-purpose flour
Salt and pepper to taste

1. Rinse turkey; pat dry. Spoon Oyster Dressing into body and neck cavities, packing loosely. Skewer or sew openings closed; truss turkey. Place turkey, breast side up, on rack in roasting pan. Insert meat thermometer in thickest part of thigh, not touching bone. Brush with butter.

2. Roast turkey, uncovered, in preheated 325°F oven, basting every 30 to 45 minutes with butter, until thermometer registers 180°F, 3½ to 4 hours. Remove turkey to platter; keep warm, loosely covered.

3. Transfer drippings to 4-cup measure; skim fat, reserving ⅓ cup. Add stock to drippings if necessary to make 3 cups.

4. Mix reserved fat and the flour in medium saucepan until smooth; cook and stir over medium heat until light brown, 5 to 10 minutes. Gradually whisk in 3 cups drippings; cook and stir over medium-low heat until gravy thickens and bubbles for 1 minute. Stir in salt and pepper.

5. Carve turkey; serve with dressing and gravy.

OYSTER DRESSING

Reserved turkey liver, chopped
2 medium onions, finely chopped
2 stalks celery, finely chopped
½ cup butter or margarine
7 cups cubed day-old French bread
1 cup shucked fresh oysters, drained, coarsely
  chopped, or 1 jar (8 ounces) small oysters,
  drained, coarsely chopped
⅓ cup minced parsley
1 teaspoon poultry seasoning
1 teaspoon salt
⅛ teaspoon white pepper
¼ to ⅓ cup chicken broth

Saute liver, onions and celery in butter in large skillet over medium heat until vegetables are soft, about 5 minutes. Combine with remaining ingredients except broth in large bowl; toss to mix well. Drizzle with broth; toss until evenly moistened.

Makes about 8 cups

CHICKEN PORTUGUAISE

Makes 4 servings

1 broiler-fryer chicken (about 3 pounds), cut up
2 small green bell peppers, thinly sliced
1 large onion, thinly sliced
¼ pound mushrooms, thinly sliced
1 stalk celery, chopped
1 can (16 ounces) tomatoes, undrained, chopped
¼ cup dry rosé or white wine
3 to 4 cloves garlic, minced
   Salt and ground black pepper to taste

1. Broil chicken skin side up in preheated broiler, 6 inches from heat source, until skin is crisp, 10 to 15 minutes. Drain off fat.

2. Place green bell pepper, onion, mushrooms and celery in shallow baking dish; top with chicken. Mix tomatoes, wine, garlic, salt and ground pepper in medium bowl; pour over chicken.

3. Bake, uncovered, in preheated 400°F oven, basting frequently, until chicken is tender and sauce is thick, 50 to 60 minutes.

CHICKEN A LA KING

The King for whom this dish was named was not foreign royalty; he was Charles King, who operated the old Brighton Beach Hotel outside New York City.

Makes 4 to 6 servings

1 package (10 ounces) frozen patty shells
1 package (10 ounces) frozen small peas with
   butter in pouch
1 envelope (0.87 ounces) chicken gravy mix
1¾ cups diced cooked chicken
1 cup sour cream
1 jar (2 ounces) diced pimiento, drained
⅛ teaspoon rubbed sage

1. Prepare patty shells according to package directions.

2. Place unopened vegetable pouch in vigorously boiling water in saucepan; do not cover pan. Heat water to second vigorous boil; cook 15 minutes.

3. Meanwhile, prepare gravy mix according to package directions in medium saucepan. Stir in chicken, sour cream, pimiento and sage. Cook and stir over low heat until hot; do not boil. Stir in peas; serve over patty shells.

Chicken Portuguaise

Chicken Cordon Bleu

CHICKEN CORDON BLEU

Tender chicken wrapped around smoked ham and melting cheese makes a great dinner for eight.

Makes 8 servings

    4 boneless chicken breasts (about 2 pounds),
        skinned, split (8 pieces)
    8 teaspoons chopped parsley
    8 thin slices mozzarella cheese
    4 thin slices boiled ham, cut into halves
    1 tablespoon mayonnaise
    1 tablespoon warm water
 ½ cup seasoned breadcrumbs
        White Wine Sauce (recipe follows)
        Parsley sprigs, chopped parsley and lemon
            wedges for garnish

1. Pound chicken with meat mallet to ¼-inch thickness. Sprinkle each piece with 1 teaspoon of the parsley. Top each with 1 slice cheese and ½ slice ham. Roll up tightly; secure with wooden picks.

2. Mix mayonnaise and water in shallow dish. Roll chicken in mayonnaise mixture, then in breadcrumbs to coat. Place in greased baking pan.

3. Bake in a preheated 425°F oven until cooked through, 15 to 20 minutes. Remove wooden picks.

4. To serve, spoon White Wine Sauce over chicken rolls. Garnish with parsley and lemon wedges.

WHITE WINE SAUCE

    3 tablespoons butter or margarine
    3 tablespoons all-purpose flour
    1 cup chicken stock
 ⅔ cup milk
    3 tablespoons dry white wine
        Onion salt and pepper to taste
        Pinch nutmeg, if desired   *(Continued)*

1. Melt butter in medium saucepan over medium heat; stir in flour until smooth. Cook and stir 1 minute.

2. Gradually whisk in stock and milk until smooth. Stir in remaining ingredients; cook and stir until sauce thickens and bubbles for 1 minute.

Makes about 2 cups

ROAST CHICKEN WITH APPLE STUFFING

Makes 4 to 6 servings

 ¾ cup plus 2 tablespoons butter or margarine,
        melted
    3 cups unseasoned stuffing mix
    2 cups chopped pared apples
    1 cup chopped celery
 ½ cup raisins
 ¼ cup minced onion
    1 teaspoon salt
 ½ teaspoon ground sage
 ⅛ teaspoon pepper
    1 whole broiler-fryer chicken (3½ pounds)
    2 teaspoons lemon juice
 1½ cups chicken stock

1. Pour ¾ cup of the butter over stuffing mix in large bowl; toss to moisten evenly. Add apples, celery, raisins, onion, salt, sage and pepper; mix well.

2. Spoon stuffing into body and neck cavities, packing loosely. Truss chicken; place in roasting pan. Brush with remaining 2 tablespoons butter and the lemon juice.

3. Roast in preheated 350°F oven, basting occasionally with stock, until meat thermometer inserted into thickest part of thigh not touching bone registers 190°F, about 1½ hours. Let stand 10 minutes before carving.

Note: Leftover stuffing can be baked in a glass baking dish alongside chicken. Add ¼ cup chicken broth for each 2 cups stuffing; cover and bake until done.

ROTINI WITH TWO CHEESES

Intriguing spiral-shaped pasta gives a new look to this savory Cheddar and Swiss cheese casserole.

Makes 6 to 8 servings

- 12 ounces rotini pasta
- 1½ tablespoons salt
- ¼ cup butter
- ¼ cup all-purpose flour
- 1 tablespoon seasoned salt
- 2 teaspoons dry mustard
- ¼ teaspoon white pepper
- 3½ cups milk
- ½ pound mushrooms, sliced
- 1 jar (4 ounces) pimientos, drained, chopped
- 4 green onions, sliced
- 1 tablespoon Worcestershire sauce
- 4 ounces Swiss cheese, shredded
- 4 ounces Cheddar cheese, shredded

1. Add rotini and salt to large pan of boiling water; cook, stirring occasionally, until almost but not quite tender, 6 to 7 minutes. Drain well.

2. Meanwhile, melt butter in medium saucepan over medium heat. Stir in flour, seasoned salt, mustard and pepper until smooth; cook and stir until bubbly. Gradually whisk in milk; cook and stir until mixture thickens and bubbles for 1 minute.

3. Add mushrooms, pimientos, 3 of the onions and the Worcestershire sauce to saucepan; mix well. Add Swiss and Cheddar cheeses; cook and stir over medium-low heat until cheeses are melted.

4. Combine rotini and cheese sauce in large bowl; mix well. Transfer to greased 2-quart baking dish. Bake in preheated 350°F oven 45 minutes. Garnish with the remaining green onion.

CHICKEN ON SPINACH NOODLE NESTS

Makes 4 servings

- 2 tablespoons butter
- 1 tablespoon olive oil
- 8 chicken thighs, boned
- 1 teaspoon salt
- ½ teaspoon ground black pepper
- 8 spinach noodle nests (1 ounce each)*
- ½ cup large-curd cottage cheese
- 1 cup chopped green onions
- ⅔ cup chopped red bell pepper
- ⅓ cup all-purpose flour
- 3 cups chicken broth, warm
- 3 tablespoons dry white wine

1. Heat butter and oil in large skillet over medium heat. Sprinkle chicken with salt and ground pepper; add to skillet. Cook, turning once, until brown, about 10 minutes.

2. Cook noodle nests according to package directions, keeping nests intact. Carefully remove from water; drain. Arrange nests in single layer in 2-quart shallow baking dish.

3. Place 1 tablespoon of the cottage cheese in each nest; top each with 1 chicken thigh. Keep warm.

4. Remove and discard all but 4 tablespoons drippings from skillet. Add onions and bell pepper to skillet; saute over medium heat 2 minutes. Add flour; cook and stir until golden, about 2 minutes. Gradually whisk in broth until smooth; cook and stir until thick, about 2 minutes. Stir in wine; heat to boiling. Spoon sauce over chicken.

5. Bake in preheated 350°F oven until chicken is tender, about 20 minutes.

*Note: If spinach noodle nests are not available, use plain or spinach noodles; arrange in nest-shaped circles after cooking.

Rotini with Two Cheeses

COUNTRY CHICKEN PIE

The secret of a top crust that bakes all the way through is to have the chicken mixture underneath hot when the pastry is put in place.

Makes 4 servings

1½ **cups sliced carrots**
½ **cup chopped onion**
½ **cup chopped celery**
⅓ **cup finely chopped green bell pepper**
⅓ **cup boiling water**
¼ **cup chicken fat, butter or margarine**
¼ **cup all-purpose flour**
1 **teaspoon salt**
Pinch ground black pepper
1 **cup chicken broth**
1 **cup milk**
2 **cups diced cooked chicken**
1 **package (10 ounces) frozen peas, thawed**
Dilly Pastry (recipe follows)

1. Combine carrots, onion, celery, green bell pepper and water in medium saucepan; cook, covered, over medium-high heat 3 minutes. Drain well.

2. Melt chicken fat in large saucepan over medium heat;

(Continued)

stir in flour, salt and ground pepper until smooth. Gradually whisk in broth and milk; cook and stir until mixture thickens and bubbles for 1 minute.

3. Reduce heat to low; add chicken, peas and carrot mixture to sauce. Cook and stir until hot throughout; pour into greased 8-inch square baking dish.

4. Roll out Dilly Pastry on lightly floured surface into 7-inch square. Cut pastry into 4 squares; cut out center of each square with decorative cutter, if desired. Place on top of chicken mixture. Bake in preheated 400°F oven until pastry is golden, 25 to 30 minutes.

DILLY PASTRY

¾ **cup all-purpose flour**
½ **teaspoon dried dill weed**
¼ **teaspoon salt**
¼ **cup solid vegetable shortening**
2 **to 3 tablespoons cold water**

Mix flour, dill and salt in small bowl; cut in shortening until pieces are size of small peas. Gradually add water, stirring and tossing with fork until mixture cleans side of bowl. Gather dough into ball; refrigerate, wrapped in plastic wrap, at least 1 hour or overnight.

Country Chicken Pie

FRENCH TURKEY RAGOUT

Makes 4 servings

1 cup chopped onion
2 tablespoons butter or margarine
1¼ pounds turkey thighs, boned, cut into 2-inch pieces
1 tablespoon tomato paste
1 clove garlic, minced
2½ cups turkey or chicken stock
½ teaspoon salt
¼ teaspoon pepper
1 bay leaf
4 carrots, sliced
2 medium potatoes, pared, cut into halves, sliced
2 tablespoons all-purpose flour
¼ cup cold water
½ cup whipping cream
Chopped parsley for garnish

1. Saute onion in butter in Dutch oven over medium heat until soft, about 4 minutes. Add turkey; cook, turning occasionally, 5 minutes. Add tomato paste and garlic; cook and stir 30 seconds.

2. Add stock, salt, pepper and bay leaf to pan; heat to boiling. Reduce heat; simmer, covered, 25 minutes. Stir in carrots and potatoes; continue cooking, covered, until turkey and vegetables are tender, about 20 minutes longer. Remove and discard bay leaf.

3. Mix flour with cold water in small bowl until smooth; stir into turkey mixture. Cook, stirring constantly, until liquid thickens and bubbles for 1 minute; reduce heat to low. Stir in cream; cook just until hot. Transfer to tureen; garnish with parsley.

French Turkey Ragout

DIAMOND JIM FLOUNDER

New York financier James Brady was noted for a flamboyant lifestyle and the enormous quantities of food he could put away at one sitting. This version of his particular favorite, Flounder à la Marguèry, became identified forever with him.

Makes 6 servings

2 pounds fresh or thawed frozen flounder, sole or other white fish fillets, cut into serving-size pieces
1 teaspoon salt
¼ teaspoon pepper
18 shucked raw oysters
18 shelled deveined shrimp
2 cups Fish Stock (recipe follows)
1 cup butter or margarine
8 large egg yolks, beaten
¼ cup dry white wine
2 tablespoons lemon juice
Paprika

1. Sprinkle fish with salt and pepper; place in well-greased 12×8×2-inch baking dish. Top with oysters and shrimp; add 1 cup of the Fish Stock.

2. Bake in preheated 350°F oven, basting occasionally, until fish is opaque, about 15 minutes. Remove oysters and shrimp from baking dish. Carefully remove fish with slotted spatula; arrange in single layer on flame-proof platter. Top each piece of fish with 3 oysters and 3 shrimp; keep warm.

(Continued)

3. Transfer liquid from baking dish to medium saucepan; add remaining 1 cup Fish Stock. Cook over medium-high heat until reduced to ½ cup; reduce heat to medium. Add butter; whisk until melted.

4. Gradually whisk stock mixture into egg yolks in medium bowl; return to saucepan. Cook over low heat, whisking constantly, until sauce thickens; do not boil. Stir in wine and lemon juice; heat just until hot.

5. Pour sauce over fish in even layer. Broil 4 inches from heat source until light brown, 1 to 3 minutes. Sprinkle with paprika; serve immediately.

FISH STOCK

1½ quarts water
2 medium onions, cut into quarters
1 cup sliced carrots
8 peppercorns
¼ teaspoon dried thyme
1 bay leaf
1½ pounds fresh or thawed frozen inexpensive white fish fillets, cut into 1-inch pieces

1. Combine water, onions, carrots, peppercorns, thyme and bay leaf in large skillet; heat over medium heat to boiling. Reduce heat; simmer, uncovered, 5 minutes.

2. Stir in fish; simmer, uncovered, until liquid is reduced to 2 cups. Strain through sieve lined with dampened cheesecloth; discard solids.

Makes 2 cups

Whiting with Polenta

WHITING WITH POLENTA

Italians cook cornmeal very thick, call it polenta and serve it topped with a variety of vegetables, meat or seafood and special sauces.

Makes 4 to 6 servings

    4 cups water
    1 cup yellow cornmeal
1½ teaspoons salt
    ¼ pound grated Parmesan cheese
    ¼ cup butter
    ⅛ teaspoon pepper
    2 packages (10 ounces each) frozen chopped
        spinach
    1 tablespoon lemon juice
    1 teaspoon dried oregano, crumbled
1½ pounds whiting fillets
    All-purpose flour
    3 tablespoons vegetable oil
    ⅓ cup chopped parsley
    ½ cup dry white wine
    ½ cup tomato puree

1. Mix 1 cup of the water, the cornmeal and 1 teaspoon of the salt in small bowl. Heat remaining 3 cups water in large saucepan to boiling; gradually whisk in cornmeal mixture until smooth. Cook over medium heat, stirring frequently, until thickened. Cook, covered, over low heat 10 minutes longer.

2. Remove from heat. Add cheese, butter and pepper; stir until butter and cheese are melted. Spread on greased oven-proof serving platter.

3. Cook spinach according to package directions; drain well. Mix with lemon juice, oregano and remaining ½ teaspoon salt. Spread on top of cornmeal mixture; keep warm in 200°F oven. *(Continued)*

4. Dip fish in flour to coat lightly. Saute in oil in large skillet over medium heat, turning once, until golden brown. Arrange on top of spinach; sprinkle with parsley.

5. Add wine and tomato puree to skillet; heat, scraping up bits from bottom, to boiling. Pour over fish; serve immediately.

NEW BEDFORD FLOUNDER ROLL-UPS

Bake up a packaged mix to make cornbread in a hurry for the flavorful bacon-herb stuffing.

Makes 12 servings

    8 slices bacon
    ½ cup butter or margarine, melted
    6 cups cornbread crumbs
    ½ teaspoon dried chervil, crumbled
    ½ teaspoon dried tarragon, crumbled
        Hot water
  12 large skinless flounder fillets
        White pepper to taste
        Butter or margarine
        Lemon slices or wedges

1. Cook bacon in large skillet over medium heat until crisp; drain on paper toweling. Crumble.

2. Measure ¼ cup bacon drippings; combine with melted butter in large bowl. Add cornbread crumbs, bacon, chervil and tarragon; mix well. Add enough hot water to make stuffing as moist as desired.

3. Place ¹⁄₁₂ of the stuffing at large end of each flounder fillet; roll up firmly. Place roll-ups, seam side down, in baking pan lined with greased aluminum foil. Sprinkle with pepper; dot generously with butter.

4. Bake in preheated 375°F oven until fish flakes easily with fork, about 25 minutes. Serve with lemon.

SPAGHETTI WITH CLAM SAUCE

Makes 8 servings

4 dozen medium cherrystone clams, scrubbed*
Boiling water
1 cup chopped onion
4 to 5 cloves garlic, minced
½ cup butter
2 tablespoons plus 1 teaspoon salt
1 teaspoon dried basil, crumbled
Freshly ground pepper to taste
1 pound spaghetti
1 tablespoon chopped fresh dill
Fluted lemon slices and dill sprigs for garnish

1. Add clams to 3 cups boiling water in large pot; steam, covered, over medium-high heat, just until clams open. Remove clams, draining well; discard any unopened shells.

2. Strain clam broth; reserve 3 cups. Remove clams from shells; chop.

3. Saute onion and garlic in butter in large skillet over medium heat until onion is soft, about 4 minutes; stir in clams, reserved broth, 1 teaspoon of the salt, the basil and pepper. Heat to boiling; boil 1 minute. Remove from heat; keep warm.

4. Add spaghetti and remaining 2 tablespoons salt to large kettle of boiling water. Cook, stirring occasionally, until firm-tender; drain well. *(Continued)*

5. Place spaghetti on warm platter; top with clam sauce. Sprinkle with chopped dill; garnish with lemon slices and dill sprigs. Toss before serving.

*Note: 2 cups canned minced clams and 3 cups bottled clam juice can be substituted; omit steps 1 and 2.

OVEN-POACHED SCALLOPS

Makes 4 servings

1 pound scallops
2 teaspoons lemon juice
½ teaspoon salt
⅛ teaspoon pepper
1 cup chopped mushrooms
½ cup butter or margarine, melted
½ cup soft breadcrumbs
2 tablespoons chopped parsley for garnish

1. Pat scallops dry with paper toweling; cut into halves. Place in 4 greased large scallop shells or individual flame-proof ramekins or 9-inch flame-proof pie plate.

2. Sprinkle scallops with lemon juice, salt and pepper; top with mushrooms. Drizzle with ¼ cup of the butter.

3. Mix remaining ¼ cup butter with breadcrumbs in small bowl; sprinkle over mushrooms.

4. Broil in preheated broiler, 6 inches from heat source, until scallops are opaque throughout, 10 to 12 minutes. Garnish with parsley.

Spaghetti with Clam Sauce

CHATHAM SCROD A LA KING

Patrons of fish markets and restaurants around Boston know scrod as the special name for young cod and haddock.

Makes 6 servings

¼ cup plus 2 tablespoons butter or margarine
¼ cup all-purpose flour
1 teaspoon salt
¼ teaspoon ground black pepper
2 cups milk
¼ cup dry sherry
1 cup sliced mushrooms
1 green bell pepper, coarsely chopped
2 tablespoons vegetable oil
1 cup cooked peas
⅓ cup slivered pimiento
3 pounds scrod fillets, cut into 6 even pieces
Lemon slices, pickle slices and parsley sprigs
    for garnish   *(Continued)*

1. Melt ¼ cup of the butter in medium saucepan. Stir in flour, ½ teaspoon of the salt and ⅛ teaspoon of the ground pepper until smooth; cook and stir over medium heat until bubbly. Whisk in milk until smooth; cook and stir until sauce thickens and bubbles for 1 minute. Stir in sherry; remove from heat.

2. Saute mushrooms and green bell pepper in oil in medium skillet over medium heat until mushrooms are golden, 6 to 8 minutes. Add to sauce; stir in peas and pimiento. Keep warm, covered, over hot water.

3. Place scrod on foil-lined broiler pan. Sprinkle with remaining ½ teaspoon salt and ⅛ teaspoon ground pepper; dot with remaining 2 tablespoons butter. Broil in preheated broiler, 4 inches from heat source, turning once, until opaque throughout, about 5 minutes per side.

4. Remove scrod to serving dish. Garnish with lemon slices, pickle slices and parsley; serve with sauce.

Chatham Scrod à la King

Maine Lobster Boil

COD FILLETS KIEV

A surprise pocket of herb-seasoned butter awaits the touch of a fork to each golden-brown piece of sesame-coated fish.

Makes 6 to 8 servings

- 2 pounds thick cod, haddock or grouper fillets
- ¼ cup butter, room temperature
- ¼ cup finely chopped green onion
- ¼ cup minced parsley
- 1 tablespoon chopped fresh dill
- ½ teaspoon salt
- ½ cup sesame seeds
- ⅓ cup cornstarch
- 2 large eggs, beaten
- 2 to 4 tablespoons butter
- 2 to 3 tablespoons vegetable oil
  Parsley sprig for garnish

1. Pat fish dry; cut into 6 or 8 even-size pieces. With thin sharp knife, cut horizontal pocket in side of each piece.

2. Combine ¼ cup butter, the onion, minced parsley, dill and salt in small bowl; mix well. Spread butter mixture in fish pockets, dividing evenly.

3. Spread ¼ cup of the sesame seeds in thin layer on large piece of waxed paper. Dip fish in cornstarch to coat. Dip in eggs; place on sesame seeds on waxed paper. Sprinkle remaining ¼ cup sesame seeds on top of fish; let stand 15 minutes. *(Continued)*

4. Heat 2 tablespoons butter and 2 tablespoons oil in large heavy skillet over medium heat until hot. Add ½ of the fish pieces; cook, turning once, just until fish flakes with a fork, 3 to 5 minutes per side. Remove to serving dish. Keep warm. Repeat with remaining fish, adding remaining butter and oil to skillet if needed. Garnish with parsley sprig.

MAINE LOBSTER BOIL

Makes 6 servings

- 1½ gallons water
- ⅓ cup salt
- 6 live lobsters (1 pound each)
  Parsley sprigs for garnish
  Melted butter or margarine
  Lemon wedges

1. Combine water and salt in large kettle; cover kettle. Heat over hot coals to boiling.

2. Plunge lobsters head first into boiling water; cook, covered, until lobsters are done, 5 to 6 minutes after water returns to boiling. Drain well.

3. Garnish with parsley; serve with butter and lemon wedges.

Note: *Unless kettle is extra large, cook only 2 or 3 lobsters at a time.*

SPAGHETTI WITH EGGPLANT SAUCE

Oregano and basil subtly season an all-vegetable sauce as it bubbles to a rich, satisfying thickness.

Makes 4 servings

 1 eggplant (about 1 pound), pared, diced (¾-inch)
¼ cup vegetable oil
 1 can (16 ounces) tomatoes, undrained, chopped
 1 can (8 ounces) tomato sauce
¼ teaspoon dried oregano, crumbled
¼ teaspoon dried basil, crumbled
   Pinch crushed red pepper
 8 ounces spaghetti
 1 tablespoon salt
   Grated Parmesan cheese

1. Saute eggplant in oil in large skillet over medium heat until light brown, about 6 minutes. Stir in tomatoes, tomato sauce, oregano, basil and red pepper. Cook, uncovered, stirring occasionally, until thickened, about 25 minutes. Reduce heat to low; simmer, covered, 15 minutes longer.

2. Meanwhile, add spaghetti and salt to rapidly boiling water in large kettle. Cook, uncovered, stirring occasionally, until tender, 8 to 12 minutes; drain well.

3. Pour eggplant sauce over spaghetti on large platter; toss before serving. Serve with cheese.

CHERRY SALAD SUPREME

This party-perfect layered gelatin beauty needs no fancy mold. Make it in a rectangular pan and cut in squares.

Makes 12 servings

 1 package (3 ounces) raspberry flavor gelatin
 2 cups boiling water
 1 can (21 ounces) tart cherry pie filling
 1 package (3 ounces) lemon flavor gelatin
 4 ounces cream cheese, softened
⅓ cup mayonnaise
 1 can (8 ounces) crushed pineapple in juice, undrained
½ cup whipping cream, whipped
 1 cup miniature marshmallows
¼ cup chopped nuts

1. Dissolve raspberry gelatin in 1 cup of the boiling water in medium bowl; stir in pie filling. Pour into 13 × 9-inch baking pan; refrigerate until nearly set.

2. Dissolve lemon gelatin in remaining 1 cup boiling water in small bowl. Beat cream cheese and mayonnaise in large mixer bowl until smooth; gradually beat in lemon gelatin. Stir in pineapple and juice; fold in whipped cream and marshmallows.

3. Spread lemon mixture on top of cherry layer; refrigerate until set. Sprinkle with nuts before serving.

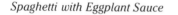

Spaghetti with Eggplant Sauce

Apple Pecan Molded Salad

APPLE PECAN MOLDED SALAD

Makes 8 servings

- 2 envelopes unflavored gelatin
- 3 tablespoons sugar
- 1 cup boiling water
- 2 cups fruity white wine
- ¾ cup white grape juice
- 1 tablespoon white wine vinegar
- 1 teaspoon salt
- 16 pecan halves
- 1 Granny Smith apple
- 1 cup finely shredded heart of romaine lettuce
- ½ cup coarsely chopped pecans

1. Mix gelatin and sugar in medium bowl. Add boiling water; stir until gelatin and sugar are dissolved. Stir in wine, grape juice, vinegar and salt; refrigerate, stirring occasionally, until as thick as unbeaten egg white.

2. Spoon ¼ of the gelatin mixture into lightly oiled 5-cup ring mold. Arrange 8 pecan halves, evenly spaced, on top of gelatin. Return to refrigerator.

3. Core apple; cut lengthwise in half. Cut ½ apple into 8 thin slices; arrange slices on top of pecan halves. Arrange remaining 8 pecan halves vertically around outer edge of mold.

4. Gently spoon another ¼ of the gelatin mixture into mold to cover apples; refrigerate until set.

5. Add lettuce to mold; cover with thin layer of gelatin mixture; return to refrigerator.

6. Chop remaining ½ apple; toss with chopped pecans. Sprinkle in even layer in mold. Top with remaining gelatin mixture; refrigerate, covered, until set, at least 4 hours. Unmold just before serving.

SUMMERHOUSE LAMB SALAD

Enjoy leftover leg of lamb roast down to the last delicious sliver in this taste-tempting curry-dressing salad.

Makes 4 servings

- 1 large tart apple
- 1 pound frozen imported boneless lamb, thawed, cooked, slivered (about 2 cups)
- 1 can (16 ounces) kidney beans, drained
- 1 medium cucumber, pared, seeded, sliced
- ¼ cup thinly sliced green onions
- ½ cup vegetable oil
- 3 tablespoons lemon juice
- 1 teaspoon curry powder
- ½ teaspoon ground cumin
- ½ teaspoon salt
- ⅛ teaspoon pepper
  Lettuce leaves
  Cucumber slices for garnish
- ½ cup broken walnuts, if desired

1. Cut apple lengthwise into quarters and core. Cut quarters lengthwise into slices; cut slices crosswise into halves.

2. Combine apple, lamb, beans, seeded cucumber and green onions in large bowl; toss to mix well.

3. Whisk oil, lemon juice, curry powder, cumin, salt and pepper in small bowl until blended. Add to lamb mixture; toss. Refrigerate, covered, stirring occasionally, 3 to 6 hours.

4. To serve, spoon lamb mixture onto plate lined with lettuce; garnish with cucumber slices. Sprinkle with nuts.

Mushroom Strata

MUSHROOM STRATA

Purchase mushrooms with caps closed tightly around the stems as an indication of freshness for cooked dishes or salads.

Makes 6 servings

   8 ounces mushrooms, sliced
   4 tablespoons butter or margarine
   6 slices bread, diced (½-inch)
  ½ **cup chopped onion**
  ½ **cup chopped celery**
  1 cup milk
  ½ **cup mayonnaise**
  2 large eggs, beaten
  1 teaspoon salt
  ½ **teaspoon pepper**
  ½ **teaspoon dried tarragon, crumbled**
  1 cup shredded Cheddar cheese   *(Continued)*

1. Saute mushrooms in 3 tablespoons of the butter in medium skillet over medium-high heat 2 minutes. Spoon mushrooms over ½ of the bread in greased 1½-quart baking dish.

2. Saute onion and celery in remaining 1 tablespoon butter in skillet over medium heat until soft, about 4 minutes. Spoon onion mixture evenly over mushrooms; top with remaining bread.

3. Whisk milk, mayonnaise, eggs, salt, pepper and tarragon in medium bowl until smooth; pour evenly over layers in baking dish. Sprinkle with cheese.

4. Refrigerate, covered, several hours or overnight, or let stand at room temperature until bread absorbs milk mixture, about 30 minutes.

5. Bake in preheated 325°F oven until top is golden and knife inserted into center is withdrawn clean, 45 to 60 minutes.

WINTER VEGETABLE MELANGE

Count on three root vegetables—carrots, rutabagas and turnips—to give winter meals a flavor lift.

Makes 6 servings

¾ **pound rutabagas, pared, cut into 2 × ⅓ × ⅓-inch julienne strips**
¾ **pound carrots, pared, cut into 2 × ⅓ × ⅓-inch julienne strips**
½ **pound white turnips, pared, cut into 2 × ⅓ × ⅓-inch julienne strips**
½ **teaspoon salt**
¼ **cup butter or margarine, melted**
1 **tablespoon chopped parsley**
2 **teaspoons fresh lemon juice**

1. Combine rutabagas, carrots and turnips in large saucepan; add 2 inches water and the salt. Heat to boiling; reduce heat. Simmer, covered, until vegetables are tender, 15 to 20 minutes; drain well.

2. Combine vegetables with remaining ingredients; mix well. Transfer to serving dish.

NORTH SEA POTATO SALAD

A uniquely elegant salad with creamy-dressed potatoes against dark romaine or spinach leaves and sieved egg yolk and caviar for a garnish.

Makes 6 servings

1 **pound medium red-skinned potatoes, unpared**
Salt
1 **small to medium onion**
1 **large sprig parsley**
½ **cup creamy cheese- or sour-cream-based salad dressing or mayonnaise**
½ **cup whipping cream**
3 **tablespoons chopped chives or green onion**
Spinach or romaine lettuce leaves
2 **hard-cooked eggs**
1 **jar (2 ounces) red or black lumpfish caviar**
Fresh dill sprigs for garnish *(Continued)*

1. Cook potatoes in boiling salted water with onion and parsley until fork-tender, about 25 minutes. Drain; discard onion and parsley.

2. Pare potatoes; cut into thin slices. Combine potatoes and dressing in large bowl; toss gently to mix. Refrigerate, covered, 1 to 4 hours.

3. At serving time, beat cream in small mixer bowl until stiff; fold cream and chives into potatoes. Spoon onto plate lined with spinach leaves. Chop egg whites; sieve egg yolks. Spoon caviar on top of potatoes; top with egg whites and yolks. Garnish with dill.

NEW ENGLAND BAKED BEANS

Makes 6 servings

1 **pound dried Great Northern, small white or navy beans**
Boiling water
1½ **teaspoons salt**
1 **teaspoon dry mustard**
½ **teaspoon pepper**
½ **cup chopped onion**
¼ **cup molasses**
¼ **cup packed brown sugar**
¼ **cup cider vinegar**
¼ **pound salt pork, diced**

1. Add beans to 1 quart boiling water in large saucepan; boil 2 minutes. Remove from heat; let stand, covered, at room temperature 1 hour.

2. Drain beans; mix with salt, mustard and pepper in large bowl. Add onion, molasses, sugar and vinegar; mix well.

3. Spoon ½ of the bean mixture into greased 1½- to 2-quart bean pot or baking dish. Top with ½ of the salt pork. Repeat bean and salt pork layers once. Add enough boiling water to just cover beans.

4. Bake, covered, in preheated 300°F oven 6 hours. Check beans occasionally and add boiling water as needed to prevent top from drying.

Winter Vegetable Melange

EGG AND MACARONI SALAD

Here's a golden egg salad with confetti bits of green pepper and red pimiento, plus a generous measure of creamy pasta.

Makes 6 to 8 servings

⅔ cup mayonnaise
2 teaspoons lemon juice
1 teaspoon instant minced onion
½ teaspoon salt
¼ teaspoon pepper
1 package (7 ounces) elbow macaroni, cooked, drained
6 hard-cooked eggs, chopped
½ cup finely chopped celery
½ cup chopped green bell pepper
½ cup chopped red bell pepper
Leaf lettuce leaves

1. Mix mayonnaise, lemon juice, onion, salt and pepper in large bowl. Add remaining ingredients except lettuce; mix well. Refrigerate, covered, 1 to 4 hours.

2. To serve, spoon salad onto lettuce-lined plates.

NEW ENGLAND PARSNIP SLAW

The smaller the parsnip the sweeter the slaw. Save the larger roots for delicious cooked vegetable combinations.

Makes 6 to 8 servings

½ cup sour cream
2 tablespoons finely chopped onion
2 tablespoons finely chopped parsley
1 tablespoon lemon juice
1 teaspoon sugar
1 teaspoon salt
⅛ teaspoon pepper
8 parsnips
2 apples

1. Mix sour cream, onion, parsley, lemon juice, sugar, salt and pepper in medium bowl.

2. Pare and shred parsnips; add to sour cream dressing. Mix well; refrigerate, covered, several hours.

3. Just before serving, core and dice apples; do not pare. Add to parsnip mixture; mix well.

Egg and Macaroni Salad

Shrimp and Rice Salad

SHRIMP AND RICE SALAD

Butterfly shrimp give a beautiful finishing touch to a salad plate. After removing the vein from peeled, fresh shrimp, make a deeper cut along the back of the shrimp, cutting not quite through. When cooked, the sides of the shrimp open up to look like a butterfly.

Makes 4 servings

  1 pound shrimp, shelled, deveined, butterflied
  2 cloves garlic, minced
  2 tablespoons vegetable oil
  1 medium head romaine lettuce
  4 cups cooked California long-grain rice, room
     temperature
  1 large tomato, coarsely chopped
  4 hard-cooked eggs, coarsely chopped
  ½ cup feta or goat cheese, crumbled
  ½ cup Calamata or ripe olives, pitted
  ¼ pound snow peas, julienned
  ¼ cup chopped red onion
  ¼ cup diced pared cucumber
  3 tablespoons capers, drained
    Herb Dressing (recipe follows)
    French bread, if desired   *(Continued)*

1. Saute shrimp and garlic in oil in large skillet over medium-high heat until opaque throughout, 3 to 5 minutes. Remove shrimp to bowl; refrigerate, covered, until cold.

2. Remove dark green outer leaves from lettuce; reserve. Chop pale green and yellow lettuce heart.

3. Combine chopped lettuce with remaining ingredients except Herb Dressing and bread in large bowl; toss to mix well. Add shrimp; mix well.

4. Line 4 salad plates with reserved lettuce leaves; top with rice mixture. Serve with Herb Dressing and bread.

HERB DRESSING

  1 tablespoon lemon juice
  1 tablespoon Dijon-style mustard
  1 teaspoon anchovy paste
  1 teaspoon dried oregano, crumbled
  1 teaspoon dried basil, crumbled
  1 teaspoon dried chives
  ½ teaspoon salt
  ¼ teaspoon pepper
  ½ cup vegetable oil

Mix all ingredients except oil in small bowl; gradually whisk in oil until blended.

Makes about ⅔ cup

Blushing Beet Salad Ring

SNAPPY CARROT SALAD

Snippets of fresh ginger root, together with a tart lime dressing, add a special zing to this carrot-raisin salad tossed with walnuts and sliced green onions.

Makes 6 to 8 servings

  4 cups shredded carrots
  6 green onions, sliced diagonally
¾ cup chopped walnuts
½ cup raisins
  1 teaspoon minced fresh ginger root
  3 tablespoons vegetable oil
  3 tablespoons lime juice
½ teaspoon salt
⅛ teaspoon pepper
  3 cups broken mixed salad greens

1. Combine carrots, green onions, nuts, raisins and ginger in large bowl; toss to mix.

2. Whisk oil, lime juice, salt and pepper in small bowl until blended. Add to carrot mixture; toss. Serve on salad greens.

BLUSHING BEET SALAD RING

No shy beauty is this deep-red gelatin mold. Pickled beets and horseradish give it plenty of spunk to complement the tasty chicken mixture in the center.

Makes 6 to 8 servings

  1 can (16 ounces) pickled beets
  1 envelope unflavored gelatin
¼ cup cold water
2¾ cups boiling water
  2 packages (3 ounces each) lemon flavor gelatin
  2 tablespoons red wine vinegar
  2 tablespoons prepared horseradish
  1 teaspoon salt
  2 tablespoons finely chopped onion
    Chicken Macaroni Salad (recipe follows)

1. Drain beets, reserving liquid; dice beets.

2. Sprinkle unflavored gelatin over cold water in large bowl; let stand 5 minutes to soften. Add boiling water and lemon gelatin; stir until gelatin is dissolved. Stir in reserved beet

(Continued)

liquid, the vinegar, horseradish and salt. Refrigerate, stirring occasionally, until as thick as unbeaten egg white, 30 to 45 minutes.

3. Fold beets and onion into gelatin mixture; pour into oiled 6-cup ring mold. Refrigerate until set, at least 4 hours.

4. To serve, unmold gelatin ring onto serving plate; spoon Chicken Macaroni Salad into center.

CHICKEN MACARONI SALAD

2 cups diced cooked chicken
¾ cup sliced celery
½ cup small elbow or shell macaroni, cooked, drained
2 hard-cooked eggs, chopped
3 tablespoons chopped green bell pepper
3 tablespoons shredded carrot
2 to 3 tablespoons finely chopped onion
¾ cup mayonnaise
½ cup sour cream
2 tablespoons white wine vinegar
1 teaspoon lemon juice
½ teaspoon Dijon-style mustard
¼ teaspoon salt
    Dash hot red pepper sauce

1. Combine chicken, celery, macaroni, eggs, green bell pepper, carrot and onion in large bowl; toss lightly.

2. Mix remaining ingredients in small bowl; pour over chicken mixture. Toss to coat; refrigerate, covered, at least 1 hour or up to 8 hours.

Makes about 4 cups

RINGED WALDORF SALAD

A shimmering gelatin mold encircles the apple-celery-walnut combination that made a hit when the Waldorf-Astoria Hotel opened in New York in 1893.

Makes 8 servings
2 packages (3 ounces each) strawberry flavor gelatin*
1 quart apple juice, hot
¼ cup lemon juice
5 apples, pared, cored, diced
½ cup diced celery
½ cup chopped walnuts
½ cup mayonnaise
½ cup sour cream or plain yogurt
    Lettuce leaves
    Apple slices for garnish

1. Prepare strawberry gelatin according to package directions, using apple juice instead of water; stir in lemon juice.

2. Rinse 5-cup ring mold with cold water. Add gelatin mixture to mold; refrigerate until set, several hours.

3. Just before serving, combine diced apples, celery, walnuts, mayonnaise and sour cream in medium bowl; mix well.

4. Unmold gelatin onto plate lined with lettuce; spoon apple mixture into center. Garnish with apple slices.

Note: *Cherry or raspberry flavor gelatin can be substituted for strawberry.*

COLORFUL COLESLAW

A slightly tart, homemade dressing that is low in calories makes this crunchy slaw a favorite with salad lovers.
Makes 6 servings
5 cups finely shredded green cabbage
1 cup shredded carrot
1 apple, pared, cored, diced
¼ cup chopped green bell pepper
½ cup evaporated milk
¼ teaspoon salt
⅛ teaspoon ground pepper
¼ cup cider vinegar

1. Combine cabbage, carrot, apple and green bell pepper in large bowl; toss to mix well.

2. Mix milk, salt and ground pepper in small bowl; gradually stir in vinegar. Pour over cabbage mixture; toss. Refrigerate, covered, until serving time.

Colorful Coleslaw

CHALLAH

Challah is a traditional yeast bread baked for the Jewish Sabbath. The dough is often braided and poppy seeds or sesame seeds sprinkled over the egg-glazed top.

Makes 1 loaf

⅔ cup warm water (105 to 115°F)
1 tablespoon sugar
1 package (¼ ounce) active dry yeast
1 large egg
1 tablespoon butter or margarine, melted
1 teaspoon salt
2½ to 3 cups all-purpose flour
   Vegetable oil
1 large egg yolk
2 tablespoons cold water
   Sesame seeds, if desired

1. Combine warm water, sugar and yeast in large bowl; stir to dissolve yeast. Let stand until bubbly, about 5 minutes.

2. Add egg, butter and salt to yeast mixture; whisk until blended. Whisk in 1 cup of the flour; whisk 1 minute. Gradually stir in as much of the remaining flour as needed to make soft dough, about 1½ cups.

3. Knead dough on floured surface, using as much of the remaining flour as needed to prevent sticking, until smooth and elastic, 8 to 10 minutes. *(Continued)*

Challah

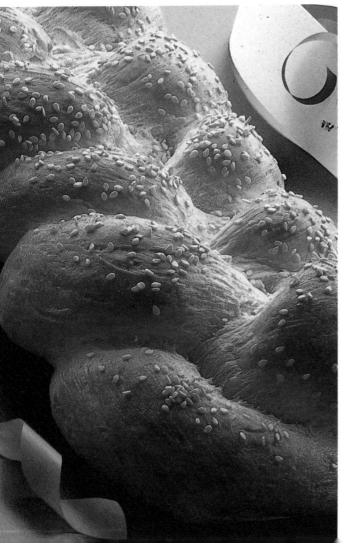

4. Place in greased bowl; turn dough over. Let rise, covered, in warm place until doubled, about 1 hour.

5. Punch down dough; divide into 3 equal pieces. Roll each piece into 24-inch-long rope. Loosely braid ropes together; tuck ends under and pinch to seal. Place on greased baking sheet; brush with oil. Let rise, loosely covered, until almost doubled, about 40 minutes.

6. Beat egg yolk with cold water in small bowl; brush on top and sides of loaf. Sprinkle with sesame seeds. Bake in preheated 375°F oven until top is light brown and bottom sounds hollow when tapped, 25 to 30 minutes. Remove from baking sheet; cool on wire rack.

CINNAMON BRAID

Makes 1 loaf

⅓ cup instant mashed potato flakes
⅓ cup boiling water
⅓ cup warm water (105 to 115°F)
4 tablespoons granulated sugar
1 package (¼ ounce) active dry yeast
1 large egg
¼ cup instant nonfat dry milk solids
¼ cup butter or margarine, melted
1 teaspoon salt
2½ to 3 cups all-purpose flour
   Cinnamon Sugar (recipe follows)

1. Mix potato flakes and boiling water in small bowl; let cool to 105 to 115°F.

2. Combine ⅓ cup warm water, 1 tablespoon of the granulated sugar and the yeast in large bowl; stir to dissolve yeast. Let stand until bubbly, about 5 minutes.

3. Add potato mixture, remaining 3 tablespoons granulated sugar, the egg, milk solids, butter and salt to yeast mixture; whisk until smooth. Whisk in 1½ cups flour until smooth. Stir in as much of the remaining flour as needed to make soft dough, about 1 cup.

4. Knead on floured surface, adding as much of the remaining flour as needed to prevent sticking, until dough is smooth and elastic, about 10 minutes.

5. Place in greased bowl; turn dough over. Let rise, covered, in warm place until doubled, about 1 hour.

6. Punch down dough; divide into 3 even pieces. Roll each piece into 20-inch long strand; roll each strand in Cinnamon Sugar to coat. Braid strands together; pinch ends to seal and tuck under. Place in greased 9 × 5 × 3-inch loaf pan. Let rise again, covered, until almost doubled, about 45 minutes.

7. Bake in preheated 350°F oven until bottom sounds hollow when tapped, 35 to 40 minutes. Immediately remove from pan; cool completely on wire rack.

CINNAMON RAISIN BRAID: Knead ½ cup raisins into dough in Step 4.

CINNAMON SUGAR

¼ cup sugar
2 teaspoons ground cinnamon
1 tablespoon butter or margarine, room temperature

Mix sugar and cinnamon in small bowl. Add butter; mix well.

Prune Nut Swirl

PRUNE NUT SWIRL

Maple-flavored glaze drizzles down the sides of a rich sweet bread to serve for brunch and morning or afternoon coffee get-togethers.

Makes 12 servings

½ cup milk
⅓ cup butter
3½ to 4 cups all-purpose flour
¼ cup sugar
1 package (¼ ounce) active dry yeast
½ teaspoon salt
4 large eggs
Prune Walnut Filling (recipe follows)
Maple Glaze (recipe follows)
Pitted prune halves and walnut halves for garnish

1. Heat milk and butter in small saucepan over low heat to 120 to 130°F; butter need not be completely melted.

2. Mix 1 cup of the flour, the sugar, yeast and salt in large mixer bowl. Gradually add warm milk mixture, beating at medium speed; beat 2 minutes. Beat in 3 of the eggs. Beat in 1 cup of the remaining flour; beat 2 minutes. Stir in as much of the remaining flour as needed to make smooth firm dough, about 1½ cups.

3. Knead dough on floured surface, using as much of the remaining flour as needed to prevent sticking, until smooth, elastic and not sticky, 8 to 10 minutes.

4. Place in greased bowl; turn dough over. Let rise, covered, in warm place until almost doubled, about 1½ hours.

(Continued)

5. Punch down dough. Roll out on lightly floured surface into 16 × 12-inch rectangle. Spread Prune Walnut Filling on dough, leaving ½ inch of edges uncovered. Roll up dough, jelly-roll fashion; pinch bottom seam to seal. Tuck ends under; pinch to seal. Place seam side down on greased baking sheet. Let rise, covered, until almost doubled, about 1 hour.

6. Beat remaining egg in small bowl. Brush top and sides of loaf evenly with egg. Bake in preheated 350°F oven until top is brown and bottom sounds hollow when tapped, 25 to 35 minutes. Remove from baking sheet; cool completely on wire rack.

7. Drizzle with Maple Glaze; garnish with prunes and walnuts. To serve, cut diagonally into thin slices.

PRUNE WALNUT FILLING

1½ cups pitted prunes (9 ounces)
½ cup water
½ teaspoon maple flavoring
1 cup chopped walnuts

Combine prunes, water and flavoring in blender container; process until almost smooth. Transfer to medium bowl; stir in walnuts.

MAPLE GLAZE

1 cup sifted powdered sugar
1 to 2 tablespoons milk
¼ teaspoon maple flavoring

Mix sugar and as much of the milk as needed to make glaze consistency in small bowl until smooth; stir in flavoring.

Olive Pizza Bread

OLIVE PIZZA BREAD

Makes 6 to 8 servings

1 package (13¾ ounces) hot roll mix
1 can (10½ ounces) pizza sauce
2 tablespoons vegetable oil
1 clove garlic, minced
½ teaspoon dried oregano, crumbled
½ teaspoon dried basil, crumbled
⅓ cup grated Parmesan cheese
1½ cups pitted California ripe olives, sliced
¼ cup minced parsley

1. Prepare hot roll mix according to package directions to form dough. Pat out dough on greased baking sheet into 15 × 10 × ¼-inch rectangle. Make deep indentations in dough at 1-inch intervals with finger. Let rise, covered, in warm place until doubled, about 45 minutes.

2. Mix pizza sauce, oil, garlic, oregano and basil in small bowl. Spread ½ of the sauce on top of dough; sprinkle with cheese.

3. Bake in preheated 450°F oven 8 minutes.

4. Sprinkle olives over partially baked dough; drizzle with remaining sauce. Sprinkle with parsley. Bake until edges are light brown, about 5 minutes longer. Serve hot.

Note: Wrap bread well and freeze, if desired. To reheat, unwrap and place on baking sheet; bake in 350°F oven about 25 minutes.

PARKER HOUSE ROLLS

These light, tender dinner rolls, easily recognized by their folded-over tops, originated at a famous Boston hotel.
Makes 15 to 18 rolls

⅔ cup warm water (105 to 115°F)
3 tablespoons sugar
1 package (¼ ounce) active dry yeast
3 tablespoons butter or margarine, melted
3 tablespoons instant nonfat dry milk solids
1 large egg, beaten
1 teaspoon salt
2½ to 3 cups all-purpose flour
Melted butter

1. Combine water, 1 tablespoon of the sugar and the yeast in large bowl; stir to dissolve yeast. Let stand until bubbly, about 5 minutes.

2. Add the remaining 2 tablespoons sugar, 3 tablespoons butter, the milk solids, egg and salt to yeast mixture; mix well. Beat in 1 cup of the flour. Stir in as much of the remaining flour as needed to make soft dough, about 1½ cups.

3. Knead dough on floured surface, using as much of the remaining flour as needed to prevent sticking, until dough is smooth and elastic, about 10 minutes.

4. Place in greased bowl; turn dough over. Let rise, covered, in warm place until doubled, 1 to 1½ hours.

(Continued)

5. Punch down dough. Roll out ¼ inch thick on floured surface. Cut dough with 3-inch round cutter. Make crease with dull edge of knife, just off center, on each round. Fold larger side over smaller side; pinch rounded edge just at center point to seal.

6. Gather dough trimmings; roll out, cut and shape as in step 5 until all dough has been used.

7. Place rolls on greased baking sheets; brush with butter. Let rise, loosely covered, until doubled, 30 to 40 minutes.

8. Bake in preheated 375°F oven until rolls are golden, 12 to 15 minutes. Remove from baking sheets. Serve warm, or cool on wire racks.

APPLE PECAN MUFFINS

Bake up a batch of crunchy muffins to serve warm from the oven for a weekend breakfast or with a soup or salad lunch.
Makes 12 muffins

2 cups buttermilk baking mix
½ cup chopped pecans
¼ cup sugar
¼ teaspoon ground cinnamon
½ cup water
1 large egg, lightly beaten
¼ cup frozen apple juice concentrate, thawed, undiluted
2 tablespoons butter or margarine, melted

1. Mix baking mix, pecans, sugar and cinnamon in large bowl. Mix remaining ingredients in medium bowl; add to dry ingredients. Stir just until moistened; do not overmix.

2. Spoon batter into greased muffin tin cups, filling about ⅔ full. Bake in preheated 400°F oven until wooden pick inserted into center is withdrawn clean, 12 to 15 minutes. Cool in pan on wire rack 5 minutes. Remove from pan; serve warm, or cool completely on rack.

BANANA PUMPKIN BREAD

Fruit-nut breads slice more easily if wrapped in aluminum foil when cool and allowed to stand several hours or overnight. Since this recipe makes 3 loaves, you may want to foil-wrap one or more for the freezer.
Makes 3 loaves

3 to 4 very ripe medium bananas
1½ cups sugar
1 cup solid-pack pumpkin
3 large eggs
1 cup vegetable oil
5 cups all-purpose flour
1 tablespoon baking soda
2 teaspoons ground cinnamon
½ teaspoon ground cloves
2 cups chopped walnuts
Orange Cream Cheese Spread (recipe follows)

1. Process enough bananas in blender until smooth to make 2 cups. Combine banana puree, sugar, pumpkin and eggs in large mixer bowl; beat well. Beat in oil.

(Continued)

2. Mix flour, baking soda, cinnamon and cloves in medium bowl; add to banana mixture, ¼ at a time, mixing well after each addition. Stir in walnuts.

3. Pour batter into 3 greased 8½ × 4½ × 3-inch loaf pans. Bake in preheated 350°F oven until wooden pick inserted into center is withdrawn clean, 50 to 60 minutes.

4. Cool in pans on wire racks 10 minutes. Remove from pans; cool completely on racks. Serve with Orange Cream Cheese Spread.

ORANGE CREAM CHEESE SPREAD

1 package (8 ounces) cream cheese, room temperature
3 tablespoons orange juice
1 tablespoon grated orange rind

Combine all ingredients in small mixer bowl; beat until smooth.

Makes about 1 cup

EGG BAGELS

It's the boiling before baking that gives bagels their delightfully chewy texture. Split these doughnut-shaped rolls and spread with cream cheese and top with smoked salmon or other savory sandwich fillings.
Makes 1 dozen bagels

⅔ cup warm water (105 to 115°F)
1 package (¼ ounce) active dry yeast
2 tablespoons plus 1 teaspoon sugar
2 large eggs
1 tablespoon vegetable oil
1 teaspoon salt
2¼ to 2¾ cups all-purpose flour
2 tablespoons cold water

1. Combine warm water, yeast and 1 teaspoon of the sugar in large bowl; stir to dissolve yeast. Let stand until bubbly, about 5 minutes.

2. Add 1 of the eggs, the oil and salt to yeast mixture; whisk until blended. Whisk in 1½ cups of the flour until smooth. Stir in as much of the remaining flour as needed to make soft dough, about ¾ cup.

3. Knead on floured surface, adding as much of the remaining flour as needed to prevent sticking, until dough is smooth and elastic, about 10 minutes. Let stand, covered with plastic wrap, 15 minutes.

4. Divide dough into 12 equal pieces; roll each piece into 6-inch-long strand. Moisten ends of each strand; pinch together to seal, forming doughnut shape. Place on greased baking sheet; let stand at room temperature 15 minutes.

5. Add remaining 2 tablespoons sugar to 2 quarts water in large pot; heat to boiling. Carefully place 3 or 4 bagels into boiling water. When bagels rise to surface, turn them over; cook until puffed, 1½ to 2 minutes longer. Remove with slotted spoon; place on greased baking sheet. Repeat until all bagels have been boiled.

6. Beat remaining egg and cold water in small bowl; brush on tops of bagels. Bake in preheated 425°F oven until tops are golden and crisp, 20 to 25 minutes. Remove from baking sheets; cool on wire racks.

BELGIAN WAFFLES WITH CHERRY SAUCE

Most Americans first tasted these crisp waffles with the big, deep squares at the 1964 New York World's Fair. Today Belgian wafflemakers are a popular countertop appliance.
Makes 8 servings

    4 large eggs, separated
    3 tablespoons margarine, melted
    1 tablespoon plus ½ teaspoon vanilla
    1 cup all-purpose flour
    1 cup milk
    ½ teaspoon salt
    2 pounds ricotta cheese
 1½ cups powdered sugar
       Cherry Sauce (recipe follows)

1. Beat egg yolks, margarine and ½ teaspoon of the vanilla in large bowl until blended. Whisk in flour until smooth; whisk in milk and salt.

2. Beat egg whites in large mixer bowl until stiff but not dry; fold into egg yolk mixture. Bake batter in Belgian waffle iron according to manufacturer's instructions; keep waffles warm.

(Continued)

3. Combine cheese, sugar and remaining 1 tablespoon vanilla in large bowl; beat until smooth. Break or cut each waffle into 2 sections. For each serving, spread 1 section with ¼ cup cheese filling; top with second section. Top each stack with ½ cup Cherry Sauce.

CHERRY SAUCE

    ½ cup sugar
 1½ tablespoons cornstarch
 1½ cups cold water
    2 cups dark sweet cherries, pitted
    2 teaspoons rum extract
    1 teaspoon lemon juice
    3 drops red food coloring

1. Mix sugar and cornstarch in medium saucepan; stir in water. Cook, stirring constantly, over medium heat until mixture thickens and bubbles for 3 minutes.

2. Stir in cherries; cook just until hot. Do not boil. Stir in rum extract, lemon juice and food coloring. Let stand at room temperature 2 to 3 hours before serving.

Makes 1 quart

Belgian Waffles with Cherry Sauce

STRAWBERRY RIPPLE COFFEE CAKE

Makes 8 servings

⅔ cup butter or margarine, room temperature
⅔ cup sugar
2 cups all-purpose flour
2 large eggs
2 teaspoons baking powder
½ teaspoon salt
½ teaspoon baking soda
½ teaspoon ground cinnamon
¼ teaspoon ground nutmeg
⅔ cup buttermilk
⅓ cup strawberry jam

1. Beat butter and sugar in large mixer bowl until light and fluffy. Add ¾ cup of the flour; mix slowly just until mixture forms coarse crumbs. Remove ⅔ cup of the crumb mixture and reserve.

2. Add eggs, baking powder, salt, baking soda, cinnamon and nutmeg to remaining mixture in bowl; beat until smooth. Add remaining 1¼ cups flour ½ at a time, alternating with buttermilk, beating until smooth after each addition.

3. Spread batter in greased 9 × 9 × 2-inch baking pan. Drop jam by teaspoons onto batter; pull knife through batter to give marbled effect. Sprinkle reserved crumb mixture on top.

4. Bake in preheated 350°F oven until wooden pick inserted into center is withdrawn clean, 30 to 35 minutes. Serve warm.

Strawberry Ripple Coffee Cake

SOFT PRETZELS

Pretzels will keep their unique twist during cooking if you will let each one float off a wide spatula into the boiling water.

Makes 12 pretzels

¾ cup warm water (105 to 115°F)
1 tablespoon sugar
1 package (¼ ounce) active dry yeast
1 teaspoon table salt
2½ to 3 cups all-purpose flour
¼ cup baking soda
6 cups boiling water
1 large egg white, beaten
Coarse (kosher) salt

1. Combine warm water, sugar and yeast in large bowl; stir to dissolve yeast. Let stand until bubbly, about 5 minutes.

2. Add table salt and 1 cup of the flour to yeast mixture; beat well. Stir in as much of the remaining flour as needed to make soft dough, about 1½ cups.

3. Knead dough on floured surface, using as much of the remaining flour as needed to prevent sticking, until smooth and elastic, about 10 minutes. Cover dough with inverted bowl; let stand 10 minutes.

4. Divide dough into 12 equal pieces; roll each piece into 20-inch-long rope. Twist ropes into pretzel shapes; place on well-greased baking sheets. Let rise, uncovered, until almost doubled, about 30 minutes.

5. Add baking soda to 6 cups boiling water in nonaluminum Dutch oven over medium-high heat.   *(Continued)*

6. Cook 1 or 2 pretzels at a time. Carefully lift from baking sheet with wide metal spatula; lower into boiling water. Cook until puffed, about 15 seconds. Remove from water, draining well; place pretzels ½ inch apart on greased baking sheets.

7. Brush pretzels with egg white; sprinkle lightly with coarse salt. Bake in preheated 400°F oven until golden, about 20 minutes. Remove from baking sheets; cool on wire racks.

SOFT RYE PRETZEL VARIATION: Prepare recipe as above, substituting ½ cup rye flour for ½ cup of the all-purpose flour and adding 1 tablespoon caraway seeds.

POPOVERS

It's the steam from the milk and eggs that makes the batter "pop" during baking and produce the hollow in the middle of a crusty shell. Serve as a delightful hot bread any time, or break open to fill with creamed chicken or seafood.

Makes 6 large or 12 small popovers

1 cup milk
1 cup all-purpose flour
3 large eggs, beaten
1 tablespoon butter or margarine, melted
½ teaspoon salt

1. Grease and flour six 6-ounce custard cups or 12 muffin cups.

2. Combine all ingredients in medium bowl; beat just until smooth. Pour into prepared cups, dividing evenly.

3. Bake in preheated 375°F oven until dark brown and crisp, 45 to 50 minutes. Serve immediately.

CHEESE VARIATION: Substitute garlic salt for salt. Stir ½ cup shredded Cheddar or Swiss cheese into batter.

Boston Brown Bread

OLD-FASHIONED OATMEAL BREAD

Makes 1 loaf

1 cup water
½ teaspoon salt
⅓ cup plus 2 teaspoons rolled oats
⅓ cup warm water (105 to 115°F)
3 tablespoons packed light brown sugar or light molasses
1 package (¼ ounce) active dry yeast
2 tablespoons vegetable oil
2½ to 3 cups all-purpose flour

1. Combine 1 cup water and the salt in small saucepan; heat to boiling. Stir in ⅓ cup of the oats; cook, uncovered, over medium heat 5 minutes. Let cool to 105 to 115°F.

2. Combine ⅓ cup warm water, 1 tablespoon of the sugar and the yeast in large bowl; stir to dissolve yeast. Let stand until bubbly, about 5 minutes.

3. Add cooked oatmeal, remaining 2 tablespoons sugar and the oil to yeast mixture; mix well. Whisk in 1½ cups of the flour until blended. Stir in as much of the remaining flour as needed to make soft dough, about 1 cup.

4. Knead on floured surface, adding as much of the remaining flour as needed to prevent sticking, until dough is smooth and elastic, about 10 minutes.

5. Place in greased bowl; turn dough over. Let rise, covered, in warm place until doubled, about 1 hour.

6. Punch down dough; shape into loaf. Place in greased 8½ × 4½ × 2½-inch loaf pan; sprinkle with remaining 2 teaspoons oats. Let rise, covered, until almost doubled, about 45 minutes.

7. Bake in preheated 375°F oven until bottom sounds hollow when tapped, 25 to 30 minutes. Immediately remove loaf from pan; cool completely on wire rack.

BOSTON BROWN BREAD

Makes about 16 servings

⅔ cup dark molasses
2 large eggs, well beaten
2 tablespoons butter or margarine, melted
1 teaspoon baking soda
1 cup buttermilk
1 cup all-purpose flour
1 cup whole wheat flour
1 cup rye flour
1 teaspoon baking powder
½ teaspoon salt
½ cup golden raisins
½ cup chopped nuts
    Boiling water
    Cream cheese, butter and preserves, if desired

1. Mix molasses, eggs and butter in large bowl. Stir baking soda into buttermilk in small bowl. Mix all-purpose, whole wheat and rye flours, baking powder and salt in medium bowl.

2. Add ⅓ of the flour mixture at a time to molasses mixture, alternating with buttermilk mixture, mixing well after each addition. Stir in raisins and nuts.

3. Spoon batter into 3 or 4 greased tin cans (16- to 20-ounce size), filling ½ full. Cover cans with double thickness of greased aluminum foil; tie securely with kitchen string.

4. Place cans on rack in large kettle; add boiling water to kettle to come halfway up sides of cans. Cover kettle; adjust heat to maintain steady steam.

5. Steam until wooden pick inserted into center is withdrawn clean, 1 to 1½ hours. Remove cans from water; cool on wire rack 2 to 3 minutes. Remove breads from cans; serve warm, or cool completely on racks. Serve with cream cheese, butter and preserves.

BLUEBERRY ALMOND LOAF

Bran cereal, nuts and fruit in a breakfast bread flavored with orange get the day off to a super start.

Makes 2 small loaves

  ¾ **cup sugar**
  ¾ **cup orange juice**
  1 **large egg, beaten**
  3 **tablespoons vegetable oil**
  2 **teaspoons grated orange rind**
1¾ **cups all-purpose flour**
  ¾ **cup unprocessed miller's bran or bran cereal**
  3 **teaspoons baking powder**
  1 **teaspoon ground cinnamon**
  ½ **teaspoon salt**
  1 **cup whole unblanched almonds, finely chopped**
  1 **cup fresh or frozen blueberries**

1. Combine sugar, orange juice, egg, oil and orange rind in large bowl; beat well.

2. Mix flour, bran, baking powder, cinnamon and salt in medium bowl. Add to sugar mixture; stir just until evenly moistened. Stir in almonds and blueberries.

3. Pour batter into 2 greased and floured 7½ × 3½ × 2½-inch loaf pans. Bake in preheated 350°F oven until wooden pick inserted into center is withdrawn clean, about 35 minutes. Cool in pans on wire rack 5 minutes. Remove from pans; cool completely on rack.

MAPLE SYRUP DOUGHNUTS

Maintain 375°F as the temperature of the oil in the fry kettle for doughnut making. Cook only a few at a time to avoid a temperature drop when fresh doughnuts are added.

Makes about 1 dozen

1 **cup maple syrup**
1 **tablespoon solid vegetable shortening**
2 **large eggs**
4 **cups all-purpose flour**
1 **teaspoon baking powder**
1 **teaspoon baking soda**
½ **teaspoon salt**
½ **teaspoon ground nutmeg**
⅔ **cup buttermilk**
  Vegetable oil for frying

1. Beat syrup and shortening in large mixer bowl until blended. Beat in eggs until smooth.

2. Sift flour, baking powder, baking soda, salt and nutmeg into medium bowl. Add flour mixture, ⅓ at a time, to syrup mixture, alternating with buttermilk, mixing well after each addition. Refrigerate dough, covered, 1 hour.

3. Heat 2 inches oil in Dutch oven to 375°F. Roll out dough on lightly floured surface to ½-inch thickness. Cut out dough with doughnut cutter.

4. Fry 3 or 4 doughnuts at a time in oil, turning once, until golden brown and cooked through, about 2½ minutes per side. Drain on wire racks lined with paper toweling.

Blueberry Almond Loaf

Celestial Brownies

CELESTIAL BROWNIES

A heavenly confection with the most chocolate, nuts and chewy goodness of any brownie under the sun.

Makes 16 brownies

  8 ounces semisweet chocolate, chopped
  7 tablespoons butter
  2 large eggs, room temperature
  ¾ cup granulated sugar
  1 teaspoon vanilla
  ¼ cup all-purpose flour
  1 cup coarsely chopped toasted walnuts or pecans
  Powdered sugar, if desired

1. Melt chocolate and butter in top of double boiler over hot water; stir until smooth.

2. Beat eggs in large mixer bowl at high speed 1 minute. Gradually beat in granulated sugar. Continue beating until mixture is pale yellow and has consistency of soft-peaked whipped cream, 4 to 5 minutes.

3. Reduce mixer speed to medium; beat in chocolate mixture and vanilla until thoroughly blended. Add flour; beat at low speed just until flour is absorbed. Stir in nuts; spread batter evenly in well-greased 8-inch square baking pan.

4. Bake in preheated 375°F oven until wooden pick inserted into center is withdrawn clean, about 30 minutes. Cool completely in pan on wire rack. Cut into squares; sprinkle with powdered sugar.

Note: *For extra-chewy texture, cover brownies and let stand at room temperature overnight.*

OATMEAL DATE BARS

A buttery mixture of brown sugar and oats surrounds a smooth date filling in these rich cookie squares.

Makes about 16 bars

  1½ cups chopped pitted dates
  ¾ cup water
  2 tablespoons granulated sugar
  1 cup all-purpose flour
  1 cup quick-cooking oats
  ½ cup packed brown sugar
  ½ teaspoon baking soda
  ½ teaspoon salt
  ½ cup butter or margarine, cold

1. Combine dates, water and granulated sugar in medium saucepan; cook over medium-high heat to boiling. Cook, stirring constantly, until dates are soft, about 5 minutes; remove from heat.

2. Mix flour, oats, brown sugar, baking soda and salt in medium bowl. Cut in butter until mixture resembles coarse crumbs.

3. Press ½ of the oat mixture on bottom of greased 8-inch square baking pan; spread evenly with date mixture. Cover date mixture evenly with remaining oat mixture; press firmly with spatula.

4. Bake in preheated 400°F oven until top is light brown, 40 to 45 minutes. Cool completely on wire rack; cut into bars.

HOLIDAY STEAMED PUDDING

Makes 10 to 12 servings

2½ cups all-purpose flour
  1 teaspoon ground cinnamon
  ¾ teaspoon baking soda
  ½ teaspoon ground ginger
  ½ teaspoon ground nutmeg
  ½ teaspoon salt
  ¼ teaspoon ground cloves
1⅔ cups maraschino cherries, drained, cut into
      halves
  1 cup chopped dried apricots
  1 cup chopped dried figs
  1 cup chopped prunes
  1 cup chopped walnuts
  ¾ cup currants
  ⅞ cup finely ground suet
  ¾ cup light molasses
  ¾ cup milk
      Boiling water
      Brandied figs, red candied cherries and
        maraschino cherry slices for garnish
      Hard Sauce (see Index) or whipped cream, if
        desired

1. Sift flour, cinnamon, baking soda, ginger, nutmeg, salt and cloves into large bowl. Add cherry halves, apricots, dried figs, prunes, walnuts and currants; toss to mix well.

2. Add suet, molasses and milk to bowl; mix well. Pour into well-buttered 2-quart mold. *(Continued)*

3. Cover mold with heavy-duty aluminum foil; tie securely with string. Place mold on rack in large kettle; add boiling water to come halfway up sides of mold.

4. Cover kettle; adjust heat to maintain simmer. Steam until metal skewer inserted into center of pudding is withdrawn clean, 2 to 2½ hours. Add water to kettle, if needed, during cooking.

5. Unmold pudding onto platter; garnish with brandied figs and cherries. Serve with Hard Sauce or whipped cream.

PETITE PRUNE TARTS

Miniature-muffin pans are the size to use for baking the small pastry shells for this sophisticated dessert.
Makes 16 tartlets

16 pitted prunes
  ¼ cup sherry
  ½ cup sour cream
  1 to 2 tablespoons packed brown sugar
16 baked 2-inch tartlet shells
16 candied violets for garnish

1. Combine prunes and sherry in small bowl; let stand, stirring occasionally, 1 to 2 hours.

2. Mix sour cream with brown sugar to taste in small bowl. Drain prunes.

3. Spoon sour cream mixture into tartlet shells, dividing evenly. Top each with 1 prune; garnish with candied violets.

Holiday Steamed Pudding

POACHED PEARS IN RUM SAUCE

Makes 4 servings

4 medium firm-ripe pears
¾ cup boiling water
¼ cup rum
¼ teaspoon ground mace or nutmeg
½ cup packed brown sugar
¼ cup butter
½ cup whipping cream

1. Pare pears, leaving stems on. Carefully core pears from bottom, leaving tops intact. Stand pears upright in saucepan just large enough to hold them; add water and rum to pan. Sprinkle pears with mace, then with sugar; dot with butter.

2. Cook, covered, over low heat, basting frequently, until pears are just tender, 15 to 20 minutes. Carefully remove pears to serving dish; keep warm.

3. Add cream to saucepan; cook over medium-high heat, stirring frequently, until sauce is reduced and thickened. Pour sauce over pears; serve hot.

CHERRY MOUSSE

Makes 8 servings

3 large eggs, separated, room temperature
¼ cup sugar
3 tablespoons water
3 cups whipping cream
1¾ cups pitted tart or sweet cherries, pureed
Sliced almonds for garnish

1. Beat egg whites in large mixer bowl until stiff but not dry; transfer to another large bowl. Place egg yolks in large mixer bowl.

2. Combine sugar and water in small saucepan; heat over high heat until sugar dissolves and syrup boils for 1 minute. Add syrup to egg yolks in thin stream while beating; beat at high speed until stiff and shiny, 5 to 6 minutes. Fold into egg whites.

3. Beat cream in large mixer bowl until stiff; fold into egg mixture. Fold in cherry puree. Pour into individual serving dishes; refrigerate, covered, at least 2 hours. Garnish with almonds.

Poached Pears in Rum Sauce

CHARLOTTE RUSSE

Ladyfingers, those small split sponge cakes about a finger's length long, form the outer layer in this classic molded dessert.

Makes 6 to 8 servings

2 envelopes unflavored gelatin
¼ cup cold water
1⅓ cups milk
⅔ cup sugar
4 large egg yolks
1 teaspoon vanilla
14 ladyfingers, split
½ cup sour cream
⅓ cup chopped blanched almonds
1 cup whipping cream

1. Sprinkle gelatin over cold water in small bowl; let stand 5 minutes to soften.

2. Heat milk in heavy medium saucepan until warm. Beat sugar and egg yolks in small bowl until blended; gradually whisk into warm milk. Cook, stirring constantly, over low heat until thick enough to coat spoon, about 10 minutes; do not boil. Remove from heat.

3. Add gelatin mixture to hot custard; stir until gelatin is completely dissolved. Stir in vanilla. Refrigerate, stirring occasionally, until mixture thickens enough to mound from a spoon, about 1 hour.

4. Meanwhile, butter 2-quart charlotte mold or souffle dish. Line bottom with circle of waxed paper; butter paper. Line bottom and sides of mold with ladyfingers, cut sides facing in, cutting to fit.

5. Stir sour cream and almonds into gelatin mixture. Beat cream in small mixer bowl until stiff; fold into gelatin mixture. Pour into mold.

6. Refrigerate until completely set, at least 5 hours. Unmold just before serving.

EGGNOG PRALINE PIE

Here's a holiday dessert that heaps eggnog's good cheer over brown-sugar candy in a graham cracker crust.

Makes 8 servings

4 tablespoons butter or margarine
¼ cup packed brown sugar
⅓ cup chopped pecans
1 packaged graham cracker crumb crust (6-ounce)
¼ cup granulated sugar
¼ cup all-purpose flour
¼ teaspoon salt
2 cups eggnog
Whipped cream and ground nutmeg for garnish

1. Combine 3 tablespoons of the butter, the brown sugar and pecans in small saucepan; cook and stir over medium heat until mixture comes to full boil. Spread mixture in bottom of pie crust.

2. Mix granulated sugar, flour and salt in medium saucepan; stir in eggnog. Cook, stirring constantly, over medium heat until mixture thickens and bubbles for 1 minute; remove from heat. Stir in remaining 1 tablespoon butter until melted; pour into pie crust.

3. Refrigerate, covered, until set, several hours. Garnish with whipped cream and nutmeg.

Cheese Blintzes

CHEESE BLINTZES

Thin egg pancakes filled with cottage cheese and topped with fruit for brunch or dessert.

Makes 6 to 9 servings

1 cup all-purpose flour
1½ teaspoons salt
1 cup milk
4 large eggs, beaten
2 to 3 tablespoons butter
3 cups cottage cheese
3 tablespoons sugar
1 large egg yolk
2 teaspoons vanilla
½ teaspoon grated lemon rind
Preserves and fresh or canned fruit

1. Mix flour and 1 teaspoon of the salt in medium bowl; gradually stir in milk until smooth. Whisk in eggs.

2. Heat 6-inch nonstick skillet over medium heat until hot. Add 1 teaspoon of the butter. Add 2 tablespoons of the batter; rotate pan to cover bottom evenly with batter. Cook until top of pancake is set and dry, about 1 minute. Turn pancake out onto clean towel, brown side up. Repeat, adding butter to pan as needed, until all batter is used. (You should have 18 pancakes.)

3. Combine cottage cheese, sugar, egg yolk, vanilla, lemon rind and remaining ½ teaspoon salt in medium bowl; mix well.

4. Place 2 to 3 tablespoons of the cottage cheese mixture in center of each pancake. Fold sides over filling; roll up ends. Place blintzes in baking pan. Heat in preheated 350°F oven until hot, about 10 minutes. Serve with preserves and fruit.

Festive Christmas Cake

FESTIVE CHRISTMAS CAKE

Treat carolers and tree-trimmers to slices of tender yellow cake decked out with bright red cherries and nuts.

Makes 12 to 16 servings

  1 cup finely chopped pecans
  1 jar (8 ounces) maraschino cherries, drained
  1 package (8 ounces) cream cheese, room
    temperature
  1 cup butter or margarine, room temperature
1½ cups granulated sugar
1½ teaspoons vanilla
1½ teaspoons ground cinnamon
  ¼ teaspoon ground nutmeg
  4 large eggs
2¼ cups sifted cake flour
1½ teaspoons baking powder
1½ cups sifted powdered sugar
  1 to 2 tablespoons milk
    Pecan halves for garnish

1. Sprinkle ½ cup of the finely chopped pecans evenly in bottom of greased 10-inch Bundt or tube pan. Reserve 4 cherries for garnish; chop remaining cherries.

2. Combine cream cheese, butter, granulated sugar, vanilla, cinnamon and nutmeg in large mixer bowl; beat until light and fluffy. Add eggs, 1 at a time, beating well after each addition.

3. Sift 2 cups of the flour with baking powder; gradually beat into butter mixture. Combine remaining ¼ cup flour, ½ cup pecans and chopped cherries in medium bowl; mix well. Fold into batter.

4. Pour batter into prepared pan. Bake in preheated 325°F oven until wooden pick inserted into center is withdrawn
(Continued)

clean, about 1 hour and 15 minutes. Cool in pan on wire rack 5 minutes. Remove from pan; cool completely on rack.

5. Before serving, cut reserved cherries into halves. Mix powdered sugar with as much milk as needed to form thick glaze consistency in small bowl until smooth. Spoon glaze on top of cake; garnish with cherry and pecan halves.

APPLE STREUSEL MINCE PIE

With its nutty streusel topping, this pie saves the fuss of rolling out a top crust. Choose firm all-purpose apples for the filling.

Makes one 9-inch pie

  3 apples, pared, thinly sliced
  ½ cup plus 3 tablespoons all-purpose flour
  2 tablespoons butter or margarine, melted
  1 unbaked 9-inch pastry shell
  1 jar (28 ounces) mincemeat
  ¼ cup packed light brown sugar
  1 teaspoon ground cinnamon
  ⅓ cup butter or margarine, cold
  ¼ cup chopped nuts

1. Toss apple slices with 3 tablespoons of the flour and the melted butter in large bowl. Arrange in pastry shell; top with mincemeat.

2. Combine remaining ½ cup flour, the sugar and cinnamon in medium bowl; cut in cold butter until crumbly. Stir in nuts. Sprinkle over mincemeat.

3. Bake in preheated 425°F oven 10 minutes. Reduce oven setting to 375°F; bake until golden brown, 25 to 30 minutes longer. Cool slightly before serving.

FIG AND NUT CAKE

A luscious, fruit-packed loaf with chopped chocolate, diced candied orange and lemon peels but no shortening.

Makes 12 to 16 servings

¾ cup hazelnuts (about 4 ounces)
¾ cup whole dried figs (about 4 ounces)
⅔ cup slivered blanched almonds (about 3 ounces)
⅓ cup diced candied orange peel
⅓ cup diced candied lemon peel
3 ounces semisweet chocolate, finely chopped
3 large eggs
½ cup sugar
1¼ cups all-purpose flour
1¾ teaspoons baking powder
¾ teaspoon salt

1. Toast hazelnuts in small baking pan in preheated 350°F oven 12 minutes; let cool slightly. Rub a few hazelnuts at a time between palms of hands to remove as much of the skins as possible.

2. Coarsely chop hazelnuts, figs, almonds and candied orange and lemon peels. Combine with chocolate in medium bowl; mix well.

3. Beat eggs and sugar in large mixer bowl at high speed until very pale yellow and thick and fluffy, at least 5 minutes. Gently fold nut mixture into egg mixture.

4. Combine flour, baking powder and salt in sieve. Sift ½ of the flour mixture over egg mixture; gently fold in. Repeat with remaining flour mixture. Spread batter in greased 8½ × 4½ × 3-inch loaf pan.

5. Bake until top is deep golden brown and center is firm to touch, 60 to 70 minutes. Cool in pan on wire rack 5 minutes. Remove from pan; cool completely on rack, at least 4 hours, before cutting.

ZABAGLIONE

A marvelous Italian custard dessert made with wine and cooked with care in a double boiler. Delicious served with any fresh berries.

Makes 4 servings

5 large egg yolks, room temperature
¼ cup sugar
½ cup Marsala
¼ cup dry white wine
Sliced fresh fruit and cookies, if desired

1. Combine egg yolks and sugar in top of double boiler; beat with portable electric mixer or rotary beaters until mixture is pale yellow and creamy.

2. Place top of double boiler over simmering water over low heat. Gradually beat ½ of the Marsala into egg yolk mixture; beat 1 minute. Gradually beat in remaining Marsala and the white wine.

3. Reduce heat to very low; continue cooking custard over gently simmering water, beating constantly and scraping bottom and sides of pan frequently, until mixture is fluffy and thick enough to form soft mounds when dropped from beaters, 6 to 10 minutes. Watch very carefully and do not overcook or custard will curdle.

4. Immediately remove top of double boiler from water. Whisk custard briefly; pour into individual dishes. Serve at once with fruit and cookies.

BLUEBERRY GRUNT

A good old Down East name for biscuit-topped blueberry cobbler often spiced with nutmeg.

Makes 8 servings

2 cups fresh blueberries*
1 cup water
½ cup sugar
1½ cups all-purpose flour
2 teaspoons baking powder
2 teaspoons grated orange rind
¼ teaspoon ground nutmeg
¼ teaspoon salt
¾ cup milk
Whipped cream, if desired

1. Combine blueberries, water and sugar in medium skillet; cook and stir over medium heat until mixture just starts to bubble. Reduce heat.

2. Mix flour, baking powder, orange rind, nutmeg and salt in medium bowl. Add milk; stir just until moistened.

3. Drop batter by spoonfuls on top of simmering blueberries. Cover skillet; simmer until dumplings are puffed, 10 to 15 minutes. Serve with cream.

Note: *2 cans (15 ounces each) blueberries in syrup can be substituted for fresh; omit water and sugar.*

Blueberry Grunt

VIENNESE ALMOND TORTE

Serve this exquisite Austrian pastry as the Austrian-Americans do. Accompany each wedge with a cup of coffee topped with a dollop of unsweetened whipped cream.

Makes 10 servings

  2 cups all-purpose flour
  ⅓ cup plus ¼ cup plus 1 tablespoon sugar
  1 teaspoon grated orange rind
  ½ teaspoon salt
  ¾ cup butter or margarine, cold
  1 large egg, separated
  1 tablespoon rum
  ¼ cup whipping cream
  1 teaspoon almond extract
  1¼ cups whole blanched almonds, ground
  ½ cup raspberry jam
  1 large whole egg
  1 tablespoon water

1. Mix flour, ⅓ cup of the sugar, the orange rind and salt in medium bowl; cut in butter until mixture resembles fine crumbs. Mix egg yolk and rum in small bowl; drizzle over flour mixture, stirring and tossing with fork. Knead dough

(Continued)

in bowl briefly until smooth; refrigerate, wrapped in plastic, 30 minutes.

2. Press ¾ of the dough on bottom and 1¼ inches up side of 9-inch springform pan.

3. Whisk egg white in medium bowl until foamy; whisk in ¼ cup of the sugar, the cream and almond extract. Stir in almonds.

4. Spread almond mixture evenly in bottom of pastry shell. Drop jam by spoonfuls on top of almond mixture; spread in even layer.

5. Roll out remaining dough on lightly floured surface into 9×5-inch rectangle; cut with fluted pastry wheel into ten 9×½-inch strips. Weave strips in lattice pattern on top of jam. Trim ends of strips; press against side pastry to seal. Flute edge.

6. Beat remaining whole egg with water in small bowl. Brush pastry strips with egg wash; sprinkle with remaining 1 tablespoon sugar.

7. Bake in preheated 350°F oven until pastry is golden and crisp, 25 to 30 minutes. Cool completely in pan on wire rack. Remove sides of pan before serving.

Viennese Almond Torte

POTS DE CREME

Small cups of a rich chocolate and peanut butter dessert put a sweet finish to an elegant dinner.

Makes 6 servings

½ cup milk
2 ounces unsweetened chocolate, chopped
1 teaspoon butter
¾ cup powdered sugar
½ cup peanut butter
1 teaspoon vanilla
2 large eggs, separated
½ cup whipping cream
Whipped cream and chopped peanuts for garnish

1. Combine milk, chocolate and butter in small saucepan; cook, stirring occasionally, over low heat until chocolate is melted and mixture is smooth. Add sugar, peanut butter and vanilla; whisk until smooth.

2. Gradually whisk hot chocolate mixture into egg yolks in small bowl; return to saucepan. Cook, stirring constantly, over low heat until thickened, about 1 minute. Do not boil. Immediately transfer to medium bowl; let cool, covered.

3. Beat egg whites in small mixer bowl until stiff but not dry; fold into chocolate mixture. Beat ½ cup cream in small mixer bowl until stiff; fold into chocolate mixture.

4. Spoon into 6 pot de creme cups or custard cups; refrigerate, covered, until cold. Garnish with whipped cream and peanuts before serving.

RIESLING CHIFFON CAKE

A tall, pale gold cake with a lightness in texture to match the delicate flavor of the white wine in the batter.

Makes 12 servings

2¼ cups sifted cake flour
1½ cups granulated sugar
1 cup blanched almonds, finely ground
3 teaspoons baking powder
1 teaspoon salt
¾ cup Riesling wine
½ cup vegetable oil
5 large egg yolks
1 teaspoon grated lemon rind
½ teaspoon almond extract
1 cup egg whites (7 or 8)
1 teaspoon cream of tartar
Powdered sugar

1. Combine flour, granulated sugar, almonds, baking powder and salt in large mixer bowl; mix well. Add wine, oil, egg yolks, lemon rind and almond extract; beat until smooth.

2. In second large clean mixer bowl with clean beaters, beat egg whites and cream of tartar until stiff but not dry. Gradually fold egg yolk mixture into egg whites just until blended.

3. Pour batter into ungreased 10-inch tube pan. Bake in preheated 325°F oven until wooden pick inserted into center is withdrawn clean, about 1 hour.

4. Invert cake in pan with center tube placed on funnel or bottle so cake does not touch counter; cool completely. Loosen sides with knife; remove from pan. Dust top with powdered sugar.

Pots de Creme

CAPE COD CRANBERRY VELVET PIE

A luscious pink freeze-ahead pie with a no-bake cranberry cheesecake filling in a graham cracker crust.

Makes 8 servings

1 package (8 ounces) cream cheese, room temperature
1 cup whipping cream
¼ cup sugar
½ teaspoon vanilla
1 can (16 ounces) whole-berry cranberry sauce
1 packaged graham cracker crumb crust (6-ounce)

1. Beat cream cheese in large mixer bowl until fluffy.

2. Beat cream in small mixer bowl, gradually adding sugar and vanilla, until soft peaks form. Gradually beat cream mixture into cream cheese; beat until smooth and creamy.

3. Reserve a few whole cranberries for garnish; fold remaining cranberry sauce into cream cheese mixture. Spoon into pie crust; freeze until firm, 1 to 2 hours.

4. Remove pie from freezer 15 minutes before serving; garnish with reserved berries.

Sour Cream Gingerbread

SOUR CREAM GINGERBREAD

A moist, family-style cake so rich in spicy goodness it needs neither frosting nor topping.

Makes 8 servings

   Granulated sugar
1½ cups all-purpose flour
  1 teaspoon baking soda
  ½ cup packed light brown sugar
  ⅓ cup butter or margarine, softened
  ¾ teaspoon ground ginger
  ¾ teaspoon ground cinnamon
  ¾ teaspoon dry mustard
  ½ teaspoon ground cloves
  ¼ teaspoon salt
  ½ cup unsulphured molasses
  2 large eggs
  ½ cup sour cream
  2 cups whipped cream, if desired
  ¼ cup powdered sugar, if desired

1. Grease 8×8×2-inch baking pan. Sprinkle with granulated sugar; shake out excess. Mix flour and baking soda in small bowl.

2. Combine brown sugar, butter, ginger, cinnamon, mustard, cloves and salt in large mixer bowl; beat until light and fluffy. Beat in molasses. Add eggs, 1 at a time, beating well after each addition. Add ½ of the flour mixture at a time, alternating with sour cream, beating well after each addition.

3. Transfer batter to prepared pan. Bake in preheated 350°F oven until wooden pick inserted into center is withdrawn clean, about 25 minutes.

4. Cool cake in pan on wire rack 10 minutes. Remove from pan; cool completely on rack.

5. Cut cake horizontally in half with serrated knife. Place bottom half on serving plate; spread with whipped cream. Cover with top half of cake. Place paper lace doily on top; sprinkle with powdered sugar. Remove doily.

MAPLE BUTTERNUT PIE

Two native American trees provide the makings for a delightful pie. There's sweetness from the sugar maple and nutmeats from the butternut.

Makes 8 servings

  ½ cup maple syrup
  ¼ cup all-purpose flour
  2 large egg yolks, lightly beaten
  ½ teaspoon salt
  2 cups milk, scalded
  ½ cup toasted chopped butternuts or pecans
  1 baked 9-inch pie shell
  3 large egg whites
  6 tablespoons sugar

1. Whisk maple syrup, flour, egg yolks and salt in top of double boiler until smooth; gradually whisk in milk. Cook, stirring constantly, over simmering water until thick, about 10 minutes; remove from water.

2. Stir in nuts; pour into pie shell. Refrigerate until cold.

3. Beat egg whites in large mixer bowl until soft peaks form; gradually beat in sugar. Beat until stiff peaks form. Spread meringue on pie filling, sealing to edges.

4. Bake in preheated 425°F oven until meringue is golden, 3 to 5 minutes; cool completely on wire rack.

INDIAN PUDDING

Makes 6 to 8 servings

  ¾ cup yellow cornmeal
  4 cups milk
  ½ cup sugar
  ⅓ cup molasses
  1 teaspoon ground cinnamon
  1 teaspoon salt
  ½ teaspoon ground ginger
  Whipped cream

1. Mix cornmeal with 1 cup of the milk in small bowl.

2. Heat remaining 3 cups milk in medium saucepan to boiling; reduce heat to low. Gradually whisk in cornmeal mixture until smooth. Stir in sugar, molasses, cinnamon, salt and ginger; cook and stir over medium heat until mixture thickens, 2 to 3 minutes.

3. Pour batter into greased 1½-quart baking dish. Bake in preheated 325°F oven until knife inserted midway between center and edge is withdrawn clean, 1 to 1½ hours.

4. Cool pudding on wire rack 30 minutes. Serve with whipped cream.

SPICED CHOCOLATE RING

Makes 8 to 10 servings

1¼ cups sugar
¾ cup butter or margarine, room temperature
¾ teaspoon ground cinnamon
¾ teaspoon ground allspice
2 large eggs
2 ounces unsweetened chocolate, melted, cooled
¾ teaspoon vanilla
1¼ cups all-purpose flour
¾ teaspoon baking powder
¾ cup boiling water
Chocolate Glaze (recipe follows)

1. Combine sugar, butter, cinnamon and allspice in large mixer bowl; beat until light and fluffy. Add eggs, 1 at a time, beating well after each addition. Beat in chocolate and vanilla.

2. Mix flour and baking powder in small bowl; add to butter mixture, ⅓ at a time, beating well after each addition. Add

(Continued)

water, ⅓ at a time, beating after each addition until smooth.

3. Pour batter into greased and floured 6-cup ring mold. Bake in preheated 350°F oven until wooden pick inserted into center is withdrawn clean, about 50 minutes.

4. Cool cake in pan on wire rack 10 minutes. Remove from pan; cool completely on rack.

5. Spoon warm Chocolate Glaze on top of cake; let stand until glaze sets.

CHOCOLATE GLAZE

2 ounces semisweet chocolate, chopped
2 tablespoons butter or margarine
2 tablespoons powdered sugar
½ teaspoon ground cinnamon

Combine chocolate and butter in top of double boiler; cook and stir over simmering water until melted and smooth. Remove from water; stir in sugar and cinnamon until smooth. Keep warm.

Spiced Chocolate Ring

BLUEBERRY FLUMMERY

The Shaker communities have given us a legacy of good food with amusing names made with simple ingredients.
Makes 4 servings

½ cup sugar
2 tablespoons cornstarch
2⅓ cups fresh blueberries
1½ cups water
2 tablespoons lemon juice
1 teaspoon grated lemon rind
4 orange or lemon rind curls for garnish
   Soft-whipped cream, if desired

1. Mix sugar and cornstarch in medium saucepan; stir in 2 cups of the blueberries, the water, lemon juice and grated lemon rind.

2. Cook and stir over medium-low heat until mixture thickens and bubbles for 3 minutes. Spoon into dessert cups; refrigerate, covered, until cold.

3. Before serving, top with remaining ⅓ cup blueberries. Garnish with orange rind curls; serve with cream.

Blueberry Flummery

PUMPKIN PIE WITH SOUR CREAM TOPPING

Makes one 9-inch pie

1 can (16 ounces) solid-pack pumpkin
2 large eggs
1 teaspoon ground cinnamon
½ teaspoon ground ginger
½ teaspoon ground nutmeg
½ teaspoon salt
1 can (14 ounces) sweetened condensed milk
1 unbaked 9-inch pastry shell
1½ cups sour cream
2 tablespoons sugar
1 teaspoon vanilla

1. Combine pumpkin, eggs, cinnamon, ginger, nutmeg and salt in large bowl; mix well. Stir in sweetened condensed milk until well blended. Pour into pastry shell.

2. Bake in preheated 425°F oven 15 minutes. Reduce oven setting to 350°F; bake 15 minutes longer.

3. Meanwhile, combine sour cream, sugar and vanilla in medium bowl. Spread evenly over top of pie; bake 10 minutes longer. Cool on wire rack.

APPLE DUMPLINGS

Makes 10 dumplings

½ cup margarine
1 cup plus 1 tablespoon all-purpose flour
½ cup plus 1 tablespoon small-curd cottage cheese
1 to 2 tablespoons water
5 small cooking apples, pared, cored, cut
   crosswise into halves
¼ cup dark corn syrup
1 tablespoon packed brown sugar
1 tablespoon granulated sugar
½ teaspoon ground cinnamon
10 teaspoons red jam or jelly
1 large egg
2 tablespoons milk
¼ teaspoon almond extract

1. Cut margarine into flour in medium bowl until mixture resembles fine crumbs. Stir in cottage cheese; stir in water until mixture cleans sides of bowl. Refrigerate, wrapped in plastic wrap, 1 hour.

2. Place apples in corn syrup in large skillet; sprinkle with brown sugar. Cook, uncovered, over low heat, turning once, until tender. Mix granulated sugar and cinnamon; sprinkle over apples. Let cool completely.

3. Roll out ½ of the dough on floured surface to ¼-inch thickness; cut out 10 circles ¼ inch larger on all sides than apples. Place pastry circles on greased baking sheets; top each with 1 apple half.

4. Roll out remaining dough to ⅛-inch thickness; cut out 10 circles, ¾ inches larger on all sides than apples; cut out hole from center of each. Place 1 pastry circle on top of each apple; press firmly to seal. Spoon 1 teaspoon jam into center of each.

5. Beat egg, milk and almond extract in small bowl; brush dumplings with egg wash. Bake in preheated 450°F oven until crisp and golden, 12 to 15 minutes. Serve warm, or cool completely on wire racks.

Almond Butter Cookie Hearts

ALMOND BUTTER COOKIE HEARTS

A rolled cookie dough with plenty of possibilities. Make cut-out hearts or shape into balls and finger cookies.

Makes about 4 dozen cookies

1 cup butter or margarine
⅔ cup sugar
1 large egg yolk
1 teaspoon almond extract
¼ teaspoon salt
2⅓ cups all-purpose flour
1 cup finely chopped blanched almonds
    Tubes of red decorating icing or homemade butter-cream frosting, tinted red

1. Beat butter and sugar in large mixer bowl until light and fluffy; beat in egg yolk, almond extract and salt. Gradually stir in flour and almonds.

2. Roll out dough on lightly floured surface to ⅛-inch thickness. Cut dough with 3-inch heart-shaped cutter; place on ungreased baking sheets.

3. Bake in preheated 350°F oven until golden, 8 to 10 minutes. Remove from baking sheets; cool on wire racks.

4. Decorate cookies with icing. *(Continued)*

GRATED CHOCOLATE BALLS: Combine ¾ cup whole blanched almonds and 1 ounce unsweetened chocolate in food processor or blender container; process until grated. Shape cookie dough into 1-inch balls; roll in almond-chocolate mixture to coat. Place on baking sheets. Bake in preheated 350°F oven until firm, 8 to 10 minutes; cool on wire racks. Makes about 4½ dozen.

CHOCOLATE HALF-DIPS: Shape cookie dough into 1½-inch diameter log; refrigerate, wrapped in plastic wrap, until firm, several hours. Cut crosswise into ¼-inch-thick slices; place on baking sheets. Bake in preheated 350°F oven until golden, 10 to 12 minutes; cool on wire racks. Melt 6 ounces semisweet chocolate and 3 tablespoons solid vegetable shortening in top of double boiler over hot water; mix well. Dip 1 side of each cookie into chocolate and shake off excess; place on wire racks lined with waxed paper. Sprinkle chocolate with finely chopped almonds; let stand until chocolate is set. Makes about 6 dozen.

DOUBLE-DIPS: Prepare Chocolate Half-Dips as above, omitting almond topping. When chocolate is set, mix enough milk (1 to 3 tablespoons) with 2 cups sifted powdered sugar to make glaze consistency; tint pink with red food coloring. Dip opposite side of cookies into glaze and shake off excess; let stand until glaze sets. Makes about 6 dozen.

Pineapple Upside Down Cake

PINEAPPLE UPSIDE DOWN CAKE

Makes 8 servings

- ¼ cup butter
- ⅔ cup packed brown sugar
- 1 can (20 ounces) pineapple slices in syrup
- 10 maraschino cherries
- 1½ cups all-purpose flour
- ¾ cup granulated sugar
- 1½ teaspoons baking powder
- ½ teaspoon salt
- ½ cup milk
- ¼ cup solid vegetable shortening
- 1 large egg
- 1 teaspoon lemon juice
- 1 teaspoon vanilla
- ¼ teaspoon grated lemon rind

1. Melt butter in 10-inch cast iron skillet; stir in brown sugar until blended. Remove from heat.

2. Drain pineapple, reserving 2 tablespoons syrup. Arrange pineapple slices in brown sugar mixture to cover bottom of skillet, overlapping as necessary. Place 1 maraschino cherry in center of each slice.

3. Combine flour, granulated sugar, baking powder and salt in large mixer bowl. Add milk and shortening; beat for 2 minutes.

4. Add egg, reserved syrup, the lemon juice, vanilla and lemon rind. Beat 2 minutes. Pour batter over pineapple in skillet, spreading evenly.

5. Bake in preheated 350°F oven 40 minutes, or until wooden pick inserted into center is withdrawn clean. Cool in skillet on wire rack 5 minutes. Invert onto serving plate; serve warm.

STEAMED CARROT PUDDING

Everyday puddings were steamed rather than baked in the days of open-hearth cookery. Bake ovens were heated only when there were enough foods to fill them.

Makes 4 servings

- 1 cup shredded carrot
- 1 small potato, pared, shredded
- 1 cup raisins
- ⅔ cup all-purpose flour
- ⅓ cup sugar
- 1 teaspoon baking powder
- 1 teaspoon ground allspice
- ½ teaspoon salt
- ½ teaspoon baking soda
- ⅓ cup honey
- ⅓ cup milk
  - Boiling water
  - Hard Sauce (see Index), if desired

1. Combine all ingredients except honey, milk, water and Hard Sauce in medium bowl; toss to mix. Stir in honey and milk just until all ingredients are evenly moistened.

2. Pour batter into well-greased 4-cup metal mold or oven-proof bowl. Cover with double thickness of aluminum foil; tie foil in place tightly with string. Place mold on rack in large kettle.

3. Add enough boiling water to kettle to come halfway up sides of mold; adjust heat to maintain steady simmer. Cover kettle tightly.

4. Steam pudding until metal skewer inserted into center is withdrawn clean, 1½ to 2 hours. Remove mold to wire rack; carefully remove foil. Let cool 3 to 5 minutes before unmolding. Serve warm with Hard Sauce.

BANANA CREAM PIE

Spread pie weights or dry beans in the bottom of a pie shell that is baked without a filling. This will keep the tender pastry from shrinking or puffing up too much in the oven.
Makes 8 servings

⅔ cup packed brown sugar
¼ cup cornstarch
¼ teaspoon salt
3 cups whipping cream, half-and-half or milk
3 large eggs, separated
2 tablespoons butter or margarine
2 tablespoons dark rum or 1 teaspoon rum
    flavoring
2 or 3 bananas
    Butter Pastry Pie Shell (recipe follows)
⅛ teaspoon cream of tartar
⅓ cup granulated sugar

1. Mix brown sugar, cornstarch and salt in medium saucepan; stir in cream. Cook over medium heat, stirring constantly, until mixture thickens and bubbles for 3 minutes.

2. Gradually whisk 1 cup of the hot mixture into egg yolks in small bowl; gradually whisk egg yolk mixture into remaining hot mixture in pan. Cook, stirring constantly, over low heat until thickened. Remove from heat; stir in butter and rum.

3. Slice bananas; arrange in cooled Butter Pastry Pie Shell. Pour custard mixture over bananas.

4. Beat egg whites and cream of tartar in large mixer bowl until foamy; gradually beat in granulated sugar. Beat until

(Continued)

stiff and glossy. Spread over filling, sealing well to edge of pastry.

5. Bake in preheated 425°F oven until meringue is golden, 3 to 5 minutes. Cool completely on wire rack.

BUTTER PASTRY PIE SHELL

1 cup all-purpose flour
¼ teaspoon salt
⅓ cup butter or margarine, cold
1 large egg yolk
1 tablespoon vegetable oil
2 teaspoons cider vinegar
1 to 3 tablespoons ice water

1. Mix flour and salt in medium bowl; cut in butter until pieces are size of small peas.

2. Mix egg yolk, oil, vinegar and 1 tablespoon of the water in small bowl. Gradually sprinkle yolk mixture over flour mixture, tossing lightly with fork, until dough begins to hold together, adding more water if necessary. Press into ball; refrigerate, wrapped in plastic wrap, 1 hour.

3. Roll out dough on lightly floured surface into 12-inch circle; fit into 9-inch pie pan. Pierce bottom and sides all over with fork; trim and flute edge.

4. Line pastry with parchment or waxed paper; fill with dry beans or pie weights. Bake in preheated 425°F oven until pastry is set, about 12 minutes. Remove paper and beans or weights. Continue baking until pastry is crisp and golden, 8 to 10 minutes longer. Cool completely on wire rack.
Makes one 9-inch pie shell

Banana Cream Pie

NEW YORK CHEESECAKE

A scrumptious cream cheese creation with a cake-crumb crust and smooth texture made famous in New York restaurants.

Makes 8 to 10 servings

  2 tablespoons butter, room temperature
1⅓ cups fine cake crumbs (from white, yellow or pound cake)
1¼ pounds cream cheese, room temperature
  ¾ cup whipping cream
  3 tablespoons fresh lemon juice
  2 teaspoons vanilla
  ¾ cup sour cream
1¼ cups sugar
  4 large eggs, room temperature, lightly beaten

1. Coat 8-inch springform pan evenly with butter. Place cake crumbs in pan; rotate pan to coat bottom and sides evenly. Press crumbs gently in place.

2. Beat cream cheese in large mixer bowl at medium speed until completely smooth. Gradually beat in cream, lemon juice and vanilla; beat until smooth.

3. Add sour cream; beat at medium speed until blended. Continue beating while slowly adding sugar; beat until sugar is absorbed. Add eggs, ¼ at a time, beating well after each addition. Pour batter into prepared pan; gently rotate pan several quarter-turns to settle batter.

(Continued)

4. Bake in middle of preheated 325°F oven until cake is set 2 inches in from edges and center is still puddinglike, about 1 hour and 15 minutes, for creamy center. For firmer center, bake until center is just set, 8 to 10 minutes longer. Turn oven off; let cake stand in oven, with door propped open 8 inches, 30 minutes.

5. Place pan on wire rack away from drafts; let cool completely. Remove sides of pan; refrigerate cake, uncovered, overnight or at least 8 hours. Cover cake loosely with plastic wrap; refrigerate until serving time.

POPPY SEED TEA LOAF

Brew a fresh pot of hot tea or one of the herbal combinations to sip with thin slices of this lemon-glazed loaf.

Makes 8 to 12 servings

  1 cup sugar
  ¼ cup plus 2 tablespoons butter or margarine, room temperature
  2 large eggs
  ¼ cup poppy seeds
  ½ teaspoon almond extract
1½ cups all-purpose flour
  1 teaspoon baking powder
  ½ teaspoon salt
  ½ cup liquid non-dairy creamer
  Lemon Glaze (recipe follows)

(Continued)

New York Cheesecake

1. Beat sugar and butter in large mixer bowl until light and fluffy. Add eggs, poppy seeds and almond extract; beat until fluffy.

2. Mix flour, baking powder and salt in medium bowl. Add flour mixture to butter mixture, ⅓ at a time, alternating with non-dairy creamer, mixing well after each addition. Spread batter in greased 8½ × 4½ × 3-inch loaf pan.

3. Bake in preheated 350°F oven until wooden pick inserted into center is withdrawn clean, about 50 minutes. Cool in pan on wire rack 10 minutes. Top with Lemon Glaze; cool completely in pan.

LEMON GLAZE

  1 cup powdered sugar, sifted
1½ to 3 tablespoons lemon juice
  ½ teaspoon almond extract

Mix sugar, 1½ tablespoons of the lemon juice and the almond extract in small bowl; stir in as much of the remaining 1½ tablespoons lemon juice as needed to make smooth thick glaze.

GRAHAM CRACKER CAKE WITH CINNAMON SYRUP

Sylvester Graham's name is attached to the cracker and the whole wheat flour he introduced in the mid-1800s. He advocated "high fiber" and "whole grain" nearly 150 years ago.

Makes 6 to 8 servings

1¾ cups fine graham cracker crumbs
  1 cup sugar
  ⅓ cup all-purpose flour
  2 teaspoons baking powder
  1 cup milk
  ½ cup butter or margarine, room temperature
  2 large eggs
  1 teaspoon vanilla
  ¾ cup finely chopped walnuts
  Cinnamon Syrup (recipe follows)

1. Mix graham cracker crumbs, sugar, flour and baking powder in large mixer bowl. Add milk, butter, eggs and vanilla; beat at medium speed until thoroughly blended. Fold in walnuts; spread batter in greased and floured 13 × 9 × 2-inch baking pan.

2. Bake in preheated 350°F oven until wooden pick inserted into center is withdrawn clean, about 30 minutes. Place on wire rack.

3. Pierce surface of warm cake all over with fork. Slowly pour Cinnamon Syrup over cake; let stand 15 minutes to allow syrup to soak in. Serve warm.

CINNAMON SYRUP

½ cup sugar
½ teaspoon ground cinnamon
½ cup whipping cream
¼ cup butter or margarine

Mix sugar and cinnamon in small saucepan; stir in cream and butter. Cook and stir over medium-high heat to boiling; boil 1 minute. Keep warm until ready to use.

Star-Spangled Cherry Pie

STAR-SPANGLED CHERRY PIE

Letting pie dough rest so that the flour absorbs the liquid is one of the secrets of easy-to-handle pastry.

Makes 6 servings

1½ cups all-purpose flour
  ½ teaspoon salt
  ½ cup solid vegetable shortening
  4 to 5 tablespoons cold water
  1 can (21 ounces) tart cherry pie filling
  1 tablespoon margarine
  1 teaspoon sugar

1. Mix flour and salt in medium bowl; cut in shortening until pieces are the size of small peas. Gradually add water, stirring and tossing with fork, until mixture cleans sides of bowl. Refrigerate, wrapped in plastic wrap, 1 hour.

2. Roll out ½ of the dough on lightly floured surface into 11-inch circle; fit into 8-inch pie pan.

3. Spread pie filling in pastry shell; dot with margarine.

4. Roll out remaining dough into 9-inch circle; cut out 6 evenly spaced star shapes with cookie cutter. Place pastry circle on top of filling; trim edges, leaving ½-inch overhang. Fold edges under; pinch to seal. Flute edge; sprinkle top with sugar.

5. Bake in preheated 450°F oven 10 minutes. Reduce oven setting to 350°F; bake 30 minutes longer. Star-shaped cutouts can be baked on baking sheet until crisp, 10 to 15 minutes.

Deep Dish Apple Pie

DEEP DISH APPLE PIE

Clay cooking gives this deep dish apple pie a wonderfully old-fashioned flavor, and the traditional top crust is as crisp and flaky as anyone could wish.

Makes 6 to 8 servings

1 cup packed brown sugar
2 tablespoons all-purpose flour
1 teaspoon ground cinnamon
1 teaspoon grated lemon rind
¼ teaspoon ground mace or nutmeg
⅛ teaspoon salt
6 medium tart apples, pared, cored, thinly sliced
  (about 8 cups)
2 tablespoons butter or margarine
Cinnamon Pastry (recipe follows)

1. Soak top and bottom of square 2-quart clay cooker in water 15 minutes; drain.

2. Mix sugar, flour, cinnamon, lemon rind, mace and salt in large bowl. Add apples; toss to coat. Spread apple mixture in cooker; dot with butter.

3. Roll out Cinnamon Pastry on floured surface into square slightly larger than upper edge of cooker. Place pastry on top of apples; turn edges under and press firmly against cooker with fork. Cut several steam vents in top of pastry.

4. Place covered cooker in cold oven; set oven at 450°F. Bake until apples are tender and crust is brown, about 1 hour. If necessary, remove cover and bake until crust is brown, about 5 minutes longer. Serve warm or at room temperature.

CINNAMON PASTRY

1 cup all-purpose flour
1 tablespoon powdered sugar
½ to 1 teaspoon ground cinnamon
¼ cup butter or margarine, cold
1 tablespoon lard, cold
2 to 3 tablespoons cold water

(Continued)

Mix flour, sugar and cinnamon in medium bowl; cut in butter and lard until mixture resembles coarse crumbs. Stir in cold water until dough cleans side of bowl. Refrigerate, wrapped in plastic wrap, 1 hour.

ANISE COOKIES

A sweet, rusklike cookie baked in two stages. First the dough is shaped and baked in foot-long loaves; then it is sliced and toasted to a golden brown in the oven.

Makes about 4 dozen cookies

4 ounces whole blanched almonds (about ¾ cup)
2¼ cups all-purpose flour
1 teaspoon baking powder
¾ teaspoon salt
¾ cup sugar
½ cup unsalted butter, room temperature
3 large eggs, room temperature
2 tablespoons brandy
2 teaspoons grated lemon rind
1 tablespoon whole anise seeds

1. Toast almonds in small baking pan in preheated 375°F oven until light brown, 6 to 8 minutes. Cool almonds completely; chop coarsely.

2. Mix flour, baking powder and salt in small bowl. Beat sugar and butter in large mixer bowl until light and fluffy. Add eggs, 1 at a time, beating well after each addition. Stir in brandy and lemon rind. Add flour mixture; stir until smooth. Stir in almonds and anise seeds. Refrigerate, covered, 1 hour to firm and to blend flavors.

3. Spoon ½ of the dough lengthwise in row on one side of greased baking sheet; spread top and sides even with spatula, forming 12 × 2-inch log. Dough will be fairly soft. Pat surface smooth with lightly floured fingertips. Repeat with remaining ½ of the dough to form second log.

4. Bake in preheated 375°F oven until logs are light golden brown, 20 to 25 minutes. Cool logs completely on baking sheet on wire rack. *(Continued)*

5. Reduce oven setting to 350°F. Cut logs diagonally with serrated knife into ½-inch-thick slices. Place slices flat in single layer on 2 ungreased baking sheets. Bake 8 minutes. Turn slices over; bake until cut surfaces are light brown and cookies are dry, 10 to 12 minutes longer. Remove cookies from baking sheets to wire racks; cool completely. Anise Cookies will keep several weeks in tightly covered container.

PUMPKIN CREAM CHEESE TART

Glazed orange slices and glistening cranberry sauce top pumpkin and spice and everything nice in a smooth cheese-cake filling.

Makes 10 to 12 servings

Pie crust mix for single 9-inch crust
4 packages (3 ounces each) cream cheese, room temperature
¾ cup packed light brown sugar
2 large eggs
1 teaspoon ground cinnamon
1 teaspoon grated orange rind
¼ teaspoon ground nutmeg
1 can (16 ounces) solid-pack pumpkin
1 can (16 ounces) whole-berry cranberry sauce
Glazed Orange Slices (recipe follows), if desired

(Continued)

1. Prepare pie crust mix according to package directions. Press dough evenly on bottom and 1½ inches up side of 9-inch springform pan; refrigerate.

2. Beat cream cheese and brown sugar in large mixer bowl until light and fluffy. Beat in eggs, one at a time. Stir in cinnamon, orange rind and nutmeg; stir in pumpkin until smooth.

3. Transfer pumpkin mixture to pastry-lined pan. Place in preheated 425°F oven; immediately reduce oven setting to 350°F. Bake until center is almost set, about 35 minutes. Cool completely on wire rack.

4. Top pumpkin layer with cranberry sauce. Arrange Glazed Orange Slices in ring on top of tart. Refrigerate until serving time. Remove side of springform pan before serving.

GLAZED ORANGE SLICES

1 cup granulated sugar
¼ cup water
12 thin orange slices

1. Heat sugar and water in large skillet over medium heat to boiling; boil 1 minute.

2. Add orange slices to skillet. Cook over low heat, turning frequently, until the slices are almost translucent, about 5 minutes.

Pumpkin Cream Cheese Tart

Chesapeake Bay to the Bayou
THE SOUTH

Since Colonial times, hospitality has been a byword in the South. Just a gathering of family and friends is reason enough for a celebration featuring the finest of Southern cooking. Some of the recipes in this chapter reflect the down-home goodness of family and community suppers. Other recipes shine in more formal settings.

Like other regions of America, the South has developed its own traditional ingredients and preparation methods, beginning with native foodstuffs and adding French, Spanish, African, Caribbean, English and other ethnic influences. This process has produced the diversity of foods and cooking styles enjoyed today by those who call the South home.

One of the best known of these styles can be found in and around New Orleans, an area with a well-deserved reputation for excellent food. Today, Cajun and Creole cooking is a wonderful culinary mixture that reflects its complex cultural background.

But whether it's the French Quarter in Louisiana or Richmond in Virginia, what the South is probably most famous for is the easy, yet elegant, hospitality you can find all across the region.

Begin any get-together with Bacon Baked Oysters or with toast or crackers spread with Biloxi Butter, a peppy version of what the British call potted shrimp. In summer, serve Citrus Blossom Punch or Orange-Strawberry Slush—both designed to provide relief from the sultry summer heat. For festive winter holiday celebrations, the Cream Cheese Christmas Tree will certainly add a cheery note.

The soup course offers wonderful possibilities. For a light meal, you may wish to serve a delicious Orange Fruit Soup or a distinctively Southern Peanut Soup. Heartier offerings are Beef & Barley Soup Monticello (an updated version of a dish often served at Thomas Jefferson's plantation), Black Bean and Sausage Soup (a dish Floridians have inherited from the large Cuban population there), or Shrimp Gumbo (a New Orleans dish chock full of gulf shrimp, sausage and okra).

Fish and shellfish abound in this region, and recipes are as diverse as the seafood itself. Crabs are plentiful off the coast of Maryland, where Devilish Blue Crab and Maryland Crab Cakes are the order of the day.

South Atlantic seafish are used to great effect in Pompano en Papillote and in Red Snapper with Seafood Sauce. Oysters from the waters of the Gulf of Mexico near New Orleans make tasty Oyster Beignets; and crawfish (sometimes called crayfish) from the Mississippi Delta are transformed into Crawfish Etouffée. Southern catfish were never better than when prepared for Catfish Bienville.

Main dishes of meat and poultry are also plentiful. Savor the Bourbon-Laced Beef Roast or Dixie Pork Loin Roast with a crunchy peanut coating. And you must try the unique Yam-Ham Souffle or even George Washington's Beef and Kidney Pie from yesteryear. Ham is, of course, a Southern tradition, and you'll find a perfect Citrus-Glazed Ham recipe here. And don't forget that all-time favorite—choosing between Picnic Fried Chicken and Batter-Fried Chicken can be a real dilemma. Even deciding among poultry stuffings is no easy task; Peanut Stuffing, Cornbread-Rice Stuffing and Tangy Poultry Stuffing are all destined for Sunday-dinner stardom.

Any number of salads, vegetables and side dishes round out the Southern table. You'll find Hot Seafood Salad, fresh Garden Potato Salad and cool Calico Salad Mold. And just wait for the rave reviews of Sweet Potato Fritters, Pattypan Squash Casserole and Cheese-Frosted Cauliflower, plus many more carrot, sweet potato, corn, spinach, and green bean dishes.

There's almost no end to the desserts to be enjoyed. Included in this chapter are two kinds of Pecan Pie (Chocolate and just plain Superb), Bourbon Pecan Cake, Cherried Fruit Cake, Lemon Mousse, Elegant Orange Cake, Tangerine Souffle, Watsonia Peach Ice Cream, Spiced Sweet Potato Pie, Double Peach Melba and Key Lime Pie.

Southerners offer their families and friends a variety of sweets and treats. Cherry-studded Creole Fudge, delicate Praline Lace Crisps and Spiced Pecans can be holiday specialties. Dixie Peanut Brittle and Southern Country Crunch are fun to serve at any time.

When your guests gather after dinner, serve them Cafe Brulot—coffee as they might have it in the French Quarter of New Orleans—made mellow with brandy and orange liqueur.

CREAM CHEESE CHRISTMAS TREE

Trace the outline of the tree on the green pepper and pimiento-flecked cheese with the tip of a sharp knife before cutting.

Makes 15 to 20 appetizer servings

2 packages (8 ounces each) cream cheese, room temperature
6 ounces blue cheese, room temperature
¼ cup finely chopped green bell pepper
¼ cup finely chopped pimiento
½ teaspoon garlic salt
   Pecan halves
   Curly endive or parsley sprigs
   Assorted crackers   *(Continued)*

1. Beat cream cheese and blue cheese in large mixer bowl until light and fluffy. Stir in green bell pepper, pimiento and garlic salt.

2. Spread mixture evenly on piece of aluminum foil in ¾-inch-thick rectangle; refrigerate until firm.

3. Cut cheese rectangle into Christmas tree shape with knife; save trimmings for snacking.* Place tree, on foil, on serving dish; trim foil flush with edges of tree.

4. Arrange pecan halves in rows across surface of tree; arrange endive around sides. Serve with crackers.

Note: *Recipe can be prepared ahead to this point; refrigerate, covered, up to 24 hours.*

Cream Cheese Christmas Tree

ORANGE-STRAWBERRY SLUSH

Makes 4 servings

1½ cups ginger ale
1 cup crushed ice
1 can (6 ounces) frozen orange juice concentrate, thawed
¼ cup grenadine
1 package (10 ounces) frozen strawberries, partially thawed

1. Combine ginger ale, crushed ice, orange juice concentrate and grenadine in blender container; process for 10 seconds.

2. Add strawberries; process 5 seconds; serve immediately.

CITRUS BLOSSOM PUNCH

Makes 3 quarts

1 quart apple juice, cold
1 bottle (28 ounces) ginger ale, cold
2 cups cold water
2 cans (6 ounces each) frozen grapefruit juice concentrate, thawed
1 can (6 ounces) frozen orange juice concentrate, thawed
Orange Ice Ring (recipe follows)

Combine all ingredients except Orange Ice Ring in large pitcher. To serve, place Orange Ice Ring in punch bowl; pour punch over ice.

ORANGE ICE RING

1 orange, thinly sliced
1 red apple, cored, sliced into thin wedges
3 cups orange juice

1. Cut orange slices into halves. Arrange orange slices and apple wedges in 4-cup ring mold. Add enough orange juice just to cover fruit; freeze until firm. Add remaining orange juice; freeze until firm.

2. To unmold, dip mold briefly in warm water; invert onto plate.

ORANGE 'N' SPICE ICED TEA

Makes six 8-ounce servings

6 cups cold water
3 sticks cinnamon (2 inches each)
½ teaspoon whole cloves
10 tea bags
1 can (6 ounces) frozen orange juice concentrate, thawed
¼ cup sugar
Orange slices and mint sprigs for garnish

1. Combine 3 cups of the water, the cinnamon sticks and cloves in medium saucepan. Heat to boiling; remove from heat. Add tea bags; let brew 5 minutes.

2. Remove and discard tea bags; strain tea into heat-proof pitcher. Add remaining 3 cups water, the orange juice concentrate and sugar; mix well. Refrigerate until cold.

3. To serve, pour over ice cubes in tall glasses; garnish with orange slices and mint.

Citrus Blossom Punch (top); Orange 'n' Spice Iced Tea (center); Orange-Strawberry Slush (bottom)

CAFE BRULOT

A specialty in the French Quarter of New Orleans, this after-dinner coffee laced with brandy and orange liqueur is flamed before serving.

Makes 8 to 10 servings

Rind from 2 oranges, slivered
Rind from 2 lemons, slivered
2 tablespoons sugar
3 sticks cinnamon (about 3 inches each)
6 whole cloves
6 whole allspice
8 ounces brandy
2 ounces orange-flavored liqueur
1 quart hot strong black coffee
8 to 10 sticks cinnamon sticks (about 3 inches each) for garnish

1. Combine orange and lemon rinds, sugar, 3 sticks cinnamon, the cloves and allspice in chafing dish; add brandy and liqueur. Heat and stir until hot.

2. Carefully ignite brandy with long match; stir until sugar is dissolved and flames die out.

3. Gradually stir in coffee; pour into coffee cups. Garnish with cinnamon sticks.

Bayou Seafood Hors d'Oeuvres

BAYOU SEAFOOD HORS D'OEUVRES

Treat your guests to tiny crab meat fritters prepared Cajun style with both black and red pepper.

Makes 12 to 16 servings

¼ cup instant minced onion
¼ cup water
2 cans (6 ounces each) crab meat or 2 cans (7 ounces each) tuna, drained, flaked
2 large eggs, lightly beaten
½ cup dry breadcrumbs
2 tablespoons dried parsley flakes
1½ teaspoons dry mustard
¼ teaspoon black pepper
  Pinch ground red pepper
  Vegetable oil for frying or ½ cup butter or margarine
  Cucumber slices for garnish

1. Mix onion and water in medium bowl; let stand 10 minutes to rehydrate.

2. Add crab meat, eggs, breadcrumbs, parsley, mustard, black and red peppers to onion; mix well. Shape into 1-inch balls, about 4 dozen.

3. Heat 2 inches oil in Dutch oven to 375°F; fry a few balls at a time until golden, about 1 minute. Or, melt butter in large skillet; add as many balls as will fit in single layer without crowding and fry, turning occasionally, until brown on all sides, about 3 minutes. Remove with slotted spoon; drain on paper toweling.

4. Serve at once, or keep warm in single layer in shallow baking pan, covered with foil, in preheated 250°F oven up to 30 minutes. Garnish with cucumber.

OYSTER BEIGNETS

Makes about 60 puffs

1 cup milk
¼ cup margarine or butter
1 cup all-purpose flour
½ teaspoon sugar
4 large eggs
1 pint fresh shucked oysters, drained, chopped
  Vegetable oil for frying
  Zesty Sauce (recipe follows)

1. Heat milk and margarine in medium saucepan to boiling. Add flour and sugar all at once; beat vigorously until smooth. Cook and stir over medium heat until mixture forms ball and cleans sides of pan; remove from heat.

2. Add eggs, 1 at a time, beating until smooth and shiny after each addition. Add oysters; mix well.

3. Heat 2 to 3 inches oil in large saucepan to 365°F. Drop batter by teaspoonfuls into oil; fry 6 to 8 at a time, turning occasionally, until brown, 4 to 5 minutes. Drain on paper toweling. Serve immediately with Zesty Sauce.

ZESTY SAUCE

¾ cup chili sauce
¼ cup minced celery
1 tablespoon horseradish
1 tablespoon lemon juice
½ teaspoon salt

Mix all ingredients in small bowl; refrigerate, covered.

Makes about 1 cup

SHRIMP & MUSHROOM BISQUE

Florida rock shrimp have the hard shell of a lobster tail. The flavor is something like both shrimp and lobster, making it a superb choice for a rich creamy soup.

Makes 6 servings

 2 tablespoons salt
1½ pounds shelled deveined rock shrimp
 2 cups sliced mushrooms
½ cup sliced green onions
½ cup butter or margarine, melted
 1 can (10¾ ounces) condensed cream of
   mushroom soup
 2 cups milk
 1 tablespoon dry sherry

1. Heat 2 quarts water and the salt in large saucepan to boiling. Add shrimp; cook 30 seconds. Drain; rinse under cold running water until cool. Cut shrimp into halves.

2. Saute mushrooms and green onions in butter in large saucepan over medium heat until tender but not brown, about 5 minutes. Stir in soup, then milk; cook, stirring occasionally, over medium heat until hot. Do not boil.

3. Stir in shrimp; cook, stirring occasionally, over low heat 4 minutes. Stir in sherry; serve immediately.

SHRIMP GUMBO

Some say this spicy Louisiana dish with African origins gets its name from gumbo, the folk word for okra. The sliced pods of this green vegetable thicken the peppery seafood mixture made with tomatoes, onions and hot sausage.

Makes 6 servings

 3 large onions, sliced
 1 package (16 ounces) frozen cut okra
 1 can (16 ounces) stewed tomatoes, undrained
 2 cups water
½ pound dry hot sausage, diced or sliced
 1 can (8 ounces) tomato sauce
 2 tablespoons bacon drippings or butter
 2 cloves garlic, chopped
½ teaspoon crushed red pepper
 1 bay leaf
   Salt and pepper to taste
 2 pounds frozen shelled deveined shrimp

1. Combine all ingredients except shrimp in Dutch oven; heat to boiling. Reduce heat; simmer, partially covered, 30 minutes.

2. Add shrimp; mix well. Cook, partially covered, stirring occasionally, until shrimp are cooked through, 10 to 15 minutes longer.

Shrimp & Mushroom Bisque

BLACK BEAN AND SAUSAGE SOUP

Makes 4 to 6 servings

1 pound dried black beans (about 2 cups), rinsed, drained
7 to 7½ cups water
2 stalks celery with leaves, finely chopped
2 medium onions, chopped
3 cloves garlic, minced
1 small dried hot red pepper, crumbled
2 teaspoons salt
1 teaspoon ground coriander
¼ teaspoon ground cloves
1½ pounds Polish sausage or smoked bratwurst, cut into 1-inch pieces
Sour cream
Coriander sprigs for garnish

1. Soak beans in 4 cups of the water in large bowl overnight. (Or, heat beans and 4 cups water in Dutch oven to boiling; boil 2 minutes, then let stand, covered, 1 hour.) Do not drain beans.

2. Combine beans and their liquid and 3 cups of the remaining water in Dutch oven; stir in celery, onions, garlic, pepper, salt, ground coriander and cloves. Heat to boiling; reduce heat to very low. Simmer, covered, until beans are tender but not soft, 1½ to 2 hours.

3. Remove 1 cup of the beans; mash coarsely and return to soup. Stir in sausage and remaining ½ cup water if soup is too thick. Simmer, covered, stirring occasionally, until beans are soft, about 30 minutes longer. Serve with sour cream; garnish with coriander sprigs.

SHRIMP SOUP WITH PASTA

Makes 6 servings

2 onions, coarsely chopped
2 carrots, coarsely chopped
2 stalks celery, coarsely chopped
1 clove garlic, minced
2 tablespoons butter or margarine
2 tablespoons olive oil
5 cups chicken stock
1 cup dry sherry or white wine
¼ cup tomato paste
2 tablespoons chopped parsley
1 teaspoon dried basil, crumbled
½ teaspoon dried oregano, crumbled
¼ teaspoon salt
⅛ teaspoon pepper
½ cup soup pasta
1 pound shrimp in shells
⅓ cup dry Marsala

1. Saute onions, carrots, celery and garlic in butter and oil in large saucepan over medium heat until soft, about 8 minutes.

2. Stir in stock, sherry, tomato paste, parsley, basil, oregano, salt and pepper; heat to boiling. Stir in pasta; reduce heat. Simmer, covered, 15 minutes. Add shrimp; simmer, covered, until shrimp turn pink, about 5 minutes.

3. Remove shrimp from soup; shell and devein shrimp. Return shrimp to soup; stir in Marsala. Heat just until hot.

Black Bean and Sausage Soup

Beef & Barley Soup Monticello

BEEF & BARLEY SOUP MONTICELLO

At the Virginia plantation of notable gourmet Thomas Jefferson, food was prepared with great attention to flavor and ingredients, whether the dish was elegant or plain. In this barley soup, cloves and allspice season the hearty broth as they did in Jefferson's day.

Makes about 4 quarts; 8 servings
  4 **pounds beef marrow bones**
  4 **quarts water**
  1 **pound beef flanken or short ribs**
½ **pound pearl barley**
  6 **whole cloves**
  6 **whole allspice**
  2 **bay leaves**
  1 **teaspoon salt**
¼ **teaspoon pepper**
  2 **cups sliced carrots**
½ **cup raisins, if desired**
  2 **cups packed torn fresh spinach (½ pound)**
  1 **teaspoon paprika**

1. Heat marrow bones and water in Dutch oven over medium heat to boiling; reduce heat to low. Skim foam; simmer, covered, 1 hour. Skim fat and foam.

2. Add beef flanken, barley, cloves, allspice, bay leaves, salt and pepper to Dutch oven; mix well. Heat to boiling; reduce heat. Simmer, covered, stirring occasionally, 2 hours.

(Continued)

3. Stir in carrots and raisins; simmer, covered, 30 minutes.

4. Remove marrow bones and flanken from soup; skim fat. Remove marrow from bones; remove meat from flanken. Discard all bones. Cut marrow and meat into bite-size pieces; return to soup.

5. Stir spinach and paprika into soup; simmer, covered, 10 minutes.

SPICY CHEDDAR BEEF SPREAD

Pack this nippy concoction in a small earthenware crock to take tailgating before a football game.

Makes 2 cups; 8 servings
  8 **ounces sharp Cheddar cheese, shredded**
½ **cup beer**
¼ **cup mayonnaise**
  1 **teaspoon Worcestershire sauce**
¼ **teaspoon ground red pepper**
  3 **ounces dried beef, finely snipped**
    Assorted crackers

1. Combine all ingredients except beef and crackers in blender container; process until smooth. Transfer to medium bowl.

2. Stir in dried beef; refrigerate, covered, at least 1 hour. Serve with crackers.

Peanut Soup

VEGETABLE MEDLEY SOUP

Makes 8 servings

  7 cups water
  ⅓ cup tomato paste
  ⅓ cup bottled salsa
  2¼ cups cut green beans
  ½ cup chopped turnips
  ½ cup chopped rutabagas
  ½ cup chopped onions
  ½ cup chopped celery
  ½ cup chopped carrots
  ½ cup chopped green bell pepper
  ½ cup chopped crookneck squash
  ½ teaspoon garlic powder
  ½ teaspoon onion powder
  ½ teaspoon ground oregano
  ¼ teaspoon ground cumin
  ⅔ cup chopped zucchini

1. Combine water, tomato paste and salsa in large saucepan; heat to boiling. Stir in remaining ingredients except zucchini; reduce heat. Simmer, covered, 8 minutes.

2. Stir in zucchini; continue cooking, uncovered, until vegetables are tender, about 5 minutes longer.

PEANUT SOUP

Chopped peanuts play a three-star vegetable, protein, and flavor role in production of a creamy first-course or luncheon soup.

Makes 5 to 6 servings

  1 cup chopped peanuts
  1 cup chopped carrots
  ½ cup chopped celery
  ¼ cup chopped green onion
  1 clove garlic, minced
  ½ cup butter
  ¼ cup all-purpose flour
  2 cans (13¾ ounces each) chicken broth
  1 cup milk
  1 tablespoon chopped parsley   *(Continued)*

1. Saute peanuts, carrots, celery, green onion and garlic in butter in large saucepan over medium heat until vegetables are soft, about 4 minutes. Stir in flour; cook and stir 1 minute.

2. Gradually stir in broth; heat to boiling. Reduce heat; simmer 15 minutes.

3. Stir in milk; heat just until hot. Stir in parsley.

CORN AND CHICKEN CHOWDER

The smoky goodness of crumbled bacon mingles with thyme-seasoned vegetables and diced chicken in a thick soup that is a meal in itself.

Makes 6 to 8 servings

  5 slices bacon, cut into 1-inch pieces
  ½ cup sliced mushrooms
  ¾ cup chopped sweet onion
  ½ teaspoon dried thyme, crumbled
  2 cups diced cooked chicken
  1 can (10¾ ounces) condensed cream of celery
      soup, undiluted
  1 can (10½ ounces) condensed chicken vegetable
      soup, undiluted
  1 can (8 ounces) whole kernel corn, undrained
  1 cup water
  ½ cup chopped fresh or canned tomatoes
  ¼ teaspoon paprika
  1 soup can milk
  1 cup coarsely chopped pecans

1. Cook bacon in large saucepan over medium heat until crisp; drain on paper toweling. Discard all but 2 tablespoons of the drippings.

2. Saute mushrooms in reserved drippings over medium heat 5 minutes. Add onion and thyme; saute until mushrooms are brown and onion is soft, about 4 minutes.

3. Stir in bacon, chicken, soups, corn, water, tomatoes and paprika. Cook over low heat, stirring occasionally, 20 minutes. Stir in milk; heat just to boiling. Garnish with pecans.

BACON BAKED OYSTERS

The layer of coarse salt in the baking pan stabilizes and insulates the half-shells containing the succulent oysters.

Makes 4 to 6 servings

6 slices bacon, cut into 1-inch pieces
½ cup mayonnaise
1 cup buttery cracker crumbs
2 tablespoons minced chives
1 teaspoon hot red pepper sauce
1 teaspoon lemon juice
½ teaspoon Dijon-style mustard
Rock salt or coarse (kosher) salt
24 fresh oysters, shucked, ½ of the shells reserved
¼ cup grated Parmesan cheese

1. Cook bacon in large skillet over medium heat just until limp; drain.

2. Combine mayonnaise, cracker crumbs, chives, red pepper sauce, lemon juice and mustard in small bowl; mix well.

3. Place ½ inch rock salt in bottoms of 4 to 6 baking dishes. Place oysters in half-shells securely in salt.

4. Top oysters with crumb mixture, dividing evenly; sprinkle with cheese. Top each with 1 piece of bacon.

5. Bake in preheated 400°F oven until oysters are hot and edges begin to curl, about 8 minutes; serve immediately.

BILOXI BUTTER

Enjoy the buttery elegance of this chilled shrimp cocktail spread turned out of a mold and ready to serve with crackers and vegetables.

Makes about 1½ cups

½ cup butter or margarine, room temperature
½ pound cooked shelled deveined shrimp, ground*
2 tablespoons lemon juice
2 teaspoons horseradish
¼ teaspoon salt
⅛ teaspoon ground nutmeg
⅛ teaspoon hot red pepper sauce
Tiny shrimp and chopped parsley for garnish
Assorted party breads, crackers and/or raw vegetables

1. Beat butter in small mixer bowl until light and fluffy. Add ground shrimp, lemon juice, horseradish, salt, nutmeg and red pepper sauce; beat until blended. Pack into 1½-cup mold or two 6-ounce custard cups; refrigerate, covered, until firm, several hours.

2. To serve, unmold shrimp butter onto serving plate; garnish with tiny shrimp and parsley. Serve with bread, crackers and/or vegetables.

Note: *2 cans (4½ ounces each) shrimp, rinsed and drained, can be substituted; omit salt.*

Bacon Baked Oysters

TROPICAL AMBROSIA

There's no sugar needed or added to this glorious combination of naturally sweet orange and banana, juice-packed pineapple and unsweetened juice concentrate topped with flaked coconut.

Makes 4 servings

2 oranges, peeled, seeded, cut into chunks
1 ripe banana, sliced
1 can (8 ounces) juice-packed pineapple chunks, undrained
1 tablespoon frozen pineapple juice concentrate, thawed
2 tablespoons flaked coconut

Combine all ingredients except coconut in medium bowl; mix well. Spoon into dessert dishes; sprinkle with coconut.

CUCUMBER DIP

Makes 4 to 6 servings

1 large cucumber, pared, seeded, minced
½ teaspoon salt
1 package (3 ounces) cream cheese, room temperature
2 tablespoons sour cream
2 tablespoons chopped canned green chilies
Sliced zucchini, celery and carrot sticks, cauliflower flowerets and cherry tomatoes

1. Mix cucumber and salt in medium bowl; refrigerate 1 hour. Drain cucumber; squeeze to extract moisture.

2. Beat cream cheese in small mixer bowl until smooth; beat in sour cream. Stir in cucumber and chilies.

3. Serve dip with assorted vegetables.

Tropical Ambrosia

ZESTY CRAB SPREAD

Makes 10 to 12 servings

- 1 envelope unflavored gelatin
- ¼ cup cold water
- 1 cup clam juice, heated to boiling
- 1 cup mayonnaise
- 2 tablespoons Dijon-style mustard
- ½ teaspoon salt
- ½ teaspoon liquid pepper sauce
- 1 can (6½ ounces) white crab meat, drained, flaked
- ½ cup finely chopped seeded pared cucumber
- ½ cup finely chopped red bell pepper
- ½ cup finely chopped yellow bell or banana pepper
- ½ cup finely chopped green onions
- ¾ cup whipping cream, whipped
  Assorted crackers

1. Sprinkle gelatin over water in medium bowl; let stand 1 minute to soften. Pour boiling clam juice over gelatin; stir until gelatin is completely dissolved.

2. Mix mayonnaise, mustard, salt and pepper sauce in small bowl; stir into gelatin mixture. Refrigerate, stirring occasionally, until thickened to consistency of unbeaten egg whites.

3. Add crab meat, cucumber, red and yellow peppers and green onions to gelatin mixture; mix well. Fold in whipped cream.

4. Pour mixture into lightly oiled 4-cup mold. Refrigerate until set, at least 4 hours, preferably overnight to blend flavors. Unmold onto serving plate; serve with crackers.

CARROT SOUP WITH PEAS

Two favorite vegetables in a brilliant new guise. The carrots blend into a thick herb-splashed puree dotted with tiny green peas for color and flavor contrast.

Makes 8 to 10 servings

- 1 pound carrots, shredded
- 8 green onions, minced
- 1 cup finely chopped potato
- 1 small clove garlic, minced
- ¼ cup butter or margarine
- ¼ teaspoon dried chervil
- ¼ teaspoon dried marjoram
- ¼ teaspoon dried thyme
- ⅛ teaspoon dried tarragon
- 1½ quarts chicken stock
- 3 cups frozen non-dairy creamer, thawed
- 1 package (10 ounces) frozen tiny peas, thawed
- ½ teaspoon salt
- ¼ teaspoon pepper

1. Saute carrots, green onions, potato and garlic in butter in Dutch oven over medium-low heat until vegetables are wilted, about 10 minutes. Stir in chervil, marjoram, thyme and tarragon.

2. Add stock; cook, uncovered, over medium-high heat until potato is tender, about 10 minutes.

3. Process vegetable mixture in batches in blender until smooth; return to Dutch oven.

4. Gradually stir in non-dairy creamer and peas; cook just until soup is hot. Stir in salt and pepper.

Orange Fruit Soup

ORANGE FRUIT SOUP

A delicate luncheon soup lightly seasoned with cardamom, a sweetly pungent spice of the ginger family and a favorite with fruit.

Makes 8 to 10 servings

- 3 cans (16 ounces each) pears, drained
- 6 cups orange juice
- ¾ cup sour cream
- 1½ teaspoons ground cardamom
- 5 oranges, peeled, sectioned
  Orange slice and toasted coconut for garnish
  Assorted toppings: creme fraiche, toasted coconut, avocado slices, macadamia nuts

1. Process pears in blender until smooth; transfer to large bowl.

2. Stir in orange juice, sour cream and cardamom; refrigerate, covered, several hours.

3. Just before serving, stir orange sections into soup. Garnish with orange slice and coconut; serve with assorted toppings.

SEAFOOD CHOWDER

This is some fine kettle of fish! Cod, oysters, clams and shrimp in a creamy wine and herb broth—with shell macaroni for good measure.

Makes 8 servings

2 stalks celery, chopped
1 medium onion, chopped
1 clove garlic, minced
¼ cup butter
6 fresh shucked oysters or 1 can (10 ounces)
    oysters
1 can (8 ounces) minced clams
1 can (4 ounces) tiny shrimp
Water
⅓ cup dry white wine
1 teaspoon chicken bouillon granules
1 teaspoon salt
½ teaspoon dried thyme, crumbled
½ teaspoon ground nutmeg
½ teaspoon ground black pepper
1 bay leaf
5 tablespoons all-purpose flour
1 pound codfish fillets, cubed
½ medium green bell pepper, chopped
1½ cups small shell macaroni, cooked, drained
1 cup evaporated milk
1 jar (2 ounces) pimiento, drained, chopped
2 tablespoons chopped parsley

1. Saute celery, onion and garlic in butter in Dutch oven until soft, about 4 minutes.

2. Drain liquid from oysters, clams and shrimp into 4-cup measure; add enough water to make 3 cups liquid. Add to pan; stir in wine, bouillon granules, salt, thyme, nutmeg, ground pepper and bay leaf. Heat to boiling; reduce heat. Simmer, covered, 15 minutes.   *(Continued)*

French Onion Soup

3. Mix flour with ⅓ cup water in small bowl until smooth; gradually whisk into soup. Cook and stir until soup thickens and bubbles for 1 minute.

4. Add codfish, oysters and green bell pepper to soup; mix. Simmer, uncovered, 10 minutes; remove and discard bay leaf.

5. Add clams, shrimp, macaroni, milk, pimiento and parsley to soup. Heat over medium-low heat just to simmering; serve immediately.

FRENCH ONION SOUP

Makes 4 servings

1 envelope onion soup mix
¼ cup dry white wine, if desired
½ pound Swiss cheese, diced
4 slices French bread, toasted
½ cup grated Parmesan cheese
1 tablespoon butter or margarine, melted

1. Prepare onion soup mix according to package directions; remove from heat. Stir in wine, then Swiss cheese. Ladle into 4 individual ovenproof soup crocks or pour into 1½-quart baking dish.

2. Float bread on top of soup. Sprinkle bread with Parmesan cheese; drizzle with butter.

3. Bake in preheated 400°F oven until cheese topping is golden, about 7 minutes.

STRIPED BASS ITALIAN

For a casual dinner, enjoy charcoal-grilled fish over spaghetti to serve al fresco with a bottle of chilled white wine, a green salad and garlic bread.

Makes 6 servings

2 pounds fresh or thawed frozen striped bass,
    snapper, grouper or other thick fish fillets
¼ cup vegetable oil
1 tablespoon lemon juice
½ teaspoon salt
½ teaspoon dried oregano, crumbled
1 clove garlic, sliced
1 jar (32 ounces) spaghetti sauce
12 ounces spaghetti
½ cup shredded or grated Parmesan cheese
    Celery hearts and parsley sprigs for garnish

1. Cut fish into serving-size portions; place in single layer in shallow baking dish. Mix oil, lemon juice, salt, oregano and garlic in small bowl; pour over fish. Refrigerate, covered, turning once, 1 hour.

2. Drain fish, reserving marinade. Place fish in well-greased hinged wire baskets. Grill 5 inches from medium-hot coals 8 minutes; baste with reserved marinade. Turn over; grill until fish flakes with fork, 7 to 8 minutes longer.

3. While fish is cooking, heat spaghetti sauce; cook spaghetti according to package directions and drain well.

4. To serve, place fish on top of spaghetti on plates; spoon sauce over fish and spaghetti. Sprinkle with cheese; garnish with celery and parsley.

Striped Bass Italian

Shrimply Delicious Creole

RED SNAPPER WITH SEAFOOD SAUCE

Makes 6 servings

6 fresh or thawed frozen red snapper or other
    white fish fillets (about 1½ pounds)
1 teaspoon salt
¼ teaspoon pepper
6 tablespoons lemon juice
1 cup fine dry breadcrumbs
4 tablespoons butter
2 tablespoons vegetable oil
1 can (4 ounces) sliced mushrooms, drained
½ cup sliced green onions
3 tablespoons minced parsley
1 package (6 ounces) frozen crab meat or shrimp
    or mixture of both, thawed
1 tablespoon dry sherry
3 cups hot cooked rice (cooked in chicken broth)

1. Sprinkle fillets with ½ teaspoon of the salt and ⅛ teaspoon of the pepper. Drizzle with 3 tablespoons of the
lemon juice. Dip in breadcrumbs to coat evenly.

2. Heat 2 tablespoons of the butter and the oil in large
skillet over medium heat until hot. Add as many fillets as
will fit in single layer without crowding. Cook, turning
once, until fish is golden brown and flakes with fork, 4 to 5
minutes per side. Remove fish to platter; keep warm. Repeat until all fillets have been cooked.

3. Add remaining 2 tablespoons butter to skillet; cook until
light brown. Add mushrooms, onions and parsley; saute 2
minutes.
(Continued)

4. Add crab meat, sherry, remaining 3 tablespoons lemon
juice, ½ teaspoon salt and ⅛ teaspoon pepper to skillet;
cook and stir until hot. Spoon sauce over fish; serve with
rice.

SHRIMPLY DELICIOUS CREOLE

*When "Creole" isn't describing the French cooking style of
New Orleans, it identifies a versatile sauce of tomatoes,
green peppers and onions.*

Makes 4 servings

¾ cup chopped green bell pepper
½ cup chopped celery
2 tablespoons butter or margarine
1 can (16 ounces) tomatoes, undrained, chopped
½ cup water
1 envelope golden onion soup mix
1 tablespoon chopped parsley
1 pound shelled deveined medium shrimp
    Hot cooked rice

1. Saute green bell pepper and celery in butter in large
skillet over medium heat until soft, about 5 minutes.

2. Add tomatoes, water, soup mix and parsley; mix well.
Heat to boiling; reduce heat. Simmer, covered, stirring occasionally, 20 minutes.

3. Stir shrimp into skillet; cook, stirring occasionally, until
shrimp are opaque throughout, 3 to 5 minutes. Serve over
rice.

MARYLAND CRAB CAKES

Makes 4 to 6 servings

½ cup minced onion
¼ cup minced green bell pepper
2 tablespoons margarine or vegetable oil
1 tablespoon dry mustard
1 teaspoon Worcestershire sauce
¾ teaspoon salt
¼ teaspoon hot red pepper sauce
¼ teaspoon ground black pepper
  Pinch ground red pepper
¼ cup all-purpose flour
1¼ cups half-and-half
1 pound blue crab meat, flaked
2 large egg yolks, beaten
½ cup fresh breadcrumbs
½ teaspoon paprika
1 tablespoon butter, melted
2 to 4 tablespoons vegetable oil
  Cherry tomatoes and watercress for garnish
  Lemon wedges

1. Saute onion and green bell pepper in margarine in large skillet over medium heat until soft, about 4 minutes. Stir in mustard, Worcestershire sauce, salt, red pepper sauce, black pepper and red pepper. Stir in flour; cook and stir until bubbly.

2. Gradually stir in half-and-half until smooth; cook and stir until sauce thickens and bubbles for 1 minute. Stir in crab meat; remove from heat. *(Continued)*

3. Gradually stir ½ of the hot sauce into egg yolks in medium bowl; stir egg yolk mixture into remaining sauce in pan. Cook, stirring constantly, over low heat until thickened. Refrigerate crab meat mixture until cold.

4. Mix breadcrumbs, paprika and butter in small bowl. Shape crab meat mixture into 6 or 8 patties; dip in crumb mixture to coat evenly. Fry in oil in large skillet over medium heat until golden brown, 3 to 4 minutes per side. Garnish with tomatoes and watercress; serve with lemon wedges.

RAMPART STREET SHRIMP

Makes 6 servings

1½ pounds large shrimp, shelled, deveined
¼ cup butter or margarine
2 cloves garlic, minced
½ teaspoon dried oregano, crumbled
  Salt and ground red pepper to taste
½ cup dry vermouth
2 tablespoons lemon juice
3 cups hot cooked rice

1. Saute shrimp in butter in large skillet over medium-high heat 3 minutes. Stir in garlic, oregano, salt and pepper. Stir in vermouth.

2. Cook and stir over medium-low heat until shrimp are opaque throughout, 2 to 3 minutes longer. Stir in lemon juice. Serve over rice.

Maryland Crab Cakes

TROUT WELLINGTON

Inside this golden-brown packet shaped like a fish are fillets of sea trout spread with elegant crab meat paté.

Makes 4 servings

2 fresh or thawed frozen sea trout fillets
    (½ pound each)
1 tablespoon lemon juice
1 teaspoon salt
½ teaspoon pepper
1 container (8 ounces) refrigerated crescent roll
    dough
    Crab Stuffing (recipe follows)
1 large egg yolk mixed with 2 tablespoons water
    Orange and lime slices and green onion curls
      for garnish

1. Sprinkle fish with lemon juice, salt and pepper.

2. Unroll dough and separate into 2 equal pieces. Roll out each piece on lightly floured surface to ⅛-inch thickness. Cut 1 piece of dough with knife into fish shape 2 inches longer and 1 inch wider than fillet. Cut second piece of dough into fish shape 2 inches longer and 3 inches wider than fillet.

3. Spead thin layer of Crab Stuffing on smaller piece of dough; top with 1 fillet. Spread fillet with ½ of the remaining stuffing; top with remaining fillet. Spread remaining stuffing over top and sides of fish to cover. Top with larger piece of dough; pinch edges to seal.   *(Continued)*

4. Roll out dough scraps and cut into shapes for fins, eye and gills; arrange on top of fish. Make scale impressions in dough with ½-inch round cutter.

5. Place on floured baking sheet; brush with egg yolk and water mixture. Refrigerate 1 hour.

6. Transfer fish to greased shallow baking pan. Bake in preheated 425°F oven 10 minutes. Reduce oven setting to 350°F; continue baking until dough is brown, about 10 minutes longer. Carefully transfer fish to platter; garnish with orange and lime slices and green onion curls.

CRAB STUFFING

⅓ to ½ cup whipping cream
½ pound fresh or thawed frozen crab meat
½ cup chopped celery
½ cup breadcrumbs
¼ cup butter, melted
1 large egg white
1 teaspoon lemon pepper seasoning
¼ teaspoon salt

Combine ⅓ cup of the cream and the remaining ingredients in blender or food processor container; process until smooth. Add remaining cream if needed to form spreading consistency.

Trout Wellington

Baked Fish in Tomato Cups

BAKED FISH IN TOMATO CUPS

Here's a triple-treat entree with tender baked fish, colorful cooked vegetable and fluffy mashed potatoes, all cooked in the same dish.

Makes 6 servings

  6 medium tomatoes
  3 tablespoons butter or margarine, room
     temperature
  1 tablespoon chopped parsley
  1 tablespoon lemon juice
  ½ teaspoon Worcestershire sauce
  ½ teaspoon grated onion
  ½ teaspoon salt
  ⅛ teaspoon hot red pepper sauce
  6 fresh or thawed frozen croaker or other fish
     fillets (4 to 6 ounces each)
  4 cups mashed potatoes
    Chopped parsley and watercress sprigs for
     garnish

1. Cut top off each tomato; scoop out and discard centers. Drain tomato cups, inverted on paper toweling.

2. Combine butter, 1 tablespoon parsley, the lemon juice, Worcestershire sauce, onion, salt and red pepper sauce in small bowl; mix well.

3. Roll up fillets; secure with wooden picks. Stand rolls on end in well-greased 8 × 8 × 2-inch baking dish. Bake in preheated 350°F oven 10 minutes.

4. Remove wooden picks; place fish in tomato cups. Arrange tomatoes, evenly spaced, in well-greased shallow 12 × 8-inch baking dish. Dot fish and tomatoes with butter mixture, dividing evenly. *(Continued)*

5. Pipe potatoes through pastry bag fitted with large star tip around tomatoes. Bake at 350°F until fish is opaque throughout and potatoes and tomatoes are heated through, 12 to 15 minutes. Garnish with parsley and watercress.

FISH FILLETS WITH MUSTARD BUTTER

Makes 6 servings

  2 pounds fresh or thawed frozen fish fillets
  3 cups water
  ¾ cup plus 3 tablespoons lemon juice
  6 tablespoons margarine or butter, melted
  4 teaspoons prepared mustard
  ¾ teaspoon salt
  ½ teaspoon paprika
    Chopped parsley

1. Cut fillets into serving-size pieces; place in single layer in well-greased 12 × 8 × 2-inch baking dish. Mix water and ¾ cup of the lemon juice in small bowl; pour over fish. Refrigerate 20 minutes.

2. Drain fish well; arrange in single layer on well-greased rack of broiler pan. Mix margarine, remaining 3 tablespoons lemon juice, the mustard, salt and paprika in small bowl. Brush fish generously with margarine mixture.

3. Broil 4 inches from heat source 4 to 6 minutes. Carefully turn fish over; baste generously with margarine mixture. Broil until fish is opaque throughout, 4 to 6 minutes longer. Sprinkle with parsley. Heat remaining margarine mixture; serve with fish.

Jambalaya

OYSTER SANDWICH LOAVES

In New Orleans of an earlier era this wonderful sandwich of fried oysters piled high on a long loaf of French bread was called a peacemaker, because it was carried home by a husband who stayed out on the town too late.

Makes 6 servings

1 pint fresh or thawed frozen shucked oysters
½ teaspoon salt
⅛ teaspoon pepper
2 large eggs, beaten
¼ cup milk
¾ cup all-purpose flour
2 cups soft breadcrumbs
2 loaves French bread (15 × 3 inches each)
½ cup margarine or butter, melted
  Vegetable oil for frying
½ cup prepared tartar sauce
1½ cups shredded lettuce
18 thin tomato slices

1. Drain oysters; pat dry with paper toweling. Sprinkle with salt and pepper. Mix eggs and milk in small bowl. Roll oysters in flour, dip into egg mixture, then roll in breadcrumbs to coat evenly. Refrigerate at least 30 minutes to firm coating.

2. Cut bread loaves horizontally into halves; pull out soft bread from insides of halves. Brush insides of bread shells with margarine. Place on baking sheet; bake in preheated 350°F oven until warm and crisp, 3 to 5 minutes.

3. Heat 2 to 3 inches oil in deep fryer to 350°F. Place oysters in single layer in fry basket. Fry until golden brown, 2 to 3 minutes; drain on paper toweling. Repeat until all oysters have been fried.

4. Spread insides of bread shells with tartar sauce. Place lettuce in bottom halves of bread; top with tomato slices, then with oysters. Cover with top halves of bread. Cut each loaf crosswise into 3 portions.

JAMBALAYA

Makes 6 to 8 servings

1 can (28 ounces) tomatoes, undrained, crushed
1¼ cups water
1 cup rice
¼ cup instant minced onion
1 teaspoon salt
¾ teaspoon dried thyme, crumbled
¼ teaspoon instant minced garlic
⅛ teaspoon ground red pepper
1 bay leaf
1 pound cooked ham, cut into 1½ × 1 × ¼-inch pieces
1 package (10 ounces) frozen peas, thawed
2½ pounds medium shrimp, shelled, deveined
1 tablespoon minced parsley

1. Combine tomatoes, water, rice, onion, salt, thyme, garlic, red pepper and bay leaf in Dutch oven; mix well. Heat to boiling; reduce heat. Simmer, covered, 15 minutes.

2. Stir in ham and peas; simmer 5 minutes. Stir in shrimp and parsley; simmer, covered, just until shrimp turn opaque throughout, about 4 minutes. Remove bay leaf before serving.

Note: *2 pounds fish fillets, cut into 1-inch pieces, can be substituted for shrimp.*

CELERY-TUNA STIR FRY

Choose solid-pack tuna for this easy supper dish and handle the chunks gently as you combine them with vegetables and sauce.

Makes 4 to 6 servings

2 cans (7 ounces each) solid white tuna, packed in oil
3 tablespoons water
1 tablespoon soy sauce
1 tablespoon dry sherry
1½ teaspoons prepared mustard
¼ teaspoon garlic powder
3 cups diagonally sliced celery
2 cups onion wedges
2 large tomatoes, cut into wedges
  Hot cooked rice, if desired

1. Drain oil from tuna into wok or large skillet; break tuna into chunks. Mix water, soy sauce, sherry, mustard and garlic powder in small bowl.

2. Heat oil over medium heat until hot. Add celery and onion; stir-fry until crisp-tender, 6 to 8 minutes. Add tomatoes and tuna; stir-fry 1 minute.

3. Add soy sauce mixture; cook and stir until hot throughout. Serve over rice.

CATFISH BIENVILLE

Like many elegant sauces, this version of the one named for the French colonial governor and founder of New Orleans is thickened with a roux. Fat and flour are cooked together before any liquid is added.

Makes 6 to 8 servings

1 tablespoon butter or margarine, melted
1 tablespoon lemon juice
1 teaspoon salt
⅛ teaspoon white pepper
2 pounds fresh or thawed frozen farm-raised
    catfish fillets (4 to 5 ounces each)
Bienville Sauce (recipe follows)
Parsley sprigs and tomato roses for garnish

1. Mix butter, lemon juice, salt and pepper in small bowl.

2. Place fish on well-greased broiler pan; brush with butter mixture. Broil in preheated broiler, 6 inches from heat source, until opaque throughout, 6 to 8 minutes. Remove to serving plates.

3. Spoon Bienville Sauce over fish. Garnish with parsley and tomato roses. *(Continued)*

BIENVILLE SAUCE

3 slices bacon, chopped
⅓ cup chopped green onions
2 tablespoons butter or margarine
¼ cup all-purpose flour
2 cups milk
½ pound process cheese spread, diced
¼ cup dry sherry
1 can (4 ounces) sliced mushrooms, drained
½ pound cooked shelled deveined shrimp,
    chopped
¼ teaspoon Worcestershire sauce
¼ teaspoon white pepper
Dash hot red pepper sauce

1. Saute bacon and green onions in medium saucepan over medium heat until bacon is light brown. Stir in butter until melted. Stir in flour; cook and stir until bubbly.

2. Gradually whisk in milk until smooth; cook and stir over medium-low heat until sauce thickens and bubbles for 1 minute. Stir in cheese; cook and stir until melted and smooth. Stir in remaining ingredients; cook and stir until hot.

Makes about 3 cups

Catfish Bienville

CRAWFISH ETOUFFÉE

Looking like miniature Northern lobsters, crawfish are a variety of shellfish plentiful in southern waters. They're especially popular smothered in a blanket of vegetables in a Cajun stew made with a browned-flour roux and served with rice.

Makes 6 servings

¼ cup butter or margarine
⅓ cup all-purpose flour
1 cup chopped onion
1 cup chopped celery
1 cup chopped green bell pepper
2 cloves garlic, minced
3 cups crawfish tails (12 ounces)
2 cups chicken broth
¼ cup minced parsley
1 teaspoon salt
⅛ teaspoon ground black pepper
⅛ teaspoon ground red pepper
  Hot red pepper sauce to taste
3 cups hot cooked rice

1. Melt butter in large heavy saucepan. Stir in flour; cook and stir over medium-low heat until roux is dark brown, 10 to 15 minutes.

2. Add onion, celery, green bell pepper and garlic; cook and stir until crisp-tender, 2 to 3 minutes.

3. Stir in remaining ingredients except rice; heat over medium heat to simmering. Reduce heat to medium-low; simmer, stirring frequently, 20 minutes. Ladle etouffée into soup bowls; top each serving with ½ cup of the rice.

SKEWERED SEAFOOD BOATS

Warmed fresh pineapple shells carry a tasty cargo of broiled shrimps and scallops basted in a ginger-sweet Russian dressing.

Makes 4 servings

2 medium pineapples
1 cup bottled red Russian dressing
¼ cup packed brown sugar
½ teaspoon ground ginger
½ pound large shrimp, shelled, deveined
½ pound scallops
1 large green bell pepper, cut into 1¼-inch pieces
4 cups hot cooked rice
3 tablespoons chopped green onion

1. Cut pineapples lengthwise into halves. Cut pineapple from shells; reserve shells. Cut pineapple into 1-inch chunks; measure and reserve 1 cup chunks. Reserve remaining pineapple for other use.

2. Mix dressing, sugar and ginger in small bowl.

3. Thread shrimp, scallops, green bell pepper and the reserved 1 cup pineapple chunks onto skewers in alternating order. Grill or broil 6 inches from heat source, turning and basting frequently with dressing mixture, until seafood is cooked through, about 5 minutes.

4. Meanwhile, wrap leaves of reserved pineapple shells in aluminum foil; grill or broil with cut surfaces toward heat source until light brown, about 5 minutes. Remove foil.

5. Mix rice and green onion in medium bowl; spoon into hot pineapple shells. Top with skewers.

PARADE-DRESSED MULLET

Enjoy golden Cheddar cheese and parsley-seasoned bread cubes sandwiched between pairs of lean fish fillets.

Makes 6 servings

2 pounds fresh or thawed frozen mullet fillets
1 teaspoon salt
  Pinch pepper
  Cheese Stuffing (recipe follows)
2 tablespoons melted butter or vegetable oil
  Paprika

1. Sprinkle fish with salt and pepper. Place ½ of the fillets, skin side down, in well-greased 12 × 8 × 2-inch baking dish.

2. Place Cheese Stuffing on top of fish; cover with remaining fillets, skin side up. Brush with butter; sprinkle with paprika.

3. Bake in preheated 350°F oven until fish is opaque throughout, 30 to 35 minutes.

CHEESE STUFFING

1 cup chopped onion
¼ cup butter or vegetable oil
2 cups toasted or dry bread cubes
1 cup shredded Cheddar cheese
2 tablespoons chopped parsley
2 teaspoons dry mustard
½ teaspoon salt
  Pinch pepper

Saute onion in butter in medium skillet over medium heat until soft, about 4 minutes. Combine with remaining ingredients in medium bowl; toss to mix well.

QUICK SEAFOOD NEWBURG

Makes 4 servings

2 tablespoons butter
2 tablespoons all-purpose flour
1 cup milk
¼ cup dry sherry
  Salt
  Ground black pepper to taste
  Pinch ground nutmeg
  Pinch ground red pepper
2 cups diced, cooked, shelled lobster or shrimp or 2 cans (7 ounces each) tuna, drained, flaked
4 slices toasted bread, cut diagonally into halves
2 tablespoons minced parsley
  Paprika
  Lemon wedges for garnish

1. Melt butter in large saucepan. Stir in flour; cook and stir over medium-low heat until bubbly. Gradually whisk in milk until smooth; cook and stir until sauce thickens and bubbles for 1 minute.

2. Stir in sherry, salt, black pepper, nutmeg, and red pepper. Stir in lobster; cook just until hot.

3. To serve, spoon lobster mixture over toast triangles; sprinkle with parsley and paprika. Garnish with lemon wedges.

Skewered Seafood Boats

Devilish Blue Crab

DEVILISH BLUE CRAB

Claws with brilliant touches of blue give the Atlantic crab its name. The shell gives it a double existence. As the crab grows, it molts, leaving the hard shell behind and exposing a new soft one which hardens later. Soft-shell crabs are usually grilled or pan-fried and consumed shell and all. Hard-shell crabs are steamed or simmered or purchased as cooked crab meat.

Makes 6 servings

  2 slices bacon
  ½ cup chopped onion
  ½ cup chopped celery
  ¼ cup chopped green bell pepper
  1 clove garlic, minced
  1 pound blue crab meat, flaked
1½ cups cracker crumbs
  ½ cup margarine or butter, melted
  1 large egg, beaten
  ¼ cup milk
  2 tablespoons chopped parsley
  1 teaspoon dry mustard
  1 teaspoon Worcestershire sauce
  ½ teaspoon salt
  ⅛ teaspoon ground red pepper
  Parsley sprigs and lemon slices for garnish

1. Cook bacon in medium skillet over medium heat until crisp. Drain bacon on paper toweling; reserve drippings.

2. Saute onion, celery, green bell pepper and garlic in reserved drippings over medium heat until vegetables are soft, about 4 minutes. *(Continued)*

3. Crumble bacon. Combine bacon, onion mixture and remaining ingredients except garnish in large bowl; mix well.

4. Divide mixture evenly among 6 well-greased crab shells or 6-ounce ramekins. Bake in preheated 350°F oven 25 to 30 minutes. Garnish with parsley sprigs and lemon slices.

Note: *Mixture can be baked in well-greased 1½-quart baking dish, if desired.*

OYSTER & HAM CASSEROLE

Makes 6 servings

  2 cups cracker crumbs
  ½ cup chopped cooked ham
  ½ cup chopped green bell pepper
  Pinch ground black pepper
  2 cans (12 ounces each) fresh or thawed frozen
     oysters, drained
  ½ cup margarine or butter
  ¼ cup dry sherry
  Oyster crackers

1. Combine cracker crumbs, ham, green bell pepper and ground pepper in medium bowl; mix well.

2. Arrange ½ of the oysters in a well-greased 12 × 8 × 2-inch baking dish. Dot with ½ of the margarine; sprinkle with ½ of the sherry. Cover with ½ of the crumb mixture. Repeat layers once; arrange oyster crackers on top.

3. Bake in preheated 450°F oven until light brown, 20 to 25 minutes.

POMPANO EN PAPILLOTE

X marks the spot for cutting open the parchment packet of fish and seafood in a superb wine sauce created at Antoine's Restaurant in New Orleans.

Makes 6 servings

3 cups water
2 lemon slices
1¼ teaspoons salt
1 bay leaf
⅛ teaspoon dried thyme, crumbled
2 pounds fresh or thawed frozen pompano or other fish fillets
½ cup chopped green onions
1 clove garlic, minced
2 tablespoons margarine or butter
3 tablespoons all-purpose flour
2 large egg yolks, beaten
3 tablespoons dry white wine
1 can (6½ or 7 ounces) crab meat, drained, flaked
¼ pound cooked shelled deveined shrimp
2 tablespoons vegetable oil
Lemon wedges

1. Combine water, lemon slices, 1 teaspoon of the salt, the bay leaf and thyme in 10-inch skillet; heat to boiling. Add fish; reduce heat. Simmer, covered, until fish is opaque throughout, 5 to 10 minutes.

2. Carefully remove fish to plate, draining well. Strain and reserve 1½ cups of the poaching liquid. Carefully remove any skin and bones from fish.

3. Saute green onions and garlic in margarine in medium saucepan over medium heat until soft, about 3 minutes. Stir in flour and remaining ¼ teaspoon salt until smooth. Gradually whisk in reserved poaching liquid until smooth. Cook and stir over medium heat until sauce thickens and bubbles for 1 minute; remove from heat.

4. Gradually whisk about ½ cup of the hot sauce into egg yolks in small bowl. Gradually whisk egg yolk mixture into remaining sauce in saucepan. Cook and stir over low heat until sauce thickens; do not boil. Remove from heat; stir in wine. Stir in crab meat and shrimp. *(Continued)*

5. Cut 6 pieces of parchment paper into 12 × 10-inch heart shapes. Brush parchment paper with oil. Place 1 portion of fish on 1 side of each paper heart; top each with about ½ cup of the crab-shrimp sauce. Fold other side of paper over fish to enclose. To seal, start at top of heart, fold edges over and crease sharply at ½-inch intervals; twist tip of heart tightly.

6. Place hearts in single layer in shallow baking pan. Bake in preheated 400°F oven until puffed with steam, 10 to 15 minutes. To serve, cut hearts open with large X; fold paper back. Serve with lemon wedges.

GRILLED FISH TURNOVERS

A hinged wire grill basket is a dandy piece of barbecuing equipment which makes it easy to baste and turn tender fish fillets being charcoal broiled.

Makes 12 servings

4 pounds fresh or thawed frozen flounder, sole or other skinless fish fillets
6 slices (1 ounce each) sharp cheese, cut into halves
½ cup butter or margarine, melted
½ cup fresh lemon juice
2 teaspoons salt
2 teaspoons paprika
½ teaspoon pepper
Lemon wedges

1. Cut fish into 12 even pieces. Place ½ slice cheese at one end of each piece of fish; fold other end of fish over cheese. Place fish turnovers in single layer in well-greased hinged wire grill basket.

2. Mix remaining ingredients except lemon wedges in small bowl. Brush fish with butter sauce.

3. Grill 4 inches from medium-hot coals 5 to 8 minutes. Baste fish with sauce; turn wire grill over. Grill until fish is opaque throughout, 5 to 8 minutes longer. Serve with lemon wedges.

Pompano en Papillote

BOURBON-LACED BEEF ROAST

Makes 8 to 12 servings

½ cup bourbon
½ cup soy sauce
1 small onion, finely chopped
3 tablespoons packed brown sugar
3 tablespoons lemon juice
2 tablespoons water
1 teaspoon Worcestershire sauce
1 beef top round roast (4 to 6 pounds)

1. Combine all ingredients except beef in small bowl; mix well. Place beef in heavy-duty plastic bag; add marinade, turning beef to coat. Close bag securely; refrigerate, turning at least once, 6 hours or overnight.

2. Remove beef from marinade. Insert rotisserie rod lengthwise through center of roast; balance roast and tighten spit forks so that roast turns only with rod.

3. Place beef on rotisserie; roast over low- to medium-hot coals to desired degree of doneness: 140°F for rare or 155°F for medium. Insert instant-registering thermometer into thickest part of meat to test for doneness; allow 22 to 27 minutes per pound.

LIVER IN TOMATO SAUCE

Makes 2 servings

1 can (8 ounces) tomato sauce with tomato bits
¼ cup chopped green bell pepper
¼ cup chopped celery
¼ cup chopped onion
¼ cup water
¼ teaspoon dried basil, crumbled
⅛ teaspoon ground black pepper
1 slice bacon, cut into 1-inch pieces
½ pound beef liver (½ inch thick)
1 cup hot cooked rice

(Continued)

1. Combine tomato sauce, green bell pepper, celery, onion, water, basil and ground pepper in medium saucepan; heat to boiling. Reduce heat; simmer 15 minutes.

2. Meanwhile, cook bacon over medium heat in medium skillet until crisp. Remove bacon; add to sauce.

3. Saute liver in bacon drippings over medium heat, 2 minutes per side. Remove liver to cutting board; cut into ½-inch-wide strips.

4. Return liver to skillet; stir in sauce and rice. Simmer 5 minutes.

GEORGE WASHINGTON'S BEEF AND KIDNEY PIE

Still a Southern tradition is the pairing of meats and herbs in a red-wine gravy surrounded by flaky pastry in a deep baking dish.

Makes 6 to 8 servings

1 pound beef kidney, soaked, drained*
2 pounds boneless beef shoulder, cut into 1-inch cubes
¼ cup all-purpose flour
2 teaspoons salt
¼ teaspoon pepper
¼ cup rendered suet or vegetable oil
¼ cup instant minced onion
1¼ cups water
½ cup dry red wine
1½ teaspoons dried marjoram, crumbled
¼ teaspoon dried thyme, crumbled
½ pound mushrooms, sliced
1 package (10 ounces) pie crust mix
1 large egg yolk mixed with 2 teaspoons water

1. Split kidney lengthwise in half; remove all fat, membranes and veins. Cut into 1-inch cubes; combine with beef in large bowl.

2. Mix flour, salt and pepper in small bowl; sprinkle over meat. Toss to coat evenly. Cook meat, part at a time, in rendered suet in Dutch oven over medium heat until brown on all sides; remove to plate.

3. Mix onion and ¼ cup of the water in small bowl; let stand 10 minutes to rehydrate. Add to Dutch oven; saute over medium heat 2 minutes. Stir in remaining 1 cup water, the wine, marjoram and thyme; cook and stir to loosen particles clinging to bottom of pan.

4. Return meat to Dutch oven; heat to boiling. Reduce heat; simmer, covered, stirring occasionally, until meat is tender, about 1½ hours.

5. Stir in mushrooms; simmer, covered, 20 minutes. Transfer mixture to 2-quart baking dish with rim.

6. Prepare pie crust mix according to package directions; roll out pastry on lightly floured surface and trim to 1 inch wider on all sides than edge of baking dish. Moisten rim of baking dish; top with pastry, folding edge under itself. Press edge to seal; flute edge.

7. Brush pastry with egg yolk wash. Decorate top with leaf shapes cut from pastry trimmings; brush with egg wash. Cut steam vents in top of pastry. Bake in preheated 425°F until pastry is golden, 20 to 25 minutes.

*Note: Kidney can be omitted if desired; increase beef shoulder to 3 pounds.

George Washington's Beef and Kidney Pie

Sausage-Spinach Quiche

SAUSAGE-SPINACH QUICHE

Makes 8 servings

  8 ounces bulk pork sausage
¼ cup chopped onion
  1 clove garlic, minced
  1 package (10 ounces) frozen chopped spinach,
      cooked, squeezed dry
1½ cups shredded Cheddar cheese
      Pastry Shell (recipe follows)
  2 cups half-and-half
  3 large eggs, lightly beaten
¼ teaspoon salt
⅛ teaspoon pepper
      Cherry tomatoes and watercress sprigs for
      garnish

1. Crumble sausage in medium skillet; add onion and garlic. Saute over medium heat until sausage is brown, about 8 minutes; drain well.

2. Add spinach to sausage mixture; mix well. Sprinkle cheese evenly in bottom of Pastry Shell; top with sausage mixture.

3. Whisk half-and-half, eggs, salt and pepper in medium bowl until blended; pour over sausage mixture.

(Continued)

4. Bake in preheated 375°F oven until knife inserted near center is withdrawn clean, about 45 minutes. Cool on wire rack 10 minutes before serving; garnish with tomatoes and watercress.

PASTRY SHELL

1⅓ cups all-purpose flour
½ teaspoon salt
½ cup lard or vegetable shortening, cold
  3 to 4 tablespoons ice water

1. Mix flour and salt in medium bowl; cut in lard until mixture resembles coarse crumbs. Gradually add water, stirring and tossing with fork, until mixture holds together when squeezed. Refrigerate, wrapped in plastic, 1 hour.

2. Roll out dough on lightly floured surface into 12-inch circle. Ease into 9-inch quiche pan; trim flush with edge of pan. Pierce bottom in several places with fork.

3. Line pastry with parchment paper; fill with pie weights or dry beans. Bake in preheated 400°F oven until pastry is set, 10 to 12 minutes. Remove paper and weights; bake just until pastry begins to color, about 5 minutes longer. Cool completely on wire rack.

Scotch Eggs

COUNTRY JAMBALAYA

Hot and spicy sausage frequently fuels the fire in Cajun and Creole recipes such as this bayou favorite with ham (jambon in French) in its name.

Makes 8 to 10 servings

  ¾ pound broiler-fryer chicken pieces
  2 tablespoons butter
  1 pound hot Italian sausage, crumbled
  1 cup diced ham or smoked pork
  ½ cup all-purpose flour
  2 cups chopped celery
  ⅓ cup chopped onion
  3 cloves garlic, minced
  1 teaspoon seasoned salt
  ¼ teaspoon ground black pepper
  ¼ teaspoon ground white pepper
  ¼ teaspoon dried rosemary, crumbled
  ⅛ teaspoon dried thyme, crumbled
2½ cups water
  1 beef bouillon cube
  ½ cup white rice
1½ cups chopped fresh or canned tomatoes
  2 cups chopped bell or banana peppers
  6 to 8 ounces cooked or canned crab meat
  1 cup chopped green onions
  ½ cup chopped parsley

1. Cook chicken in butter in large Dutch oven over medium heat until golden brown, about 4 minutes per side; remove from pan. Add sausage and smoked pork to pan; cook until brown. Remove from pan; drain fat, reserving ¼ cup.

2. Mix reserved ¼ cup fat and the flour in Dutch oven. Cook and stir over very low heat until rich brown in color, about 20 minutes. *(Continued)*

3. Add celery, onion and garlic; cook and stir 3 minutes. Stir in salt, black and white peppers, rosemary and thyme. Add water and bouillon cube; heat to boiling. Stir in rice; reduce heat. Simmer, covered, 15 minutes.

4. Remove skin and bones from chicken; add chicken, sausage and smoked pork to rice mixture. Stir in tomatoes; simmer, covered, at least 15 minutes but no longer than 30 minutes.

5. Stir in remaining ingredients; heat just to boiling. Reduce heat; simmer until peppers are tender, about 10 minutes.

SCOTCH EGGS

Makes 6 servings

  1 pound bulk pork sausage
  6 hard-cooked eggs, shelled, patted dry
  1 large egg, beaten
  ⅔ cup fine dry breadcrumbs
    Vegetable oil for frying
    Prepared mustard, if desired

1. Divide sausage into 6 even portions; wrap 1 portion of the sausage around each hard-cooked egg to encase completely. Dip each in beaten egg, then roll in breadcrumbs to coat completely.

2. Heat 2 inches oil in large saucepan to 350°F. Fry 3 eggs at a time, turning occasionally, until golden brown, 3 to 4 minutes. Remove eggs with slotted spoon; drain on paper toweling.

3. Place eggs in shallow baking pan. Bake in preheated 400°F oven until sausage is cooked through, 10 to 15 minutes. Serve hot or room temperature with mustard.

BATTER-FRIED CHICKEN

Makes 4 servings

1 broiler-fryer chicken (about 3 pounds), cut up
1 cup water
1 stalk celery, cut into 2-inch lengths
1 small onion, cut in half
1 clove garlic, cut in half
½ teaspoon salt
⅛ teaspoon pepper
 Vegetable oil for frying
 Fluffy Egg Batter (recipe follows)

1. Combine chicken, water, celery, onion, garlic, salt and pepper in 5-quart Dutch oven; heat to boiling. Reduce heat; simmer, covered, until chicken is almost tender, 20 to 25 minutes.

2. Remove chicken from Dutch oven; drain and pat dry with paper toweling. Let cool slightly. Strain and reserve broth for other use.

(Continued)

3. Heat 3 inches of oil in clean Dutch oven to 350°F. Fry 2 or 3 pieces of chicken at a time as follows: Dip chicken into Fluffy Egg Batter to coat all sides; fry, turning occasionally, until golden, 5 to 7 minutes. Drain on paper toweling; keep warm on baking sheet lined with paper toweling in preheated 200°F oven until all chicken is cooked.

FLUFFY EGG BATTER

1 cup all-purpose flour
1 teaspoon baking powder
1 teaspoon salt
¼ teaspoon white pepper
¾ cup milk
2 large eggs
1 tablespoon vegetable oil

Mix flour, baking powder, salt and pepper in medium bowl. Add milk, eggs and oil; whisk until smooth.

Makes about 1½ cups

Batter-Fried Chicken

SAUSAGE CREOLE WITH OKRA

Makes 6 to 8 servings

1 pound hot breakfast pork sausage
⅔ cup all-purpose flour
½ cup chopped onion
¼ cup chopped green bell pepper
1 large clove garlic, minced
1½ cups tomato juice
1 cup water
1 beef bouillon cube
1 chicken bouillon cube
⅛ teaspoon hot red pepper sauce
1 pound bratwurst, cut into 1-inch slices
1 cup sliced okra
1 cup chopped tomatoes
Hot cooked rice

(Continued)

1. Crumble breakfast sausage into Dutch oven; cook over medium heat until brown, about 8 minutes. Remove sausage with slotted spoon to plate. Drain and discard all but ⅓ cup fat.

2. Stir flour into ⅓ cup fat until smooth; cook, stirring constantly, over low heat until roux is rich golden brown, about 15 minutes.

3. Add onion, pepper and garlic to roux; cook and stir until onion is tender, about 4 minutes. Add breakfast sausage, tomato juice, water, bouillon cubes and red pepper sauce. Heat, stirring frequently, to boiling; reduce heat. Simmer, covered, 20 minutes.

4. Stir in bratwurst, okra and tomatoes; simmer, stirring frequently, 15 minutes. Serve over rice.

Sausage Creole with Okra (top); Sausage & Broccoli Casserole (bottom)

SAUSAGE & BROCCOLI CASSEROLE

Makes 6 servings

1 package (20 ounces) frozen chopped broccoli, thawed
1 can (8 ounces) sliced mushrooms, drained
½ pound smoked sausage, thinly sliced
1 jar (16 ounces) pasteurized process cheese spread
⅓ cup evaporated milk
¾ teaspoon seasoned salt
¼ teaspoon garlic powder

1. Combine broccoli and mushrooms in 1½-quart baking dish; mix well. Top with sausage.

2. Heat cheese spread in medium saucepan over medium heat; gradually stir in milk until smooth. Remove from heat; stir in salt and garlic powder. Pour over broccoli mixture.

3. Bake, covered, in preheated 350°F oven 30 minutes. Uncover dish; continue baking until edges of sausage begin to brown, 5 to 10 minutes longer.

BEEF AND CORNBREAD BAKE

Golden cornbread in squares or as an ingredient holds a special place in Southern cookery. When it is not served drenched with butter or syrup as a hot bread, it's crumbled in stuffing for turkey or baked as the top crust on a tasty casserole.

Makes 4 to 6 servings

1 pound ground beef
1 small onion, chopped
1 can (15 ounces) tomato sauce
1 to 2 teaspoons chili powder
½ teaspoon ground cumin
¼ teaspoon garlic salt
1 cup whole kernel corn, drained
1 can (3½ ounces) pitted ripe olives, drained, sliced
1 package (8 ounces) cornbread muffin mix
½ cup shredded Cheddar cheese

1. Cook and stir beef in large skillet over medium heat 5 minutes. Add onion; cook and stir until beef is brown, about 5 minutes longer.

2. Stir in tomato sauce, chili powder, cumin and garlic salt; heat to boiling. Stir in corn and olives; remove from heat. Transfer to 3-quart baking dish.

3. Prepare cornbread mix according to package directions. Spoon over beef mixture in even layer. Bake in preheated 375°F oven until cornbread is cooked through, about 25 minutes.

4. Sprinkle top with cheese; bake until melted, about 2 minutes longer.

To microwave: Crumble beef into 3-quart microwave-safe bowl; add onion. Microwave, covered, on HIGH stirring once, 4 to 5 minutes; drain. Stir in remaining ingredients except cornbread mix and cheese. Microwave, covered, on HIGH until bubbly, 3 to 4 minutes. Prepare cornbread mix; spoon on top of beef mixture. Microwave, uncovered, on HIGH, 3 minutes. Rotate bowl ¼ turn. Microwave on MEDIUM (50% power) until cornbread is done, about 6 minutes. Sprinkle with cheese; let stand 5 minutes.

TARRAGON CHICKEN

Makes 4 servings

1 broiler-fryer chicken (about 3 pounds), cut up
1 teaspoon salt
¼ teaspoon pepper
2 tablespoons butter or margarine
1 tablespoon vegetable oil
⅓ cup chopped onion
2 tablespoons chopped fresh tarragon or 2 teaspoons dried tarragon, crumbled
1 tablespoon minced parsley
1 clove garlic, minced
½ cup dry white wine
3 tablespoons all-purpose flour
1 cup milk

1. Sprinkle chicken with salt and pepper; cook in butter and oil in large skillet over medium heat, turning once, until light brown, 10 to 12 minutes. Remove chicken to plate.

2. Saute onion in drippings until golden, about 6 minutes. Stir in tarragon, parsley and garlic; saute 30 seconds. Stir in wine.

3. Return chicken to skillet; spoon wine mixture over chicken. Heat to boiling; reduce heat. Simmer, covered, 20 minutes. Remove chicken to plate.

4. Mix flour with ¼ cup of the milk in small bowl until smooth; gradually whisk into liquid in skillet until smooth. Stir in remaining ¾ cup milk. Cook and stir until sauce thickens and bubbles for 1 minute.

5. Return chicken to skillet; simmer, covered, over low heat until chicken is tender, 8 to 10 minutes longer.

DELICIOUS SURPRISE CHICKEN

Makes 4 servings

1 broiler-fryer chicken (about 3 pounds), cut up
1 tablespoon vegetable oil
½ cup chopped onion
½ cup chopped green bell pepper
1 clove garlic, sliced
1 teaspoon salt
¼ teaspoon ground black pepper
½ cup unsweetened pineapple juice
2 tablespoons lemon juice
½ teaspoon Worcestershire sauce
½ teaspoon dry mustard
¼ teaspoon dried oregano, crumbled
Hot cooked noodles

1. Cook chicken in oil in large skillet over medium-high heat until brown on all sides, about 10 minutes. Reduce heat to medium; push chicken to side of skillet. Add onion, green bell pepper and garlic; saute 5 minutes.

2. Arrange chicken on top of vegetables; sprinkle with ½ teaspoon of the salt and ⅛ teaspoon of the ground pepper.

3. Mix pineapple juice, lemon juice, Worcestershire sauce, mustard, oregano and remaining ½ teaspoon salt and ⅛ teaspoon ground pepper in small bowl. Pour over chicken; cook, covered, over low heat 30 minutes.

4. Uncover skillet; cook until sauce is thick and chicken is fork-tender, about 10 minutes longer. Serve over noodles.

FLORIDIAN CHICKEN

Makes 4 servings

    8 chicken thighs, skinned, boned
 ½ teaspoon salt
 ⅛ teaspoon pepper
    1 tablespoon butter or margarine
    1 tablespoon vegetable oil
    3 large carrots, cut diagonally into thin slices
 1½ cups thinly sliced celery
    1 medium onion, thinly sliced
    1 cup chicken broth
 ½ cup grapefruit juice
 ¼ cup dry sherry
    1 teaspoon dried tarragon
    2 tablespoons water
 1½ teaspoons cornstarch
    1 grapefruit, peeled, sectioned
      Mint sprig for garnish

1. Sprinkle chicken with salt and pepper. Cook in butter and oil in large skillet over medium heat until golden, 4 to 5 minutes per side.

2. Add carrots, celery, onion, broth, grapefruit juice, sherry and tarragon; heat to boiling. Reduce heat; simmer, covered, until chicken is tender, 30 to 40 minutes.

3. Remove chicken and vegetables with slotted spoon to platter; keep warm.

4. Mix water and cornstarch in small bowl until smooth; stir into broth in skillet. Cook, stirring constantly, until sauce thickens and bubbles for 3 minutes. Add grapefruit; cook until grapefruit is hot.

5. Arrange grapefruit around edges of platter; spoon sauce all over. Garnish with mint.

PATCHWORK CASSEROLE

An easy meat and potato casserole popular to carry to a covered-dish supper. Squares or triangles of cheese arranged checkerboard fashion on top when the dish comes out of the oven melt on the way to the social hall.

Makes 8 to 10 servings

    2 pounds ground beef
    2 cups chopped green bell pepper
    1 cup chopped onion
    2 pounds frozen Southern-style hash-brown
      potatoes, thawed
    2 cans (8 ounces each) tomato sauce
    1 cup water
    1 can (6 ounces) tomato paste
    1 teaspoon salt
 ½ teaspoon dried basil, crumbled
 ¼ teaspoon ground black pepper
    1 pound pasteurized process American cheese,
      thinly sliced

1. Cook and stir beef in large skillet over medium heat until crumbled and brown, about 10 minutes; drain off fat.

2. Add green pepper and onion; saute until soft, about 4 minutes. Stir in remaining ingredients except cheese.

3. Spoon ½ of the meat mixture into 13 × 9 × 2-inch baking pan or 3-quart baking dish; top with ½ of the cheese. Spoon remaining meat mixture evenly on top of cheese.

4. Cover pan with aluminum foil. Bake in preheated 350°F oven 45 minutes.

5. Cut remaining cheese into decorative shapes; arrange in patchwork design on top of casserole. Let stand, loosely covered, until cheese melts, about 5 minutes.

Floridian Chicken

Christmas Beef Rib Roast

CHRISTMAS BEEF RIB ROAST

Wreathe the stately holiday roast with a medley of colorful vegetables dressed simply with lemon butter.

Makes 10 to 12 servings

1 standing beef rib roast (5 to 6 pounds), room temperature
Mixed buttered cooked vegetables, if desired

1. Place roast, fat side up, in shallow roasting pan; do not add water or cover pan. Insert meat thermometer into thickest part of meat, not touching bone.

2. Roast in preheated 325°F oven. For rare, roast until thermometer registers 130 to 135°F, 20 to 25 minutes per pound. For medium, roast to 150 to 155°F, 30 to 35 minutes per pound. For well done, roast to 160 to 165°F, 35 to 40 minutes per pound.

3. Let roast stand, loosely covered, in warm place 15 to 20 minutes before carving. Serve with vegetables.

INDIVIDUAL YORKSHIRE PUDDINGS

First cousins to popovers, these decidedly English "puddings" are savory rather than sweet. Made with pan drippings from a beef roast, they traditionally accompany the meat course.

Makes 12 servings

1 cup all-purpose flour
¾ teaspoon salt
2 large eggs
1 cup milk
¼ cup hot roast beef drippings

1. Heat muffin pan in preheated 400°F oven until hot. Sift flour and salt into small bowl.

2. Beat eggs and milk in medium bowl until blended. Gradually beat in flour mixture until smooth.

3. Place 1 teaspoon hot drippings in each of 12 preheated muffin cups; add batter, dividing evenly.

4. Bake at 400°F until golden, about 30 minutes. Serve immediately.

Dixie Pork Loin Roast

DIXIE PORK LOIN ROAST

Ground peanuts bring a special crunchiness to the robust molasses basting mixture that builds up layers of rich flavor as the meat roasts.

Makes 6 to 8 servings

12 ounces beer
½ cup molasses
⅓ cup ground dry-roasted peanuts
¼ cup lemon juice
2 tablespoons coarse-grain mustard
1 tablespoon sugar
½ teaspoon salt
½ teaspoon dried oregano, crumbled
¼ teaspoon ground cumin
⅛ teaspoon ground red pepper
1 pork loin roast (4 pounds), trimmed
Chopped peanuts and watercress for garnish

1. Combine all ingredients except pork and garnish in medium saucepan; heat to boiling. Reduce heat to medium; cook and stir until slightly thickened, about 15 minutes.

2. Insert meat thermometer into thickest part of pork not touching bone. Place pork on rack in aluminum-foil-lined roasting pan. Roast in preheated 400°F oven 30 minutes.

3. Reduce oven setting to 325°F. Continue roasting, basting every 15 minutes with beer mixture, until thermometer registers 170°F, about 1½ hours. Let stand 15 minutes before carving.

4. To serve, cut pork into individual chops; place on platter. Spoon remaining basting sauce over pork; garnish with chopped peanuts and watercress.

PORK TENDERLOIN WITH DILLED MUSHROOM SAUCE

Tenderloins are the leanest, most tender cut of pork. Steaks sliced from them and pounded flat deserve gentle cooking and an elegant mushroom and wine sauce.

Makes 4 to 5 servings

2 pork tenderloins (1¼ to 1½ pounds total)
3 cups sliced mushrooms
2 tablespoons butter or margarine
2 tablespoons vegetable oil
¼ teaspoon salt
⅛ teaspoon pepper
½ cup chablis wine
¼ cup sour cream
¼ teaspoon dill weed

1. Cut each tenderloin crosswise into 4 pieces. Place each piece cut side down on flat surface; pound with meat mallet to ½-inch thickness.

2. Saute mushrooms in butter in large skillet over medium heat until golden, 5 to 7 minutes; remove from skillet with slotted spoon.

3. Cook 4 tenderloin patties at a time in oil in same skillet over medium heat until brown, 3 to 4 minutes per side.

4. Return all browned patties to skillet; sprinkle with salt and pepper. Add wine; simmer, covered, 12 minutes. Remove patties to platter; keep warm.

5. Whisk sour cream and dill weed into juices in pan; stir in mushrooms. Cook over low heat until hot; do not boil. Serve sauce with pork patties.

CAJUN CHEESE SOUFFLE

Makes 4 to 6 servings

¼ cup butter
¼ cup all-purpose flour
1½ cups milk
¼ teaspoon salt
   Pinch ground red pepper
½ pound Cheddar cheese, shredded
4 large eggs, separated
¼ pound bacon, cut into 1-inch pieces
1 medium green bell pepper

1. Melt butter in medium saucepan over medium-low heat. Stir in flour; cook and stir until bubbly. Gradually whisk in milk until smooth; cook and stir until sauce thickens and bubbles for 1 minute. Stir in salt and red pepper; remove from heat.

2. Add cheese to hot sauce; stir until melted. Stir in egg yolks, 1 at a time; reserve, covered.

3. Cook bacon in large skillet over medium heat until crisp. Remove with slotted spoon; drain on paper toweling. Reserve drippings.

4. Chop ½ of the green bell pepper; slice remaining ½. Saute chopped green pepper in reserved drippings until soft, about 4 minutes. Remove with slotted spoon; drain on paper toweling. Stir chopped green pepper and ¾ of the bacon into reserved sauce.

5. Beat egg whites in large mixer bowl until stiff but not dry; fold into cheese sauce. Pour into 2-quart souffle dish or straight-sided baking dish.

6. Bake in preheated 375°F oven until top is puffed and brown, 30 to 45 minutes. Garnish with remaining bacon and sliced green pepper; serve immediately.

FRENCH PICNIC LOAF

Three meats and three herbs blended expertly in a long loaf to pack with French bread, fresh fruit and red wine for a special lunch in the park.

Makes 12 servings

1½ pounds ground beef
1 pound ground pork
1 pound cooked ham, diced (¼-inch)
3 cups soft breadcrumbs
3 large eggs
⅔ cup catsup
1 can (4 ounces) sliced mushrooms, drained
1 medium green bell pepper, finely chopped
1 envelope onion soup mix
1 teaspoon ground allspice
½ teaspoon ground thyme
½ teaspoon garlic powder
   Watercress for garnish
   French bread

1. Combine all ingredients except watercress and French bread in large bowl; mix well. Shape into loaf in rectangular baking pan.

2. Bake in preheated 325°F oven until meat thermometer inserted into center registers 170°F, about 1½ hours. Cool on wire rack; refrigerate until cold. Garnish with watercress; serve with French bread.

HAM & GRITS PUFF

Hominy grits are a popular Southern form of dried hulled corn, cooked and served with eggs for breakfast or baked with ham and cheese in a casserole for brunch or supper.

Makes 6 servings

4 cups water
1¼ cups quick-cooking grits
1 teaspoon salt
1½ cups shredded Swiss cheese
1 cup diced cooked ham
⅓ cup butter
⅛ teaspoon garlic powder
2 large eggs
⅓ cup milk

1. Heat water in large saucepan to boiling; gradually stir in grits and salt. Heat to boiling; reduce heat. Simmer, stirring constantly, 10 minutes; remove from heat.

2. Add cheese, ham, butter and garlic powder to saucepan; stir until cheese and butter are melted.

3. Whisk eggs and milk in small bowl until blended; quickly stir into hot grits mixture. Pour into well-buttered 1½-quart rectangular baking dish.

4. Bake in preheated 325°F oven until top is golden and center is set, about 1 hour. Let stand 10 minutes before serving.

French Picnic Loaf

OVEN-BARBECUED RIBS

Country-style ribs are the meaty ones cut from the back rather than the side and containing some of the pork loin muscle. Back ribs are next in line but without meat from the loin.

Makes 4 to 6 servings

  3 pounds country-style pork loin or back ribs
  2 tablespoons vegetable oil
  1 teaspoon salt
 ½ teaspoon pepper
  1 to 1½ cups prepared barbecue sauce

1. Cut ribs into serving-size pieces about 5 inches long. Brush with oil on all sides; sprinkle with salt and pepper.

2. Arrange ribs in single layer in large shallow roasting pan. Bake in preheated 350°F oven 1 hour; drain off drippings.

3. Brush ribs with barbecue sauce. Continue baking, basting with sauce every 15 minutes, until ribs are tender and richly glazed, 1 to 1¼ hours longer.

HAM AND CHEESE DINNER

Crisp sliced celery teamed with leftover ham in a hurry-up cheese sauce to spoon over noodles or cornbread.

Makes 4 servings

 1½ cups sliced celery
  2 tablespoons butter or margarine
  1 can (11 ounces) condensed Cheddar cheese
    soup
  1 cup diced cooked ham
  1 can (4 ounces) sliced mushrooms, drained
 ½ cup milk
  1 teaspoon prepared mustard
  8 ounces egg noodles, cooked, drained
    Celery leaves for garnish

1. Saute celery in butter in medium saucepan over medium heat until crisp-tender, about 7 minutes.

2. Stir in soup, ham, mushrooms, milk and mustard. Cook and stir until hot, about 5 minutes. Serve over noodles; garnish with celery leaves.

Oven-Barbecued Ribs

Brunswick Stew

BRUNSWICK STEW

Makes 6 to 8 servings

1 stewing chicken (about 4½ pounds), cut up
2 quarts water
1 stalk celery with leaves, cut into 2-inch lengths
1 small onion, cut into quarters
1 small clove garlic, cut in half
2 teaspoons salt
1 teaspoon whole peppercorns
1 can (16 ounces) tomatoes, cut into 1-inch pieces, undrained
2 medium potatoes, pared, diced
1 onion, thinly sliced
¼ cup tomato paste
1 teaspoon sugar
½ teaspoon ground pepper
½ teaspoon dried thyme, crumbled
⅛ teaspoon garlic powder
   Dash hot red pepper sauce
1 package (10 ounces) frozen lima beans
1 package (10 ounces) frozen whole kernel corn

1. Combine chicken, giblets and neck in Dutch oven; add water. Heat to boiling; reduce heat and skim off foam. Add celery, quartered onion, garlic, salt and peppercorns; simmer, covered, until thighs are tender, 2½ to 3 hours.

2. Remove chicken pieces from broth; cool slightly. Remove meat from chicken, discarding bones and skin. Cut enough chicken into 1-inch pieces to measure 3 cups; reserve remaining chicken for other use.

3. Strain broth, discarding solids; skim off fat. Return 1 quart of the broth to Dutch oven. Reserve remaining broth for other use. *(Continued)*

4. Add tomatoes, potatoes, sliced onion, tomato paste, sugar, ground pepper, thyme, garlic powder and red pepper sauce to Dutch oven. Heat to boiling; reduce heat. Simmer, covered, 30 minutes.

5. Add beans and corn to stew; heat to boiling. Reduce heat; simmer, covered, 5 minutes. Add chicken pieces; cook 5 minutes longer.

CHICKEN MEDITERRANEAN

Makes 4 servings

½ cup water
¼ cup lemon juice
1 tablespoon grated lemon rind
1 teaspoon dried oregano, crumbled
1 teaspoon garlic salt
½ teaspoon pepper
1 broiler-fryer chicken (3 pounds), cut into quarters
   Lemon slices and ¼ cup chopped parsley for garnish

1. Combine water, lemon juice, lemon rind, oregano, garlic salt and pepper in small bowl; mix well. Pour over chicken in large bowl. Refrigerate, covered, turning chicken frequently, 3 to 4 hours.

2. Drain chicken, reserving marinade. Arrange chicken in single layer in shallow baking dish.

3. Bake chicken, uncovered, in preheated 425°F oven 25 minutes. Reduce oven setting to 350°F; brush chicken with reserved marinade. Continue baking, basting occasionally, until chicken is tender and golden brown, 25 to 35 minutes longer. Garnish with lemon slices and parsley.

Picnic Fried Chicken

CITRUS-GLAZED HAM

Makes 12 to 16 servings

1 fully-cooked ham with bone (12 to 15 pounds)
1 cup dark corn syrup
2 tablespoons orange or lemon juice
1 tablespoon grated orange or lemon rind
  Toasted pecan halves
  Whole cloves

1. Place ham, fat side up, on rack in large roasting pan. Bake in preheated 325°F oven 1 hour and 15 minutes.

2. Mix corn syrup, orange juice and orange rind in small bowl.

3. Remove ham from oven; score fat with sharp knife ⅛ inch deep in diamond pattern. Brush ham with ½ of the syrup mixture.

4. Continue baking ham, basting frequently, until well glazed and heated through, about 45 minutes longer.

5. Place 1 pecan half in center of ½ of the diamonds; insert 1 clove in remaining diamonds. Baste ham once more; bake 10 minutes longer.

PICNIC FRIED CHICKEN

Makes 4 servings

1 tablespoon seasoned salt
1½ teaspoons lemon pepper
½ teaspoon dried thyme, crumbled
¾ cup all-purpose flour
1 broiler-fryer chicken (about 3 pounds), cut up
¼ cup butter or margarine
¼ cup peanut oil

1. Mix salt, pepper and thyme in shallow dish. Place flour in second shallow dish.

2. Pat chicken very dry. Dip in salt mixture; shake off excess. Dip in flour to coat; shake off excess.

3. Heat butter and oil in large skillet over medium heat until hot. Add chicken; fry, turning occasionally, until brown on all sides and fork-tender, 20 to 30 minutes.

4. Serve hot, or refrigerate immediately until cold to carry on picnic.

Note: *Recipe can be doubled, if desired; use 2 large skillets.*

YAM-HAM SOUFFLE

Makes 6 servings

6 tablespoons butter or margarine
5 tablespoons all-purpose flour
1 teaspoon salt
1 teaspoon dry mustard
1 teaspoon ground ginger
2 cups milk
6 large eggs, separated
2 cups ground cooked ham (about ¾ pound)
1½ cups cooked mashed Louisiana yams (about 3 medium sweet potatoes)

1. Melt butter in medium saucepan over medium heat; stir in flour, salt, mustard and ginger until smooth. Cook and stir until bubbly. Gradually whisk in milk; cook and stir until sauce thickens and bubbles for 1 minute. Remove from heat.

2. Gradually whisk 1 cup of the hot sauce into egg yolks in small bowl; gradually whisk egg yolk mixture into remaining sauce in pan. Cook, stirring constantly, over low heat 2 minutes; do not boil. Remove from heat; stir in ham and yams.

3. Beat egg whites in large mixer bowl until stiff but not dry; fold into yam mixture. Pour into 2-quart buttered souffle dish or baking dish.

4. Bake in preheated 375°F oven until knife inserted near center is withdrawn clean, 50 to 60 minutes. Serve immediately.

SHERRIED PORK ROAST

Makes 8 servings

⅔ cup pitted prunes
¾ cup dry sherry
1 boneless pork loin roast (about 3 pounds)
2 ounces crystallized ginger
¼ cup honey
¼ cup grated onion
2½ tablespoons soy sauce
Salt and pepper to taste
Parsley sprigs for garnish

1. Combine prunes and sherry in small bowl; let stand, stirring occasionally, 1 to 2 hours or overnight. Drain prunes, reserving sherry.

2. Cut 2½-inch-deep slit lengthwise in boned side of roast. Arrange prunes in row in center of roast; tie roast securely with kitchen string to enclose prunes.

3. Chop 1 ounce of the ginger; combine with reserved sherry, the honey, onion, soy sauce, salt and pepper in small bowl. Mix well; pour over pork in shallow bowl. Marinate, turning occasionally, 2 to 4 hours.

4. Drain pork, reserving marinade. Roast pork in preheated 350°F oven, basting frequently with reserved marinade, until meat thermometer inserted into thickest part of meat registers 160°F, 1½ to 2 hours. (Cover roast with foil as needed to prevent burning.)

5. Slice remaining 1 ounce ginger. Garnish roast with sliced ginger and parsley.

Yam-Ham Souffle

ZUCCHINI LASAGNE

Thinly sliced zucchini stands in for the wide flat noodles in this satisfying Italian-style baked dish.

Makes 8 servings

2½ pounds zucchini
1¼ cups grated Parmesan cheese
  1 package (8 ounces) cream cheese, room
      temperature
  1 cup cottage cheese, sieved
  1 cup sour cream
  3 large eggs, beaten
  2 tablespoons chopped parsley
  1 clove garlic, minced, if desired
1½ pounds ground beef
  ½ cup chopped onion
  ¼ cup chopped green bell pepper
  2 teaspoons dried basil, crumbled
  ½ teaspoon dried oregano, crumbled
  ½ teaspoon dried rosemary, crumbled
  ½ teaspoon salt
  1 can (15 ounces) Italian-style marinara sauce
  1 can (8 ounces) tomato sauce
  4 to 6 slices Monterey Jack cheese
    Paprika

1. Cut zucchini lengthwise into thin slices.

2. Mix 1 cup of the Parmesan cheese, the cream cheese, cottage cheese, sour cream, eggs, parsley and garlic in medium bowl.

3. Cook and stir beef in large skillet over medium heat 5 minutes. Add onion and green pepper; continue cooking until beef is brown and onion is soft, about 5 minutes longer. Drain off fat.

4. Add basil, oregano, rosemary and salt to skillet; mix well. Stir in marinara sauce and tomato sauce. Simmer over low heat, stirring occasionally, 30 minutes.

5. Spread ⅓ of the meat sauce in bottom of buttered 12 × 9-inch baking dish; top with ½ of the zucchini, then with ½ of the cheese mixture. Repeat layers once; spread remaining

(Continued)

⅓ meat sauce on top. Top with Jack cheese; sprinkle with remaining ¼ cup Parmesan cheese.

6. Bake, covered, in preheated 350°F oven 30 minutes. Uncover dish; sprinkle with paprika. Bake 30 minutes longer; let stand 10 minutes before serving.

CORNBREAD-RICE STUFFING

A sensational stuffing packed with the delightful color and texture contrasts of yellow cornbread with white rice and soft, dark raisins with crunchy pine nuts.

Makes about 8 cups; 10 to 12 servings

  1 large onion, chopped
  ½ cup olive oil
  ¾ pound ground pork
2¼ cups water
  ⅔ cup long-grain rice
  4 cups cornbread stuffing mix
  ½ cup pine nuts
  ⅓ cup raisins
  ⅓ cup chopped parsley
  2 teaspoons dried thyme, crumbled
  ½ teaspoon salt
  ⅛ teaspoon pepper

1. Saute onion in oil in large skillet over medium heat until soft, about 4 minutes. Add pork; cook and stir until crumbled and light brown, about 8 minutes.

2. Add 1¼ cups of the water and the rice to skillet; cook, covered, over medium-low heat until water is absorbed, about 10 minutes. Remove from heat.

3. Toss stuffing mix with remaining 1 cup water in large bowl; let stand 5 minutes. Add pork-rice mixture and remaining ingredients; toss to mix well.*

4. To serve as side dish, transfer mixture to greased 2½-quart baking dish. Bake in preheated 325°F oven, covered, 30 minutes. Uncover dish; continue baking until top is golden, about 15 minutes longer.

***Note:** Recipe can be used to stuff turkey or chicken.*

Cornbread-Rice Stuffing

Fresh Tomato Pie Floridian

FRESH TOMATO PIE FLORIDIAN

Cartwheel slices of juicy red tomatoes nestle in a rich cheese custard baked in a flaky pastry crust.

Makes 6 to 8 servings

Pastry dough for single-crust 9-inch pie
1 cup chopped onion
1 cup diced green bell pepper
1 clove garlic, minced
3 tablespoons butter or margarine
4 large eggs
1 cup milk
1½ cups shredded Cheddar cheese
1 teaspoon salt
¼ teaspoon ground black pepper
2 ripe medium tomatoes, sliced, drained
Parsley sprigs for garnish

(Continued)

1. Roll out dough on lightly floured surface into 12-inch circle; fit into 9-inch pie pan. Fold edges under and pinch to seal; flute edge. Pierce bottom and sides with fork.

2. Line pie shell with parchment; fill with pie weights or dry beans. Bake in preheated 425°F oven until pastry is set, 8 to 10 minutes. Remove paper and weights; continue baking until golden, about 8 minutes longer. Cool on wire rack. Reduce oven setting to 325°F.

3. Saute onion, green bell pepper and garlic in butter in large skillet over medium heat 5 minutes.

4. Lightly beat eggs in large bowl; stir in milk. Add cheese, salt, ground pepper and onion mixture; mix well.

5. Arrange all but 4 of the tomato slices in bottom of pie shell; pour egg mixture over tomatoes. Top with remaining tomato slices.

6. Bake at 325°F until knife inserted in center of custard is withdrawn clean, about 50 minutes. Cool on wire rack 10 to 15 minutes before cutting; garnish with parsley.

Vegetable & Pork Skillet

VEGETABLE & PORK SKILLET

Makes 4 servings

  1 bunch fresh broccoli (about 1¼ pounds)
  1 pound lean boneless pork
  2 carrots, pared
  1 medium onion
 ¾ cup water
 ¼ cup soy sauce
  2 tablespoons dry sherry
  1 tablespoon cornstarch
  2 teaspoons sugar
 ⅛ teaspoon ground ginger
 ⅛ teaspoon salt
  2 tablespoons vegetable oil
  1 clove garlic, minced

1. Cut broccoli stems crosswise into ⅛-inch-thick slices. Cut broccoli flowerets into 1-inch pieces. Cut pork into 3 × ¼ × ¼-inch strips. Cut carrots crosswise into halves; cut lengthwise into ¼ × ¼-inch-thick strips. Cut onion lengthwise into ¼-inch-thick slivers.

2. Mix water, soy sauce, sherry, cornstarch, sugar, ginger and salt in small bowl.

3. Heat oil in wok or large skillet over high heat until hot. Add garlic; cook and stir 5 seconds. Add pork and broccoli stem pieces; cook, stirring and tossing constantly, until pork is no longer pink, about 3 minutes.

4. Stir in broccoli flowerets, carrot and onion; reduce heat to medium. Cook, covered, stirring occasionally, just until vegetables are crisp-tender, about 5 minutes.

(Continued)

5. Stir soy sauce mixture; add to pan. Heat, stirring constantly, to boiling; reduce heat. Simmer and stir until sauce is thickened, about 2 minutes.

Note: *Beef or chicken can be substituted for pork. Cauliflower, green beans, zucchini, yellow squash or cabbage can be substituted for broccoli.*

PEANUT STUFFING

Makes about 3½ cups; 6 servings

 ¼ cup finely chopped onion
 ¼ cup chopped celery
 ¼ cup butter or margarine
  1 teaspoon salt
 ½ teaspoon dried thyme, crumbled
 ¼ teaspoon poultry seasoning
    Pinch ground red pepper, if desired
  3 cups day-old breadcrumbs
 ½ cup turkey or chicken stock
 ¾ cup chopped roasted peanuts

1. Saute onion and celery in butter in small skillet over medium heat until soft, about 4 minutes. Stir in salt, thyme, poultry seasoning and red pepper.

2. Combine onion mixture and remaining ingredients in medium bowl; toss to mix well.*

3. To serve as a side dish, transfer mixture to greased 1-quart baking dish. Bake, uncovered, in preheated 325°F oven until top is light brown, 25 to 30 minutes.

Note: *Dressing can be used to stuff pork chops or poultry.*

SPINACH CUSTARD BAKE

Makes 6 servings

1 pound spinach, rinsed, stemmed
1 cup plain yogurt or sour cream or 1 package
   (8 ounces) cream cheese, diced
3 large eggs
1 small onion, chopped
½ teaspoon salt
½ teaspoon dried basil
   Pinch pepper
1 cherry tomato, sliced, for garnish

1. Cook spinach with water that clings to leaves in large saucepan, covered, over medium heat just until limp, about 3 minutes.

2. Combine spinach with remaining ingredients except tomato in food processor or blender container; process until smooth. Pour into buttered 1-quart baking dish or souffle dish.

3. Bake in preheated 325°F oven until knife inserted near center is withdrawn clean, about 35 minutes. Garnish with tomato.

TANGY POULTRY STUFFING

Makes about 6 cups; 10 to 12 servings

¾ cup chopped onion
¾ cup chopped celery
6 tablespoons corn oil
3¾ cups toasted bread cubes
9 tablespoons grapefruit juice
¼ cup chopped parsley
2 to 3 teaspoons ground sage
½ teaspoon pepper
½ teaspoon salt

1. Saute onion and celery in oil in medium skillet over medium heat until soft, about 5 minutes.

2. Combine bread cubes, onion mixture and remaining ingredients in large bowl; toss to mix.*

3. To serve as side dish, transfer mixture to a greased 2½-quart baking dish. Bake, covered, in preheated 325°F oven 30 to 40 minutes.

Note: Recipe can be used to stuff turkey or chicken.

Spinach Custard Bake

HOT SEAFOOD SALAD

Makes 6 servings

1 pound shelled deveined cooked shrimp
2 tablespoons butter, melted
½ cup cornflake crumbs
1 cup sour cream
2 ounces blue cheese, finely crumbled
1½ tablespoons lemon juice
1 teaspoon salt
½ teaspoon grated lemon rind
8 ounces brick cheese, coarsely shredded
3 stalks celery, chopped
¼ cup chopped green bell pepper
¼ cup toasted slivered almonds
2 tablespoons chopped onion
Lemon wedges and parsley sprigs for garnish

1. Reserve 6 whole shrimp for garnish; coarsely chop remaining shrimp. Drizzle butter over cornflake crumbs in small bowl; toss to mix well.

2. Combine sour cream, blue cheese, lemon juice, salt and lemon rind in large bowl; mix well. Add chopped shrimp, brick cheese, celery, green bell pepper, almonds and onion; mix well.

3. Spoon mixture into 6 individual shallow baking dishes, dividing evenly; sprinkle with cornflake crumb mixture. Bake in preheated 300°F oven just until heated through, 10 to 15 minutes. Garnish with reserved shrimp, lemon wedges and parsley.

FRESH ASPARAGUS MIMOSA

Vegetables or salads garnished with chopped hard-cooked egg or egg yolks are entitled to be called "mimosa."

Makes 8 servings

4 pounds asparagus
¼ cup butter or margarine, melted
1 tablespoon fresh lemon juice
3 hard-cooked eggs, sieved, room temperature

1. Snap off and discard bottom of each asparagus stalk. Cook, covered, in small amount of boiling water in large skillet just until crisp-tender, 5 to 10 minutes; drain.

2. Mix butter and lemon juice in small bowl. Pour over asparagus; transfer to serving dish. Sprinkle with eggs.

Fresh Asparagus Mimosa

NEW ORLEANS BLACKEYE SALAD

Bean salad with a Southern difference. Blackeyes, red-edged radishes, green onions tossed with almost-white artichoke hearts and celery crescents in a sharp dressing make for a delightful taste treat.

Makes 8 servings

1 pound dried blackeye beans
6 cups cold water
2 tablespoons solid vegetable shortening
3 chicken bouillon cubes
1 teaspoon onion salt
¼ teaspoon garlic salt
¼ teaspoon white pepper
6 cups hot water
2 jars (4 ounces each) marinated artichoke hearts
1 cup thinly sliced celery
½ cup sliced radishes
½ cup sliced green onions
4 to 8 drops hot red pepper sauce
Bottled French or Italian dressing
Chopped parsley and pimiento strips for garnish

1. Soak beans in 6 cups cold water in large bowl at room temperature overnight. Drain beans; rinse well.

2. Combine beans, shortening, bouillon cubes, onion salt, garlic salt, pepper and 6 cups hot water in large kettle. Heat to boiling; reduce heat. Simmer, partially covered, until beans are tender, about 1 hour. Add water if needed to keep beans immersed.

3. Drain beans; refrigerate, covered, until cold.

4. Pour marinade from artichoke hearts over beans. Dice hearts; add to beans. Add celery, radishes, green onions and red pepper sauce. Add just enough salad dressing to coat; toss to mix.

5. Refrigerate, covered, 1 to 4 hours before serving. Garnish with parsley and pimiento strips.

ORANGE-CARROT PUFF

Here's a light-as-a-cloud souffle, sunny orange in color and flavor. It's perfect for lunch with a green salad or spectacular as a dinner vegetable.

Makes 8 servings

2 pounds carrots, pared, cut into 1-inch lengths
1 cup orange juice
3 large eggs, separated
¼ cup all-purpose flour
¼ cup butter or margarine, melted
2 tablespoons honey
¾ teaspoon grated orange rind
¾ teaspoon ground cinnamon
¾ teaspoon ground cardamom
½ teaspoon salt

1. Cook carrots in small amount of boiling water in large saucepan, covered, until tender, 15 to 20 minutes; drain well.

2. Combine ⅓ of the carrots and ⅓ of the orange juice in blender container; process until smooth. Repeat 2 more times with remaining carrots and orange juice.

3. Lightly whisk egg yolks in large bowl; whisk in carrot puree and remaining ingredients except egg whites.

(Continued)

Sweet Potato Fritters (top); Hot Pickled Okra (bottom)

4. Beat egg whites in small mixer bowl until stiff but not dry; fold into carrot mixture. Pour into buttered 2½-quart baking dish.

5. Bake in preheated 350°F oven until top is puffed and set, about 45 minutes. Serve immediately.

HOT PICKLED OKRA

Enjoy these intriguing hot and vinegary okra pods alongside roast pork, chops or a cold meat platter.

Makes 8 servings

1½ cups cider vinegar
½ cup water
⅓ cup sugar
2 teaspoons hot red pepper sauce
1 teaspoon dry mustard
1 teaspoon salt
1 pound whole okra, cooked, or 2 packages (10 ounces each) frozen whole okra, thawed

1. Combine vinegar, water, sugar, red pepper sauce, mustard and salt in medium noncorrosive saucepan; heat to boiling. Stir in okra; simmer 5 minutes.

2. Transfer mixture to heat-proof glass bowl. Refrigerate, covered, at least 3 hours or up to 1 week.

SWEET POTATO FRITTERS

Makes 6 to 8 servings

Vegetable oil for frying
6 medium sweet potatoes, pared
1½ cups self-rising flour
½ cup yellow cornmeal
1½ cups water
3 tablespoons minced green onion
½ teaspoon salt
½ teaspoon ground mace
⅛ teaspoon ground red pepper
Hot red chilies and whole green onions, if desired

1. Heat 1 inch oil in large deep skillet to 350°F. Cut potatoes diagonally into ¼-inch-thick slices.

2. Mix flour, cornmeal, water, minced green onion, salt, mace and ground red pepper in medium bowl until smooth.

3. Fry as many potato slices at a time as will fit in skillet without crowding as follows: Dip slices into batter to coat, letting excess drain off. Fry, turning once, until golden brown, about 3 minutes per side. Drain on paper toweling; serve immediately with chilies and whole green onions.

Broccoli Spoon Bread

BROCCOLI SPOON BREAD

A bread in name only, this traditional cornmeal favorite that's too soft to slice is a lovely vegetable side dish and a Southern alternative for rice or potatoes.

Makes 4 to 6 servings

1½ cups broccoli flowerets (about 1-inch pieces)
¾ cup yellow cornmeal
2 tablespoons all-purpose flour
1 teaspoon salt
2 cups water
4 tablespoons butter or margarine
1 cup sliced celery
¼ cup chopped onion
4 large eggs, separated
1 cup milk
1 cup shredded Cheddar cheese
¼ teaspoon hot red pepper sauce
    Lemon slice twist for garnish   *(Continued)*

1. Cook broccoli in 1 inch boiling water in medium saucepan, covered, just until crisp-tender, 6 to 8 minutes; drain well.

2. Mix cornmeal, flour and salt in medium saucepan; gradually stir in water until smooth. Heat to boiling; cook and stir until thickened. Transfer to large bowl; stir in 2 tablespoons of the butter.

3. Saute celery and onion in remaining 2 tablespoons butter in medium skillet over medium heat until soft, about 4 minutes. Add to cornmeal mixture; mix well.

4. Add egg yolks to cornmeal mixture; mix well. Stir in milk, cheese and red pepper sauce. Reserve 2 broccoli flowerets for garnish if desired; stir remaining broccoli into cornmeal mixture.

5. Beat egg whites in large mixer bowl until stiff but not dry; fold into cornmeal mixture. Spoon into 2-quart baking dish.

6. Bake in preheated 375°F oven until top is crusty and light brown, 55 to 60 minutes. Garnish with reserved broccoli flowerets and lemon slice; serve immediately.

PEACHES & CREAM GELATIN SALAD

Makes 8 to 10 servings

First Layer
   1 package (3 ounces) orange or peach flavor
      gelatin
   1 cup boiling water
   ¾ cup cold water
   3 cups sliced pared fresh peaches
   1 small banana, sliced
   ½ medium apple, pared, shredded

Second Layer
   1 envelope unflavored gelatin
   3 tablespoons cold water
   ½ cup half-and-half
   1 package (8 ounces) cream cheese, room
      temperature
   ⅔ cup sugar
   1 cup whipping cream
   1 cup fresh peach puree

1. For first layer, mix gelatin and boiling water in large bowl until gelatin is dissolved. Stir in cold water; refrigerate, stirring occasionally, until partially set, about 30 minutes.

2. Fold in peaches, banana and apple; pour into 6-cup mold. Refrigerate until surface is sticky-firm, about 1 hour.

3. Meanwhile, make second layer. Sprinkle gelatin over cold water in small saucepan; let stand 1 minute to soften. Stir in half-and-half; cook and stir over medium-low heat until gelatin is dissolved.

4. Beat cream cheese and sugar in large mixer bowl until smooth. Gradually beat in whipping cream, then gelatin mixture. Stir in peach puree.

5. Pour cream cheese mixture over sticky-firm layer in mold. Refrigerate until completely set, several hours. Unmold before serving.

CALICO SALAD MOLD

Potatoes vinaigrette with sweet pickle relish and shreds of green and orange vegetables set a tasty pattern against a lime gelatin background.

Makes 10 to 12 servings

   1 cup water
   ¼ cup cider vinegar
   1 teaspoon salt
   1 pound frozen Southern-style hash-brown
      potatoes
   2 cups boiling water
   2 packages (3 ounces each) lime or lemon flavor
      gelatin
   2 cups cold water
   2 cups finely shredded cabbage
   1 cup finely shredded carrot
   1 cup finely chopped celery
   ¼ cup sweet pickle relish, drained
      Lettuce leaves
      Carrot curls for garnish
      Mayonnaise

1. Mix 1 cup water, the vinegar and salt in large skillet; add potatoes. Heat to boiling; reduce heat. Simmer, covered, until potatoes are tender and liquid is absorbed, 5 to 10 minutes. Let cool completely.

2. Pour boiling water over gelatin in large bowl; stir until gelatin is dissolved. Stir in cold water; refrigerate, stirring occasionally, until slightly thickened but not set.

3. Stir potatoes, cabbage, carrot, celery and relish into gelatin. Spoon into 8-cup mold; refrigerate until set, several hours.

4. To serve, unmold onto plate lined with lettuce leaves; garnish with carrot curls. Serve with mayonnaise.

Peaches & Cream Gelatin Salad

PEACHY GREEN BEANS

A green and gold skillet saute featuring luscious fresh sliced peaches in a vegetable accompaniment for baked ham or chicken.

Makes 6 to 8 servings

3 pounds fresh green beans, cut into 1-inch
    pieces*
1 teaspoon salt
4 cups boiling water
½ cup slivered almonds
¼ cup butter
3 medium peaches, pared, pitted, sliced
1 tablespoon lemon juice

1. Add green beans and salt to boiling water in large saucepan. Cook until crisp-tender, about 8 minutes; drain.

2. Saute almonds in butter in large skillet over medium heat 1 minute. Add peaches; saute 1 minute. Sprinkle with lemon juice.

3. Add beans; toss gently. Cook just until heated through.

Note: *Three cans (16 ounces each) cut green beans can be substituted; omit salt and boiling water. Heat beans just to boiling in Step 1; drain. Proceed with recipe.*

POTATO & ONION KABOBS

Makes 4 servings

2 large potatoes, unpared (1½ pounds)
1 large sweet onion
3 tablespoons butter, melted
1 teaspoon paprika
½ teaspoon celery salt
¼ teaspoon garlic powder
⅛ teaspoon pepper

1. Cook potatoes in boiling water in medium saucepan, 20 minutes; drain and cool slightly.

2. Cut each potato crosswise into four 1-inch-thick slices. Cut onion crosswise into four 1-inch-thick slices. Thread 2 potato slices alternating with 1 onion slice onto each of four 8-inch skewers, piercing vegetables through skin sides.

3. Mix remaining ingredients in small bowl. Brush both sides of vegetables with seasoned butter.

4. Grill kabobs over medium coals 20 minutes, brushing occasionally with seasoned butter and turning kabobs over after 10 minutes.

Peachy Green Beans

Broccoli with Cheese

BROCCOLI WITH CHEESE

Makes 4 servings

- 1 pound fresh broccoli
- ½ cup cottage cheese
- 1 large egg, beaten
- 2 tablespoons instant minced onion
- 2 tablespoons shredded Swiss cheese
- ½ teaspoon salt
- ⅛ teaspoon white pepper
- 2 drops hot red pepper sauce
- 3 tablespoons breadcrumbs
- 1 tablespoon butter or margarine, melted
  Paprika

1. Cut broccoli stalks lengthwise into halves; cook in large saucepan of boiling water until crisp-tender, about 8 minutes. Drain well; arrange in greased 1-quart baking dish.

2. Combine cottage cheese, egg, onion, Swiss cheese, salt, pepper and red pepper sauce in small bowl; mix well. Spoon over broccoli.

3. Mix breadcrumbs and butter in small bowl; sprinkle over cheese mixture. Cover baking dish tightly with aluminum foil.

4. Bake in preheated 325°F oven until cheese topping is set, about 20 minutes. Remove foil; sprinkle top of casserole with paprika.

EGGPLANT & RICE FRITTERS

Steam or bake unpeeled eggplant halves as you would winter squash (but remember eggplant becomes fork-tender in 10 to 15 minutes); it is easier to scoop the cooked vegetable out of the shell than to peel it first.

Makes 1 dozen fritters

- 2 cups mashed cooked eggplant (about 1 pound uncooked)
- 1½ cups cooked rice
- 1 cup shredded sharp Cheddar cheese
- 2 large eggs, lightly beaten
- ¼ cup all-purpose flour
- 2 teaspoons grated onion
- 1½ teaspoons salt
- ½ teaspoon pepper
- 1 drop hot red pepper sauce
- 2 to 6 tablespoons vegetable oil

1. Combine all ingredients except oil in large bowl; mix well.

2. Heat 2 tablespoons of the oil in large skillet over medium heat. Drop eggplant mixture by tablespoonfuls into skillet. Cook, turning once, until golden brown and cooked through, about 3 minutes per side. Remove to plate; keep warm. Repeat until all batter is cooked, adding oil to pan as needed.

Orange-Spiked Zucchini and Carrots

RED BEANS AND RICE

Makes 6 to 8 servings

1 cup chopped onion
1 cup chopped green bell pepper
1 clove garlic, minced
2 tablespoons bacon drippings or vegetable oil
1 can (15 ounces) red kidney beans or pinto beans seasoned with jalapeno pepper, undrained
1 can (8 ounces) tomato sauce
1 teaspoon salt
3 to 4 cups hot cooked rice

1. Saute onion, green bell pepper and garlic in drippings in large saucepan until crisp-tender, about 3 minutes.

2. Stir in beans, tomato sauce and salt; heat to boiling. Reduce heat; simmer, uncovered, 10 minutes. Serve over rice.

ORANGE-SPIKED ZUCCHINI AND CARROTS

Makes 6 to 8 servings

1 pound zucchini, cut into ¼-inch slices
1 package (10 ounces) frozen sliced carrots, thawed
1 cup unsweetened orange juice
1 stalk celery, finely chopped
2 tablespoons chopped onion
Salt and pepper to taste

1. Combine all ingredients in large saucepan; heat to boiling. Reduce heat; simmer, covered, stirring occasionally, until zucchini is firm-tender, about 6 minutes.

2. Uncover pan; simmer vegetables until most of the liquid is evaporated.

THREE-FRUIT CONSERVE

Makes about 4 cups

1 cup drained crushed canned pineapple
1 cup diced drained canned pears
½ cup chopped dates
2 tablespoons lemon juice
3½ cups sugar
1 cup chopped pecans
½ cup water
½ cup liquid pectin

1. Combine pineapple, pears, dates and lemon juice in large saucepan; heat to boiling. Add sugar, pecans and water; stir to mix. Simmer, uncovered, until pineapple and pears are translucent, about 10 minutes.

2. Remove from heat; stir in liquid pectin. Immediately pour into sterilized ½-pint canning jars, leaving ¼ inch head space; adjust caps.

3. Process jars 15 minutes in boiling water bath canner. Cool jars completely on wire rack.

SAVORY CORN

Frozen orange juice concentrate adds a mellow touch to hot or smoky barbecue sauce for yellow kernels of corn.

Makes 4 servings

1 package (10 ounces) frozen corn
¼ cup chopped onion
¼ cup bottled barbecue sauce
2 tablespoons frozen orange juice concentrate, thawed
⅛ teaspoon garlic powder
Salt to taste

1. Cook corn and onion in boiling water in medium saucepan until tender, about 10 minutes; drain well. Return to saucepan.

2. Stir in remaining ingredients; cook just until hot.

CHICKEN CITRUS PLATTER

Like colors on an artist's palette, strips of white breast of chicken share the plate with deep red beets, orange and grapefruit sections, pea pods, avocado slices and shredded red cabbage.

Makes 4 to 6 servings

1½ pounds skinned boned chicken breasts
1 onion, cut into quarters
1 carrot, cut into 2-inch lengths
1 stalk celery, cut into 2-inch lengths
½ teaspoon salt
4 peppercorns
1 bay leaf
3 cups shredded red cabbage
½ pound pea pods, blanched, drained
2 grapefruit, peeled, sectioned
3 oranges, peeled, sectioned
1 avocado, pared, pitted, sliced
1 cup sliced cooked beets
Lettuce leaves
Citrus Dressing (recipe follows)

(Continued)

1. Combine chicken, onion, carrot, celery, salt, peppercorns and bay leaf in large saucepan; add water to barely cover. Heat over medium heat to simmering; reduce heat. Simmer, covered, until chicken is cooked through, 12 to 15 minutes.

2. Drain chicken; let cool. Tear into shreds.

3. Arrange chicken, cabbage, pea pods, grapefruit, oranges, avocado and beets on platter lined with lettuce. Serve with Citrus Dressing.

CITRUS DRESSING

½ cup orange juice
1 large egg yolk
1 tablespoon white wine vinegar
2 teaspoons Dijon-style mustard
1 teaspoon fennel seeds, crushed
¼ teaspoon salt
⅛ teaspoon pepper
½ cup vegetable oil

Whisk orange juice, egg yolk, vinegar, mustard, fennel seeds, salt and pepper in medium bowl until blended. Gradually whisk in oil until blended.

Makes about 1¼ cups

Three-Fruit Conserve

SKILLET PEPPERS AND ONIONS

Sliced red and green bell peppers and sweet onion slices make a great hot vegetable combo. A little oil, a splash of wine and they simmer crisp-tender in just a few minutes.
Makes 4 servings

> 2 tablespoons vegetable oil
> 1 large red bell pepper, thinly sliced
> 1 large green bell pepper, thinly sliced
> 1 large Spanish onion, thinly sliced
> 2 tablespoons soy sauce
> 2 tablespoons dry white wine

1. Heat oil in large skillet over medium-high heat until hot. Add red and green bell peppers and onion; stir-fry for 2 minutes.

2. Add soy sauce and wine; simmer, covered, until vegetables are crisp-tender, about 2 minutes. Uncover pan; simmer until most of the liquid is evaporated.

DELECTABLE CARROT CASSEROLE

Herbed stuffing mix spreads a crunchy blanket over bright carrot coins in a smooth cheesy sauce.
Makes 8 to 10 servings

> ½ cup chopped onion
> 7 tablespoons butter or margarine
> 4 cups cooked sliced carrots
> 1 can (10¾ ounces) condensed cream of celery soup
> ¾ cup shredded Cheddar cheese
> 3 cups herb-flavored stuffing mix

1. Saute onion in 3 tablespoons of the butter in large skillet over medium heat until soft, about 4 minutes.

2. Add carrots, soup and cheese; mix well. Transfer to 2-quart baking dish; top with stuffing mix. Melt remaining butter; pour over stuffing mix.

3. Bake in preheated 350°F oven until hot throughout, about 20 minutes.

Skillet Peppers and Onions

Cold Rock Shrimp and Pasta Salad

COLD ROCK SHRIMP AND PASTA SALAD

Since the hard shell of fresh rock shrimp is cut open and removed before cooking, the shrimp meat cooks more quickly than other varieties. Simmer peeled rock shrimp in boiling water only 20 to 45 seconds and rinse immediately in cold water.

Makes 6 servings

1 pound cooked shelled deveined rock shrimp
6 ounces yellow and green linguine, cooked, drained
1 cup diagonally sliced celery
Summer Dressing (recipe follows)
Tomato wedges and avocado slices for garnish

1. Combine shrimp, linguine and celery in medium bowl. Add ¼ cup of the Summer Dressing; toss to mix.

2. Transfer salad to platter. Garnish with tomato and avocado; serve with remaining dressing. *(Continued)*

SUMMER DRESSING

1 cup vegetable oil
½ cup half-and-half
3 tablespoons white wine vinegar
2 hard-cooked egg yolks, sieved
1 tablespoon chopped capers
2 teaspoons sugar
½ teaspoon salt
½ teaspoon onion salt
½ teaspoon pepper
½ teaspoon dry mustard
½ teaspoon lemon juice
1 or 2 small cloves garlic, minced
⅛ teaspoon Worcestershire sauce

Combine all ingredients in jar with tight-fitting lid; shake until blended.

Plantation Fish in Aspic

PLANTATION FISH IN ASPIC

Makes 6 servings

    Water
1 cup dry sauterne wine
1 medium onion, cut into quarters
1 stalk celery, cut into quarters
2 bay leaves
1½ teaspoons salt
  ¼ teaspoon dried thyme, crumbled
  1 lemon
2 pounds fresh or thawed frozen grouper or other
    fish fillets
2 envelopes unflavored gelatin
  ¼ cup tarragon vinegar
2 tablespoons lemon juice
1 teaspoon dry mustard
  ¼ cup chopped celery
  ¼ cup chopped green onion
  ¼ cup chopped green bell pepper
2 tablespoons chopped pimiento
2 tablespoons chopped parsley
    Lettuce leaves
    Cucumber slices for garnish
    Mayonnaise   *(Continued)*

1. Combine 2 cups water, the wine, quartered onion and celery stalk, the bay leaves, salt and thyme in well-greased 10-inch skillet. Cut lemon in half; squeeze juice into skillet, then drop in halves. Heat to boiling.

2. Add fish to skillet; reduce heat. Simmer, covered, until fish is opaque throughout, 5 to 10 minutes. Remove fish to plate, draining well; let cool. Strain and reserve poaching liquid.

3. Sprinkle gelatin over ½ cup water in medium saucepan; let stand 1 minute to soften. Add reserved poaching liquid; heat and stir over medium heat until gelatin is dissolved. Transfer to 4-cup measure; add vinegar, lemon juice and enough water to make 4 cups liquid.

4. Mix mustard with small amount of the liquid until smooth; stir into remaining liquid. Refrigerate, stirring occasionally, until as thick as unbeaten egg white.

5. Flake fish, removing any skin and bones. Combine fish, chopped celery, green onion, green bell pepper, pimiento and parsley in large bowl; toss gently to mix. Add gelatin mixture; mix well. Pour into 7-cup mold or loaf pan. Refrigerate until completely set, several hours.

6. To serve, unmold onto platter lined with lettuce leaves; garnish with cucumber slices. Serve with mayonnaise.

PATTYPAN SQUASH CASSEROLE

Pattypan are the disc-shaped, pale green summer squash with a scalloped edge called cymling in old cookbooks.

Makes 6 servings

½ cup minced onion
3 cloves garlic, minced
3 tablespoons butter or margarine
2 pounds small pattypan squash, pared, seeded, diced (½-inch)
½ teaspoon salt
⅛ teaspoon pepper
2 large eggs, beaten
⅓ cup half-and-half
⅓ cup soft breadcrumbs

1. Saute onion and garlic in butter in large skillet over medium heat until soft, about 4 minutes. Add squash, salt and pepper; toss to coat. Transfer to well-greased 2-quart baking dish.

2. Mix eggs and half-and-half in small bowl; pour over squash. Sprinkle with breadcrumbs.

3. Bake in preheated 350°F oven just until squash is tender, about 30 minutes.

REFRIGERATOR GRAPE CHUTNEY

Makes about 1½ cups

⅔ cup white wine vinegar
½ cup chopped onion
½ cup seedless raisins
2 tablespoons chopped crystallized ginger
¼ cup packed brown sugar
1 tablespoon shredded coconut
½ cup red or green grapes, seedless or seeded

(Continued)

1. Combine vinegar, onion, raisins and ginger in small saucepan; heat to boiling. Reduce heat; simmer 5 minutes. Stir in sugar; cook 3 minutes longer. Remove from heat. Stir in coconut; let cool completely.

2. Stir in grapes. Store, covered, in refrigerator up to two weeks. (Serve as condiment with roasts, chops or poultry.)

CARROT-PARSNIP TART

An impressive gold and white vegetable filling in a pastry shell to serve with cold sliced roast beef or lean ham.

Makes 6 servings

4 medium carrots, coarsely chopped
1 small parsnip, coarsely chopped
1¼ teaspoons salt
3 large eggs
½ cup soft breadcrumbs
3 tablespoons butter
2 tablespoons lemon juice
Pinch white pepper
1 unbaked 8-inch pie shell
3 tablespoons packed brown sugar, if desired
Carrot and parsnip slices and parsley sprig for garnish

1. Combine carrots, parsnip and ¾ teaspoon of the salt in medium saucepan; add water to cover. Cook, covered, until tender, 20 to 25 minutes; drain well.

2. Combine cooked vegetables, remaining ½ teaspoon salt, the eggs, breadcrumbs, butter, lemon juice and pepper in blender container; process until smooth. Pour into pie shell.

3. Bake in preheated 375°F oven 15 minutes. Sprinkle top of pie with sugar; continue baking until knife inserted near center is withdrawn clean, about 15 minutes longer. Cool on wire rack 10 minutes before serving. Garnish with carrot and parsnip slices and parsley.

Carrot-Parsnip Tart

OVERNIGHT VEGETABLE AND EGG SALAD

Dip deep into the bowl with salad servers to lift out some of each crisp vegetable along with the creamy dressing sparked with dill and thyme.

Makes 8 to 10 servings

  8 cups fresh spinach, torn into bite-size pieces
  2 medium ripe tomatoes, cut into wedges
1½ cups sliced zucchini
  ½ pound mushrooms, sliced, cut into halves
  4 hard-cooked eggs, sliced
  ½ cup mayonnaise
  ½ cup sour cream
  ¾ teaspoon salt   *(Continued)*

  ½ teaspoon dried dill weed, crumbled
  ½ teaspoon onion powder
  ¼ teaspoon dried thyme, crumbled
1/16 teaspoon white pepper
  2 tablespoons water
  1 teaspoon distilled white vinegar
  1 teaspoon dried parsley flakes

1. Layer spinach, tomatoes, zucchini, mushrooms and eggs in attractive pattern in 3-quart glass bowl.

2. Mix mayonnaise, sour cream, salt, dill, onion powder, thyme and pepper in small bowl; stir in water and vinegar. Spread in thin layer on top of salad, making sure it reaches edges of bowl. Refrigerate, covered, overnight.

3. Bring salad to room temperature before serving; sprinkle with parsley.

Overnight Vegetable and Egg Salad

Cheddar-Stuffed Louisiana Yams

CHEDDAR-STUFFED LOUISIANA YAMS

Makes 4 servings

4 medium Louisiana yams (sweet potatoes)
¾ cup shredded Cheddar cheese
¼ cup milk
1½ tablespoons butter or margarine, melted
¾ teaspoon salt
   Pinch pepper
   Paprika

1. Pierce yams in a few places with skewer. Bake yams in preheated 400°F oven 15 minutes. Reduce oven setting to 375°F; continue baking until yams are tender, about 35 minutes longer.

2. Cut thin slice from top of each yam; scoop out centers, leaving 1¼-inch-thick shells. Combine yam centers, ½ cup of the cheese, the milk, butter, salt and pepper in small mixer bowl; beat until fluffy.

3. Spoon mixture into yam shells; sprinkle with remaining ¼ cup cheese. Sprinkle with paprika. Broil 4 inches from heat source until light brown.

CHEESE-FROSTED CAULIFLOWER

Makes 4 to 5 servings

1 medium head cauliflower, trimmed, cored
½ teaspoon salt
½ cup mayonnaise
2 teaspoons prepared mustard
¾ cup shredded sharp cheese

1. Cook whole cauliflower in boiling water to cover in large saucepan until crisp-tender, 12 to 15 minutes; drain.

(Continued)

2. Place cauliflower in ungreased shallow baking pan; sprinkle with salt. Mix mayonnaise and mustard in small bowl; spread evenly over cauliflower. Sprinkle with cheese.

3. Bake in preheated 375°F oven until cheese is melted and bubbly, about 10 minutes.

CORN FRITTERS

Fresh sweet corn kernels right off the cob, all wrapped up in quick-bread batter and fried golden brown to be served with pancake syrup or powdered sugar, are a staple in the South.

Makes about 12 fritters

¼ cup all-purpose flour
3 tablespoons cornstarch
½ teaspoon baking powder
¼ teaspoon salt
   Pinch ground red pepper
1 large egg, beaten
2 tablespoons milk
1½ cups fresh corn kernels (about 3 ears)
   Corn oil
   Pancake syrup or powdered sugar

1. Mix flour, cornstarch, baking powder, salt and red pepper in medium bowl.

2. Mix egg and milk in small bowl until blended. Add to flour mixture; stir just until mixed. Stir in corn.

3. Heat 1 inch oil in large deep skillet to 375°F.

4. Carefully add batter by tablespoonfuls, a few at a time; fry, turning occasionally, until golden brown, about 3 minutes. Remove with slotted spoon; drain on paper toweling. Serve hot with syrup or sugar.

Garden Potato Salad

GARDEN POTATO SALAD

Colorful carrots, corn and green beans join red-skinned potatoes in a tangy yogurt dressing pleasingly seasoned with tarragon.

Makes 6 servings

¼ cup plain yogurt
¼ cup low-fat cottage cheese
2 teaspoons milk
½ teaspoon cider vinegar
½ teaspoon onion powder
¼ teaspoon dried tarragon
¼ teaspoon salt
⅛ teaspoon pepper
2 pounds small red-skinned potatoes, scrubbed
1 cup green beans, cut in 1-inch lengths
½ cup corn kernels, uncooked
½ cup shredded carrot
Lettuce leaves

1. For dressing, combine yogurt, cottage cheese, milk, vinegar, onion powder, tarragon, salt and pepper in blender container; process until smooth. Refrigerate, covered.

2. Cook potatoes in large saucepan of boiling water until fork-tender, about 15 minutes; drain. Cut potatoes into quarters; place in large bowl.

3. Cook beans in boiling water until crisp-tender, 2 to 3 minutes. Drain; add to potatoes.

4. Add corn and carrot; toss lightly. Refrigerate, covered, until cold, 1 to 2 hours.

5. To serve, spoon vegetables into lettuce-lined bowl; top with dressing. Toss before serving.

ONIONS AU GRATIN

Small whole onions bake and bubble in a pimiento and cheese sauce under an ever-so-light blanket of buttery crumbs.

Makes 6 to 8 servings

2 pounds small white onions
1 teaspoon salt
¼ cup plus 2 tablespoons butter or margarine, melted
¼ cup all-purpose flour
2 cups milk
1 cup shredded sharp cheese
¼ cup chopped pimiento
¼ cup chopped parsley
¼ teaspoon pepper
½ cup soft breadcrumbs

1. Add onions and ½ teaspoon of the salt to large saucepan of boiling water; cook until onions are tender, about 15 minutes. Drain well; place in 2-quart baking dish.

2. Mix ¼ cup of the butter and the flour in medium saucepan; cook and stir over medium heat until bubbly. Gradually whisk in milk; cook and stir until sauce thickens and bubbles for 1 minute. Remove from heat.

3. Add cheese, pimiento, parsley, remaining ½ teaspoon salt and the pepper to sauce; stir until cheese is melted. Pour sauce over onions.

4. Mix breadcrumbs with remaining 2 tablespoons butter; sprinkle over onions. Bake in preheated 375°F oven until top is golden, about 15 minutes.

CAESAR BEAN SALAD

Warmed kidney beans absorb more of the good cheese and garlic flavor of the dressing-marinade than they would if chilled right out of the can.

Makes 6 to 8 servings

- 2 cans (16 ounces each) kidney beans
- ¼ cup fresh lemon juice
- ¼ cup grated Parmesan cheese
- ½ teaspoon salt
- 1 clove garlic, minced
- ¼ teaspoon pepper
- ¼ teaspoon dry mustard
- ½ cup olive oil
  Romaine lettuce
- 3 hard-cooked eggs, cut into wedges
- 1 cup seasoned croutons
  Parsley sprigs for garnish

1. Heat beans in medium saucepan until hot; drain well.

2. Combine lemon juice, cheese, salt, garlic, pepper and mustard in medium bowl; whisk in oil until blended. Add warm beans; mix gently. Refrigerate, covered, until cold.

3. To serve, place bean mixture in bowl lined with lettuce; arrange eggs around edge. Sprinkle with croutons; garnish with parsley.

GREEN BEANS DIABLO

A zippy salad fix-up for canned green beans, crumbled bacon and hard-cooked eggs fired with chili peppers.

Makes 4 to 5 servings

- 6 tablespoons vegetable oil
- 3 tablespoons cider vinegar
- ½ teaspoon salt
- ½ teaspoon pepper
- 2 teaspoons chopped hot chilies
- 1 can (16 ounces) green beans, drained
- 4 hard-cooked eggs, chopped
- 1 tablespoon mayonnaise
- 2 teaspoons wine vinegar
- 1 teaspoon prepared mustard
- 4 slices crisp-cooked bacon, crumbled
- 1 small onion, minced
  Lettuce leaves

1. Whisk oil, cider vinegar, salt and pepper in small bowl until blended; stir in chilies. Add to green beans in medium bowl; refrigerate, covered, 2 to 3 hours.

2. Combine eggs, mayonnaise, wine vinegar and mustard in small bowl; mix well. Refrigerate, covered, 2 to 3 hours.

3. To serve, toss bacon and onion lightly with beans. Spoon into bowl lined with lettuce leaves; top with egg mixture.

Caesar Bean Salad

MORAVIAN SUGAR CAKE

Although called a cake, this is a yeast-raised bread that originated with a religious group from eastern Europe who came to evangelize in the American colonies.

Makes 1 coffee cake; 8 to 10 servings

⅓ cup warm water (105 to 115°F)
4 tablespoons granulated sugar
1 package (¼ ounce) active dry yeast
2 large eggs, beaten
¼ cup butter or margarine, melted, cooled
2 tablespoons instant nonfat dry milk solids
2 teaspoons ground cinnamon
1 teaspoon salt
2½ to 3 cups all-purpose flour
¼ cup packed brown sugar
¼ cup finely chopped walnuts
2 tablespoons butter or margarine, room
    temperature

1. Combine warm water, 1 tablespoon of the granulated sugar and the yeast in large bowl; stir to dissolve yeast. Let stand until bubbly, about 5 minutes.

2. Add remaining 3 tablespoons granulated sugar, the eggs, ¼ cup melted butter, the milk solids, 1½ teaspoons of the cinnamon and the salt to yeast mixture; mix well. Whisk in 1½ cups of the flour until smooth. Stir in as much of the remaining flour as needed to make soft dough, about 1 cup.

3. Knead on floured surface, adding as much of the remaining flour as needed to prevent sticking, until dough is smooth and elastic, about 10 minutes. Cover dough with inverted bowl; let stand 20 minutes.

4. Combine brown sugar, walnuts, 2 tablespoons butter and remaining ½ teaspoon cinnamon in small bowl; mix well.

5. Roll dough into 36-inch-long strand. Coil strand in loose spiral in greased 9-inch round cake pan; sprinkle with wal-

(Continued)

nut mixture. Let rise, covered, in warm place until doubled, about 1 hour.

6. Bake in preheated 350°F oven until top is evenly browned and bottom sounds hollow when tapped, 30 to 35 minutes. Immediately remove from pan; cool completely on wire rack.

DAFFODIL BREAD

A delicate English tea bread, richly yellow with eggs and flavored with bits of finely diced candied citron. Slice thinly and toast lightly, and serve with fruit preserves.

Makes 10 to 12 servings

¾ cup liquid non-dairy creamer
1 cake active yeast
¼ cup butter, room temperature
¼ cup granulated sugar
3 large eggs
1 teaspoon salt
3 cups all-purpose flour
½ cup diced candied citron
    Powdered sugar

1. Heat non-dairy creamer in small saucepan to 80 to 90°F. Mix with yeast in small bowl until yeast is dissolved.

2. Beat butter and granulated sugar in large mixer bowl until light and fluffy. Add eggs, 1 at a time, beating well after each addition. Beat in yeast mixture and salt. Gradually beat in flour until smooth. Stir in citron.

3. Pour batter into well-greased 9-inch tube pan. Let rise, loosely covered, in warm place until doubled, 1 to 3 hours.

4. Bake in preheated 350°F oven until bread sounds hollow when tapped, about 30 minutes. Cool in pan on wire rack 10 minutes. Remove from pan; cool completely on rack. Sprinkle with powdered sugar before serving.

Moravian Sugar Cake

Sour Cream Coffee Ring

SOUR CREAM COFFEE RING

Makes 1 coffee cake; 12 to 16 servings
   1 cup finely chopped walnuts
   2 tablespoons packed brown sugar
   1 teaspoon ground cinnamon
1¼ cups granulated sugar
   ¾ cup butter or margarine, room temperature
   2 large eggs
   1 cup sour cream
   1 teaspoon vanilla
   2 cups all-purpose flour
1½ teaspoons baking powder
   ½ teaspoon baking soda

1. Combine nuts, brown sugar and cinnamon in small bowl; mix well. *(Continued)*

2. Beat granulated sugar and butter in large mixer bowl until light and fluffy. Add eggs, 1 at a time, beating well after each addition. Beat in sour cream and vanilla.

3. Mix flour, baking powder and baking soda in medium bowl. Add flour mixture, ⅓ at a time, to sour cream mixture, mixing on low speed after each addition just until blended.

4. Pour ½ of the batter into greased and floured 9-inch Bundt or tube pan; sprinkle with ½ of the nut mixture. Repeat layers once more.

5. Bake in preheated 350°F oven until wooden pick inserted into center is withdrawn clean, 45 to 55 minutes. Cool cake in pan on wire rack 10 minutes. Remove from pan; cool completely on rack.

Bran Muffins (top); Banana Nut Bread (center); Baking Powder Biscuits (bottom)

BANANA NUT BREAD

Makes 8 to 12 servings

⅔ cup sugar
½ cup butter or margarine, room temperature
2 large eggs
2 ripe medium bananas, mashed
1 tablespoon lemon juice
⅓ cup milk
1¾ cups all-purpose flour
1 teaspoon baking soda
½ teaspoon salt
½ cup chopped pecans or walnuts

1. Combine sugar and butter in large mixer bowl; beat until light and fluffy. Beat in eggs, 1 at a time. Beat in bananas and lemon juice; beat in milk.

2. Mix flour, baking soda and salt in medium bowl. Add to banana mixture; mix well. Stir in ¼ cup of the nuts. Pour batter into greased 8½ × 4½ × 2½-inch loaf pan; sprinkle with remaining ¼ cup nuts.

3. Bake in preheated 350°F oven until wooden pick inserted into center is withdrawn clean, 55 to 65 minutes. Cool in pan on wire rack 15 minutes. Remove from pan; cool completely on rack.

(Continued)

BRAN MUFFINS

Makes 10 to 12 muffins

1¼ cups all-purpose flour
 ½ cup sugar
 1 tablespoon baking powder
 ½ teaspoon salt
1½ cups whole-bran cereal
 1 cup chopped nuts, dates or raisins
1¼ cups milk
 1 large egg, beaten
 ¼ cup butter or margarine, melted

1. Mix flour, sugar, baking powder and salt in medium bowl; stir in cereal and nuts. Make a well in center of mixture.

2. Mix milk, egg, and butter in small bowl; add all at once to flour mixture. Stir with fork just until moistened; batter will be lumpy.

3. Spoon batter into greased muffin tin cups, filling ¾ full. Bake in preheated 400°F oven until golden, 20 to 25 minutes. Remove from muffin tin; serve warm, or cool on wire rack.

SOUTHERN CRESCENTS

Makes 3 dozen

 1 cup butter or margarine, room temperature
 1 package (8 ounces) cream cheese, room
    temperature
 2 cups all-purpose flour
 ¼ teaspoon salt
 ¾ cup finely chopped pecans
 ⅓ cup sugar
1½ teaspoons ground cinnamon
 1 teaspoon ground nutmeg
 2 tablespoons milk
 1 large egg yolk

(Continued)

1. Beat butter and cream cheese in large mixer bowl until smooth. Add flour and salt; mix well. Divide dough into 6 even pieces; refrigerate, wrapped in plastic, 2 hours.

2. Mix pecans, sugar, cinnamon and nutmeg in small bowl.

3. Working with 1 piece of dough at a time, roll out dough on lightly floured surface into 8-inch circle. Sprinkle circle with 2 tablespoons of the pecan mixture; cut into 6 wedges. Starting at wide edge, roll up each wedge; shape into crescent. Place point side down on ungreased baking sheets.

4. Mix milk and egg yolk in small bowl until blended. Brush crescents with egg yolk wash, being careful not to drip on baking sheet; sprinkle with remaining pecan mixture.

5. Bake in preheated 350°F oven until golden brown, about 12 minutes. Remove from baking sheets; serve warm, or cool on wire racks.

BAKING POWDER BISCUITS

Makes 1 dozen biscuits

2¼ cups all-purpose flour
 1 tablespoon baking powder
 ½ teaspoon salt
 ¼ cup butter or margarine, cold
 ¾ cup milk

1. Mix flour, baking powder and salt in medium bowl. Cut in butter until mixture resembles coarse crumbs; make a well in center. Add milk; stir with fork just until dough holds together.

2. Gently knead dough on lightly floured surface 6 to 8 times. Roll or pat out dough until ½ inch thick. Cut out dough with 2½-inch round cutter. Reroll dough scraps and cut out.

3. Place biscuits on ungreased baking sheet. Bake in preheated 450°F oven until golden, 12 to 15 minutes. Serve hot.

Southern Crescents

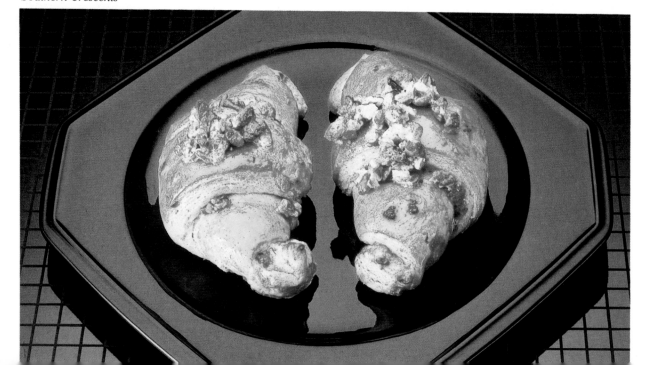

LEMON LOAF

There's lemon rind mixed into the batter and a lemon juice glaze on top to carry the fresh citrus flavor through every delicious bite.

Makes 8 to 12 servings

1½ cups sugar
½ cup butter, room temperature
1 tablespoon grated lemon rind
2 cups all-purpose flour
2 teaspoons baking powder
1 teaspoon baking soda
½ teaspoon salt
¾ cup buttermilk
1 cup walnuts, chopped
¼ cup lemon juice

1. Combine 1 cup of the sugar and the butter in large mixer bowl; beat until light and fluffy. Beat in lemon rind.

2. Mix flour, baking powder, baking soda and salt in medium bowl. Add flour mixture, ½ at a time, to butter mixture, alternating with buttermilk, beating well after each addition. Stir in nuts.

3. Pour batter into greased and floured 8½ × 4½ × 2½-inch loaf pan. Bake in preheated 375°F oven until wooden pick inserted into center is withdrawn clean, about 1 hour. Cool in pan on wire rack 10 minutes.

4. While loaf is cooling, mix lemon juice and remaining ½ cup sugar in small saucepan. Heat until sugar dissolves.

5. Unmold loaf onto wire rack; place rack over waxed paper. Pierce top of loaf all over with 2-tined fork or skewer. Gradually spoon lemon syrup on top of loaf, letting syrup soak in. Cool completely.

TWO-TONE BROWNIES

Cream cheese marbling ripples through the chocolate batter and swirls to the surface in this large pan of moist walnutty brownies.

Makes 18 brownies

1 package (8 ounces) cream cheese, room temperature
2⅓ cups sugar
5 large eggs
½ teaspoon vanilla
1 cup butter, room temperature
1 cup all-purpose flour
1 cup unsweetened cocoa powder
¼ teaspoon salt
1½ cups chopped walnuts

1. Beat cream cheese and ⅓ cup of the sugar in small mixer bowl until smooth; beat in 1 egg and the vanilla.

2. Beat butter and remaining 2 cups sugar in large mixer bowl until light and fluffy. Add remaining 4 eggs, 1 at a time, beating well after each addition.

3. Mix flour, cocoa powder and salt in medium bowl. Add flour mixture, ⅓ at a time, to butter mixture, mixing on low speed after each addition just until blended. Stir in nuts.

4. Spread ½ of the cocoa batter in greased 13 × 9 × 2-inch baking pan; top with cream cheese mixture in even layer. Top with remaining batter; swirl with spatula to marble slightly.

5. Bake in preheated 350°F oven until set in center, 35 to 40 minutes. Cool completely in pan on wire rack. Cut into 18 bars.

Lemon Loaf

Bourbon Pecan Cake

BOURBON PECAN CAKE

Makes 12 to 16 servings

2½ cups granulated sugar
 1 cup butter, room temperature
 6 large eggs
 3 cups sifted cake flour
 2 teaspoons baking powder
 1 teaspoon salt
 1 teaspoon ground nutmeg
 1 cup sour cream
 ½ cup plus 1 tablespoon bourbon
 1½ cups coarsely chopped pecans
 2 cups sifted powdered sugar
 1 to 2 tablespoons water
   Pecan halves for garnish

1. Beat granulated sugar and butter in large mixer bowl until light and fluffy. Add eggs, 1 at a time, beating well after each addition.

2. Mix flour, baking powder, salt and nutmeg in medium bowl. Mix sour cream and ½ cup of the bourbon in small bowl.

3. Add ⅓ of the flour mixture at a time to butter mixture, alternating with sour cream mixture, beating well after each addition. Stir in chopped pecans.

4. Pour batter into greased 10-inch tube or Bundt pan. Bake in preheated 325°F oven until wooden pick inserted into center is withdrawn clean, about 1½ hours. Test cake frequently after first hour and 15 minutes.

(Continued)

5. Cool cake in pan on wire rack 15 minutes. Remove from pan; cool completely on rack.

6. In medium bowl, mix powdered sugar, remaining 1 tablespoon bourbon and as much of the water as needed to make smooth thick glaze. Pour glaze on top of cake, letting it run down the sides. Garnish with pecan halves.

BANANAS FOSTER

You don't have to visit New Orleans to enjoy this flambéed dessert. Prepare it in the kitchen or dazzle dinner guests by flaming the sauce table-side in a chafing dish.

Makes 4 servings

½ cup packed brown sugar
 ¼ cup butter or margarine
 4 firm-ripe small bananas, cut lengthwise into
   halves
   Pinch ground cinnamon
 ⅓ cup light rum
 4 scoops vanilla or coffee ice cream

1. Cook sugar and butter in 10-inch skillet over medium heat until melted. Cook and stir until slightly thickened, about 2 minutes.

2. Add bananas; cook and stir gently until heated and glazed, 1 to 2 minutes. Sprinkle with cinnamon.

3. Add rum; carefully ignite with long match. Spoon sauce over bananas until flames subside, about 1 minute. Serve warm over ice cream.

Pina Colada Cheesecake

PINA COLADA CHEESECAKE

A Caribbean cooler inspires a tropical cheesecake with juicy sweet pineapple and coconut rum baked in a superb nut-coconut crust.

Makes 8 to 10 servings

2¼ **pounds cream cheese, room temperature**
 ¾ **cup juice-packed crushed canned pineapple,**
     drained well, ½ cup juice reserved
 ⅓ **cup coconut rum**
 ¼ **cup sour cream**
1½ **cups sugar**
 4 **large eggs, room temperature**
   Coco-Nut Crust (recipe follows)
   Fresh pineapple slices for garnish

1. Beat cream cheese in large mixer bowl on medium speed until completely smooth. Gradually beat in crushed pineapple. Gradually beat in reserved pineapple juice and coconut rum until blended.

2. Add sour cream; beat on medium speed until blended. Continue beating while slowly adding sugar. Add eggs, 1 at a time, beating well after each addition. Batter will be thin. Pour into Coco-Nut Crust; gently rotate pan several quarter-turns to settle batter.   *(Continued)*

3. Bake in middle of preheated 350°F oven until cake is set 2½ inches in from edges and center is still puddinglike, 60 to 65 minutes, for creamy center. For firmer center, bake until center is just set, about 10 minutes longer. (Cake may crack at sides.)

4. Place pan on wire rack away from drafts; let cool completely. Remove sides of pan; refrigerate cake, uncovered, overnight or at least 8 hours. Cover cake loosely with plastic wrap; refrigerate until serving time. Garnish with pineapple slices.

COCO-NUT CRUST

1 **cup desiccated flaked coconut**
1 **cup ground toasted Brazil nuts or hazelnuts***
¼ **cup sugar**
¼ **cup butter, melted**

1. Combine coconut, Brazil nuts and sugar in medium bowl. Drizzle with butter; stir and toss with fork until uniformly moistened. Press mixture evenly on bottom and sides of well-buttered 9-inch springform pan; refrigerate 5 minutes.

2. Bake crust in preheated 350°F oven 7 minutes. Cool completely on wire rack.

***Note:** To toast whole nuts, bake in ungreased shallow baking pan at 350°F until skins begin to crack, 5 to 8 minutes. Rub in coarse sieve to remove loose skins; cool.*

MARTHA WASHINGTON'S FRUITED CAKE

The spices nutmeg and mace, favorites in Colonial kitchens, both come from the nutmeg tree. Mace comes from a weblike covering on the seed, while nutmeg is ground from the seed itself.

Makes 16 servings

2¼ cups all-purpose flour
  1 teaspoon ground mace
  ¼ teaspoon ground nutmeg
  ¼ teaspoon salt
  2 tablespoons milk
  2 tablespoons brandy
  1 cup butter or margarine, room temperature
  1 cup granulated sugar
  5 large eggs, separated
  1 cup mixed chopped candied fruits
  ½ cup golden raisins
    Powdered sugar

(Continued)

1. Mix flour, mace, nutmeg and salt in medium bowl. Mix milk and brandy in small bowl.

2. Beat butter and granulated sugar in large mixer bowl until light and fluffy. Add egg yolks, 1 at a time, beating well after each addition.

3. Add flour mixture, ½ at a time, alternating with milk mixture, mixing on low speed after each addition. Stir in candied fruits and raisins.

4. Beat egg whites in clean large mixer bowl until stiff but not dry; fold into batter. Pour into greased and floured 9-inch tube pan.

5. Bake in preheated 325°F oven until wooden pick inserted into center is withdrawn clean, about 1 hour and 10 minutes. Cool in pan on wire rack 10 minutes. Remove from pan; cool completely on rack. Sprinkle with powdered sugar before serving.

Martha Washington's Fruited Cake

CHERRIED FRUIT CAKE

There's just enough batter to hold all of the luscious fruit and nuts together for slicing in this fabulous holiday treat.

Makes 1 loaf

¾ cup sifted all-purpose flour
½ teaspoon baking powder
½ teaspoon salt
1 jar (16 ounces) maraschino cherries, drained well
9 ounces pecan halves
8 ounces pitted dates
8 ounces candied pineapple, sliced
3 large eggs
3 tablespoons rum
¼ cup light corn syrup

1. Grease 9×5×3-inch loaf pan. Line bottom and sides with parchment paper; grease paper. Sift flour, baking powder and salt into large bowl. Add cherries, pecans, dates and pineapple; toss to coat evenly with flour mixture.

2. Beat eggs and rum in small bowl until blended; pour over fruit mixture; mix well. Transfer to prepared pan; press with spatula to pack tightly.

3. Bake in preheated 300°F oven until wooden pick inserted in center is withdrawn clean, about 1 hour and 45 minutes.

4. Cool cake in pan on wire rack 15 minutes. Remove cake from pan; remove paper. Brush warm cake with corn syrup; cool completely on rack.

LEMON MOUSSE

It's much easier to grate the rind from the whole lemon before the fruit is cut and the juice extracted.

Makes 8 to 10 servings

1 envelope unflavored gelatin
¼ cup cold water
1 cup sugar
6 large eggs, separated
¾ cup fresh lemon juice
1½ tablespoons grated lemon rind
1½ cups whipping cream

1. Sprinkle gelatin over water in small bowl; let stand 1 minute to soften.

2. Beat sugar and egg yolks in top of double boiler until blended; whisk in lemon juice and lemon rind. Cook over barely simmering water, whisking constantly, until thick enough to coat a spoon, about 10 minutes; remove from water.

3. Add gelatin mixture; stir until gelatin is dissolved. Let cool completely.

4. Beat egg whites in large mixer bowl until stiff but not dry; fold into gelatin mixture. Beat cream in large mixer bowl until soft peaks form; fold into gelatin mixture.

5. Spoon mixture into 1½-quart souffle dish. Refrigerate until completely set, several hours.

Cherried Fruit Cake

TANGERINE SOUFFLE

As members of the mandarin orange family, tangerines are small, with a distinctive flavor and juiciness. Because tangerines are so easy to peel and the sections pull apart without effort, they have the nickname "zipperfruit."

Makes 10 to 12 servings

- 6 large eggs, separated
- 1½ cups tangerine juice (5 to 6 tangerines)
- 2 tablespoons grated tangerine rind
- 1¼ cups sugar
- 2 envelopes unflavored gelatin
- ⅛ teaspoon salt
- 2 cups whipping cream
- 3 tangerines, peeled, sectioned, seeded

1. Fold 30-inch-long piece of waxed paper lengthwise in half; tape securely around 2-quart souffle dish forming 3-inch collar above rim of dish.

2. Beat egg yolks lightly in small bowl; stir in tangerine juice and tangerine rind.

3. Mix ¾ cup of the sugar, the gelatin and salt in top of double boiler. Gradually stir in egg yolk mixture. Cook, stirring constantly, over simmering water until mixture thickens, about 10 minutes.

4. Immediately transfer to large bowl; refrigerate until mixture mounds slightly when dropped from a spoon, about 40 minutes. Remove from refrigerator.

5. Beat egg whites in large mixer bowl until foamy. Gradually beat in remaining ½ cup sugar; beat until stiff and shiny. Fold into gelatin mixture.

6. Beat cream in large mixer bowl until soft peaks form; fold into gelatin mixture.

7. Spoon ⅓ of the gelatin mixture into souffle dish; top with ⅓ of the tangerine sections. Repeat layers 2 more times; refrigerate until set, 3 to 4 hours. Carefully remove collar before serving.

VERY CHOCOLATE BROWNIES

An absolutely scrumptious chocolate syrup and cocoa variation of America's favorite bar cookie.

Makes 16 brownies

- ½ cup butter or margarine
- 1 cup sugar
- 2 large eggs
- 1 teaspoon vanilla
- 1 cup all-purpose flour
- ¼ cup unsweetened cocoa powder
- ¼ teaspoon baking soda
- ¾ cup chocolate-flavored syrup
- ¾ cup chopped nuts

1. Beat butter, sugar, eggs and vanilla in large mixer bowl until light and fluffy.

2. Mix flour, cocoa powder and baking soda in medium bowl. Add flour mixture, ½ at a time, to butter mixture, alternating with chocolate syrup, mixing well after each addition. Stir in nuts.

3. Spread batter in greased 9 × 9 × 2-inch baking pan. Bake in preheated 350°F oven until wooden pick inserted into center is withdrawn clean, 30 to 35 minutes. Cool in pan on wire rack; cut into squares.

Strawberry Coconut Freeze

STRAWBERRY COCONUT FREEZE

Use a sharp knife dipped in warm water to carve slices from this light and elegant frozen fruit and rum dessert.

Makes 8 to 10 servings

- 1 envelope unflavored gelatin
- ⅔ cup orange juice
- 1 pint strawberries, pureed (about 1½ cups)
- ¾ cup coconut rum
- 2 large egg whites
- ¼ cup sugar
- Sliced strawberries for garnish

1. Sprinkle gelatin over orange juice in small saucepan; let stand 1 minute to soften. Cook and stir over medium heat until gelatin is completely dissolved; remove from heat.

2. Add strawberry puree and coconut rum to gelatin mixture; mix well. Transfer to shallow metal pan; freeze until frozen 1½ inches in from edges of pan.

3. Beat egg whites in small mixer bowl until foamy; gradually beat in sugar. Beat until stiff but not dry.

4. Beat strawberry mixture in large mixer bowl until smooth but still icy; fold in egg whites. Pour into 5-cup mold; freeze, covered, until firm, several hours or overnight.

5. Before serving, transfer mold to refrigerator for 20 minutes. Unmold onto serving dish; garnish with sliced strawberries.

Superb Pecan Pie

DOUBLE PEACH MELBA

Makes 4 servings

1 package (10 ounces) frozen raspberries, thawed
1 tablespoon cornstarch
½ cup red currant or raspberry jelly
4 pared fresh peach halves
4 scoops peach ice cream
  Whipped cream, if desired

1. Drain liquid from raspberries into small saucepan; stir in cornstarch until smooth. Add jelly; cook, stirring constantly, over medium heat until sauce thickens and bubbles for 1 minute. Transfer to medium bowl.

2. Stir berries into sauce; refrigerate, covered, until cold.

3. To serve, place 1 peach half in each of 4 dessert dishes; top each with 1 scoop ice cream. Spoon sauce over ice cream; top with whipped cream.

SUPERB PECAN PIE

Makes 8 servings

1 cup sugar
3 large eggs, beaten
½ cup dark corn syrup
6 tablespoons butter or margarine, melted
1 teaspoon vanilla
1 cup chopped pecans
1 unbaked 9-inch pie shell   *(Continued)*

1. Beat sugar into eggs in medium bowl; beat in corn syrup, butter and vanilla. Stir in pecans; pour into pie shell.

2. Bake in preheated 350°F oven until knife inserted midway between center and edge is withdrawn clean, 45 to 60 minutes. Cool completely on wire rack.

CREOLE FUDGE

This Southern confection is more than chocolatey. Chock full of candied cherries, pecans and raisins, it's also fruity, nutty and chewy.

Makes about 2 pounds

¼ pound large marshmallows (12 to 14)
¼ pound butter or margarine
2 cups sugar
¾ cup evaporated milk
1½ cups semisweet chocolate morsels
½ cup chopped pecans
½ cup raisins
⅓ cup chopped candied cherries

1. Combine marshmallows and butter in large heavy saucepan; cook and stir over very low heat until marshmallows melt and mixture is smooth.

2. Mix sugar and milk in medium saucepan; heat over medium heat to simmering. Reduce heat; simmer, stirring constantly, 5 minutes. Add to marshmallow mixture; mix well.

3. Add chocolate; beat until thick and creamy. Stir in pecans, raisins and cherries; pour into buttered 8-inch square pan. Refrigerate until firm; cut into squares.

CITRUS TART AUGUSTINE

Here's a fresh fruit pie with a citrus twist. Tart grapefruit and orange sections sweetly surrounded by warmed currant jelly in a buttery orange pastry.

Makes 8 servings

⅓ cup sugar
2 tablespoons cornstarch
⅛ teaspoon salt
¾ cup milk
⅓ cup fresh grapefruit juice
⅓ cup fresh orange juice
2 large eggs, lightly beaten
1 teaspoon grated orange rind
¼ cup red currant jelly
  Orange Pastry Crust (recipe follows)
3 oranges, peeled, sectioned
2 grapefruit, peeled, sectioned
  Whipped cream for garnish

1. Mix sugar, cornstarch and salt in medium saucepan; gradually stir in milk, grapefruit juice and orange juice. Cook and stir over low heat until mixture thickens and bubbles for 1 minute; remove from heat.

2. Gradually whisk ½ of the hot mixture into eggs in small bowl; whisk egg mixture into remaining hot mixture in pan. Stir in orange rind. Cook, stirring constantly, over low heat until filling thickens, 3 to 5 minutes; do not boil. Let cool to room temperature.

3. Heat jelly in small saucepan over low heat until melted and smooth; cool slightly.

(Continued)

4. Brush inside of Orange Pastry Crust with some of the jelly; spread with filling. Arrange orange and grapefruit sections on top of filling; brush with remaining jelly. Refrigerate at least 30 minutes before serving. Remove sides of pan; garnish with whipped cream.

ORANGE PASTRY CRUST

1 cup all-purpose flour
½ cup ground walnuts, almonds or pecans
3 tablespoons sugar
1 teaspoon grated orange rind
¼ teaspoon salt
⅓ cup butter or margarine, cold
3 to 4 tablespoons fresh orange juice, cold

1. Mix flour, nuts, sugar, orange rind and salt in medium bowl; cut in butter until mixture resembles fine crumbs. Gradually add orange juice, stirring and tossing with fork until mixture holds together when squeezed. Refrigerate, wrapped in plastic, 1 hour.

2. Roll out dough on lightly floured surface into 12-inch circle. Ease into 9-inch fluted tart pan with removable bottom; trim flush with edge of pan. Pierce bottom in several places with fork; refrigerate 30 minutes.

3. Line pastry with parchment paper; fill with pie weights or dry beans. Bake in preheated 375°F oven 8 minutes. Remove paper and weights; bake until light brown, 10 to 12 minutes longer. Cool completely on wire rack.

Citrus Tart Augustine

LEMON CURD

A very English, very lemony, very versatile spread. Smooth it between layers of white cake, roll it up in jelly-roll, spoon it into miniature tart shells or pass with toast.

Makes about 1½ cups

 1 cup sugar
 3 large eggs, lightly beaten
 ½ cup fresh lemon juice
    Pinch salt
 ½ cup butter, room temperature
 1 tablespoon grated lemon rind

1. Combine sugar, eggs, lemon juice and salt in medium nonaluminum heavy saucepan; mix well. Cook, stirring constantly, over low heat until mixture thickens enough to coat a spoon, 10 to 12 minutes; do not boil.

2. Immediately transfer to medium bowl. Add butter, 1 tablespoon at a time, stirring after each addition until melted and blended. Stir in lemon rind. Refrigerate, covered, until cold.

ELEGANT ORANGE CAKE

Makes 10 to 12 servings

 6 large eggs, separated
 ¾ cup sugar
 3 tablespoons orange juice
 2 teaspoons grated orange rind
 ¼ teaspoon salt
 1 cup sifted cake flour
    Orange Syrup (recipe follows)
    Orange Frosting (recipe follows)
    Chocolate curls for garnish

1. Beat egg yolks in large mixer bowl; gradually beat in sugar until light and fluffy, 5 to 10 minutes. Beat in orange juice, orange rind and salt. Gradually stir in flour.

(Continued)

2. Beat egg whites in clean large mixer bowl until stiff but not dry; fold into egg yolk mixture. Spread batter in 3 greased and floured 8-inch round cake pans, dividing batter evenly.

3. Bake in preheated 325°F oven until center springs back when gently pressed with fingertip, about 30 minutes. Invert pans on wire racks; let cool completely.

4. Remove cake from pans; pierce layers all over with wooden pick or skewer. Gradually pour Orange Syrup over layers, letting syrup soak in. Spread each layer with Orange Frosting; stack layers on serving plate. Frost sides of cake; garnish with chocolate curls.

ORANGE SYRUP

 ¾ cup sugar
 ¾ cup water
 1 orange, unpeeled, sliced
 ¼ cup Marsala

1. Heat sugar and water in small saucepan to boiling; stir to dissolve sugar. Add orange slices; reduce heat to low. Simmer, uncovered, until liquid is reduced to ⅔ cup, about 15 minutes.

2. Remove and discard orange slices. Stir in Marsala; let syrup cool completely.

ORANGE FROSTING

 ⅔ cup sugar
 ½ cup orange juice
 2 large eggs, beaten
 ¼ cup all-purpose flour
 1 cup heavy cream, whipped

Combine sugar, orange juice, eggs, and flour in top of double boiler; mix well. Cook over simmering water, stirring constantly, until thick and smooth. Refrigerate, covered, until cold. Fold in whipped cream just before ready to use.

Lemon Curd

Heavenly Peanut Torte

HEAVENLY PEANUT TORTE

Makes 12 servings

　3 cups finely chopped roasted peanuts
　2 tablespoons all-purpose flour
　2 teaspoons baking powder
　6 large eggs, separated
1½ cups granulated sugar
1½ teaspoons vanilla
　¼ teaspoon salt
　1 pint whipping cream
　½ cup powdered sugar
　½ cup grated semisweet chocolate
　　Peanut halves for garnish

1. Grease bottoms of three 9-inch round cake pans; line bottoms with waxed paper; grease paper.

2. Mix chopped peanuts, flour and baking powder in large bowl. *(Continued)*

3. Beat egg yolks and 1 cup of the granulated sugar in large mixer bowl until thick and pale yellow. Beat in vanilla; fold into peanut mixture.

4. Beat egg whites with salt in clean large mixer bowl until foamy and doubled in volume. Gradually beat in remaining ½ cup granulated sugar; beat until stiff peaks form. Fold into peanut mixture.

5. Pour batter into prepared pans, dividing evenly; rap pans on counter to settle batter. Bake in preheated 325°F oven until wooden pick inserted into center is withdrawn clean, about 30 minutes.

6. Cool layers in pans on wire racks 15 minutes. Remove from pans; remove waxed paper. Cool layers on wire racks.

7. Beat cream and powdered sugar in large mixer bowl until soft peaks form.

8. Spread whipped cream on cake layers, dividing evenly; sprinkle layers with chocolate. Stack layers on serving plate; garnish top with peanut halves.

Rainbow Cream Cups

RAINBOW CREAM CUPS

Makes 6 servings

  1 envelope unflavored gelatin
1¼ cups cold water
  3 large eggs, separated
1¼ cups sugar
  ¼ cup lemon juice
  1 grated lemon rind
  1 cup whipping cream
  ¼ cup orange marmalade
  6 whole strawberries
  ½ cup blueberries
  1 banana, thinly sliced

1. Wrap waxed paper around tops of 6 individual souffle dishes to make 1-inch-high collars; tie with string or secure with rubber bands.

2. Sprinkle gelatin over ¼ cup of the water in cup; let stand 1 minute to soften.

3. Beat egg yolks in medium saucepan; stir in remaining 1 cup water, 1 cup of the sugar and the gelatin mixture. Cook over low heat, stirring constantly, until gelatin dissolves and mixture thickens enough to coat a spoon.

4. Transfer mixture to large bowl; stir in lemon juice and rind. Refrigerate, stirring occasionally, until mixture mounds softly.

5. Beat egg whites in small mixer bowl until foamy; gradually beat in remaining ¼ cup sugar until stiff but not dry. Fold into gelatin mixture.

6. Beat cream in small mixer bowl until stiff; fold into gelatin mixture. Spoon into prepared dishes; refrigerate until set, several hours.

7. Before serving, heat marmalade in small saucepan until hot; remove from heat. Remove waxed paper from souffle dishes. Arrange strawberries, blueberries and banana on top of desserts; brush with marmalade to glaze.

SOUR CREAM RAISIN PIE

Spreading the meringue clear out to the edge of the pie shell insulates the filling from the heat and prevents the meringue from shrinking as it browns.

Makes 6 to 8 servings

  ¾ cup plus 3 tablespoons sugar
1½ tablespoons cornstarch
  ½ teaspoon ground cinnamon
  ¼ teaspoon salt
  ¼ teaspoon ground cloves
  1 cup sour cream
  1 cup raisins
  3 large eggs, separated
1½ teaspoons lemon juice
  ½ cup chopped walnuts
  1 packaged graham cracker crumb crust (6-ounce)
  ¼ teaspoon cream of tartar
  ¼ teaspoon vanilla

1. Mix ¾ cup of the sugar, the cornstarch, cinnamon, salt and cloves in medium saucepan. Add sour cream, raisins, egg yolks and lemon juice; mix well. Cook, stirring constantly, over medium heat until mixture thickens; immediately remove from heat. Let cool.

2. Stir walnuts into cooled raisin mixture; spread evenly in pie crust.

3. Beat egg whites, cream of tartar and vanilla in small mixer bowl until foamy. Gradually beat in remaining 3 tablespoons sugar; beat until stiff but not dry. Spread meringue on top of pie, sealing carefully to edge of crust.

4. Place pie on baking sheet. Bake in preheated 350°F oven until meringue is golden brown, 5 to 10 minutes. Cool completely on wire rack.

FUDGE-LOVELY PIE

Like a fantastic chocolate bonbon with a strawberry center, baked in a pie plate. To serve, cut in thin wedges.

Makes 8 servings

  1 cup sugar
  ½ cup butter, room temperature
  ½ cup sifted all-purpose flour
  3 large eggs, separated
  1 teaspoon vanilla
  3 ounces unsweetened chocolate, melted
  ¼ cup strawberry preserves

1. Beat sugar and butter in large mixer bowl until light and fluffy. Add flour, egg yolks and vanilla; beat well. Add chocolate; beat 5 minutes.

2. Beat egg whites in small mixer bowl until stiff but not dry; fold into chocolate mixture.

3. Place ½ of the chocolate mixture in center of greased and floured 9-inch pie plate; do not spread to sides of plate. Spread strawberry preserves over chocolate mixture, covering completely. Cover preserves with remaining chocolate mixture; do not spread. (Mixture will spread out during baking.)

4. Bake in preheated 350°F oven until center is set, 20 to 25 minutes. Cool completely on wire rack.

BERRIED TREASURE RICE DESSERT

Creamy rice pudding conceals a cargo of blueberries beneath a sea of foamy white meringue.

Makes 8 servings

3 cups cooked rice
3 cups milk
1 cup sugar
1 tablespoon butter or margarine
¾ teaspoon salt
4 large eggs, separated
2 teaspoons vanilla
1 can (21 ounces) blueberry pie filling
1 tablespoon lemon juice

1. Combine rice, 2½ cups of the milk, ½ cup of the sugar, the butter and ½ teaspoon of the salt in medium saucepan. Cook, stirring frequently, over medium heat until thickened, 20 to 25 minutes. Remove from heat.

2. Beat egg yolks and remaining ½ cup milk in small bowl; gradually stir into rice mixture. Cook, stirring constantly, over low heat 2 minutes; stir in 1 teaspoon of the vanilla. Transfer to buttered 2½-quart baking dish.

3. Mix pie filling and lemon juice in medium bowl; spread over rice mixture. Bake in preheated 350°F oven until heated through, about 20 minutes. *(Continued)*

4. Beat egg whites in small mixer bowl until foamy; gradually beat in remaining ½ cup sugar, remaining ¼ teaspoon salt and remaining 1 teaspoon vanilla. Beat until stiff but not dry. Spread over hot filling, sealing meringue to edges of dish.

5. Bake at 350°F until meringue is golden, 12 to 15 minutes; cool completely on wire rack. Refrigerate until cold, about 3 hours.

PEACH SUNDAE SAUCE

A luscious fresh peach sauce with a lemon-orange accent, designated for desserts but wonderful on waffles.

Makes about 1½ cups

2 cups crushed pared fresh peaches
½ cup sugar
½ cup orange juice
2 teaspoons lemon juice
1 teaspoon vanilla

1. Mix peaches, sugar and orange juice in 1½-quart saucepan; cook and stir over high heat to boiling. Reduce heat to low; simmer, uncovered, until sauce thickens, about 15 minutes. Remove from heat.

2. Stir in lemon juice and vanilla; let cool slightly or completely. Sauce can be served warm or cold over ice cream. Store in refrigerator.

Berried Treasure Rice Dessert

NO-BAKE TROPICAL FRUIT CAKE

Fresh papaya and strawberries are the fruit, and cubes of angel food the cake, for this refrigerator dessert made light and frothy with whipped gelatin, egg whites and whipping cream.

Makes 12 servings

- 3 medium papayas (about 1 pound each), pared, seeded
- ½ cup sugar
- 2 envelopes unflavored gelatin
- 3 large eggs, separated
- ¾ cup milk
- ⅓ cup rum
- 1 cup whipping cream
- 4 cups cubed (¾-inch) angel food or sponge cake
- 2 cups sliced strawberries
- 1 cup whipped cream and sliced strawberries for garnish

1. Coarsely chop enough papaya to measure 4½ cups. Slice remaining papaya; reserve for garnish.

2. Cook chopped papaya in large saucepan of boiling water 5 minutes; drain well. Puree enough of the blanched papaya in blender to measure 2 cups; reserve remaining blanched papaya.

3. Mix ¼ cup of the sugar and the gelatin in medium saucepan. Whisk egg yolks and milk in small bowl until blended; stir into gelatin mixture. Let stand 1 minute.

4. Cook and stir gelatin mixture over low heat until gelatin is completely dissolved, about 5 minutes. Stir in pureed papaya and the rum. Transfer to large bowl; refrigerate, stirring occasionally, until mixture mounds slightly when dropped from spoon, about 30 minutes.

(Continued)

5. Beat egg whites in large mixer bowl until soft peaks form; gradually beat in remaining ¼ cup sugar. Beat until stiff; fold into gelatin mixture.

6. Beat 1 cup cream in small mixer bowl until stiff; fold into gelatin mixture. Fold in cake, 2 cups strawberries and the remaining blanched papaya.

7. Pour mixture into 9-inch springform pan. Refrigerate until set, at least 3 hours. Remove sides of pan before serving; garnish with reserved papaya slices, whipped cream and strawberries.

PEACH GLACÉ PIE

Makes 8 servings

- 1 envelope unflavored gelatin
- 2 tablespoons cold water
- 1 jar (12 ounces) apricot preserves
- ½ teaspoon almond extract
- 1 can (29 ounces) peach halves, drained
- 1 packaged graham cracker crumb crust (6-ounce)
  Whipped cream, if desired

1. Sprinkle gelatin over cold water in small bowl; let stand 1 minute to soften.

2. Heat preserves in small saucepan to boiling; remove from heat. Add gelatin mixture; stir until gelatin is dissolved. Stir in almond extract. Refrigerate, stirring occasionally, until slightly thickened.

3. Arrange peach halves in crust, cut sides down; pour gelatin mixture over peaches. Refrigerate until set, about 3 hours. Serve with whipped cream.

No-Bake Tropical Fruit Cake

Spiced Sweet Potato Pie

SPICED SWEET POTATO PIE

Y'all come for a slice of sweet potato pie, sweetened with brown sugar and nicely spiced with cloves and ginger as well as cinnamon and nutmeg.

Makes 8 servings

  1 cup packed light brown sugar
  1 teaspoon ground cinnamon
  ½ teaspoon ground ginger
  ½ teaspoon ground nutmeg
  ½ teaspoon salt
  ⅛ teaspoon ground cloves
  1 can (18 ounces) sweet potatoes in syrup,
     drained, mashed (2 cups)
  3 large eggs, beaten
1½ cups milk, hot
  1 unbaked 9-inch pie shell
  ½ cup pecan halves
    Whipped cream and ground nutmeg for garnish

1. Mix sugar, cinnamon, ginger, ½ teaspoon nutmeg, the salt and cloves in large bowl. Add sweet potatoes and eggs; mix well. Stir in milk; pour into pie shell.

2. Bake in preheated 375°F oven 25 minutes. Arrange pecans on top of filling. Bake until filling is set in center, about 30 minutes longer.

3. Cool pie completely on wire rack; serve at room temperature. Garnish with whipped cream and nutmeg.

RUM BARREL PRUNE BREAD PUDDING

Makes 8 to 10 servings

1½ cups pitted prunes, cut into halves
  ⅓ cup rum
12 slices (½-inch-thick) French bread (about ½
    pound)
  6 large eggs
  1 cup whipping cream
  ½ cup granulated sugar
  ¼ cup packed brown sugar
  3 cups milk
  2 teaspoons grated orange rind
    Powdered sugar
    Whipped cream, if desired

1. Combine prunes and rum in medium bowl; let stand, stirring occasionally, 1 to 2 hours.

2. Line bottom of shallow 2- to 3-quart flame-proof baking dish with ½ of the bread; top with prune mixture in even layer. Cover with remaining bread, overlapping slices slightly.

3. Whisk eggs, cream, granulated and brown sugars in large bowl until blended; stir in milk and orange rind. Pour over bread in baking dish; press down on bread until saturated.

4. Bake in lower half of preheated 400°F oven just until set, 40 to 50 minutes. Cool on wire rack 15 minutes.

5. Lightly dust top with sifted powdered sugar. Broil 4 inches from heat source until sugar is golden, a few seconds. Serve warm or cold with whipped cream.

STRAWBERRY ICE MILK

A light, airy frozen fruit dessert that is low in fat as well as low in calories.

Makes 6 to 8 servings

 2 teaspoons unflavored gelatin
 1 cup cold water
 ¾ cup instant nonfat dry milk solids
 1½ cups milk
 ½ cup plus 3 tablespoons sugar
 2 teaspoons vanilla
 1 tablespoon lemon juice
 1 cup sliced strawberries, pureed
   Whole strawberries for garnish

1. Sprinkle gelatin over ½ cup of the water in small bowl; let stand 1 minute to soften.

2. Mix ¼ cup of the milk solids with the milk in medium saucepan. Add gelatin mixture; cook and stir over medium heat until gelatin is dissolved. Add ½ cup of the sugar; cook and stir until dissolved. Stir in vanilla; transfer to medium bowl. Refrigerate, stirring occasionally, until as thick as unbeaten egg white.

3. Beat remaining ½ cup milk solids with remaining ½ cup water in small mixer bowl until slightly thickened. Add lemon juice and remaining 3 tablespoons sugar; beat until as thick as whipped cream. Fold into gelatin mixture.

4. Fold in strawberry puree; transfer to shallow metal pan. Freeze until mixture is frozen 1½ inches in from edges.

5. Transfer to chilled large mixer bowl; beat on high speed until fluffy. Return to metal pan; freeze, covered, until firm. Serve garnished with whole strawberries.

LIME SHERBET

Tiny flecks of grated peel testify to the fresh lime in this refrigerator-tray sherbet. Mound spoonfuls in a footed dish or float a scoop in a tall glass with a favorite chilled carbonated drink.

Makes 12 to 16 servings

 1 envelope unflavored gelatin
 1 cup sugar
 1½ cups water
 6 large egg whites, room temperature
 ¾ cup fresh lime juice
 1 tablespoon grated lime rind
   Lime slices for garnish

1. Mix gelatin with ½ cup of the sugar in small saucepan; stir in water. Cook and stir over medium heat until sugar and gelatin are dissolved; remove from heat.

2. Beat egg whites in large mixer bowl until soft peaks form. Gradually beat in remaining ½ cup sugar; beat until stiff peaks form.

3. Continue beating egg whites while adding warm gelatin mixture in thin stream. Beat in lime juice and lime rind; transfer to shallow metal pan. Freeze, stirring occasionally, until slushy.

4. Transfer to chilled large mixer bowl; beat on high speed until smooth and fluffy. Return to metal pan; freeze, covered, until firm. Serve garnished with lime slices.

Strawberry Ice Milk (top); Lime Sherbet (bottom)

SPICED PECANS

Makes 2 cups

¼ cup butter or margarine
2 cups pecan halves
1½ cups sugar
1 tablespoon ground cloves
1 tablespoon ground cinnamon
1 tablespoon ground nutmeg

1. Melt butter in medium skillet; add pecans. Cook and stir over medium-low heat 20 minutes; drain pecans on paper toweling.

2. Mix remaining ingredients in heavy-duty plastic bag or paper bag. Add warm pecans; shake to coat evenly.

3. Spread out in shallow baking pan to cool completely. Store in airtight containers in refrigerator several weeks or in freezer several months.

NATURAL HOLIDAY SNACK

In the weeks before Christmas, start collecting containers with tight-fitting lids to decorate and fill with this special mixture for gift-giving.

Makes about 4½ cups

1 cup coarsely chopped pecans
1 cup desiccated flaked coconut
1 cup dried apricots, cut into quarters
1 cup raisins
1 cup carob bits or semisweet chocolate morsels

Combine all ingredients in large bowl; toss to mix well. Store in cool place in airtight containers.

CREAM PUFFS WITH ALMOND CREAM

The same recipe for the crusty nonsweet puffs welcomes sweet or savory fillings. For dessert spoon in delicate Almond Cream, ice cream or fresh fruit. At lunch fill with creamed seafood or chicken salad.

Makes 12 puffs

1 cup water
½ cup butter
¼ teaspoon salt
1 cup all-purpose flour
4 large eggs
Almond Cream Filling (recipe follows)

1. Combine water, butter and salt in medium saucepan; heat to full rolling boil. Add flour all at once; beat vigorously until smooth. Cook and stir over medium heat until mixture is very firm and pulls away from sides of pan. Remove from heat.

2. Add eggs, 1 at a time, beating vigorously after each addition until smooth and shiny.

3. Drop dough by scant ¼ cupfuls onto ungreased baking sheets 2 to 3 inches apart. Bake in preheated 400°F oven until golden brown, 35 to 40 minutes. Cool completely on wire rack.

4. Cut off tops of puffs; pull out any filaments of soft dough. Fill with Almond Cream Filling. *(Continued)*

ALMOND CREAM FILLING

½ cup sugar
3 tablespoons cornstarch or ⅓ cup all-purpose flour
¼ teaspoon salt
3 cups milk
3 large egg yolks, beaten
¼ cup chopped toasted blanched almonds
1 teaspoon almond extract
¾ teaspoon vanilla

1. Mix sugar, cornstarch and salt in medium saucepan; stir in milk until smooth. Cook and stir over medium heat until sauce thickens and bubbles for 1 minute; remove from heat.

2. Gradually whisk about ½ of the hot sauce into egg yolks in medium bowl; gradually whisk egg yolk mixture into remaining sauce in pan. Cook, stirring constantly, over low heat until mixture thickens; do not boil.

3. Immediately transfer mixture to medium bowl; stir in remaining ingredients. Refrigerate, covered, until cold.

Makes 3½ to 4 cups

Spiced Pecans (left); Natural Holiday Snack (right)

DIXIE PEANUT BRITTLE

Be sure to use raw peanuts for brittle making. The nuts roast while the buttery candy mixture cooks and bubbles.

Makes about 2½ pounds

  2 cups sugar
  1 cup light corn syrup
  ½ cup water
  ½ teaspoon salt
  4 cups raw shelled peanuts, skins on
  2 tablespoons butter or margarine
  2 teaspoons baking soda

1. Combine sugar, corn syrup, water and salt in large heavy saucepan; heat over high heat to rolling boil.

2. Add peanuts; reduce heat to medium. Cook, stirring constantly, until syrup spins a thread, 293°F on candy thermometer.

(Continued)

3. Stir in butter until melted. Add baking soda; beat rapidly. Pour onto buttered baking sheet, spreading ¼ inch thick; let cool.

4. When cool, break candy into pieces; store in airtight container.

WATSONIA PEACH ICE CREAM

Makes 1 gallon

2½ quarts fresh peach puree
  3 cups half-and-half
  3 cups sugar
  1 can (14 ounces) sweetened condensed milk
  ⅓ cup lemon juice
  ½ teaspoon almond extract

Combine all ingredients in large bowl; mix well. Freeze in ice cream freezer according to manufacturer's directions. Place in freezer to ripen 2 to 3 hours before serving.

Dixie Peanut Brittle

Southern Country Crunch

CHOCOLATE PECAN PIE

*A sinfully rich pie made devastatingly delicious with choco-
late in the filling and a double measure of pecans.*

Makes 8 servings

  4 **large eggs, beaten**
  1 **cup sugar**
  1 **cup dark corn syrup**
  2 **ounces unsweetened chocolate, melted**
  2 **cups pecan halves**
  1 **unbaked 9-inch pie shell**

1. Lightly whisk eggs, sugar and corn syrup in large bowl
until blended; whisk in chocolate. Stir in pecans; pour into
pie shell.

2. Bake in preheated 350°F oven until knife inserted midway between edges and center is withdrawn clean, 30 to 35
minutes. Cool completely on wire rack.

KEY LIME PIE

*The limes grown in the Florida Keys are more yellow than
lime-green in color. The filling in the famous pie is charac-
teristically pale and sweetly tart.*

Makes 8 servings

  2 **to 3 medium or 4 small limes**
  3 **large eggs**
⅓ **cup sugar**
  1 **can (14 ounces) sweetened condensed milk**
  1 **graham cracker crumb pie shell (9-inch), cold**
   Whipped cream, if desired *(Continued)*

1. Grate rind and squeeze juice from limes. Combine lime
rind and juice, the eggs and sugar in medium bowl; whisk
until blended.

2. Stir in milk until smooth; pour into pie shell. Refrigerate
until completely set, several hours. Serve with whipped
cream.

SOUTHERN COUNTRY CRUNCH

*Chewy popcorn balls, caramel-y good with bright orange
kernels of candy corn and big pieces of pecan.*

Makes 16 popcorn balls

  2 **quarts popped popcorn**
½ **cup pecans**
½ **cup candy corn**
24 **caramels (about ½ pound)**
  1 **tablespoon water**
  1 **tablespoon sugar**
   Butter

1. Combine popcorn, pecans and candy corn in large bowl;
toss to mix.

2. Combine caramels, water and sugar in top of double
boiler. Heat over boiling water, stirring frequently, until
melted and smooth, about 20 minutes.

3. Pour caramel mixture over popcorn mixture; toss to coat
evenly. When caramel is cool enough to handle but still
soft, shape mixture with buttered hands into 16 balls, about
½ cup each. Place on buttered baking sheet until set.

To microwave: For Step 2, combine caramels, water and
sugar in microwave-safe 1-quart bowl. Microwave on
HIGH, stirring occasionally, until smooth, about 3 minutes.

Praline Lace Crisps

PRALINE LACE CRISPS

Makes about 2½ dozen

- ⅔ **cup blanched almonds or hazelnuts**
- ½ **cup sugar**
- ½ **cup unsalted butter**
- ⅓ **cup all-purpose flour**
- 2 **tablespoons whipping cream**
- ¼ **teaspoon salt**
- 4 **ounces dark confectionery coating for garnish**

1. Toast nuts in shallow baking pan in preheated 375°F oven until light brown, 5 to 7 minutes; cool completely.

2. Finely grind nuts in food processor or blender.

3. Combine nuts, sugar, butter, flour, cream and salt in small heavy saucepan. Cook, stirring constantly, over low heat, until butter melts and small bubbles form around sides, about 5 minutes. Remove from heat; stir for a few seconds.

4. Lightly grease 2 large baking sheets. Drop batter by rounded teaspoonfuls onto 1 of the baking sheets, leaving about 6 inches space between mounds to allow for spreading. There will be room for only 4 cookies per baking sheet.

(Continued)

5. Bake in center of preheated 375°F oven until golden brown (centers will be paler than edges), 6 to 8 minutes. (Prepare second sheet of batter while first sheet is baking.) Cool cookies on baking sheet on wire rack 45 to 60 seconds. Immediately remove cookies with wide metal spatula from baking sheet and shape before they harden.

6. To shape cookies, work quickly but carefully. If cookies are too hot or too soft to handle, let cool a few seconds longer. If cookies become too hard, return to oven for 15 to 30 seconds to soften. Cookies may be left flat. For taco shape, fold cookies in half over wooden dowel suspended between two cans. For tube shape, roll up cookies jelly-roll-style around handle of wooden spoon. For fluted horn shape, fold in half, then into quarters to form triangle, pressing slightly at point and separating folds at edges. Cool cookies on wire racks.

7. Repeat baking and shaping cookies, 1 sheet at a time, until all batter is used.

8. For garnish, chop confectionery coating; melt in top of double boiler over hot water. Dip edges of cookies into coating; shake off excess. Let cool on parchment or waxed paper until set.

PEANUT COCONUT COOKIES

Makes 3 dozen cookies

½ cup butter or margarine, room temperature
½ cup granulated sugar
½ cup packed brown sugar
1 large egg
1 teaspoon vanilla
1¼ cups sifted flour
1 teaspoon baking powder
1 teaspoon baking soda
½ teaspoon salt
1 cup chopped roasted peanuts
1 cup flaked coconut

1. Beat butter, granulated sugar and brown sugar in large mixer bowl until creamy. Beat in egg and vanilla.

2. Mix flour, baking powder, baking soda and salt in medium bowl. Add to butter mixture; mix well. Stir in peanuts and coconut.

3. Drop batter by teaspoonfuls onto greased baking sheets. Bake in preheated 350°F oven until centers are firm to the touch, 12 to 15 minutes. Remove from baking sheets; cool on wire racks.

CHOCOLATE BANANA CAKE

Rum-fudge frosting covers twin chocolate layers moist and marvelous with a puree of fresh tropical bananas.

Makes 10 to 12 servings

1½ cups mashed very ripe medium bananas
    (about 3)
1⅓ cups sugar
3 large eggs
3 squares (1 ounce each) unsweetened chocolate,
    chopped
½ cup solid vegetable shortening
1 tablespoon rum extract
1¾ cups all-purpose flour
1 teaspoon baking soda
½ teaspoon salt
    Rum-Fudge Frosting (recipe follows)

1. Combine ½ cup of the banana puree, ⅓ cup of the sugar, 1 egg and the chocolate in small saucepan. Cook and stir over medium heat until chocolate is melted; let cool.

2. Beat remaining 1 cup sugar and the shortening in large mixer bowl until light and fluffy; beat in rum extract. Add remaining 2 eggs, 1 at a time, beating mixture well after each addition.

3. Mix flour, baking soda and salt in medium bowl. Add flour mixture, ⅓ at a time, to shortening mixture, alternating with remaining 1 cup bananas, mixing well after each addition. Add chocolate mixture; mix well.

4. Pour batter into 2 greased and floured 9-inch round cake pans. Bake in preheated 350°F oven until wooden pick inserted into center is withdrawn clean, 25 to 30 minutes. Cool in pans on wire racks 10 minutes. Remove from pans; cool completely on racks.

5. Cut paper-thin slice from top of each cake layer so that frosting will soak in. Place 1 layer, cut side up, on plate; spread top with ¼ of the Rum-Fudge Frosting. Top with remaining layer, cut side up. Frost top and sides with remaining frosting.

(Continued)

RUM-FUDGE FROSTING

4 ounces sweet chocolate, chopped
1 tablespoon butter or margarine
3 tablespoons light corn syrup
1 tablespoon rum
½ cup whipping cream

1. Melt chocolate and butter in top of double boiler over hot water; stir in corn syrup and rum until smooth. Let cool to room temperature.

2. Add cream to chocolate mixture; whisk until smooth. Refrigerate until frosting thickens to desired spreading consistency.

Peanut Coconut Cookies

152

Great Lakes to Rolling Farmland
MIDDLE AMERICA

America's heartland contains some of the most productive farmland in the world. From this area, a vast array of cereal, dairy and meat products are shipped to all parts of the nation. Generations of cooks from many lands have utilized these ingredients to create some of America's best recipes.

For the first pioneers and the waves of immigrants who followed them, fertile and abundant land was the main attraction here. Some may have called the climate harsh, but it looked very much like home to the large numbers of Scandinavians and other Europeans who came to settle the Plains States. What farmers first planted here were cereal grains—wheat, corn and rye—and, not surprisingly, bread was a staple in their homes. Baking bread holds an important place in America's homes, and what used to be a necessity is now considered a pleasure.

Scandinavians contributed recipes for such breads as Swedish Limpa, a light rye bread flavored with orange peel, and for Norwegian Yule Loaf, a round, raisin-studded loaf. Germans brought recipes for Dresden Stollen, filled with candied fruit and shaped with a distinctive omelet-like fold, and for Fruit Kuchen, which can be made with any of a variety of fruits depending upon seasonal availability. You'll also find recipes for a classic Almond Cherry Danish and Czech Fruit Kolaches, made with your choice of apricot, prune or peach fillings.

But Midwesterners do not live by bread alone. Not when there are Kansas City strip steaks or Iowa pork chops to cook. Mustard-Broiled Rib Steak, Beef-in-Beer Stew, Onion-Plum Glazed Pork Roast, Beef Rolls with Spaetzle, and Orange Marmalade Ham are just a few examples of how Midwesterners prepare beef

and pork. The region also produces "wursts," or old-world sausages, such as bratwursts, frankfurters and salamis that are among the best anywhere. There is excellent breakfast sausage as well, and a fine recipe—Country Sausage Pinwheels—in which to use it.

Icy cold lakes provide sport fishing much of the year. You can prepare Great Lakes whitefish as they do in Wisconsin, using the recipe for a Door County Fish Boil. Or enjoy trying another freshwater favorite, Baked Walleyes with Orange-Rice Stuffing.

A food unique to this region of the country is wild rice. Grown in northern Minnesota in marshes or commercial paddies and usually harvested by native American Indians, wild rice is considered by many the caviar of grains. In the Wild Rice Chicken Salad and the Ham and Wild Rice Roll-Ups, you'll find two delicious ways to use it.

Eating corn on the cob is one of the joys of summer. Many kinds of corn are grown in the Midwest. In fact, one of America's favorite snacks comes from a variety that builds up so much steam inside when heated that it pops out of its shell all white and fluffy. Delicious buttered and seasoned, "popcorn" can be even better when you make it into Baked Caramel Corn.

Informal parties featuring hearty, rib-sticking food are a tradition in Middle America. The Chicago-style Deep Dish Pizza and the classic Cincinnati Chili are admirably suited for just such occasions. For more formal gatherings, treat your guests to such appetizers as Blue Cheese Dip—prepared with Iowa-, Wisconsin- or Illinois-made blue cheese—or the Sunshine Cheese Ball, coated with another Midwest specialty, sunflower seeds.

Fiesta Fritters

FIESTA FRITTERS

Chili powder and cumin add delightful hotness to Midwestern corn and cheese fritters. The bite-size puffs make tasty nibbling with before-dinner drinks.

Makes about 4 dozen

　1 cup water
　¼ cup unsalted butter
　1¼ teaspoons ground cumin
　1 teaspoon salt
　½ teaspoon chili powder
　1 cup all-purpose flour
　4 large eggs, room temperature
　1 cup canned whole-kernel corn, drained well
　¾ cup shredded Monterey Jack cheese
　　Vegetable oil for frying
　　Coarse (kosher) salt

1. Combine water, butter, cumin, 1 teaspoon salt and the chili powder in heavy 3-quart saucepan. Heat over medium-high heat until butter is melted and water is at full boil. Remove from heat; add flour all at once and beat until smooth.

2. Cook over medium-low heat, stirring constantly, until mixture leaves sides of pan clean and forms ball that holds together, about 2 minutes; remove from heat.

3. Add eggs, 1 at a time, beating with portable electric mixer or beating vigorously with wooden spoon after each addition until mixture is smooth and no longer slippery. Add corn and cheese; mix well.

4. Heat 3 inches of oil in large heavy saucepan over medium-high heat to 365°F. Cover large wire rack with triple thickness of paper toweling.

5. Spoon batter into oil, using about ½ tablespoon per fritter. Cook as many fritters at a time as will fit without crowding. Fry, turning occasionally, until fritters are brown on all sides and a small spurt of batter from inside begins to push to the outside and brown, 3 to 5 minutes. Remove with slotted spoon; drain on paper toweling. Repeat until all batter has been used.

6. Sprinkle fritters with coarse salt; serve immediately. Or, remove paper toweling and place fritters on rack in shallow baking pan and keep warm in 250°F oven, 20 to 30 minutes, if necessary. Fritters will become soggy if held longer.

SAUCY PEANUT BUTTER DIP

Makes about 1 cup

　½ cup peanut butter
　¼ cup mayonnaise
　1 teaspoon curry powder
　　Pinch pepper
　2 to 3 tablespoons milk
　　Crisp raw vegetables or potato chips

1. Mix peanut butter and mayonnaise in small bowl until smooth; stir in curry powder and pepper. Gradually stir in milk until desired dipping consistency.

2. Let stand, covered, at room temperature 1 to 2 hours before serving to blend flavors. Serve with vegetables or chips.

HOMESTYLE BEEF-BARLEY SOUP

A true cold weather friend—warm and sustaining—with enough meat and vegetables to serve as a main course for lunch or supper.

Makes 4 servings

　1 pound beef for stew, cut into ¾-inch cubes
　1 large onion, cut lengthwise into 8 wedges
　1 clove garlic, minced
　2 tablespoons vegetable oil
　1 quart water
　¼ cup pearl barley
　1 teaspoon salt
　⅛ teaspoon pepper
　1 bay leaf
　1 cup sliced carrots
　½ pound mushrooms, sliced
　¼ cup chopped parsley

1. Cook beef, onion and garlic in oil in Dutch oven over medium heat, stirring frequently, until brown, 10 to 15 minutes. Drain and discard excess fat.

2. Stir in water, barley, salt, pepper and bay leaf; heat to boiling. Reduce heat; simmer, covered, 30 minutes.

3. Stir in carrots; simmer, covered, 30 minutes longer. Stir in mushrooms; simmer, covered, until beef and barley are tender, about 30 minutes longer. Remove and discard bay leaf; stir in parsley just before serving.

BANDITO WINGS

"Steal" two servings from a single chicken wing by removing the tip and separating the pieces at the joint. Be generous with the snappy dipping sauce.

Makes 24 pieces

12 **chicken wings**
½ **teaspoon salt**
⅛ **teaspoon pepper**
8 **tablespoons butter or margarine**
2 **tablespoons vegetable oil**
½ **cup taco sauce**
¼ **cup barbecue sauce**
¼ **cup bottled French dressing**
⅛ **teaspoon hot red pepper sauce**
⅛ **teaspoon Worcestershire sauce**
Lime slice for garnish

(Continued)

1. Cut off and discard wing tips at first joint; cut through remaining joint to separate wings into 2 pieces. Sprinkle with salt and pepper.

2. Heat 2 tablespoons of the butter and the oil in large skillet over medium heat until hot. Add ½ of the wings; cook until golden and tender, 8 to 10 minutes per side. Remove to shallow baking pan. Repeat with remaining wings.

3. Melt remaining 6 tablespoons butter in 1-quart saucepan; whisk in remaining ingredients except lime slice.

4. Arrange wings in single layer in baking pan; brush with enough of the taco sauce mixture to coat evenly.

5. Bake in preheated 300°F oven until hot, 5 to 8 minutes. Transfer wings to serving plate; serve with remaining taco sauce mixture, garnished with lime slice, for dipping.

Bandito Wings

OAT 'N' WHEAT TREATS

An unusual cracker to serve alone as a snack or to team with sliced fresh fruit or ice cream.

Makes 35 pieces

- **2 cups quick-cooking oats**
- **½ cup sliced almonds**
- **½ cup wheat germ**
- **2 tablespoons sesame seeds**
- **1 cup soybean-oil margarine**
- **1 cup packed brown sugar**
- **35 square stone-ground wheat crackers**

1. Combine oats, almonds, wheat germ and sesame seeds in large bowl; mix well.

2. Combine margarine and sugar in large saucepan; heat over medium heat to boiling. Reduce heat to medium-low; boil, stirring constantly, 3 minutes. Remove from heat.

3. Quickly add oats mixture to saucepan all at once and fold in. Spread mixture evenly over each cracker; arrange crackers close together in single layer on baking sheets.

4. Bake in preheated 350°F oven 10 minutes. Serve warm or cool completely.

LIGHT 'N' EASY CAULIFLOWER SOUP

Robust, filling and surprisingly low in calories. For a smoother texture, try pureeing the soup in a blender or food processor.

Makes 6 to 8 servings

- **½ large head cauliflower, separated into flowerets, sliced**
- **1 medium onion, sliced**
- **3 cups water**
- **3 vegetable bouillon cubes**
- **½ teaspoon salt**
- **½ cup nonfat dry milk powder**
- **4 ounces Cheddar cheese, shredded**

1. Combine cauliflower, onion, water, bouillon cubes and salt in large saucepan; heat over medium heat to boiling. Reduce heat; simmer, covered, until cauliflower is tender, about 15 minutes.

2. Stir in dry milk powder. Stir in cheese; cook and stir until cheese is melted. Serve as is, or process in blender or food processor until smooth.

Oat 'n' Wheat Treats

SUNSHINE CHEESE BALL

Sunflowers are not just a wildflower. In North Dakota, thousands of acres of these enormous blossoms are cultivated as a source of polyunsaturated vegetable oil and for their seeds, which form the crunchy coating for this low-calorie appetizer.

Makes 16 to 18 servings

 2 packages (8 ounces each) Neufchatel or cream cheese, room temperature
 1 can (8 ounces) juice-packed crushed pineapple, drained well
 6 tablespoons diced red or green bell pepper
 3 tablespoons minced red onion
  Salt and ground pepper to taste
 ½ cup plus 1 tablespoon unsalted sunflower seeds
  Melba toast or crackers

1. Combine cream cheese and pineapple in small mixer bowl; beat until blended. Stir in bell pepper, onion, salt and ground pepper.

2. Shape into ball; roll in sunflower seeds to coat. Refrigerate, covered, until serving time. Serve with melba toast.

Sunshine Cheese Ball

SALMON SPREAD

Get a head start on party preparations with this easy-to-make spread. It's refrigerated overnight, allowing the flavors to mingle deliciously.

Makes about 3 cups

 1 can (16 ounces) red salmon
 1 package (8 ounces) cream cheese, room temperature
 ½ cup finely chopped pecans
 2 tablespoons liquid smoke
 2 tablespoons lemon juice
 2 tablespoons grated onion
 1 tablespoon prepared horseradish
 1 tablespoon minced parsley
  Crackers

1. Drain salmon; remove and discard bones and skin.

2. Combine salmon and cream cheese in medium bowl; mix well. Add ¼ cup of the pecans, the liquid smoke, lemon juice, onion, horseradish, and parsley; mix well. Refrigerate, covered, overnight.

3. Sprinkle the remaining ¼ cup pecans on top of spread before serving; serve with crackers.

IMPOSSIBLE REUBEN HORS D'OEUVRES

Here's a hot appetizer that resembles a quiche, but makes its own crust. By increasing the amount of batter, you can turn it into a brunch dish.

Makes 8 dozen

 2 packages (2½ to 3 ounces each) thinly sliced corned beef, finely chopped
 1 can (8 ounces) sauerkraut, drained, chopped
 1½ cups shredded Swiss cheese
 1 cup buttermilk baking mix
 1 cup milk
 2 large eggs, beaten
 1 tablespoon chopped parsley

(Continued)

1. Combine corned beef, sauerkraut and cheese in medium bowl; toss to mix. Spread in greased 13 × 9 × 2-inch baking pan.

2. Combine remaining ingredients in medium bowl; stir to mix. Pour evenly over corned beef mixture.

3. Bake in preheated 350°F oven until center is firm to touch, 20 to 25 minutes. Cool slightly; cut into 1-inch squares.

Note: For a more substantial brunch dish, increase baking mix and milk to 1½ cups; increase eggs to 3. Increase baking time by 5 to 10 minutes; cut into 8 pieces.

BEEFY SPINACH DIP

The serving bowl for this well-seasoned mixture is a hollowed-out loaf of bread. Dark rye bread will show off the creaminess of the dip, and the bread taken from the center yields tasty cubes to use for dippers.

Makes 10 to 12 servings

 1 package (10 ounces) frozen chopped spinach, thawed, drained well
 1 cup mayonnaise
 1 cup sour cream
 1 package (3 ounces) dried beef, finely chopped
 1 package (3 ounces) cream cheese, room temperature
 ½ cup chopped green onions
 2 teaspoons dried dill weed
 2 teaspoons seasoned salt
 1 round loaf white or dark bread, unsliced

1. Combine all ingredients except bread in large bowl; mix well. Refrigerate, covered, at least 3 hours.

2. At serving time, cut 1-inch slice off top of bread; hollow out center, leaving 1-inch-thick shell. Cut bread removed from center and the top slice into cubes.

3. Spoon spinach mixture into bread shell. Serve with bread cubes for dipping.

Cold Cherry Soup

COLD CHERRY SOUP

A splendid warm-weather offering that can be served either as a first course or as a dessert.

8 to 12 servings

  3 **pounds pitted tart cherries (canned, frozen or fresh)**
½ **cup orange juice**
   Water
  3 **tablespoons cornstarch**
½ **cup Riesling wine**
  1 **teaspoon ground cinnamon**
⅛ **teaspoon ground allspice**
¼ **cup packed brown sugar**
  1 **cup whipping cream**
  1 **to 1½ cups sour cream**
   Lemon slices and parsley leaves for garnish

1. Drain cherries, if using canned or frozen, reserving liquid. Process cherries in blender until finely chopped; drain, reserving liquid.

2. Measure reserved cherry liquid; add orange juice and enough water to make 2 quarts. Transfer to large saucepan.

3. Mix cornstarch with ½ cup of the cherry liquid in small bowl until smooth; stir into saucepan. Stir in wine, cinnamon, allspice and chopped cherries. Cook, stirring constantly, over medium heat until mixture thickens and bubbles for 3 minutes.

4. Remove from heat; stir in sugar. Transfer to large bowl. Gradually stir in whipping cream; refrigerate, covered, until cold, several hours.

5. Serve soup with sour cream; garnish with lemon slices and parsley.

Note: *To serve as a dessert, increase sugar to taste; omit sour cream and garnish. Serve with sweetened whipped cream sprinkled with ground nutmeg.*

ORIENTAL CHICKEN AND CORN SOUP

It's the thin slices of fresh ginger root cooked with the chicken broth that give the soup such a tantalizing flavor.

Makes 6 to 8 servings

6¾ **cups water**
  2 **pounds chicken pieces***
  6 **whole peppercorns**
1½ **teaspoons salt**
  2 **parsley sprigs, if desired**
  1 **medium yellow onion, thinly sliced**
  1 **piece (about 1-inch cube) fresh ginger root, pared, thinly sliced**
  1 **can (16 ounces) cream-style corn, undrained**
  4 **green onions, finely chopped**
  2 **teaspoons chicken bouillon granules**
  1 **teaspoon sesame oil**
½ **teaspoon grated pared fresh ginger root**
⅛ **teaspoon ground pepper**
¼ **cup cornstarch**
  2 **large egg whites**
  2 **ounces cooked ham, cut into 1½ × ⅛ × ⅛-inch pieces**
  4 **green onions, thinly sliced**

1. Combine 6 cups of the water, the chicken, peppercorns, 1 teaspoon of the salt and the parsley in 5-quart Dutch oven. Stir in yellow onion and sliced ginger. Heat over medium heat to boiling; reduce heat. Simmer, skimming surface occasionally, 1½ hours.

2. Strain chicken broth through sieve. Remove chicken to plate; discard remaining solids. When cool enough to handle, shred enough chicken meat to measure 1 cup. Reserve remaining cooked chicken for other use.

3. Combine broth, corn, chopped green onions, bouillon, sesame oil, grated ginger, ground pepper and remaining ½ teaspoon salt in Dutch oven; heat over medium heat to boiling. *(Continued)*

4. Mix cornstarch and ½ cup of the remaining water in small bowl; stir into soup. Cook and stir until soup thickens and bubbles for 3 minutes.

5. Lightly beat egg whites and remaining ¼ cup water with fork in small bowl. Slowly drizzle egg whites into soup while stirring soup vigorously. Stir in 1 cup chicken and the ham.

6. Pour soup into bowls; sprinkle with sliced green onions.

***Note:** Any chicken pieces can be used, including necks and backs. Enough meat should be on the pieces to yield 1 cup shredded cooked chicken needed for the soup.*

PEANUT HOT SAUCE

Makes about 1 cup

⅔ cup peanut butter
1 tablespoon packed brown sugar
½ teaspoon ground red pepper
¼ cup soy sauce
   Beef or chicken fondue or grilled pork or chicken

Mix peanut butter, sugar and pepper in small bowl; gradually stir in soy sauce until smooth. Serve as dipping sauce for fondue or grilled meat.

SWEET GREEN PEA SOUP

Leeks add a mild onion flavor to this creamy soup for all seasons.

Makes 4 to 6 servings

¾ cup sliced leeks, white part only
1 clove garlic, minced
1 tablespoon butter or margarine
2 cans (17 ounces each) unsalted sweet peas, undrained
1 cup milk or half-and-half
½ cup chicken broth
½ cup chopped parsley
1 tablespoon plus 1 teaspoon fresh lemon juice
½ teaspoon dried marjoram, crumbled
   Pinch ground nutmeg
   Salt and pepper to taste
   Parsley sprigs for garnish

1. Saute leeks and garlic in butter in large saucepan over medium heat until soft, about 6 minutes.

2. Combine leek mixture, 1 can of the peas and the milk in blender container; process until smooth. Transfer to saucepan.

3. Combine remaining 1 can peas, the broth, parsley, lemon juice, marjoram and nutmeg in blender; process until smooth. Add to saucepan.

4. Heat soup over medium-low heat to simmering; reduce heat to very low. Cook, stirring occasionally, 15 minutes; do not boil. Stir in salt and pepper; serve garnished with parsley.

To Microwave: Microwave butter in large microwave-safe bowl on HIGH until melted, about 1 minute. Stir in leeks and garlic; microwave on HIGH 2 minutes. Prepare soup as in Steps 2 and 3 above. Microwave soup in bowl, covered, on HIGH 5 minutes; stir. Microwave 5 minutes longer; stir and serve.

BLUE CHEESE DIP

Caves provide the temperature and humidity ideal for developing the streaks of blue-green mold in blue cheese. Combined with other dairy ingredients, it makes an appetizing dip that can also be used as a salad dressing or served on baked potatoes.

Makes 4 cups

2 cups cottage cheese
1 cup (4 ounces) crumbled blue cheese
2 tablespoons chopped green onion
2 tablespoons fresh lemon juice
1 teaspoon Worcestershire sauce
¼ teaspoon garlic salt
1 cup plain yogurt

Combine all ingredients except yogurt in blender container; process until mixed and almost smooth. Transfer to medium bowl; fold in yogurt. Refrigerate, covered, at least 1 hour to blend flavors.

Sweet Green Pea Soup

EASY LASAGNE

Cook the lasagne noodles al dente, *which means "to the tooth"—the pasta is still slightly firm when you bite into it.*

Makes 8 servings

1½ **pounds ground beef**
  1 **jar (48 ounces) chunky garden-style spaghetti sauce**
  2 **pounds ricotta cheese**
  3 **cups shredded mozzarella cheese**
  ½ **cup grated Parmesan cheese**
  3 **large eggs**
  1 **tablespoon chopped parsley**
  ¾ **teaspoon salt**
  ¼ **teaspoon pepper**
  1 **package (16 ounces) curly-edge lasagne noodles, cooked, drained**

1. Cook and stir beef in large skillet over medium heat until brown and finely crumbled, about 10 minutes. Drain and discard fat.

2. Stir in spaghetti sauce; heat, covered, to simmering. Remove from heat.

3. Combine ricotta cheese, 2 cups of the mozzarella cheese, ¼ cup of the Parmesan cheese, the eggs, parsley, salt and pepper in large bowl; mix well.

4. Spread 1 cup of the meat sauce in 13 × 9 × 2½-inch baking dish; top with 4 of the noodles, then with ⅓ of the cheese mixture. Repeat meat sauce, noodle and cheese layers 2 more times. Top with 4 noodles; spread remaining meat sauce over noodles; sprinkle with remaining ¼ cup Parmesan cheese.

5. Bake, covered, in preheated 350°F oven 45 minutes. Uncover; sprinkle evenly with remaining 1 cup mozzarella cheese. Bake until cheese is melted, about 10 minutes longer. Let stand 10 minutes before serving.

GROUND BEEF STUFFED ACORN SQUASH

Makes 4 servings

  2 **large acorn squash, cut lengthwise into halves, seeded**
  1 **pound extra lean ground beef**
  1 **small onion, chopped**
  ½ **cup chopped celery**
  1 **tart apple, cored, chopped**
  1 **cup cooked rice**
  ¼ **cup sunflower seeds**
  5 **teaspoons packed brown sugar**
1½ **teaspoons salt**
  1 **teaspoon curry powder**
  1 **large egg, beaten**
  4 **teaspoons butter or margarine**

1. Place squash, cut side down, in 13 × 9 × 2-inch baking pan; add ½ inch water to pan. Bake in preheated 375°F oven until squash can be pierced easily with skewer but not until limp, 45 to 55 minutes.

2. Meanwhile, cook and stir beef in large skillet over medium-high heat until brown, about 5 minutes. Stir in onion and celery; cook until vegetables are tender, about 4 minutes. Stir in apple; cook 1 minute longer.

(Continued)

Ground Beef Stuffed Acorn Squash

3. Stir rice, sunflower seeds, 1 teaspoon of the brown sugar, 1 teaspoon of the salt, the curry powder and egg into the meat mixture. Cook and stir until hot throughout, about 2 minutes longer.

4. Drain squash well; place, cut side up, in baking pan. Spoon 1 teaspoon each brown sugar and butter into center of each squash half; sprinkle with remaining ½ teaspoon salt. Spoon meat mixture into squash, dividing evenly and packing slightly.

5. Bake at 375°F until hot throughout, 5 to 10 minutes longer.

BEEF AND SPINACH ROULADES

Makes 6 servings

1½ **pounds beef round or sirloin steak**
  2 **cups Cabernet Sauvignon wine**
  5 **shallots, finely chopped**
  3 **tablespoons chopped parsley**
  2 **teaspoons chopped fresh rosemary or ½ teaspoon dried rosemary, crumbled**
  1 **teaspoon finely chopped garlic**
  6 **tablespoons butter**
1½ **cups cooked spinach, squeezed dry, chopped**
  ¼ **cup ricotta cheese**
  3 **tablespoons grated Romano cheese**
  1 **large egg**
  ½ **teaspoon dried oregano, crumbled**
  ½ **teaspoon salt**
  ¼ **teaspoon ground cumin**
  ⅛ **teaspoon pepper**
  8 **to 10 ounces small pearl onions, peeled**
   All-purpose flour
  1 **tablespoon tomato paste**
  ½ **cup beef stock**
   Cooked wild rice

1. Combine steak and wine in large bowl; refrigerate, covered, overnight.

2. Saute shallots, parsley, rosemary and garlic in 3 tablespoons of the butter in medium skillet over medium heat until soft, about 3 minutes. Stir in spinach; saute over low heat until dry, 3 to 5 minutes.

3. Combine spinach mixture, ricotta cheese, Romano cheese, egg, oregano, salt, cumin and pepper in medium bowl; mix well.

4. Drain steak, reserving marinade. Cut steak into thin pieces, 6 × 3 inches. Spread 2 tablespoons of the spinach mixture on each piece; roll up and secure with wooden pick.

5. Saute onions in remaining 3 tablespoons butter in large skillet over medium heat until light brown, about 6 minutes; remove with slotted spoon to 12 × 9-inch baking dish.

6. Roll beef rolls in flour to coat lightly. Cook in butter in skillet, turning occasionally, until brown, about 10 minutes; remove to baking dish.

7. Mix 1 tablespoon flour with ¼ cup of the reserved marinade in small bowl until smooth; stir into skillet. Heat to boiling; reduce heat. Cook and stir until mixture bubbles for 1 minute; stir in tomato paste. Stir in stock until smooth; stir in remaining reserved marinade. Pour over meat and onions in baking dish.

8. Bake, covered, in preheated 325°F oven until meat is very tender, 1 to 1½ hours. Serve over wild rice.

Beef Rolls with Spaetzle

BEEF ROLLS WITH SPAETZLE

Spaetzle are tiny dumplings that look like noodles. German cooks traditionally serve them as an accompaniment to braised meats with spicy marinades or gravies.

Makes 6 servings

2½ pounds thinly cut round steak
  2 slices pumpernickel bread
  1 cup chopped onions
  4 tablespoons butter or margarine
½ pound ground pork
¼ cup chopped parsley
  2 tablespoons drained capers
¼ teaspoon dried marjoram, crumbled
¼ teaspoon salt
¼ teaspoon pepper
  2 to 3 tablespoons Dijon-style mustard
  2 dill pickles, each cut lengthwise into 8 slices
    All-purpose flour
  2 carrots, chopped
  2 stalks celery, chopped
  2 cups beef stock
  1 cup dry red wine
    Spaetzle (recipe follows)
    Parsley sprigs for garnish

1. Pound meat with mallet until ⅛ inch thick; cut meat into 5 × 3-inch pieces. There should be 12 to 15 pieces.

2. Process bread in blender to fine crumbs.

3. Saute ½ cup of the onion in 1 tablespoon of the butter in Dutch oven over medium heat until tender, about 4 minutes. Add pork; cook and stir until brown and finely crumbled, about 8 minutes.

4. Combine pork mixture, bread crumbs, chopped parsley, capers, marjoram, salt and pepper in medium bowl; mix well.

(Continued)

5. Spread each beef slice with a little mustard; place 1 heaping tablespoon of the pork mixture and 1 pickle slice in center of each. Roll up tightly; fasten with wooden picks. Roll beef rolls in flour to coat; shake off excess.

6. Cook beef rolls in remaining 3 tablespoons butter in Dutch oven until brown, about 10 minutes; remove from pan.

7. Saute remaining ½ cup onion, the carrots and celery in drippings until soft, about 5 minutes. Place beef rolls on top of vegetables; add stock and wine. Heat to boiling; reduce heat. Simmer, covered, until meat is tender, 1 to 1½ hours.

8. Place beef rolls on top of spaetzle on platter; discard wooden picks. Pour sauce over beef. Garnish with parsley sprigs.

SPAETZLE

2½ cups all-purpose flour
  2 tablespoons plus 1 teaspoon salt
  2 large eggs
    Water
  3 tablespoons butter or margarine, melted

1. Mix flour and 1 teaspoon of the salt in medium bowl. Beat eggs and ½ cup water in small bowl; add to flour mixture and mix well. Knead dough on floured surface until smooth; let rest 5 minutes.

2. Roll out dough on lightly floured surface ⅛ inch thick. Using sharp knife, cut dough into thin slivers.

3. Heat 6 quarts water in large kettle to boiling; add the remaining 2 tablespoons salt. Drop dough slivers into boiling water; cook over high heat until spaetzle float to the surface, 5 to 10 minutes.

4. Remove spaetzle with slotted spoon to colander; drain well. Transfer to heated platter; toss with butter.

Makes 6 servings

BARBECUE STEAK OUT

Quick steak sandwiches topped with cheese and a spunky sauce. Carve steak into thin slices and pile onto crusty hard rolls.

Makes 8 servings

1 can (8 ounces) tomato sauce
¾ cup water
½ cup dry red wine
⅓ cup packed brown sugar
1 envelope beefy onion or onion soup mix
1 teaspoon chili powder
1 beef flank steak (about 2 pounds)
8 long hard rolls, split
8 slices American cheese, cut into halves
1 green bell pepper, cut into thin rings

1. Combine tomato sauce, water, wine, sugar, soup mix and chili powder in medium saucepan; mix well. Heat to boiling; reduce heat. Simmer, stirring occasionally, 10 minutes. Reserve 1¼ cups of the barbecue sauce.

2. Grill steak over hot coals or in preheated broiler, turning and basting frequently with remaining barbecue sauce, until desired doneness, 8 to 12 minutes for rare.

3. Cut steak across the grain into thin slices. Place slices on rolls; top with cheese and green pepper. Serve with heated reserved sauce.

POT ROAST WITH VEGETABLES

Get more than one meal from the same roast by planning ahead. Second-day possibilities include a biscuit-topped stew. Cube meat and simmer with gravy and vegetables. Bake refrigerator biscuits separately or on top of bubbling stew.

Makes 4 to 6 servings

1 beef chuck roast (3 pounds)
2 tablespoons vegetable oil
1 teaspoon salt
⅛ teaspoon pepper
¼ cup water
6 medium carrots, pared, cut into 1-inch pieces
4 medium potatoes, pared, cut into quarters
4 stalks celery, cut into 1-inch pieces
1 medium onion, cut into quarters

1. Cook beef in oil in Dutch oven over medium heat until brown on all sides, about 20 minutes. Sprinkle with salt and pepper; add water.

2. Simmer, covered, turning once, until beef is almost tender, about 1½ hours.

3. Add vegetables; cook, covered, over low heat until meat and vegetables are fork-tender, about 30 minutes longer.

Barbecue Steak Out

Parsleyed Oven Pot Roast

SUCCULENT SOUR CREAM POT ROAST

Now that sour cream is produced with dependable smoothness and flavor, it is a cooking staple across the nation. To prevent its curdling in sauces, keep the temperature of the mixture below boiling.

Makes 8 to 10 servings

- 1 boneless rolled beef chuck roast (4 to 5 pounds)
- 2 tablespoons all-purpose flour
- 1 tablespoon vegetable oil
- ¾ cup water
- ½ cup tomato sauce
- 2 small onions, chopped
- 1 clove garlic, minced
- 1 bay leaf
- ⅛ teaspoon dried thyme, crumbled
- ½ teaspoon salt
- ¼ teaspoon pepper
- ½ pound mushrooms, sliced
- 2 tablespoons butter
- 1 cup sour cream
  Hot buttered noodles
  Paprika

1. Sprinkle beef with flour to coat lightly; cook in oil in Dutch oven over medium heat until brown on all sides, about 20 minutes. Remove from pan.

2. Add water, tomato sauce, onions, garlic, bay leaf and thyme to Dutch oven; place rack in pan. Place beef on rack; sprinkle with salt and pepper. *(Continued)*

3. Roast, covered, in preheated 325°F oven until beef is tender, about 3½ hours.

4. Saute mushrooms in butter in medium skillet over medium heat until golden, about 8 minutes.

5. Remove beef to serving platter; keep warm. Remove rack from pan; remove and discard bay leaf.

6. Add mushrooms and sour cream to cooking liquid; cook and stir over medium heat until hot. Do not boil.

7. Cut beef into slices; serve with noodles sprinkled with paprika. Pass sour cream sauce separately.

PARSLEYED OVEN POT ROAST

Makes 8 to 12 servings

- 2 teaspoons salt
- ¼ teaspoon pepper
- 1 beef bottom round roast (4½ to 5 pounds)
- 1 can (28 ounces) tomatoes, undrained, chopped
- ¾ cup dry red wine
- ¼ cup instant minced onion
- 2 tablespoons parsley flakes
- 1 bay leaf
- ½ teaspoon instant minced garlic
- 6 medium carrots, pared, sliced
- 1½ pounds zucchini, cut into 1-inch chunks
- 2 cups cherry tomatoes, pierced with fork

(Continued)

1. Rub 1½ teaspoons of the salt and the pepper into meat; place in Dutch oven. Cook in preheated 450°F oven until brown on all sides, 50 to 60 minutes. Drain off fat.

2. Combine canned tomatoes, wine, onion, parsley, bay leaf, garlic and remaining ½ teaspoon salt in medium bowl. Pour over meat.

3. Reduce oven setting to 350°F. Cook meat, covered, 1½ hours. Add carrots; continue cooking until meat is firm-tender, 45 to 60 minutes. Add zucchini; continue cooking until meat is very tender, 20 to 30 minutes. Add cherry tomatoes; cook 5 minutes longer.

4. Remove meat to serving platter. Remove vegetables with slotted spoon; arrange around meat. Degrease cooking liquid; cook, uncovered, over high heat until slightly thickened, about 10 minutes. Serve with meat.

STUFFED CABBAGE LEAVES

Cooks of every nationality who grow cabbage in their homeland wrap the leaves around meat and vegetable stuffings. This central European version is spiced with caraway seeds and simmered in tomato sauce.

Makes 6 to 8 servings

  1 **large head green cabbage, cored**
    Boiling water
  1 **pound ground beef**
 ¾ **cup cooked rice**
  1 **medium onion, grated**
  1 **small potato, pared, shredded**
 ½ **cup tomato juice**
1½ **teaspoons salt**
  1 **teaspoon caraway seeds**
 ⅛ **teaspoon pepper**
 ⅔ **cup beef broth**
  1 **tablespoon vegetable oil**
  3 **medium tomatoes, coarsely chopped**
  1 **can (4 ounces) tomato sauce**
  1 **tablespoon sugar**

1. Place cabbage in large saucepan; add boiling water to cover. Cover pan; let stand until cool. Drain cabbage and separate leaves.

2. Cook and stir beef in large skillet over medium heat until brown, about 10 minutes. Stir in rice, onion, potato, tomato juice, 1 teaspoon of the salt, the caraway seeds and pepper.

3. Spoon about 2 tablespoons beef mixture onto each cabbage leaf (overlap smaller leaves to make use of entire cabbage, if necessary). Fold sides of leaf over filling, then roll up loosely.

4. Place rolls, seam sides down, on rack in Dutch oven. Add broth and oil; heat to boiling. Reduce heat; simmer, covered, 30 minutes.

5. Remove cabbage rolls to plate; remove rack from pan. Add tomatoes, tomato sauce, sugar and remaining ½ teaspoon salt to cooking liquid in pan; simmer, uncovered, 5 minutes.

6. Return cabbage rolls to pan, seam sides down; simmer, covered, 30 minutes.

MUSTARD-BROILED RIB STEAK

Wrapping the tender boneless steaks with bacon is an option worth trying, whether you do the broiling in the kitchen or outdoors over the coals.

Makes 2 servings

  2 **slices bacon, if desired**
  2 **boneless rib steaks, ¾ to 1 inch thick**
  1 **tablespoon butter or margarine, melted**
  1 **teaspoon Dijon-style mustard**
 ¼ **teaspoon pepper**
   Cherry tomatoes and parsley sprigs for garnish
   French-fried potatoes, if desired

1. Wrap bacon around sides of steaks; fasten with wooden picks.

2. Mix butter, mustard and pepper in small bowl; brush mixture evenly over both sides of steaks.

3. Broil steaks in preheated broiler about 4 inches from heat source, turning once, to desired degree of doneness, 8 to 10 minutes for rare. Garnish with cherry tomatoes and parsley; serve with potatoes.

Mustard-Broiled Rib Steak

Vegetable Meatloaf

VEGETABLE MEATLOAF

Stretch ground beef by adding shredded fresh vegetables; they add juiciness and nutrients to this family favorite.

Makes 6 to 8 servings

1½ pounds extra lean ground beef
　3 medium carrots, shredded (about 1½ cups)
　3 small potatoes, pared, shredded (about 1½ cups)
　1 medium onion, chopped
　2 large eggs
⅔ cup fine dry breadcrumbs
　2 teaspoons salt
¾ teaspoon dried basil, crumbled
½ teaspoon pepper
　2 tablespoons butter or margarine, melted
　　Cherry tomato halves for garnish

1. Combine beef, carrots, potatoes, onion, eggs, ⅓ cup of the breadcrumbs, 1½ teaspoons of the salt, the basil and pepper in large bowl; mix well. Pack mixture into greased 8½×4½×2½-inch loaf pan.

2. Mix remaining ⅓ cup breadcrumbs, ½ teaspoon salt and the butter in small bowl; sprinkle evenly over meatloaf.

3. Bake in preheated 375°F oven until meat pulls away from sides of pan, 1 to 1½ hours. Let stand 5 minutes before slicing. Garnish with cherry tomatoes.

CRANBERRY HAM BURGERS

Cranberry mixtures lend a delicious tartness to a basting sauce for burgers made from ground ham and grilled over charcoal.

Makes 6 burgers

　1 jar (14 ounces) cranberry-orange sauce
　1 cup chopped onion
½ cup dry white wine
½ cup soy sauce
　2 tablespoons vegetable oil
　2 teaspoons ground ginger
　2 teaspoons dry mustard
　1 clove garlic, minced
　2 pounds cooked ham, ground
　1 small pineapple, pared, cored, cut into ½-inch-thick slices
　　Lettuce leaves
　　Onion slices

1. For sauce, combine cranberry-orange sauce, chopped onion, wine, soy sauce, oil, ginger, mustard and garlic in medium bowl; mix well.

2. Shape ham into 6 even patties. Grill over hot coals or broil, basting frequently with sauce, turning once, until delicately browned. Grill or broil pineapple until tender.

3. Place pineapple on top of lettuce and onion slices on individual plates; top with burgers. Heat remaining sauce; spoon over burgers.

STUFFED PORK CHOPS

Makes 4 servings

1 small onion, chopped
1 clove garlic, minced
3½ tablespoons butter or margarine
1 cup soft rye breadcrumbs
1 large egg, lightly beaten
2 tablespoons minced parsley
2 tablespoons water
½ teaspoon salt
½ teaspoon pepper
½ teaspoon caraway seeds
4 rib or loin pork chops, 1¼ inches thick
   Salt
   Pepper
   All-purpose flour
⅔ cup boiling chicken stock or water

1. Saute onion and garlic in 1½ tablespoons of the butter in large skillet until golden, about 6 minutes. Combine with breadcrumbs, egg, parsley, 2 tablespoons water, ½ teaspoon each salt and pepper and the caraway seeds in medium bowl; mix well.

2. Cut pocket in each pork chop for stuffing. Fill pockets with stuffing mixture; skewer closed with wooden picks. Sprinkle chops with salt and pepper; dust with flour to coat lightly.

3. Cook chops in remaining 2 tablespoons butter in large skillet until brown, 6 to 8 minutes per side; remove to shallow baking pan.

4. Add boiling stock to pan; cover pan. Bake in preheated 350°F oven until pork is tender, about 1 hour.

STUFFED MEXICAN MEATLOAF

Cheddar cheese is only part of the inside story of this taco-seasoned beef loaf. The other part is tangy dairy sour cream. More cheese goes on top of the loaf, along with a garnish of avocado slices and cherry tomatoes.

Makes 8 servings

2 pounds ground beef chuck
1 can (8 ounces) tomato sauce
½ cup plus 2 tablespoons taco seasoning mix
⅓ cup chopped green bell pepper
⅓ cup finely chopped onion
1½ slices white bread, torn into crumbs
1 large egg, slightly beaten
2 cups shredded Cheddar cheese
½ cup sour cream
3 to 5 Cheddar cheese slices, cut diagonally into halves
   Avocado slices and cherry tomatoes for garnish

1. Combine beef, tomato sauce, taco seasoning mix, pepper, onion, breadcrumbs and egg in large bowl; mix well. Mix shredded cheese and sour cream in small bowl.

2. Place ½ the meat mixture in 9 × 5 × 3-inch loaf pan. Press deep well lengthwise in center of meat; spoon cheese mixture into well. Top with remaining meat mixture, pressing edges to seal well.

3. Bake in preheated 375°F oven 1½ to 1¾ hours. Pour off drippings; unmold meatloaf onto platter.

4. Top meatloaf with cheese triangles; let stand 8 to 10 minutes. Garnish with avocado and cherry tomatoes.

PORK OSCAR

Makes 4 servings

1 package (10 ounces) frozen asparagus spears
¼ pound crab legs, cooked, shelled, room temperature
4 butterflied boneless pork loin chops, ½ inch thick
   Pepper to taste
⅓ cup all-purpose flour
2 tablespoons butter or margarine
2 tablespoons vegetable oil
½ cup dry white wine
2 tablespoons fresh lemon juice
   Blender Bearnaise Sauce (recipe follows)
   Steamed snow peas, buttered baby carrots and fresh tarragon sprigs for garnish

1. Cook asparagus according to package directions; drain and keep warm. Cut crab into 1½-inch pieces.

2. Sprinkle pork with pepper. Dip in flour to coat lightly; shake off excess. Cook pork in butter and oil in large skillet over medium heat until brown, about 3 minutes per side.

3. Add wine and lemon juice to skillet; simmer, covered, until pork is tender, 10 to 15 minutes.

4. Place pork on individual serving plates; top with Bearnaise Sauce, asparagus and crab, dividing evenly. Garnish with snow peas, carrots and tarragon.

BLENDER BEARNAISE SAUCE

2 large egg yolks, room temperature
1 tablespoon fresh lemon juice
1 teaspoon tarragon-white wine vinegar
½ teaspoon dried tarragon, crumbled
¾ cup butter or margarine, melted, hot (not boiling)

1. Combine egg yolks, lemon juice, vinegar, and tarragon in blender container; process until mixed, about 5 seconds.

2. With motor running on low speed, gradually add ¼ cup of the butter in slow steady stream. Increase speed to high; slowly add remaining ½ cup butter. Process until thick. Keep warm in bowl over hot water.

Makes about 1 cup

Pork Oscar

Beef Bavarian

BEEF BAVARIAN

A wonderful cold-weather main dish of meat and vegetables simmered in beer.

Makes 4 to 6 servings

1½ pounds beef round steak
  2 tablespoons cornstarch
1½ teaspoons salt
 ¼ teaspoon pepper
 ¼ teaspoon garlic powder
  2 tablespoons vegetable oil
  1 large onion, sliced
  1 can (12 ounces) beer
  1 cup beef broth
 ¼ teaspoon hot red pepper sauce
  1 tablespoon packed brown sugar
  4 large carrots, sliced
  4 to 6 cups hot cooked rice

1. Cut beef across the grain into thin slices; pound with meat mallet to tenderize. Cut into 1-inch-wide strips; place in large bowl.

2. Mix cornstarch, salt, pepper, and garlic powder in small bowl. Sprinkle over beef; toss to coat evenly.

3. Cook beef in oil in large skillet over medium heat, stirring occasionally, until brown. Stir in onion; cook and stir 2 or 3 minutes longer.

4. Stir in beer, broth, red pepper sauce and sugar; heat to boiling. Reduce heat; simmer, covered, 15 minutes.

5. Stir in carrots; simmer until meat is tender, about 15 minutes longer. Serve over rice.

GINGER-ORANGE BEEF

An ever-increasing interest in Oriental cooking has introduced stir-frying to Midwest kitchens and snow peas to the backyard garden and local supermarket.

Makes 4 servings

  1 pound beef top round steak, trimmed
 ¼ cup soy sauce
1½ tablespoons grated orange rind
  1 tablespoon grated fresh ginger root
1½ teaspoons cornstarch
  1 teaspoon ground cinnamon
  2 tablespoons vegetable oil
  1 carrot, sliced
  1 green bell pepper, sliced
  1 red bell pepper, sliced
 ¼ pound snow peas, trimmed
 ¼ cup sliced water chestnuts
  1 small head iceberg lettuce, shredded

1. Cut steak into thin strips; combine with soy sauce, orange rind, ginger, cornstarch and cinnamon in medium bowl. Mix well; let stand 20 to 30 minutes.

2. Heat 1 tablespoon of the oil in wok or large skillet until hot. Add beef; stir-fry over high heat until brown, about 3 minutes. Remove beef to plate.

3. Add remaining 1 tablespoon oil to wok; heat until hot. Add carrot, green and red peppers, snow peas and water chestnuts; stir-fry until vegetables are crisp-tender, 3 to 4 minutes.

4. Return beef to skillet; cook and stir until beef is hot. Serve on lettuce on individual serving plates.

BEEF-IN-BEER STEW

Makes 8 to 10 servings

3 tablespoons vegetable oil
3 pounds boneless beef chuck, cut into 1½-inch
 cubes
3 medium onions, thinly sliced
4 cloves garlic, chopped
4 bottles (12 ounces each) dark beer
1 can (14½ ounces) beef broth
5 parsley sprigs
3 bay leaves
1 tablespoon vinegar
2½ teaspoons dried thyme, crumbled
1½ teaspoons sugar
½ teaspoon salt
¼ teaspoon pepper
8 to 10 small new potatoes, cut into halves
12 ounces sweet miniature carrots, trimmed
1 package (10 ounces) frozen peas
½ pound mushrooms, sliced
½ cup all-purpose flour
¾ cup water

1. Heat oil in large Dutch oven over medium heat until hot. Add ¼ of the beef; cook, turning frequently, until brown on all sides. Remove to plate. Repeat until all beef has been browned; add more oil to pan if necessary.

2. Add onions and garlic to pan; cook and stir over low heat until onions are soft and golden, 5 to 10 minutes.

3. Add beef, beer, broth, parsley, bay leaves, vinegar, thyme, sugar, salt and pepper to pan. Heat over medium-high heat to boiling; reduce heat. Simmer, covered, stirring occasionally, until beef is tender, about 1¼ hours.

4. Remove and discard parsley, bay leaves and surface fat.

5. Add potatoes and carrots to pan; simmer, covered, 15 minutes. Add peas and mushrooms; simmer, uncovered, until potatoes and carrots are tender, about 10 minutes.

6. Mix flour and water in small bowl until smooth; gradually stir into stew. Cook and stir over medium-low heat until thickened, about 3 minutes.

Note: *Stew can be prepared ahead through Step 4. Cool to room temperature; refrigerate, covered, no longer than 48 hours. To serve, heat to boiling and complete recipe.*

STEAK SANDWICHES WITH FETA CHEESE

That star of the Greek salad, feta cheese, takes on a new role as sandwich spread for marinated flank steak and peppers.

Makes 8 servings

3 green bell peppers
3 red bell peppers
½ cup olive oil
3 tablespoons finely chopped parsley
2 tablespoons lemon juice
1 tablespoon dried oregano
4 cloves garlic, finely chopped
1 teaspoon grated lemon rind
¾ teaspoon salt
1 beef flank steak (about 2 pounds)
 Feta Cheese Spread (recipe follows)
16 slices whole wheat bread   *(Continued)*

1. Roast peppers on rack in baking pan in preheated 425°F oven until light brown, 20 to 25 minutes; plunge into cold water. Peel, seed and core peppers; cut into strips.

2. Combine oil, parsley, lemon juice, oregano, garlic, lemon rind and salt in large bowl; whisk until blended. Stir in pepper strips.

3. Broil steak 7 minutes on each side; let stand 10 minutes.

4. Cut steak across the grain into thin slices; add to pepper mixture. Mix well; refrigerate, covered, at least 6 hours, or up to 48 hours. Bring to room temperature before serving.

5. To serve, spread bread with Feta Cheese Spread; top with steak and peppers.

FETA CHEESE SPREAD

2 packages (3 ounces each) cream cheese, room
 temperature
½ cup unsalted butter, room temperature
4 ounces feta cheese, crumbled

Combine all ingredients in small mixer bowl; beat until smooth. Refrigerate, covered, at least 24 hours, or up to 1 week. Bring to room temperature before serving.

Makes about 2 cups

Beef-in-Beer Stew

Stuffed Pork Burgers

STUFFED PORK BURGERS

Makes 4 servings

½ cup coarsely chopped mushrooms
¼ cup sliced green onions
¼ teaspoon garlic powder
1 tablespoon butter or margarine
1½ pounds lean ground pork
2 tablespoons Worcestershire sauce
1 teaspoon dry mustard
½ teaspoon pepper
   Leaf lettuce
   Bermuda onion slices
   Tomato slices
4 kaiser rolls, split
   Prepared mustard
   Pimiento-stuffed olives, if desired

1. Saute mushrooms, green onions and garlic powder in butter in small skillet over medium heat until tender, about 3 minutes.

2. Mix pork, Worcestershire sauce, dry mustard and pepper in medium bowl. Shape into 8 patties, each about 4 inches in diameter.

3. Spoon mushroom mixture onto center of 4 patties, dividing evenly; spread to within ½ inch of edge. Top with remaining 4 patties; press edges to seal.

4. Broil stuffed burgers about 8 inches from heat source until cooked through, 10 to 15 minutes per side.

5. Place lettuce, onion slices and tomato slices on bottom of rolls. Top with burgers; spread with prepared mustard. Cover with tops of rolls; serve with olives.

DANISH MEATBALLS

Makes about 30 meatballs; 8 servings

2½ pounds ground beef
½ cup all-purpose flour
½ cup fine dry breadcrumbs
2 tablespoons grated onion
1½ teaspoons salt
½ teaspoon pepper
3 large eggs, slightly beaten
1½ cups milk
3 to 5 tablespoons butter or margarine
   Parsley sprig for garnish

1. Combine beef, flour, breadcrumbs, onion, salt and pepper in large bowl; mix well together with wooden spoon. Stir in eggs.

2. Stir in milk, ½ cup at a time, letting mixture rest a few minutes after each addition to absorb all milk. When all milk has been added, beat with spoon until mixture is almost fluffy, 2 to 3 minutes. Spread top smooth; refrigerate, covered, until cold.

3. Heat 3 tablespoons of the butter in large skillet over medium heat until brown; dip metal spoon into hot butter to heat. Use spoon to scoop meatballs out of meat mixture; let meatball slide off spoon into skillet. Repeat until 8 to 10 meatballs have been formed. Cook, turning occasionally, until brown, about 10 minutes; remove to large shallow baking dish. Repeat until all meat mixture has been used; add remaining butter to skillet if needed.

4. Place meatballs in preheated 250°F oven to keep hot and continue slow cooking for about 20 minutes. Garnish with parsley.

ONION-PLUM GLAZED PORK ROAST

When fresh plums are out of season, replace them with the canned variety and enjoy this special pork roast any time.

Makes 6 to 8 servings

- **1 pork loin roast (about 3 pounds)**
- **1 teaspoon salt**
- **½ teaspoon garlic powder**
- **¼ teaspoon pepper**
- **2 sweet Spanish onions, cut into wedges**
- **Onion-Plum Sauce (recipe follows)**
- **3 tablespoons honey**
- **2 teaspoons soy sauce**
- **1 teaspoon dry mustard**
- **Orange slices and parsley sprigs for garnish**

1. Sprinkle pork with salt, garlic powder and pepper; place, fat side up, on rack in roasting pan. Roast in preheated 350°F oven 45 minutes.

2. Add onion wedges to roasting pan; turn to coat with pan drippings. Continue roasting 15 minutes.

3. Combine ½ cup of the Onion-Plum Sauce, the honey, soy sauce and mustard in small bowl; mix well. Spoon over pork; continue roasting until meat thermometer inserted into center of pork roast registers 170°F, about 30 minutes longer.

(Continued)

4. Transfer pork and onion wedges to serving platter; garnish with orange slices and parsley. Serve with remaining Onion-Plum Sauce.

ONION-PLUM SAUCE

- **4 cups thinly sliced sweet Spanish onions**
- **¼ cup vegetable oil**
- **1 pound fresh purple plums, pitted, chopped***
- **½ cup orange juice**
- **⅓ cup sugar**
- **1 tablespoon slivered orange rind**
- **1 stick cinnamon (about 3 inches)**
- **¼ teaspoon salt**

1. Cook onions in oil in heavy 2-quart saucepan, covered, over low heat, stirring occasionally, 20 minutes.

2. Stir in remaining ingredients; heat to boiling. Reduce heat; simmer, uncovered, stirring frequently, until thickened, about 30 minutes. Remove and discard cinnamon; serve with roast pork, chicken or ham.

Makes about 2 cups

Note: *1 can (16 ounces) purple plums, pitted and chopped, can be substituted for fresh. Add syrup from plums; decrease sugar to 3 tablespoons.*

Onion-Plum Glazed Pork Roast

HAM AND WILD RICE ROLL-UPS

Makes 6 to 8 servings

1 cup wild rice, rinsed well, drained
3 to 4 cups chicken broth
6 slices bacon, finely chopped
½ cup chopped onion
2 tablespoons chopped green bell pepper
1 cup sliced mushrooms
2 tablespoons butter
1 can (10¾ ounces) condensed cream of celery
    soup
1 cup half-and-half
1 canned ham (3 pounds), cut into 6 × 3½ × ⅛-inch
    slices
½ cup shredded Cheddar cheese

1. Mix rice and 3 cups of the broth in 1½-quart baking dish. Bake, covered, in preheated 350°F oven until tender, about 1½ hours. Check rice during last ½ hour of baking; add as much of the remaining broth as needed to keep rice moist and toss with fork to fluff.

2. Cook and stir bacon in medium skillet over medium heat until crisp; remove bacon with slotted spoon to large bowl. Drain and discard all but 2 tablespoons bacon drippings.

3. Saute onion and green pepper in bacon drippings in skillet over medium heat until soft, about 4 minutes; remove to bowl. Add mushrooms and butter to skillet. Saute until light brown, about 7 minutes; remove to bowl.

4. Add soup and half-and-half to bacon mixture in bowl; mix well. Measure and reserve 1½ cups of the bacon sauce. Add rice to remaining bacon sauce in bowl; mix well.

5. Place ¼ cup of the rice mixture at 1 end of each ham slice; roll up, jelly-roll fashion. Reserve any remaining rice mixture for other use. *(Continued)*

6. Spread 1 cup of the reserved bacon sauce in bottom of shallow glass baking dish; arrange ham rolls, seam side down, in single layer in dish. Spoon remaining ½ cup reserved bacon sauce down center of rolls; sprinkle with cheese. Cover dish with aluminum foil.*

7. Bake in preheated 350°F oven until hot throughout, about 35 minutes.

Note: *Recipe can be made ahead to this point; refrigerate up to 24 hours. Increase baking time slightly.*

ORANGE MARMALADE HAM

The spicy orange glaze coats a clove-studded ham for this American classic.

Makes 12 to 16 servings

1 fully cooked boneless ham (4 to 5 pounds)
¼ cup orange marmalade
¼ cup packed brown sugar
1 teaspoon dry mustard
    Pinch ground cloves
    Pinch ground nutmeg
1 to 2 teaspoons whole cloves
    Orange slices and parsley sprig for garnish

1. Place ham on rack in roasting pan; bake, uncovered, in preheated 325°F oven 45 minutes.

2. Meanwhile, mix remaining ingredients except whole cloves in small bowl.

3. After ham has baked 45 minutes, remove from oven. Score top of ham in diamond pattern, cutting about ¼ inch deep. Insert 1 whole clove in each diamond; brush marmalade mixture evenly over ham.

4. Bake until meat thermometer inserted into center of ham registers 135°F, 15 to 30 minutes longer. Transfer to serving platter; garnish with orange slices and parsley.

Orange Marmalade Ham

BEEF À LA LINDSTROM

"Lindstrom" in a recipe name indicates a Swedish specialty that usually combines chopped beets, potato, and capers. Beef à la Lindstrom is sometimes served topped with a fried or poached egg.

Makes 8 servings

1½ pounds ground beef round
1 large potato, pared, cooked, mashed with fork
¾ cup pickled beets, drained, minced
1 medium onion, minced
⅓ cup whipping cream
2 large egg yolks
1 tablespoon capers, drained
¾ teaspoon salt
⅛ teaspoon pepper
¼ cup butter or margarine
1 cup beef consommé

1. Combine all ingredients except butter and consommé in large bowl; mix lightly but thoroughly. Shape into 16 even patties.

2. Cook patties in butter in large skillet over medium heat until done in center, about 4 minutes per side; transfer to serving dish.

3. Add consommé to skillet; heat and stir to boiling. Pour over patties.

DEEP DISH PIZZA

To non-Italians, this popular food is also called "Chicago-style" pizza, even though both thin and thick crust versions abound in the Windy City. You don't need special deep dishes to make it at home. Use two regular pie pans.

**Makes two 8- or 9-inch pizzas;
4 to 6 servings**

2 cups all-purpose flour
1 package (¼ ounce) active dry yeast
1 teaspoon sugar
½ teaspoon salt
¾ cup hot water (120 to 130°F)
2 tablespoons vegetable oil
Pizza Sauce (recipe follows)
4 ounces pepperoni, sliced
1 small green bell pepper, sliced
1 can (3 ounces) sliced mushrooms, drained
1 small onion, sliced
¼ cup sliced pitted ripe olives
2 cups (8 ounces) shredded Mozzarella cheese
½ cup grated Parmesan cheese

1. Mix 1 cup of the flour, the yeast, sugar and salt in large mixer bowl. Add water and oil; beat until smooth. Beat in remaining 1 cup flour. Let rise, covered, in warm place until doubled, about 45 minutes.

2. Punch down dough; divide in half. Press each half evenly on bottom and sides of greased 8- or 9-inch metal pie pan. Let stand in warm place until puffy, 15 to 20 minutes.

3. Spread Pizza Sauce evenly over dough in each pan. Top each with ½ of the remaining ingredients. Let stand in warm place until dough at edges is puffy, 10 to 20 minutes.

4. Bake in preheated 425°F oven until crust is golden and cheese is light brown, 20 to 30 minutes.

(Continued)

Deep Dish Pizza

PIZZA SAUCE

1 medium onion, chopped
1 clove garlic, minced
2 tablespoons olive or vegetable oil
1 can (6 ounces) tomato paste
½ cup water
2 teaspoons packed brown sugar
1 teaspoon dried basil, crumbled
1 teaspoon dried oregano, crumbled
½ teaspoon salt
¼ teaspoon pepper

1. Saute onion and garlic in oil in medium saucepan over medium heat until tender, about 5 minutes.

2. Stir in remaining ingredients; heat to boiling. Reduce heat; simmer, uncovered, stirring frequently, 15 minutes.

Makes about 1¼ cups

Barbecued Short Ribs

BARBECUED SHORT RIBS

Makes 4 servings

4 tablespoons vegetable oil
1 cup catsup
2 tablespoons dry red wine
1 tablespoon Worcestershire sauce
1 tablespoon prepared mustard
1 tablespoon packed brown sugar
1 teaspoon chili powder
1 teaspoon salt
⅛ teaspoon pepper
2 drops hot red pepper sauce
3 pounds beef short ribs, cut into serving pieces
¼ cup finely chopped onion
   Water
   All-purpose flour

1. Mix 2 tablespoons of the oil, the catsup, wine, Worcestershire sauce, mustard, brown sugar, chili powder, salt, pepper and red pepper sauce in small bowl. Brush sauce on all sides of ribs; let stand, covered, 4 to 6 hours.

2. Saute onion in remaining 2 tablespoons oil in pressure cooker over medium heat until tender, about 3 minutes. Add ribs; cook, turning occasionally, until brown on all sides, 15 to 20 minutes. Add 1 cup water and any remaining sauce.

3. Cover pressure cooker; set control at 10. Cook over high heat until pressure is reached. Reduce heat; cook 45 minutes.*

4. Cool cooker naturally 5 minutes; place cooker under cold running water to complete pressure reduction. Remove ribs to serving dish; keep warm.

5. Measure liquid in cooker. For each cup of liquid, mix 1 tablespoon flour with ¼ cup cold water in small bowl until smooth. Mix liquid and flour mixture in cooker; cook, stirring constantly, over medium heat until mixture thickens and bubbles for 1 minute. Serve over ribs.

*Note: To cook at 15 pounds pressure, reduce cooking time to 30 to 35 minutes.

CINCINNATI CHILI

From a city famous for its chili comes the designation Two-Way, Three-Way, etc. Two-Way Chili means served on spaghetti. After that, the numbers indicate extra topping ingredients, such as Cheddar cheese, beans and chopped onions.

Makes 4 servings

1 pound ground beef
1 tablespoon vegetable oil
2 tablespoons instant minced onion
2 tablespoons chili powder
2 teaspoons unsweetened cocoa powder
½ teaspoon ground cinnamon
½ teaspoon ground cumin
¼ teaspoon instant minced garlic
¼ teaspoon salt
¼ teaspoon ground cloves
   Pinch ground red pepper
1 can (15 ounces) tomato sauce
1 can (10¾ ounces) condensed beef broth
2 tablespoons cider vinegar
½ pound spaghetti
1 cup cooked red kidney beans
¼ cup shredded Cheddar cheese

1. Cook and stir beef in oil in large saucepan over medium heat until brown, about 10 minutes; drain and discard excess fat.

2. Add onion, chili powder, cocoa powder, cinnamon, cumin, garlic, salt, cloves and red pepper to pan; mix well. Stir in tomato sauce, broth and vinegar; heat to boiling. Reduce heat; simmer, covered, stirring occasionally, 3 hours.

3. Let chili cool; refrigerate, covered, overnight.

4. Remove and discard fat layer from chili; heat chili until hot.

5. Cook spaghetti according to package directions; drain. Heat beans in small saucepan until hot.

6. To serve, spoon chili over spaghetti in individual bowls. Top with beans; sprinkle with cheese.

COUNTRY SAUSAGE PINWHEELS

Topped with herb-scented gravy, these hearty sausage-filled biscuit slices make a fine breakfast, lunch or brunch dish.

Makes 7 servings

2 cups all-purpose flour
1 tablespoon baking powder
2 teaspoons fines herbes
1 teaspoon seasoned salt
½ teaspoon sugar
2 tablespoons butter or lard
2 tablespoons vegetable shortening
¾ cup milk
1 pound spicy or mild breakfast pork sausage, room temperature

Gravy
3 tablespoons butter or margarine
4½ tablespoons all-purpose flour
1¼ teaspoons fines herbes
¼ teaspoon black pepper
Pinch crushed red pepper
2 cups milk
2 chicken bouillon cubes *(Continued)*

1. For pinwheels, mix flour, baking powder, fines herbes, seasoned salt and sugar in large bowl; cut in butter and shortening until mixture resembles coarse crumbs. Stir in milk; stir just until soft dough forms. Roll or pat out dough on lightly floured surface into 14 × 10-inch rectangle.

2. Roll or pat out sausage between pieces of waxed paper into 14 × 8-inch rectangle.

3. Peel off top piece of waxed paper. Invert sausage onto dough, leaving 2 inches of dough on one 14-inch side uncovered. Peel off remaining piece of waxed paper.

4. Starting at opposite 14-inch side, roll up dough and sausage, jelly-roll fashion; pinch bottom seam to seal. Refrigerate roll, wrapped in waxed paper, 45 minutes.

5. Unwrap roll; cut crosswise into 1-inch slices. Place slices, cut side down, in 13 × 9-inch baking pan. Bake in preheated 400°F oven until dough is golden, about 35 minutes.

6. For gravy, melt butter in medium saucepan over medium heat. Stir in flour, fines herbes, black pepper and red pepper; cook and stir 2 minutes. Gradually whisk in milk until smooth. Add bouillon cubes; cook and stir over medium heat until gravy thickens and bubbles for 1 minute.

7. To serve, ladle gravy over pinwheels.

Country Sausage Pinwheels

Linguine with Parsley Pesto

DEVILED BEEF ROAST ON THE GRILL

Makes 8 to 10 servings

1 beef eye-round roast (3½ to 4 pounds)
¾ cups horseradish-style mustard
2 to 3 cups coarse (kosher) salt

1. Pat beef dry with paper toweling. Cover entire surface of beef with mustard. Cover mustard layer with coarse salt; no meat or mustard should be visible.

2. Place beef in disposable foil roasting pan; place pan on grill rack over hot coals. Cover grill; cook until instant-registering meat thermometer, inserted into center of beef, registers 135 to 145°F, 50 to 60 minutes.

3. Crack salt casing; remove and discard. Cut beef into thin slices.

BAKED WALLEYES WITH ORANGE-RICE STUFFING

Makes 6 servings

6 dressed walleyes (1 to 1½ pounds each)
2 teaspoons salt
  Orange-Rice Stuffing (recipe follows)
2 tablespoons vegetable oil
2 tablespoons orange juice

1. Sprinkle fish inside and out with salt. Fill cavities with Orange-Rice Stuffing; close openings with wooden picks. Place fish in single layer in well-greased baking pan.

2. Mix oil and orange juice in small bowl; brush over fish.

3. Bake in preheated 350°F oven, basting occasionally, until fish flakes with fork, 30 to 35 minutes. Remove wooden picks before serving. *(Continued)*

ORANGE-RICE STUFFING

1 cup chopped celery
¼ cup chopped onion
¼ cup vegetable oil
¾ cup water
¼ cup orange juice
1 tablespoon grated orange rind
1 teaspoon salt
½ cup instant rice
½ cup toasted slivered almonds

1. Saute celery and onion in oil in medium saucepan over medium heat until soft, about 5 minutes. Stir in water, orange juice, orange rind and salt; heat to boiling.

2. Add rice; stir to moisten. Remove from heat; let stand, covered, 5 minutes. Stir in almonds.

LINGUINE WITH PARSLEY PESTO

Makes 8 servings

1 pound linguine or spaghetti
1 tablespoon salt
1 cup parsley sprigs
½ cup pine nuts
½ cup olive oil
¼ cup water
1 tablespoon dried basil
2 cloves garlic
  Pinch pepper
½ cup grated Parmesan cheese

1. Add linguine and salt to large kettle of rapidly boiling water; cook, uncovered, stirring occasionally, until firm-tender, 8 to 12 minutes. Drain well.

2. While linguine is cooking, combine parsley, nuts, oil, water, basil, garlic and pepper in blender container; process until smooth. Gradually add cheese, processing after each addition until mixed.

3. Toss linguine with sauce in serving bowl.

SWEET-SOUR SHRIMP WITH CHERRIES

For beautiful buffet entertaining, serve from a chafing dish or let guests help themselves from a platter.

Makes 8 to 10 servings

1½ pounds canned pitted tart red or sweet dark
    cherries in juice
    Water
 4 to 9 tablespoons sugar
 3 tablespoons cornstarch
⅓ cup cider vinegar
 3 tablespoons soy sauce
¾ teaspoon salt
½ teaspoon ground ginger
1½ cups slivered green bell pepper
 2 to 3 pounds cooked shrimp, shelled, deveined
 1 or 2 cans water chestnuts, drained, sliced
 4 to 6 cups hot cooked rice

1. Drain cherries, reserving juice; add enough water to juice to make 2¼ cups liquid.

2. Mix sugar and cornstarch in large saucepan, using 9 tablespoons sugar for tart cherries or 4 tablespoons sugar for sweet cherries. Stir in cherry juice mixture, vinegar, soy sauce, salt and ginger. Cook and stir over medium heat until sauce thickens and bubbles for 3 minutes. Stir in green pepper; cook 3 minutes longer.

3. Stir in shrimp, water chestnuts and cherries; cook until hot. Serve over rice.

TUNA-MUSHROOM DIVAN

Here's a casserole that adapts to a busy schedule. Make, bake and serve at once or make and bake later.

Makes 8 servings

 1 pound mushrooms, sliced
 5 tablespoons butter
 1 can (10½ ounces) condensed cream of
    mushroom soup
½ soup can of milk
 1 medium onion, chopped
 1 teaspoon prepared mustard
    Pinch white pepper
 2 cans (6 to 7 ounces each) tuna, drained, flaked
 2 tablespoons chopped parsley
 1 bunch fresh broccoli, cut in spears, or 2
    packages (10 ounces each) frozen broccoli
    spears
 2 cups medium egg noodles
½ teaspoon salt
½ cup fresh breadcrumbs
 1 ounce sharp Cheddar cheese, shredded

1. Saute mushrooms in 4 tablespoons of the butter in large skillet over medium heat, 3 minutes. Remove ½ of the mushrooms; reserve.

2. Add soup, milk, onion, mustard and pepper to skillet; mix well. Stir in tuna and parsley; remove from heat.

3. Cook broccoli in boiling water, covered, until tender, about 10 minutes; drain well.

4. Cook noodles in large saucepan of boiling water until tender; drain well.

5. Toss noodles, remaining 1 tablespoon butter and the salt in large bowl. Add tuna mixture; mix well. Spread evenly in greased 3-quart shallow baking dish. *(Continued)*

6. Arrange broccoli on top of noodles with flowerets toward ends. Arrange reserved mushrooms in center. Mix breadcrumbs and cheese; sprinkle on noodles around edges.

7. Bake in preheated 375°F oven until crumbs are golden and mixture is hot in center, 25 to 30 minutes.

Note: *Recipe can be prepared through Step 6 up to 12 hours ahead; refrigerate covered. Increase baking time to 45 minutes.*

PIGGY-BACK ROCK LOBSTER TAILS

Makes 2 servings

 2 South African rock lobster tails (4 ounces each),
    thawed
 2 tablespoons chicken broth
 1 teaspoon lemon juice
½ teaspoon dried orange rind
 2 drops imitation butter flavoring
    Ground ginger to taste
    Chili powder to taste

1. Insert point of kitchen shears between meat and hard shell on back of lobster tails. Clip shell down center, leaving tail "fan" intact; do not remove underside membrane. Gently open shell, separating it from meat. Lift lobster meat through split shell to rest on outside, leaving meat attached to fan end of shell.

2. Combine remaining ingredients in small bowl; mix well. Brush over lobster meat. Place shells, with meat riding "piggy back" on top, in shallow broiler pan.

3. Broil 4 inches from heat source until lobster meat is opaque throughout, about 10 minutes.

Sweet-Sour Shrimp with Cherries

Mushroom-Stuffed Salmon Loaf

BROILED FISH WITH DEVILED SAUCE

Makes 4 to 6 servings

2 pounds fresh or thawed frozen fish fillets
    Butter, melted
4 ounces Cheddar cheese, shredded
¼ cup bottled chili sauce
1 tablespoon prepared mustard
1½ teaspoons prepared horseradish
    Lemon and lime slice twists and fresh dill sprigs

1. Arrange fish on aluminum-foil-covered broiling pan; brush with butter. Broil several inches from heat source until fish is opaque in center and golden on top, about 8 minutes. Arrange fish in single layer in gratin dishes or flameproof serving dishes.

2. Mix cheese, chili sauce, mustard and horseradish in small bowl; spread evenly over fish.

3. Broil until cheese is melted and light brown, about 3 minutes. Garnish with lemon and lime slices and dill.

MUSHROOM-STUFFED SALMON LOAF

Salmon loaf has a long tradition at church potlucks and family suppers. This elegant version boasts a spinach-mushroom layer in the center and a delicate lemon sauce to be spooned over each slice.

Makes 6 servings

1 can (15½ ounces) salmon
2 cups soft breadcrumbs
2 large eggs, beaten
1 tablespoon lemon juice
1 tablespoon finely chopped onion
½ teaspoon salt
    Pepper to taste
1½ cups sliced mushrooms
2 tablespoons butter or margarine
1 cup packed shredded fresh spinach
    Lemon Sauce (recipe follows)
    Lemon slices and parsley sprigs for garnish

(Continued)

1. Drain salmon, reserving liquid for Lemon Sauce; flake salmon in medium bowl. Add breadcrumbs, eggs, lemon juice, onion, salt and pepper; mix well.

2. Saute mushrooms in butter in medium skillet over medium heat 2 minutes. Add spinach; saute until wilted, about 2 minutes.

3. Pat ½ of the salmon mixture into greased 8½ × 4½ × 2¾-inch loaf pan. Top with mushroom mixture in even layer, leaving 1-inch border on all sides. Top with remaining salmon mixture; spread top smooth.

4. Bake in preheated 350°F oven until center is set and top is golden, about 40 minutes. Let stand 5 minutes before slicing.

5. Serve with Lemon Sauce. Garnish with lemon slices and parsley.

LEMON SAUCE

    Reserved salmon liquid
    Milk
1 tablespoon butter
1 tablespoon flour
⅛ teaspoon salt
    Pinch white pepper
1 egg yolk, beaten
1 tablespoon lemon juice

1. Measure reserved salmon liquid; add enough milk to make ⅔ cup.

2. Melt butter in small saucepan over medium heat; stir in flour, salt and pepper until smooth. Gradually whisk in milk mixture; cook and stir until sauce thickens and bubbles for 1 minute.

3. Gradually whisk ¼ cup of the hot sauce into egg yolk in small bowl. Gradually whisk egg yolk mixture into remaining sauce in pan. Cook, stirring constantly, over low heat until thickened, about 1 minute; do not boil. Stir in lemon juice.

Makes about ¾ cup

DOOR COUNTY FISH BOIL

In the Wisconsin peninsula they prepare their fish boil outdoors in great iron kettles, adding ingredients according to how long each needs to cook. You can do a scaled-down version of this famous fish supper in your own kitchen. Don't forget the cherry pie for dessert.

Makes 6 servings

  2 pounds fresh or thawed frozen whitefish or other fish fillets
12 small red-skinned potatoes
10 cups water
⅓ cup salt
  6 medium onions
  1 small head cabbage, cut into 6 wedges
  1 can (16 ounces) small whole beets, drained
    Horseradish Sauce (recipe follows)
    Chopped parsley for garnish

1. Cut fish into serving-size pieces. Pare ½-inch-wide strip around middle of each potato.

2. Heat water and salt in large kettle to boiling. Add potatoes and onions; reduce heat. Simmer, covered, until firm-tender, about 30 minutes. Add cabbage; simmer until vegetables are fork-tender, about 10 minutes longer.

3. Add fish to kettle; do not stir. Cook just until opaque throughout, 3 to 4 minutes. Remove fish and vegetables with slotted spoon to platter; keep warm.

4. Add beets to water; cook just until hot. Remove beets to platter. Pour Horseradish Sauce over fish and vegetables; garnish with parsley. Serve immediately.

HORSERADISH SAUCE

½ cup prepared horseradish
  1 tablespoon all-purpose flour
½ teaspoon salt
¼ teaspoon paprika
  1 cup half-and-half

Combine horseradish, flour, salt and paprika in small saucepan; mix well. Stir in half-and-half; cook, stirring constantly, over medium heat until sauce thickens and bubbles for 1 minute. Serve hot.

Makes about 1½ cups

FISH WITH WILD RICE

Commercial blending of long-grain and wild rice in seasoned mixes gives cooks everywhere the opportunity to put the taste of wild rice on their own menus.

Makes 6 servings

  1 medium zucchini
6½ ounces long-grain and wild rice
⅓ cup chopped pecans
¼ cup chopped onion
  1 tablespoon vegetable oil
  1 tablespoon shredded Cheddar cheese
  6 fish fillets (8 to 10 ounces each)
  2 tablespoons grated Parmesan cheese
½ teaspoon salt
⅛ teaspoon pepper
    Lemon slice twists and parsley sprigs for garnish

(Continued)

1. Cut zucchini lengthwise into quarters; cut crosswise into thin slices. Cook zucchini in large saucepan of boiling water until tender, 1 minute; drain well.

2. Cook rice according to package directions.

3. Saute pecans and onion in oil in small skillet over medium heat until tender, about 3 minutes. Combine with zucchini, rice and Cheddar cheese in large bowl; mix well.

4. Spread rice mixture on fillets, dividing evenly; roll up fillets and fasten with wooden picks. Place in greased baking dish; sprinkle with Parmesan cheese, salt and pepper.

5. Bake in preheated 350°F oven until fish is opaque, 20 to 30 minutes. Remove to serving dish; garnish with lemon slices and parsley.

Fish with Wild Rice

OVEN-BAKED ROSEMARY CHICKEN

Buy drumsticks, thighs, wings, or split breasts in proportion to the dark-meat or light-meat preferences of the dinner guests. The basting sauce will coat 24 broiler-fryer chicken parts generously.

Makes 12 servings

24 broiler-fryer chicken pieces (wings, breasts, thighs and drumsticks)
2 green bell peppers, cut into ½-inch-wide strips
2 stalks celery, diagonally sliced
1 large onion, sliced, separated into rings
2 teaspoons salt
½ teaspoon ground black pepper
6 tablespoons margarine
1 cup catsup
½ cup cider or white wine vinegar
1 teaspoon dried rosemary, crumbled
½ teaspoon dry mustard
1 chicken bouillon cube

1. Arrange chicken in single layer, skin side down, in 2 large baking dishes. Top with green pepper, celery and onion; sprinkle with salt and ground pepper.

2. Melt margarine in small saucepan over low heat; stir in catsup, vinegar, rosemary and mustard. Heat to boiling; add bouillon cube and stir until dissolved. Spoon mixture over chicken and vegetables.

3. Refrigerate, covered, turning occasionally, at least 4 hours or overnight.

4. Bake in preheated 400°F oven 30 minutes. Turn chicken and baste generously; bake until chicken is fork-tender and juices run clear, about 30 minutes longer. Transfer to serving dish.

CRANBERRY CHICKEN WITH STUFFING

Makes 4 servings

1 broiler-fryer chicken (about 3 pounds), cut into quarters
4 tablespoons margarine, room temperature
1 package (1⅜ ounces) dry onion soup mix
1 can (16 ounces) whole-berry cranberry sauce
1 package (6 ounces) cornbread flavor top-of-stove stuffing mix
1½ cups hot water
½ teaspoon celery salt
⅛ teaspoon pepper
¼ cup sliced almonds

1. Place chicken in shallow baking pan. Rub chicken with 1 tablespoon of the margarine; sprinkle with ½ of the soup mix. Drain liquid from cranberry sauce; drizzle liquid over chicken. Reserve 1 cup cranberry sauce; spread remaining cranberry sauce over chicken.

2. Spread 1 tablespoon of the margarine on piece of aluminum foil large enough to cover pan; sprinkle with remaining soup mix. Invert foil over chicken; crimp edges to sides of pan to seal. Bake in preheated 350°F oven 40 minutes.

3. Mix vegetable-seasoning packet from stuffing mix, water and remaining 2 tablespoons margarine in large bowl, stirring until margarine melts. Stir in cornbread stuffing crumbs until moistened; stir in reserved 1 cup cranberry sauce.

4. Remove foil from pan and reserve; push chicken to side of pan. Add stuffing mix to pan in 4 individual mounds; drizzle with pan drippings. Sprinkle chicken with celery salt and pepper, then with almonds.

5. Bake, uncovered, until chicken is fork-tender, about 20 minutes longer. Remove any browned soup mix from reserved foil; sprinkle over chicken and stuffing. Serve each chicken quarter with 1 mound of stuffing.

Oven-Baked Rosemary Chicken

Chicken Skillet Supper

CHICKEN SKILLET SUPPER

Frozen mixed vegetables, added when the chicken is done, bring a colorful touch to this easy, top-of-the-range meal.

Makes 4 to 6 servings

1½ teaspoons salt
¼ teaspoon pepper
¼ teaspoon paprika
⅛ teaspoon garlic powder
1 broiler-fryer chicken (about 3 pounds), cut up
1 tablespoon vegetable oil
2 tablespoons water
1 medium onion, chopped
1 medium potato, pared, cut into 2 × ¼ × ¼-inch julienne strips
1 tablespoon slivered almonds, if desired
1 can (8 ounces) tomato sauce
1 cup chicken broth
1 teaspoon sugar
1 package (10 ounces) frozen mixed vegetables or French-style green beans

1. Mix salt, pepper, paprika and garlic powder in small bowl; rub into chicken.

2. Heat oil in large skillet over medium heat until hot; add chicken, skin side down. Cook, covered, 10 minutes. Add water; cook, covered, turning chicken over every 10 minutes, 30 minutes longer. Remove chicken to plate.

3. Add onion, potato and almonds to skillet; saute over medium heat until onion is soft, about 4 minutes. Stir in tomato sauce, broth and sugar; heat to boiling.

4. Add mixed vegetables and chicken to skillet; cook, covered, until mixed vegetables are cooked, about 10 minutes.

LEMON-HONEY FRIED CHICKEN

The touch of honey smooths out the tartness of the lemon juice and herbs without sweetening the blend.

Makes 4 servings

½ cup lemon juice
1 tablespoon honey
¼ teaspoon dried marjoram, crumbled
¼ teaspoon dried tarragon, crumbled
½ cup plus 3 tablespoons all-purpose flour
1 broiler-fryer chicken, cut up
1 teaspoon salt
½ teaspoon pepper
Vegetable oil for frying
2 cups hot water

1. Mix lemon juice, honey, marjoram and tarragon in shallow bowl. Place ½ cup of the flour in second shallow bowl.

2. Dip chicken, 1 piece at a time, into lemon mixture, turning to coat both sides; let excess lemon mixture drain off. Sprinkle chicken with salt and pepper; dip in flour to coat both sides. Reserve 2 tablespoons of the lemon mixture.

3. Heat 1 inch oil in large skillet over high heat to 400°F. Add chicken; fry 5 minutes, turning to brown all sides. Reduce heat to medium-high; continue frying until chicken is fork-tender, about 15 minutes longer. Remove chicken, draining well; keep warm.

4. Drain all but 2 tablespoons of the oil from skillet; stir in the remaining 3 tablespoons flour. Cook and stir over medium-high heat until brown, about 1 minute. Whisk in water and reserved 2 tablespoons lemon mixture. Cook and stir over medium-low heat until sauce thickens and bubbles for 1 minute. Serve with chicken.

Turkey Ballottine

TURKEY BALLOTTINE

For an elegant meal, prepare turkey breast in the French style, with finely minced turkey meat in the seasoned filling. The turkey skin is kept in one piece and wrapped and tied around the outside before the turkey is cooked.

Makes 8 servings

    1 whole turkey breast (5 to 6 pounds)
      Salt and pepper to taste
    4 slices white bread
    4 large eggs
    ½ cup pecans or walnuts
    ¼ teaspoon dried thyme
    ¼ teaspoon dried marjoram
      Cranberry-Stuffed Apples (recipe follows)
      Watercress for garnish

1. Remove bones from turkey breast using boning knife, keeping skin attached and in 1 piece. Butterfly breast; pound with mallet to flatten. Sprinkle with salt and pepper.

2. Trim remaining meat from bones; process to smooth paste in food processor and transfer to medium bowl. Combine bread, eggs, pecans, thyme and marjoram in food processor; process until smooth. Add to turkey paste; mix until smooth.

3. Spread stuffing evenly on turkey to within 1 inch of edges; roll up and tie securely in several places with kitchen string. Place on rack in roasting pan.

4. Roast in preheated 350°F oven until fork-tender, about 2½ hours. To serve, remove string from turkey. Place turkey on serving platter; surround with Cranberry-Stuffed Apples. Garnish with watercress.

CRANBERRY-STUFFED APPLES

    2 cups fresh cranberries
    ½ cup packed brown sugar
    ½ cup water
    2 tablespoons lemon juice
    ⅛ teaspoon ground cinnamon
    4 McIntosh apples, pared, cored   *(Continued)*

1. Combine all ingredients except apples in large skillet; mix well. Heat over medium heat to simmering; reduce heat to low.

2. Cut apples lengthwise into halves; place, cut sides up, in skillet. Simmer, covered, until apples are firm-tender, about 7 minutes.

3. Remove apples from skillet; top with cranberry mixture.

LAYERED TURKEY & CREPES

Crepes solve many a problem about what to do with left-over turkey. For a change, stack them with the filling layered in between. Adding a little poultry seasoning to the crepe batter is an extra nice touch.

Makes 4 to 6 servings

    ¼ cup sliced mushrooms
    ¼ cup sliced green onions
    3 tablespoons butter
    3 tablespoons all-purpose flour
    ¾ cup plus 2 tablespoons whipping cream
    ½ cup chicken or turkey broth
    2 large egg yolks
  1½ cups finely shredded cooked turkey
    8 crepes (7-inch diameter)
    1 tablespoon dry sherry

1. Saute mushrooms and green onions in butter in medium saucepan over medium heat just until tender, about 3 minutes. Stir in flour; whisk in ½ cup of the cream and the broth. Cook and stir over low heat until sauce thickens and bubbles for 1 minute; remove from heat.

2. Beat egg yolks and 2 tablespoons of the cream in small bowl; gradually whisk in ½ of the hot sauce. Gradually whisk egg yolk mixture into remaining hot sauce; cook, stirring constantly, over low heat 2 minutes. Do not let mixture boil. Stir in turkey.

3. Place 1 crepe on oven-proof serving plate. Spread with enough of the turkey sauce to coat. Repeat stacking and spreading crepes 6 more times; top stack with last crepe.

(Continued)

4. Beat remaining ¼ cup cream in small mixer bowl until stiff; fold in sherry. Fold whipped cream into remaining turkey sauce; pour over stacked crepes.

5. Bake in preheated 350°F oven until heated through, 15 to 20 minutes; cut into wedges to serve.

KRAUT WITH TURKEY ON A SPIT

Bits of chopped apple, orange, and red onion turn canned sauerkraut into a colorful relish. The kraut juices plus salad dressing mix and seasonings double as marinade and basting sauce for turkey on the grill.

Makes 8 to 10 servings

6 cups sauerkraut (about 48 ounces), drained, juice reserved
1 teaspoon poultry seasoning
1 teaspoon lemon pepper seasoning
1 envelope (0.7 ounces) garlic salad dressing mix
⅓ cup vegetable oil
1 frozen ready-to-stuff turkey (10 pounds), thawed
2 medium Golden Delicious apples, chopped
1 medium orange, peeled, coarsely chopped
1 small red onion, chopped
½ cup finely chopped celery
⅓ cup orange juice
2 tablespoons sugar
2 teaspoons dried fines herbes, crumbled
½ teaspoon salt
⅛ teaspoon pepper (Continued)

1. For marinade, combine reserved sauerkraut juice, the poultry seasoning, lemon pepper and salad dressing mix in large bowl; mix well. Whisk in oil until blended.

2. Remove neck and giblets from turkey; rinse turkey and drain well. Place turkey in marinade, turning to coat well. Let stand, turning frequently and spooning marinade into body cavity, 2 hours.

3. Remove turkey from marinade, draining well; reserve marinade. Tie turkey with heavy kitchen twine to hold legs and wings securely and maintain shape during cooking. Pass rotisserie spit through body cavity; fasten spit forks in turkey to hold securely.

4. Arrange medium-hot coals around foil drip pan in grill. Insert spit into rotisserie motor, 8 inches above coals; grill turkey, basting with reserved marinade every 30 minutes, until instant registering meat thermometer registers 180°F when inserted into thickest part of thigh muscle, 3 to 3½ hours. Add charcoal to fire as needed to maintain cooking temperature; cover any parts of turkey that become too brown with aluminum foil.

5. While turkey is cooking, make relish. Combine sauerkraut with remaining ingredients in large bowl; toss to mix well. Refrigerate, covered; toss lightly just before serving.

6. Let turkey stand 10 minutes before carving; serve with relish.

Note: *Turkey can be roasted in 325°F oven if desired; baste every 30 minutes with reserved marinade. Cooking time will be about the same.*

Kraut with Turkey on a Spit

Chicken Fruit Salad

TUNA MACARONI SALAD

Makes 6 to 8 servings

2 cans (6½ to 7 ounces each) tuna, drained, flaked
4 cups cooked elbow macaroni
1 cup mayonnaise
1 cup diced seeded cucumber
1 cup chopped celery
½ cup chopped green bell pepper
¼ cup chopped onion
1½ teaspoons dillweed
Salt and coarsely ground pepper to taste
Lettuce leaves
3 tomatoes, cut into wedges

1. Combine all ingredients except lettuce and tomatoes in large bowl; mix well. Refrigerate, covered, 1 to 4 hours before serving.

2. Spoon salad into lettuce-lined bowl; arrange tomatoes on top.

CHICKEN FRUIT SALAD

Makes 4 servings

2 cups diced (¾-inch) cooked chicken
1 cup seedless grapes, cut into halves
½ cup broken pecans
⅓ cup thinly sliced celery
¼ cup sour cream
2 teaspoons lime juice
Salt and pepper to taste
2 cantaloupes, cut into halves, seeded
Mint sprigs or lime slices for garnish
Leaf lettuce

Combine chicken, grapes, pecans, celery, sour cream, lime juice, salt and pepper in large bowl; toss to mix well. Spoon into cantaloupe halves. Garnish with mint sprigs or lime slices. Serve on lettuce-lined plates.

WILD RICE CHICKEN SALAD

Makes 6 servings

⅔ cup wild rice
2 cups water
1½ teaspoons salt
⅔ cup mayonnaise
⅓ cup milk
⅓ cup lemon juice
½ small onion, grated or minced
2 whole chicken breasts, cooked, skinned, boned, diced
1 can (8 ounces) water chestnuts, drained, sliced
2 cups seedless green grape halves
1 cup cashews
⅛ teaspoon pepper
   Lettuce leaves

1. Rinse rice thoroughly with warm water in medium saucepan; drain. Return rice to pan; add 2 cups water and 1 teaspoon of the salt. Heat to boiling; reduce heat to low. Cook, covered, until rice is tender, 45 to 60 minutes.

2. Combine mayonnaise, milk, lemon juice and onion in large bowl; mix well. Stir in rice, chicken and water chestnuts; refrigerate, covered, until cold.

3. Just before serving, stir in grapes, cashews, pepper and remaining ½ teaspoon salt; spoon onto platter lined with lettuce leaves.

SHELL SALAD

Makes 6 to 8 servings

2 tablespoons cider vinegar
1½ tablespoons dried onion flakes
1 cup mayonnaise
1 to 2 teaspoons paprika
1 teaspoon salt
¼ teaspoon ground black pepper
2 medium tomatoes, cut into wedges
8 ounces small shell macaroni, cooked, drained
½ cup chopped green bell pepper
2 tablespoons sliced pitted ripe olives
1 tablespoon minced parsley
2 hard-cooked eggs, sliced
   Parsley sprig for garnish

1. Mix vinegar and onion in large bowl; let stand 5 minutes. Stir in mayonnaise, paprika, salt and black pepper.

2. Mix tomatoes and 2 tablespoons of the mayonnaise mixture in small bowl.

3. Add macaroni, green pepper, olives and minced parsley to remaining mayonnaise mixture; mix well.

4. Refrigerate tomatoes and macaroni mixture separately, covered, several hours before serving.

5. To serve, transfer macaroni mixture to large serving bowl; arrange tomatoes and eggs on top. Garnish with parsley sprig.

Shell Salad

CUCUMBER MOUSSE

Just looking at this cool cucumber salad seems to shave several degrees off the temperature on a hot summer's day. Fresh lemon and lime bring a refreshing tart flavor to the creamy mixture.

Makes 6 to 8 servings

2 envelopes unflavored gelatin
1 cup water
½ cup sugar
1 teaspoon salt
  Pinch ground red pepper
3 tablespoons fresh lemon juice
1 tablespoon fresh lime juice
2 teaspoons grated lemon rind
1 teaspoon grated lime rind
2 large cucumbers, pared, seeded, finely
  shredded
2 stalks celery, finely chopped
2 tablespoons minced onion
2 tablespoons chopped parsley
1 cup whipping cream
  Lime slice and slivered lime rind for garnish

1. Sprinkle gelatin over water in small saucepan; let stand until softened, about 5 minutes. Add sugar, salt and pepper; cook and stir over medium-low heat until gelatin and sugar are dissolved.

2. Combine gelatin mixture, lemon juice, lime juice, lemon rind and grated lime rind in medium bowl; mix well. Refrigerate, stirring occasionally, until mixture is syrupy.

3. Add cucumbers, celery, onion and parsley to gelatin mixture; mix well. Refrigerate, stirring occasionally, until mixture mounds slightly when dropped from a spoon.

4. Beat cream in small mixer bowl until stiff; fold into cucumber mixture. Pour into 5-cup mold; refrigerate until set, several hours or overnight.

5. To serve, unmold mousse onto cold serving plate; garnish with lime slice and slivered lime rind.

Cucumber Mousse

GREEN PEAS & SHRIMP SALAD

Since the peas receive such a brief cooking time, they retain their shape, bright green color and fresh flavor in the salad.

Makes 8 servings

2 pounds peas in pods, shelled
1 cup chopped celery
½ cup slivered almonds
1 green onion, chopped
1 cup mayonnaise
2 cans (6 to 7 ounces each) shrimp, rinsed,
  drained
  Juice of 1 lemon
  Salt
  Pepper

1. Add peas to large saucepan of boiling water; heat to boiling. Cook 1 minute; drain. Rinse under cold running water; drain well.

2. Combine peas, celery, almonds and green onion in large bowl; stir in mayonnaise.

3. Mix shrimp and lemon juice in medium bowl. Add to pea mixture; mix well. Add salt and pepper to taste. Serve cold.

PECANDIED CARROTS

Makes 6 to 8 servings

¾ cup butter
½ cup chopped pecans
½ cup orange juice
¼ cup packed brown sugar
⅛ teaspoon ground cinnamon
⅛ teaspoon ground nutmeg
12 carrots, cut into 3 × ¼ × ¼-inch julienne strips

1. Melt butter in large saucepan; stir in pecans, orange juice, sugar, cinnamon and nutmeg. Cook, stirring constantly, over medium heat to boiling.

2. Add carrots to pan; stir to coat evenly. Cook, stirring frequently, over medium heat until carrots are tender and syrup is thickened, 10 to 15 minutes.

ONION CHIP PATTIES

Makes 8 to 12 patties

1½ cups finely chopped sweet Spanish onion
2 cups crushed potato chips
2 large eggs, beaten
2 tablespoons chopped parsley
½ teaspoon dried oregano, crumbled
¼ teaspoon dried chervil, crumbled
¼ teaspoon celery salt
⅛ teaspoon garlic powder
⅛ teaspoon pepper
2 to 3 tablespoons vegetable oil

1. Combine all ingredients except oil in large bowl; mix well. Let stand 15 minutes.

2. Shape mixture into 2 × ½-inch patties.

3. Heat oil in large skillet over medium heat until hot. Add patties; fry, turning once, until brown, 3 to 5 minutes per side.

Hot Fruit Salad

HOT FRUIT SALAD

Perk up a wintertime buffet by including a hot salad of assorted fruits. Bring out a chafing dish or candle warmer to keep the salad at the right serving temperature.

Makes 8 to 10 servings

  1 can (20 ounces) sliced pineapple, drained
  1 can (16 ounces) peach halves, drained
  1 can (16 ounces) pear halves, drained
  2 cups seedless grapes
  ¼ cup maraschino cherries, cut into halves
  ½ cup butter or margarine
  ½ cup packed light brown sugar
  1 teaspoon ground cinnamon
  ½ teaspoon ground nutmeg
  ¼ teaspoon ground cloves

1. Combine fruits in greased 2½-quart baking dish; mix gently.

2. Combine remaining ingredients in small saucepan. Cook and stir over medium-low heat until butter and sugar melt. Spoon over fruit.

3. Bake in preheated 325°F oven until fruit is glazed and hot throughout, 20 to 30 minutes.

MASHED POTATOES WITH RUTABAGA

Rutabaga, sometimes called Swedish turnip, is a root vegetable of considerable versatility. Cube it for soups and stews, mash it alone or with potatoes, or cut in strips to serve raw with party dips.

Makes 4 to 6 servings

  3 medium potatoes, pared
  1 medium rutabaga (about 1 pound), pared
  ⅓ cup milk, hot
  ¼ cup butter or margarine, room temperature
  ½ teaspoon salt
  Pinch pepper

1. Cut potatoes into eighths; cut rutabaga into pieces slightly smaller than potatoes.

2. Cook vegetables, covered, in 1 inch boiling salted water in large saucepan until tender, 20 to 25 minutes; drain well. Gently shake pan over low heat to dry vegetables.

3. Using a potato masher or electric mixer, mash potatoes and rutabaga until smooth. Gradually add milk, beating after each addition. Add butter, salt and pepper; beat until mixture is light and fluffy.

Potato Pancakes

POTATO PANCAKES

Makes 8 pancakes

2 large eggs
2 tablespoons all-purpose flour
2 tablespoons milk
2 tablespoons butter, melted
½ teaspoon salt
Pinch pepper
3 medium potatoes, pared, shredded
½ small onion, grated
Applesauce or sour cream
Parsley sprigs for garnish

1. Whisk eggs in large bowl; whisk in flour, milk, butter, salt and pepper until smooth. Add potatoes and onion; stir just until potato shreds are coated.

2. For each pancake, drop ¼ cup batter onto hot greased griddle; spread batter to form 4-inch pancake. Cook over medium heat, turning once, until brown on both sides. Serve immediately with applesauce or sour cream; garnish with parsley.

BANANA SALAD DRESSING

Makes about 2 cups

1 ripe medium banana, cut up
½ cup low-fat lemon yogurt
½ cup low-fat cottage cheese
4 to 5 tablespoons skim milk
1 tablespoon honey, if desired

Combine all ingredients in blender container; process until smooth. (Add more milk if thinner consistency is desired.) Refrigerate, covered; serve with cottage cheese or with fruit salads.

AMERICAN CORN SOUFFLE

Golden corn kernels and crisp crumbled bacon complement the delightful cheesiness of this light and airy supper dish.

Makes 6 servings

Butter for dish
Grated Parmesan cheese
¼ cup butter
¼ cup all-purpose flour
¼ teaspoon salt
⅛ teaspoon pepper
1 cup milk
1 cup shredded Colby cheese
4 large eggs, separated
1 package (10 ounces) frozen whole-kernel corn, cooked, drained
6 slices bacon, cooked, crumbled
¼ teaspoon cream of tartar

1. Butter 1½-quart souffle dish; sprinkle with Parmesan cheese to coat bottom and sides evenly.

2. Melt ¼ cup butter in medium saucepan over medium heat; stir in flour, salt and pepper until smooth. Gradually whisk in milk until smooth. Cook, stirring constantly, until mixture thickens and bubbles for 1 minute. Remove from heat; stir in Colby cheese until melted.

3. Gradually whisk ½ of the hot mixture into egg yolks in medium bowl; gradually whisk egg yolk mixture into remaining hot mixture in pan. Stir in corn and bacon.

4. Beat egg whites in large mixer bowl until foamy. Add cream of tartar; beat until soft peaks form. Fold cheese mixture into egg whites; spoon into prepared souffle dish.

5. Bake in preheated 350°F oven until top is puffed and brown, 45 to 50 minutes. Serve immediately.

RED CABBAGE WITH APPLES

Unsweetened apple juice and lemon juice not only give the cabbage-apple mixture a zippy, fresh taste, but they also keep the colors bright during cooking.

Makes 8 servings

- 1 small head red cabbage (about 1 pound), shredded
- 2 large apples, pared, thinly sliced
- ½ cup apple juice
- ¼ cup lemon juice
- 1 small onion, thinly sliced
- 3 tablespoons raisins
- 2 tablespoons packed brown sugar
  Salt and pepper to taste

Combine all ingredients in large nonstick saucepan; toss to mix. Heat over medium heat to simmering; reduce heat to low. Simmer, covered, stirring occasionally, 30 minutes.

ALMOND-CRUSTED CAULIFLOWER AND CARROTS

Makes 8 servings

- ¼ cup slivered blanched almonds
- 1 small head cauliflower, cut into 1-inch flowerets
- 2 cups diagonally sliced carrots (¼ inch thick)
  Salt to taste
- 2 tablespoons butter
- 2 teaspoons lemon juice
  Ground white pepper to taste

1. Toast almonds in small dry skillet over medium heat, stirring frequently, until golden, 1 to 2 minutes; remove to plate.

2. Cook cauliflower and carrots in boiling salted water in large saucepan until crisp-tender, about 10 minutes; drain well. Toss with butter, lemon juice and pepper in serving bowl; sprinkle with almonds.

Red Cabbage with Apples

MARINATED FRESH VEGETABLES

Makes 8 to 10 servings

3 stalks celery, sliced
4 large carrots, sliced
3 green bell peppers, sliced
3 small onions, sliced
3 tomatoes, cut lengthwise into halves, sliced
   Basil French Dressing (recipe follows)

1. Arrange vegetables in order listed in layers in clear glass bowl.

2. Pour Basil French Dressing over vegetables; toss gently to mix or leave vegetables in layers. Refrigerate, covered, several hours or overnight. Toss before serving.

BASIL FRENCH DRESSING

⅓ cup red wine vinegar
¼ cup tomato sauce
1 tablespoon sugar
1 teaspoon salt
1 teaspoon dried basil, crumbled
1 teaspoon Worcestershire sauce
1 clove garlic, minced
¼ teaspoon dry mustard
¼ teaspoon pepper
⅛ teaspoon hot red pepper sauce
1 cup vegetable oil

Combine all ingredients except oil in medium bowl; mix well. Gradually whisk in oil until blended.

ROCK LOBSTER SALAD

Chilled lobster meat moves the main-dish salad into a class by itself. In this version, the delicacy is tossed with apple, vegetables and rice, then dressed with creamy curried mayonnaise.

Makes 6 servings

3 frozen South African rock lobster tails (4 ounces each)
4 cups cooked rice
1 can (1 pound) cut green beans, drained
2 tart apples, pared, cored, diced
1 can (8 ounces) diced carrots, drained
1 cup sliced celery
1 cup mayonnaise
½ cup half-and-half
1 teaspoon curry powder
½ teaspoon salt
½ cup sliced green onions

1. Add frozen lobster tails to saucepan of boiling salted water; when water returns to boiling, boil 8 minutes. Drain; rinse under cold water.

2. Cut away underside membrane with kitchen shears; with fingers, work lobster meat loose from shell and pull out in one piece. Cut meat crosswise into ½-inch-thick slices.

3. Combine lobster meat, rice, beans, apples, carrots and celery in large bowl; mix well. Mix mayonnaise, half-and-half, curry powder and salt in small bowl. Add to lobster mixture; toss to mix.

4. Transfer salad to serving bowl; refrigerate, covered, until ready to serve. Sprinkle with green onions.

Marinated Fresh Vegetables

Poached Spiced Peaches

TWICE-BAKED POTATOES

These stuffed potatoes bake a second time to melt the cheese inside and lightly brown the top of the fluffy stuffing mixture.

Makes 8 servings

   4 **large baking potatoes**
   ¼ **cup whipping cream, half-and-half or milk, hot**
   1 **large egg, room temperature**
   ½ **teaspoon salt**
   ¼ **teaspoon white pepper**
   1 **cup shredded Cheddar cheese**

1. Scrub potatoes; pierce each in several places with fork. Bake in preheated 425°F oven until fork-tender, about 1 hour.

2. Remove potatoes from oven; reduce oven setting to 350°F.

3. Cut potatoes lengthwise into halves. Scoop out pulp into large mixer bowl; reserve shells. Beat potatoes until smooth. Beat in cream, egg, salt and pepper; beat in cheese.

4. Spoon mixture into reserved shells, dividing evenly. Bake at 350°F until hot throughout, 8 to 10 minutes; serve hot.

POACHED SPICED PEACHES

Whole peaches simmered gently in a spicy syrup laced with wine make a superb accompaniment to a main course of roast beef, pork or poultry.

Makes 6 to 8 servings

   1½ **cups sugar**
   1½ **cups water**
   1½ **cups burgundy wine or black grape juice**
   2 **tablespoons lemon juice**
   2 **sticks cinnamon (each about 3 inches)**
   6 **whole cloves**
   6 **whole allspice**
   8 **to 10 firm ripe peaches or nectarines**

1. Combine all ingredients except peaches in large saucepan; heat to boiling. Reduce heat; simmer, uncovered, 15 minutes.

2. Meanwhile, drop peaches into boiling water in second saucepan; blanch 30 seconds. Rinse under cold water; peel.

3. Add peaches to spiced syrup in saucepan; poach over low heat, turning once, until tender, about 20 minutes. Remove peaches with slotted spoon to heatproof serving bowl.

4. Cook syrup over high heat until reduced by half, about 3 minutes. Strain syrup, discarding cloves and allspice. Pour syrup over peaches; add cinnamon sticks. Refrigerate, covered, turning peaches once, several hours.

Hot German Potato Salad

HOT GERMAN POTATO SALAD

Baked instead of cooked in a skillet, this calorie-trimmed version of the traditional dish retains the lively sweet-and-sour dressing.

Makes 6 servings

⅓ cup finely chopped onion
2 tablespoons vegetable oil
1 tablespoon all-purpose flour
1½ teaspoons salt
¼ teaspoon dry mustard
¼ cup water
3 tablespoons cider vinegar
2½ cups diced cooked potatoes
½ cup sliced celery
¼ cup diced green bell pepper
3 tablespoons pickle relish

1. Saute onion in oil in small skillet over medium heat until soft, about 4 minutes. Stir in flour, salt and mustard until smooth; whisk in water and vinegar until smooth. Cook and stir until sauce thickens and bubbles for 1 minute.

2. Combine potatoes, celery, pepper and relish in 5-cup baking dish. Add hot sauce; mix well.

3. Bake in preheated 350°F oven until hot throughout, about 20 minutes.

BROCCOLI-CARROT SUPREME

Cooks of many nationalities use fresh cream on cooked vegetables. Adding white wine makes this vegetable dish special.

Makes 4 to 6 servings

4 to 6 carrots, pared, sliced
1 can (8 ounces) small white onions, drained
¼ cup butter or margarine
½ cup dry white wine
1 teaspoon salt
1 teaspoon dried thyme, crumbled
⅛ teaspoon pepper
1 bay leaf
1 package (10 ounces) frozen chopped broccoli, cooked, drained
½ cup chopped pecans
¼ cup whipping cream

1. Saute carrots and onions in butter in large skillet over medium heat 4 minutes. Stir in wine, salt, thyme, pepper and bay leaf; reduce heat to low. Simmer, covered, until carrots are tender, about 20 minutes.

2. Remove and discard bay leaf. Stir in broccoli, pecans, and cream; cook until broccoli is hot.

CABBAGE FRY PLUS

Old-fashioned panned cabbage gets an update with the addition of more vegetables. Keep cooking time short so that the three Cs—cabbage, celery and carrots—are crisp-tender.

Makes 6 to 8 servings

　2 large onions, sliced
　2 tablespoons vegetable oil
　4 cups shredded cabbage
　2 cups chopped celery
　2 cups shredded carrots
　1 green bell pepper, chopped
　1 cup sliced mushrooms
　2 tablespoons sugar
　½ teaspoon salt
　⅛ teaspoon ground black pepper
　2 large tomatoes, chopped

1. Saute onions in oil in large skillet over medium heat until light brown, about 8 minutes. Stir in cabbage, celery, carrots, green pepper and mushrooms; saute 2 minutes. Sprinkle with sugar, salt and pepper; mix gently.

2. Spoon tomatoes on top of vegetables. Cook, covered, over low heat, just until vegetables are crisp-tender, 6 to 8 minutes.

CHERRIED SWEET POTATO BAKE

Tart red cherries add a festive note to candied sweet potatoes at holiday dinners. What a colorful accompaniment to baked ham or roast turkey!

Makes 8 to 10 servings

3½ pounds sweet potatoes, pared
　1 pound pitted tart cherries, drained
　1 cup water
　⅔ cup packed brown sugar
　½ cup orange juice
　¼ cup granulated sugar
　¼ cup butter or margarine
1½ teaspoons salt
　¼ cup toasted slivered almonds

1. Cut sweet potatoes crosswise into ½-inch-thick slices. Cook, covered, in boiling water in large saucepan until tender, 12 to 15 minutes; drain.

2. Combine sweet potatoes and cherries in well-greased 13×9×2-inch baking dish.

3. Combine remaining ingredients except almonds in medium saucepan; cook and stir over medium heat until mixture thickens to thin syrup consistency. Pour syrup over sweet potatoes and cherries.

4. Bake in preheated 350°F oven until syrup is thick, about 30 minutes. Sprinkle with almonds before serving.

Cherried Sweet Potato Bake

WHOLE WHEAT BURGER BUNS

Makes 8 large or 12 small buns

¾ cup warm water (105 to 115°F)
1 tablespoon packed brown sugar
1 package (¼ ounce) active dry yeast
2 to 2½ cups all-purpose flour
½ cup whole wheat flour
2 tablespoons wheat germ
2 tablespoons butter, margarine or lard, melted
1 teaspoon salt
1 large egg white, lightly beaten
Sesame seeds

1. Combine water, sugar and yeast in large bowl; stir to dissolve yeast. Let stand until bubbly, about 5 minutes.

2. Whisk 1 cup of the all-purpose flour into yeast mixture; whisk in whole wheat flour, wheat germ, butter and salt. Stir in as much of the remaining all-purpose flour as needed to make soft dough, about 1 cup.

3. Knead on floured surface, adding as much of the remaining all-purpose flour as needed to prevent sticking, until smooth and elastic, 10 to 15 minutes.

4. Divide dough into 8 equal pieces for large buns or 12 equal pieces for small buns. Shape each piece into smooth ball; place on greased baking sheet. Let rise, covered, in warm place 30 minutes.

5. Flatten buns with palm of hand. Let rise in warm place until almost doubled, about 30 minutes.

6. Brush tops of buns with egg white; sprinkle with sesame seeds. Bake in preheated 350°F oven until tops are golden and bottoms sound hollow when tapped, 25 to 30 minutes. Remove from baking sheet; cool on wire racks.

HOT DOG BUNS

You don't have to settle for store-bought buns when serving the all-American frankfurter. Make it a special treat with great-tasting, good-textured rolls baked at home.

Makes 1 dozen buns

¾ cup warm water (105 to 115°F)
1 tablespoon sugar
1 package (¼ ounce) active dry yeast
2 tablespoons instant nonfat dry milk solids
1½ tablespoons butter or margarine, melted
1 teaspoon salt
2¾ to 3¼ cups all-purpose flour
1 large egg, beaten

1. Combine water, sugar and yeast in large bowl; stir to dissolve yeast. Let stand until bubbly, about 5 minutes.

2. Add milk solids, butter and salt to yeast mixture; mix well. Whisk in 1½ cups of the flour until smooth. Stir in as much of the remaining flour as needed to make soft dough, about 1¼ cups.

3. Knead on floured surface, adding as much of the remaining flour as needed to prevent sticking, until dough is smooth and elastic, about 10 minutes.

4. Place in greased bowl; turn dough over. Let rise, covered, in warm place 30 minutes.

5. Knead dough about 30 seconds. Divide into 12 equal pieces; shape each piece into smooth bun, 6 inches long; place on greased baking sheet. Let rise, covered, until almost doubled, about 30 minutes.

6. Brush tops of buns with egg. Bake in preheated 375°F oven until tops are golden and bottoms sound hollow when tapped, 20 to 25 minutes. Remove from baking sheet; cool on wire racks.

Hot Dog Buns (top); Whole Wheat Burger Buns (bottom)

PAUL BUNYAN STICKY BUNS

Tall tales of legendary lumberjack Paul Bunyan say the giant's footprints, filled with water, became the lakes of the North Woods. His voracious appetite required an acre-sized griddle, but it might have been satisfied with these big sticky buns.

Makes 4 large buns; 8 servings

1 package (13¾ ounces) hot roll mix
1 cup packed brown sugar
½ cup butter or margarine, melted
2 tablespoons water
1 cup chopped walnuts
¾ cup granulated sugar
1 tablespoon ground cinnamon

1. Prepare hot roll mix according to package directions for making rolls; knead dough gently on floured surface 1 minute. Place in greased bowl; turn dough over. Let rise, covered, until doubled, about 45 minutes.

2. Combine brown sugar, ¼ cup of the butter and the water in small saucepan; cook and stir over medium heat until sugar dissolves. Heat to boiling; simmer over low heat 1 minute.

3. Immediately pour syrup into 10-inch round cake pan; tilt to spread evenly. Sprinkle with ½ cup of the nuts.

4. Punch down dough; turn out onto lightly floured surface. Let rest 5 minutes. Stretch and roll to 30 × 5-inch rectangle; brush with remaining ¼ cup butter. Mix granulated sugar and cinnamon in small bowl; sprinkle over butter. Top with remaining ½ cup nuts.

5. Starting at 5-inch end, roll up dough loosely; pinch seam to seal. Cut roll crosswise into 4 equal pieces; place, cut sides up, in prepared pan. Spread pinwheels open slightly. Let rise, covered, until almost doubled, 35 to 45 minutes.

6. Cover lower oven rack with aluminum foil. Bake buns on rack in center of preheated 375°F oven until golden, 25 to 35 minutes. Immediately invert onto tray or serving dish; cool 5 minutes. Serve warm.

FRUIT KUCHEN

Descendants of German settlers in the Dakotas are especially fond of this coffeecake with its fruit and spicy custard topping. Any fruit in season, be it apples, blueberries, purple plums, pears or peaches, make a delicious kuchen.

Makes 2 coffeecakes; 8 servings each

Basic Sweet Dough (recipe follows)
½ cup plus 2 tablespoons sugar
3 medium apples, cored, sliced*
1 cup whipping cream
2 large eggs
1 teaspoon ground cinnamon

1. Punch down Basic Sweet Dough; divide in half. Shape each ½ into 8-inch circle; press each circle in greased 9-inch round cake pan to cover bottom completely.

2. Sprinkle dough in each pan with ¼ cup of the sugar; arrange apple slices on top of dough. Whisk cream and eggs in small bowl until smooth; pour over apples, dividing evenly. Mix remaining 2 tablespoons sugar and the cinnamon in small bowl; sprinkle evenly over apples and cream mixture.

(Continued)

Fruit Kuchen

3. Bake in preheated 350°F oven until edge of dough sounds hollow when tapped and knife inserted into center of cream mixture is withdrawn clean, 25 to 30 minutes. Cool in pans on wire racks.

***Note:** 2 cups fresh blueberries, raspberries, blackberries or sliced strawberries, peaches or pears can be substituted for apples.*

BASIC SWEET DOUGH

⅔ cup warm water (105 to 115°F)
3 tablespoons sugar
1 package (¼ ounce) active dry yeast
1 large egg, beaten
2 tablespoons instant nonfat dry milk solids
2 tablespoons butter or margarine, melted
1 teaspoon salt
2½ to 3 cups all-purpose flour

1. Combine water, 1 tablespoon of the sugar and the yeast in large mixer bowl; stir to dissolve yeast. Let stand until bubbly, about 5 minutes.

2. Add egg, milk solids, butter, salt and remaining 2 tablespoons sugar to yeast mixture; mix well. Add 1½ cups of the flour. Mix on low speed; beat on medium speed until smooth and elastic, about 5 minutes. Stir in as much of the remaining flour as needed to make soft dough, about 1 cup.

3. Knead on floured surface, adding as much of the remaining flour as needed to prevent sticking, until smooth and elastic, about 10 minutes.

4. Place in greased bowl; turn dough over. Let rise, covered, in warm place until doubled, 1 to 1½ hours.

NORWEGIAN YULE LOAF

Christmas is the season for this traditional Norwegian bread. Each round raisin- and fruit- studded loaf is brushed with egg yolk just before baking to give it a shiny surface.

Makes 1 loaf; 10 to 12 servings

¼ cup warm water (105 to 115°F)
4 tablespoons sugar
1 package (¼ ounce) active dry yeast
¼ cup butter or margarine, melted, cooled

(Continued)

Norwegian Yule Loaf (top); Dresden Stollen (bottom)

¼ cup evaporated milk or fresh milk
1 large egg, beaten
1 teaspoon ground cardamom or nutmeg
½ teaspoon salt
2½ to 3 cups all-purpose flour
1 cup raisins
¼ cup finely chopped candied citron
    Vegetable oil
1 large egg yolk
2 tablespoons cold water

1. Combine warm water, 1 tablespoon of the sugar and the yeast in large mixer bowl; stir to dissolve yeast. Let stand until bubbly, about 5 minutes.

2. Add butter, milk, 1 egg, the cardamom, salt and the remaining 3 tablespoons sugar to yeast mixture; mix well. Add 1½ cups of the flour. Mix on low speed; beat at medium speed until smooth and elastic, about 5 minutes. Stir in raisins, citron and as much of the remaining flour as needed to make soft dough, about 1 cup.

3. Knead on floured surface, adding as much of the remaining flour as needed to prevent sticking, until smooth and elastic, about 10 minutes.

4. Place in greased bowl; turn dough over. Let rise, covered, in warm place until doubled, about 1 hour.

5. Punch down dough. Roll or pat into 8-inch circle; place in greased 9-inch round cake pan. Brush top lightly with oil. Let rise until doubled, about 45 minutes.

6. Beat egg yolk and cold water in small bowl; brush over bread. Bake in preheated 350°F oven until top is evenly browned and bottom sounds hollow when tapped, 35 to 40 minutes. Immediately remove from pan; cool on wire rack.

DRESDEN STOLLEN

This holiday classic of German heritage is packed with rum- or brandy-soaked fruits and nuts. The circle of rich yeast dough is folded off-center like an omelet just before baking.

Makes 1 loaf; 12 to 16 servings

¼ cup golden raisins
¼ cup chopped candied cherries
¼ cup slivered almonds
¼ cup chopped candied orange peel
2 tablespoons brandy or dark rum
1 tablespoon grated lemon rind
¼ cup warm water (105 to 115°F)
4 tablespoons granulated sugar
2 packages (¼ ounce each) active dry yeast
¼ cup milk
1 large egg
½ teaspoon salt
½ teaspoon almond extract
2¾ to 3¼ cups all-purpose flour
⅓ cup butter or margarine, room temperature
2 tablespoons butter or margarine, melted
1 large egg white, beaten
3 tablespoons powdered sugar

1. Mix raisins, cherries, almonds, orange peel, brandy and lemon rind in small bowl.

2. Combine water, 1 tablespoon of the granulated sugar and the yeast in large mixer bowl; stir to dissolve yeast. Let stand until bubbly, about 5 minutes.   *(Continued)*

3. Add milk, 1 egg, the salt, almond extract and remaining 3 tablespoons sugar; mix well. Add 1½ cups of the flour and ⅓ cup butter. Mix on low speed; beat at medium speed until smooth and elastic, about 5 minutes. Stir in as much of the remaining flour as needed to make soft dough, about 1¼ cups.

4. Turn dough out onto floured surface; knead in raisin mixture. Knead dough, using as much of the remaining flour as needed to prevent sticking, until smooth and elastic, about 10 minutes.

5. Placed in greased bowl; turn dough over. Let rise, covered, in warm place until doubled, 1 to 1½ hours.

6. Punch down dough. Roll or pat dough on large greased baking sheet into a 7 × 9-inch oval; brush with melted butter. Make a crease lengthwise with handle of wooden spoon just off the center. Fold lengthwise, bringing smaller section over larger one. Brush top with egg white. Let rise, loosely covered, until almost doubled, about 45 minutes.

7. Bake in preheated 350°F oven until top is evenly browned and bottom sounds hollow when tapped, 25 to 30 minutes. Immediately remove from baking sheet to wire rack. Brush with melted butter; sprinkle with powdered sugar. Let cool completely.

CURRIED HAM-PINEAPPLE BREAD

Just beat the very soft dough of this batter bread with an electric mixer and let the loaves shape themselves in a casserole or baking dish.

Makes 2 casserole breads

1 package (13¾ ounces) hot roll mix
1 cup wheat germ
1 can (8 to 8¾ ounces) crushed pineapple, undrained
1 cup hot water (120°F)
1 large egg
2 teaspoons curry powder
¾ pound cooked ham, chopped
1 can (20 ounces) sliced pineapple
3 tablespoons packed brown sugar
1 tablespoon butter

1. Mix hot roll mix and contents of yeast packet in large mixer bowl; add wheat germ, crushed pineapple, water, egg and curry powder. Beat on low speed 1 minute, scraping sides of bowl often. Cover bowl with plastic wrap; let stand in warm place until doubled in bulk, about 45 minutes.

2. Stir down batter; stir in ham. Transfer to 2 well-greased 1-quart souffle dishes or casseroles, dividing evenly. Let stand in warm place until batter is spongy, about 20 minutes; do not let double in bulk.

3. Bake in preheated 375°F oven until golden, about 40 minutes.

4. Quickly drain pineapple slices, reserving 1½ teaspoons of the liquid. Cut slices into halves; arrange on tops of breads. Mix reserved 1½ teaspoons liquid with sugar and butter in small saucepan; cook and stir over low heat until butter is melted. Immediately pour hot mixture over pineapple on breads; bake 10 minutes longer.

PEANUT BUTTER BREAD

Spread slices of this delicious bread with ginger-cream cheese. They are great open-faced for brunch or made into tea sandwiches for parties.

Makes 1 loaf

1 cup all-purpose flour
½ cup whole wheat flour
2 teaspoons baking powder
½ teaspoon ground cinnamon
¼ teaspoon salt
¼ teaspoon ground nutmeg
¼ teaspoon ground allspice
¾ cup packed brown sugar
½ cup peanut butter
3 tablespoons butter
2 large eggs
⅔ cup milk
1 cup chopped peanuts
½ teaspoon vanilla
Creamy Ginger Spread (recipe follows), if desired

1. Mix all-purpose and whole wheat flours, baking powder, cinnamon, salt, nutmeg and allspice in medium bowl.

2. Beat sugar, peanut butter and butter in large mixer bowl until light and fluffy. Add eggs, 1 at a time, beating well after each addition.

3. Add flour mixture, ⅓ at a time, alternating with milk, mixing well after each addition. Stir in peanuts and vanilla; pour into greased 8½ × 4½ × 2½-inch loaf pan.

4. Bake in preheated 325°F oven until wooden pick inserted into center is withdrawn clean, about 1 hour. Cool in pan on wire rack 10 minutes. Remove from pan; cool completely on rack. Serve with Creamy Ginger Spread.

CREAMY GINGER SPREAD

1 package (3 ounces) cream cheese, room temperature
2 tablespoons butter
2 tablespoons honey or pineapple preserves
⅛ teaspoon ground ginger

Beat cream cheese and butter in small mixer bowl until smooth; beat in honey and ginger.

Makes about ⅔ cup

Peanut Butter Bread

FRUIT KOLACHES

These buns from Eastern Europe are little rounds of sweet dough baked with a filling in the center. Canned poppy seed or date filling can be substituted for the apricot, peach or prune fillings, if you wish.

Makes 12 sweet rolls

 1 cup dried apricots, peaches or pitted prunes, chopped
 1 cup water
 ⅓ cup honey
 2 teaspoons lemon juice
   Basic Sweet Dough (see Index)
 1 large egg
 2 tablespoons milk

1. For filling, combine dried fruit and water in small saucepan; cook over medium heat, stirring frequently, until fruit is soft and water has been absorbed, 20 to 25 minutes. Stir in honey and lemon juice; let cool completely.

2. Punch down Basic Sweet Dough; divide into 12 even pieces. Shape each piece into smooth ball; place on greased baking sheets. Flatten each ball to ½-inch thickness. Let rise, covered, in warm place until almost doubled, 20 to 30 minutes.

3. With thumb or back of spoon, press indentation in center of each roll; spoon fruit mixture into indentations. Let rise until doubled, 10 to 20 minutes longer.

4. Beat egg and milk in small bowl; brush over tops of rolls. Bake in preheated 350°F oven until golden, 15 to 20 minutes. Remove from baking sheets; cool on wire racks.

MAPLE APRICOT-DATE BREAD

When a quick bread contains generous amounts of fruit and nuts, the recipe may specify letting the dough stand in the pan a short time before baking. The wait helps the loaf to rise more evenly in the oven.

Makes 1 loaf

 ½ cup dried apricots
 1 cup chopped butternuts or walnuts
 ½ cup chopped pitted dates
 3 cups sifted all-purpose flour
 3 teaspoons baking powder
1½ teaspoons salt
 ¼ teaspoon baking soda
 1 cup packed brown sugar
 1 cup milk
 ½ cup maple syrup
 1 egg, beaten
 1 package (3 ounces) cream cheese, room temperature
   Nuts for garnish

1. Combine apricots with boiling water to cover in small bowl; let stand 15 minutes. Drain well; cut into small pieces. Mix apricots, chopped nuts and dates in small bowl.

2. Mix flour, baking powder, salt and baking soda in large bowl. Add sugar and apricot mixture; mix well.

3. Mix milk, maple syrup and egg in small bowl. Add to flour mixture; mix well. Pour into well-greased 9 × 5 × 3-inch loaf pan; let stand 20 minutes before baking.

4. Bake in preheated 350°F oven until wooden pick inserted in center is withdrawn clean, about 1½ hours. Cool in pan on wire rack 5 minutes; remove from pan. Cool completely on rack. Frost with cream cheese; garnish with nuts.

Fruit Kolaches

CRANBERRY NUT BREAD

Makes 1 loaf

1½ cups chopped fresh or thawed frozen
    cranberries
1½ cups sugar
  3 cups all-purpose flour
2¼ teaspoons baking powder
2¼ teaspoons ground cinnamon
  2 teaspoons grated orange rind
1½ teaspoons salt
  ¾ teaspoon baking soda
  ¼ teaspoon ground cloves
  ⅓ cup vegetable shortening
  1 cup orange juice
  2 large eggs, beaten
1½ cups chopped walnuts

1. Combine cranberries and ¼ cup of the sugar in small bowl; toss to mix.

2. Mix flour, baking powder, cinnamon, orange rind, salt, baking soda, cloves and remaining 1¼ cups sugar in large bowl. Cut in shortening until mixture resembles cornmeal.

3. Add orange juice and eggs; mix well. Stir in cranberries and walnuts; pour into greased 9×5×3-inch loaf pan.

4. Bake in preheated 350°F oven until wooden pick inserted into center is withdrawn clean, about 1 hour and 10 minutes. Remove from pan; cool on wire rack.

ALMOND CHERRY DANISH

Almond flavoring enhances the natural goodness of cherries and apricots in this elegant sour cream coffeecake.

Makes 3 coffeecakes; 18 to 24 servings

  2 packages (¼ ounce each) active dry yeast
  ½ cup warm water (105 to 115°F)
  2 cups sour cream, room temperature
  ⅓ cup granulated sugar
  2 large eggs
  ¼ cup butter, room temperature
  2 teaspoons salt
  6 cups all-purpose flour
    Almond Cherry Sauce (recipe follows)
1½ cups snipped dried apricots
  2 cups sifted powdered sugar
  2 to 4 tablespoons milk

1. Sprinkle yeast over water in large mixer bowl; stir to dissolve. Let stand 10 minutes.

2. Add sour cream, granulated sugar, eggs, butter and salt; beat until blended. Gradually beat in flour to form firm dough.

3. Knead dough on floured surface until smooth and elastic, about 10 minutes. Place in greased bowl; turn dough over. Let rise, covered, in warm place until doubled, about 1 hour.

4. Punch down dough; knead briefly. Divide into 3 equal pieces; roll out each piece on floured surface into 15×6-inch rectangle. Place each rectangle on greased baking sheet.

5. Make 2-inch cuts at ½-inch intervals down both long sides of each rectangle. Mix 3 cups of the Almond Cherry Sauce and the apricots in medium bowl; spoon ⅓ of the *(Continued)*

Almond Cherry Danish

mixture down center of each rectangle. Fold cut pieces of dough across filling in crisscross pattern. Let rise, loosely covered, until almost doubled, about 30 minutes.

6. Bake in preheated 375°F oven until dough is golden and sounds hollow when tapped, about 40 minutes. Carefully remove to wire racks; cool completely.

7. Mix powdered sugar and enough of the milk in small bowl to form glaze consistency; drizzle over coffeecakes. Serve topped with remaining Almond Cherry Sauce.

ALMOND CHERRY SAUCE

  ¾ cup sugar
1½ tablespoons cornstarch
1½ cups cold water
  2 cups pitted tart red cherries
  2 teaspoons almond extract
  1 teaspoon lemon juice
  3 drops red food coloring, if desired

1. Mix sugar and cornstarch in medium saucepan; stir in water. Cook, stirring constantly, over medium heat until mixture thickens and bubbles for 3 minutes.

2. Reduce heat to low; stir in cherries, almond extract, lemon juice and food coloring. Cook and stir just until hot; do not boil. Let cool completely.

Makes about 1 quart

Blueberry Buttermilk Muffins

BLUEBERRY BUTTERMILK MUFFINS

Makes about 18 muffins

½ cup butter
1 cup buttermilk
2 large eggs, beaten
2½ cups all-purpose flour
1 cup sugar
2½ teaspoons baking powder
¼ teaspoon salt
1½ cups fresh or dry-pack frozen blueberries

1. Heat butter in small saucepan over medium heat until melted and golden. Whisk butter, buttermilk and eggs in small bowl until blended.

2. Mix flour, sugar, baking powder and salt thoroughly in large bowl; make a well in center. Add buttermilk mixture to well; mix with fork just until flour is moistened. Fold in blueberries.

3. Spoon batter into greased muffin pan cups, filling ⅔ full. Bake in preheated 400°F oven until tops are golden and centers are firm to the touch, about 20 minutes. Remove from pan; serve warm, or cool on wire racks.

CHOCOLATE SOUR CREAM BUNS

Chocolate morsels in the filling melt lusciously while the coils of sweet roll dough bake to a delicate brown.

Makes 18 buns

1 cup sour cream
3 tablespoons granulated sugar
1 teaspoon salt
⅛ teaspoon baking soda
1 package (¼ ounce) active dry yeast
2 tablespoons warm water
1 large egg, lightly beaten
2 tablespoons vegetable shortening
3 cups all-purpose flour
  Chocolate Filling (recipe follows)
½ cup powdered sugar
2 teaspoons milk

1. Heat sour cream in medium saucepan over low heat, stirring constantly, just to lukewarm. Remove from heat; stir in granulated sugar, salt and baking soda. Transfer to large bowl.

2. Dissolve yeast in warm water in small bowl; stir into sour cream mixture. Beat in egg and shortening. Add 1 cup of the flour; beat until smooth. Stir in 1½ cups of the flour. Turn out onto floured surface; knead in remaining ½ cup flour until smooth and elastic.

3. Roll out dough into 18 × 12-inch rectangle; cut crosswise into eighteen 1-inch-wide strips. Roll each strip into 15-inch long rope. Wind each rope loosely into coil; place coils with sides just touching on greased baking sheet. Let rise, covered, in warm place until doubled, 1 to 1½ hours.

4. Pat down center of each bun, leaving outer ring to form edge. Spoon about 1 tablespoon Chocolate Filling into center of each bun.

5. Bake in preheated 375°F oven until light brown, 12 to 15 minutes. Mix powdered sugar and milk in small bowl; drizzle over tops of buns. Serve warm.

Note: *Chocolate Sour Cream Buns can be baked 1 day ahead without the powdered sugar glaze. Reheat, loosely covered with aluminum foil, in preheated 350°F oven 10 to 15 minutes; drizzle with glaze. Or, unglazed buns can be frozen; thaw, uncovered, at room temperature and reheat as directed above.*

CHOCOLATE FILLING

⅔ cup semisweet chocolate morsels
⅓ cup chopped pecans
¼ cup light corn syrup
2 tablespoons packed light brown sugar
2 tablespoons butter, melted
1 tablespoon cornstarch
½ teaspoon vanilla

Combine all ingredients in small bowl; mix well.

(Continued)

SWEDISH LIMPA

Bits of orange peel and caraway seeds give this rye bread its characteristic flavor.

Makes 1 loaf

⅔ cup warm water (105 to 115°F)
2 tablespoons molasses
1 package (¼ ounce) active dry yeast
½ cup rye flour
2 tablespoons butter or margarine, melted
1½ teaspoons grated orange rind
1 teaspoon instant coffee granules
1 teaspoon salt
½ teaspoon fennel seeds
½ teaspoon anise seeds
½ teaspoon caraway seeds
2 to 2½ cups all-purpose flour
Melted butter or margarine

1. Combine water, molasses and yeast in large mixer bowl; stir to dissolve yeast. Let stand until bubbly, about 5 minutes.

2. Add rye flour, 2 tablespoons butter, the orange rind, coffee granules, salt and fennel, anise and caraway seeds to yeast mixture; mix well. Add 1 cup of the all-purpose flour. Mix on low speed; beat on medium speed until smooth and elastic, about 5 minutes. Stir in as much of the remaining all-purpose flour as needed to make soft dough, about ¾ cup.

3. Knead on floured surface, adding as much of the remaining all-purpose flour as needed to prevent sticking, about 10 minutes.

4. Place in greased bowl; turn dough over. Let rise, covered, in warm place until doubled, about 1 hour.

5. Punch down dough. Shape into loaf; place in greased 8½ × 4½ × 2½-inch loaf pan. Let rise, covered, until almost doubled, about 45 minutes.

6. Bake in preheated 350°F oven until bottom sounds hollow when tapped, 35 to 40 minutes; remove bread from pan to wire rack. Brush with melted butter; let cool completely.

ONION & POPPY SEED RYE

Using both rye and wheat flours from the nation's breadbasket, these loaves are flavored with poppy seeds, onion and a touch of garlic.

Makes 3 loaves

¼ cup poppy seeds
Water
¼ cup instant minced onion
1 teaspoon instant minced garlic
2 packages (¼ ounce each) active dry yeast
2 cups warm water (105 to 115°F)
6 to 6½ cups all-purpose flour
2 cups rye flour
¼ cup sugar
1 tablespoon salt
2 large eggs
3 tablespoons vegetable shortening

1. Mix poppy seeds and 1 cup water in small bowl; let stand 45 minutes to soften. Drain.

2. Mix onion, garlic and ¼ cup water in small bowl; let stand 10 minutes to soften. *(Continued)*

3. Sprinkle yeast over 2 cups warm water in large mixer bowl; stir to dissolve. Let stand 5 minutes.

4. Add 3 cups of the all-purpose flour, the rye flour, sugar, salt, 1 of the eggs, the poppy seeds and onion and garlic to yeast; beat until smooth, about 2 minutes. Beat in shortening until smooth. Gradually stir in as much of the remaining all-purpose flour as needed to make soft dough, about 3 cups.

5. Knead dough on floured surface, adding as much of the remaining flour as needed to make firm dough; knead until smooth and elastic, about 10 minutes. Place in greased bowl; turn dough over. Let rise, covered, in warm place until doubled, about 1 hour.

6. Punch down dough; knead briefly on floured surface. Divide into 3 equal pieces; let stand, covered, 10 minutes.

7. Roll out each piece into 12 × 8-inch rectangle. Starting at narrow end, roll up jelly-roll fashion; place seam side down on lightly greased baking sheets. Tuck ends under; shape rolls gently upward with hands to add height. Let rise, covered, until doubled, about 45 minutes.

8. Cut 4 diagonal slashes in top of each loaf. Beat remaining egg with 1 teaspoon water in small bowl; brush evenly over each loaf.

9. Bake in preheated 350°F oven until tops are brown and bottoms sound hollow when tapped, about 30 minutes. Cool on wire racks.

Onion & Poppy Seed Rye

BLACKBERRY NUT DELIGHTS

There is no rule that says bar cookies must be cut in squares. Triangles can be particularly attractive amid the variety of shapes on a platter of party cookies.

Makes 35 two-inch squares

2 cups plus 4½ tablespoons all-purpose flour
½ cup granulated sugar
¼ teaspoon salt
1 cup butter, cold
1 cup blackberry jam or red raspberry preserves
1½ cups packed brown sugar
3 large eggs
½ teaspoon vanilla
1½ cups chopped walnuts
¾ cup flaked coconut
¾ teaspoon baking powder

1. For crust, mix 2 cups of the flour, the granulated sugar and ⅛ teaspoon of the salt in medium bowl. Cut in butter

(Continued)

until mixture resembles coarse crumbs. Lightly knead mixture in bowl until butter is evenly incorporated. Pat dough evenly in ungreased 15½ × 10½ × 1-inch jelly-roll pan.

2. Bake in preheated 350°F oven until crust is light brown, 15 to 18 minutes. Cool in pan on wire rack slightly, about 15 minutes. Spread jam evenly over warm crust.

3. Reduce oven setting to 325°F.

4. For topping, beat brown sugar, eggs and vanilla in large mixer bowl until very light and fluffy, 2 to 4 minutes. Add walnuts, coconut, the remaining 4½ tablespoons flour, the baking powder and the remaining ⅛ teaspoon salt; stir to mix. Spread evenly over jam.

5. Bake until top is brown and center is firm to the touch, about 35 minutes. Cool in pan on wire rack 25 minutes. Cut warm cookies with thin-bladed knife into 2-inch squares. (Cut squares diagonally in half to make triangles, if desired.) Remove squares from pan to wire rack; cool completely.

Blackberry Nut Delights (top); Poppy Seed Bars (bottom)

POPPY SEED BARS

Poppy seeds are favorites in baked goods from central European kitchens. The tiny, dark blue seeds are stirred into batters, sprinkled on top of crusty loaves, or made into fillings for sweet rolls and pastries.

Makes 16 two-inch squares

¾ **cup poppy seeds**
½ **cup whole blanched almonds**
½ **cup granulated sugar**
⅓ **cup milk**
½ **cup plus 2 tablespoons butter, cold**
2 **teaspoons lemon juice**
½ **teaspoon grated lemon rind**
¼ **teaspoon ground nutmeg**
1 **cup plus 3 tablespoons sifted all-purpose flour**
½ **cup powdered sugar, sifted**
1 **teaspoon baking powder**
1 **large egg yolk, cold**
¼ **teaspoon vanilla**

1. Combine poppy seeds and ¼ cup of the almonds in blender container. Process with on-off pulses until almonds are finely chopped; transfer to 2-quart saucepan.

2. Add granulated sugar, milk, 2 tablespoons of the butter, the lemon juice, lemon rind and nutmeg to pan. Cook, stirring constantly, over medium heat to boiling; reduce heat to medium low. Cook, stirring constantly, at gentle boil until mixture is very thick, holds together and pulls away from sides of pan, about 10 minutes; remove from heat.

3. Chop remaining ¼ cup almonds very fine. Mix flour, powdered sugar and baking powder in medium bowl. Cut in remaining ½ cup butter until mixture resembles coarse crumbs; stir in chopped almonds.

4. Beat egg yolk and vanilla in small bowl; drizzle over flour mixture. Stir and toss lightly with fork until egg is evenly distributed but mixture is still crumbly.

5. Remove ½ of the crumb mixture from bowl; squeeze together to form ball. Knead gently a few times on lightly floured surface. Press in even layer on bottom of ungreased 8-inch square baking pan.

6. Spread poppy seed mixture evenly over bottom crust. Sprinkle remaining crumb mixture evenly over poppy seed filling; pat lightly with fork.

7. Bake in preheated 350°F oven until topping just begins to turn golden, 20 to 25 minutes. Cool completely in pan on wire rack. To serve, cut into 2-inch squares.

HUNGARIAN ALMOND LOVE LETTERS

Dainty envelopes of tender cream-cheese pastry and a brandy-nut filling carry a sweet message with after-dinner coffee.

Makes 32 small pastries

1 **cup all-purpose flour**
½ **cup butter, cut into pats, cold**
1 **package (3 ounces) cream cheese, diced, cold**
1 **small lemon**
½ **cup whole unblanched almonds**
⅓ **cup sugar**
3 **tablespoons half-and-half**
2 **tablespoons brandy**
1 **large egg**
1 **tablespoon water**

(Continued)

Hungarian Almond Love Letters

1. Combine flour, butter and cream cheese in food processor work bowl fitted with steel blade. Process with on-off pulses until mixture resembles fine crumbs, about 20 seconds. Continue processing until dough forms large chunks, about 30 seconds.

2. Divide dough in half; shape each ½ into flat square. Refrigerate, wrapped in plastic wrap, at least 1 hour.

3. Pare enough lemon rind to equal 1½ square inches. Process almonds and lemon rind with on-off pulses until ground, about 45 seconds. Add sugar, half-and-half and brandy; process until smooth and creamy, about 5 seconds.

4. Transfer almond mixture to small saucepan; cook and stir over medium-high heat until mixture boils and thickens, about 5 minutes. Refrigerate until cold.

5. Roll out each ½ of the dough on very lightly floured surface to 12-inch square. Cut with fluted pastry wheel into 3-inch squares. Place 1 level teaspoon of the almond mixture on center of each. Fold up corners to meet at center over filling; pinch seams together.

6. Beat egg with water in small bowl; brush over tops of pastries. Place on ungreased baking sheets.

7. Bake in preheated 375°F oven until pale golden, about 10 minutes. Remove pastries to wire racks; let cool completely.

JUMBO DOUBLE CHOCOLATE CHIP COOKIES

Designed to satisfy chocoholics everywhere: oversized cocoa-flavored cookies studded with chocolate morsels and iced with melted chocolate.

Makes nine 5½-inch cookies

1¼ cups butter, room temperature
¾ cup granulated sugar
⅔ cup packed brown sugar
½ teaspoon salt
3 small eggs
3 drops red food coloring, if desired
3 cups sifted all-purpose flour
¾ cup unsweetened cocoa powder
½ teaspoon baking soda
20 ounces semisweet chocolate morsels
6 ounces semisweet chocolate or dark
    confectionery coating, if desired, chopped

(Continued)

Jumbo Double Chocolate Chip Cookies

1. Beat butter, granulated sugar, brown sugar and salt in large mixer bowl until light and fluffy. Add eggs, 1 at a time, beating well after each addition. Beat in food coloring.

2. Mix flour, cocoa powder and baking soda in sifter. Sift flour mixture over butter mixture, ¼ at a time, folding in after each addition until flour is absorbed. Fold in chocolate morsels.

3. For each cookie, drop ¾ cup batter onto baking sheet lined with parchment paper. (You will be able to get about 3 cookies on each baking sheet. Leave as much space as possible between cookies.) Flatten batter with dampened hand to make 4½-inch circles, ⅝ inch thick.

4. Bake in preheated 375°F oven until centers feel medium-firm, 12 to 14 minutes. Do not overbake; centers will firm up upon cooling and cookies will be moist and chewy. Cool cookies on baking sheets on wire racks 5 minutes. Carefully remove cookies to wire racks; cool completely.

5. To decorate cookies, melt chopped semisweet chocolate in top of double boiler over hot water. Spoon into pastry bag fitted with small plain tip. Pipe chocolate onto cookies to make face and zigzag border; let stand until chocolate is set.

CLOUDS IN CHOCOLATE

Fluffy clouds of meringue float gently on a smooth chocolate custard. The puffs of whipped egg white are poached in the same hot milk used to make the custard.

Makes 6 servings

2½ cups milk
¾ cup sugar
2 teaspoons vanilla
6 large eggs, separated, room temperature
⅓ cup Dutch process cocoa powder, sifted
½ cup grated semisweet chocolate for garnish

1. Combine milk, ¼ cup of the sugar and 1 teaspoon of the vanilla in large heavy skillet; heat over medium heat to barely simmering. Adjust heat to maintain temperature; stir until sugar is dissolved.

2. Meanwhile, beat egg whites in large mixer bowl until foamy. Gradually beat in ¼ cup of the sugar; beat until meringue is stiff but not dry.

3. Using 2 large wet spoons, shape meringue into egg-shaped puffs and slide gently onto hot milk mixture; do not let puffs touch each other. Poach gently over low heat 2 minutes per side.

4 Remove puffs with slotted spoon; drain on towel-covered baking sheet. Refrigerate puffs. Strain milk mixture; keep hot.

5. For custard, whisk egg yolks and remaining ¼ cup sugar in top of double boiler until thick and creamy. Whisk in cocoa powder and remaining 1 teaspoon vanilla; gradually whisk in hot milk mixture. Cook over hot water, stirring constantly, until custard thickens enough to coat a spoon.

6. Immediately transfer custard to bowl; cover surface with plastic wrap. Refrigerate until cold.

7. To serve, pour cold custard into shallow serving dish or individual bowls; float meringue puffs on custard. Garnish with chocolate.

FROZEN RASPBERRY YOGURT PIE

Match any flavor yogurt with its corresponding frozen fruit in this easy, make-ahead dessert.

Makes 6 to 8 servings

2 containers (8 ounces each) raspberry yogurt
1 container (8 ounces) frozen whipped topping, thawed
1 chocolate crumb pie crust
1 package (10 ounces) frozen raspberries, thawed

1. Fold yogurt into whipped topping in medium bowl; pour into pie crust. Freeze at least 3 hours.

2. Remove pie from freezer 15 minutes before serving. Spoon raspberries over each serving.

TOMATO SPICE CAKE

If you've never thought of using some of that bumper crop of garden tomatoes in a cake, remember that botanically, tomatoes are a fruit. This spicy loaf cake will freeze well, too.

Makes 8 to 10 servings

3 cups all-purpose flour
2 teaspoons baking powder
1 teaspoon baking soda
½ teaspoon salt
1 cup packed light brown sugar
½ cup butter or margarine, room temperature
1 teaspoon ground allspice
¾ teaspoon grated orange rind
½ teaspoon ground ginger
2 large eggs
3½ pounds ripe tomatoes, peeled, seeded, chopped, drained well (3 cups)
½ cup raisins
½ cup chopped dates
Powdered sugar

1. Mix flour, baking powder, baking soda and salt in large bowl.

2. Combine brown sugar, butter, allspice, orange rind and ginger in large mixer bowl; beat until light and fluffy. Add eggs; beat well. Add tomatoes, raisins and dates; stir to mix well. Mixture will look curdled. *(Continued)*

Tomato Spice Cake

Chocolate-Peanut Crunch Bars

3. Gradually add flour mixture, stirring until thoroughly blended after each addition. Pour into greased $9 \times 5 \times 3$-inch loaf pan.

4. Bake in preheated 350°F oven until wooden pick inserted into center is withdrawn clean, about 1 hour and 10 minutes. Cool in pan on wire rack, 5 minutes. Remove from pan; let cool completely on rack. Sprinkle with powdered sugar before serving.

CHOCOLATE-PEANUT CRUNCH BARS

Middle America leads the world in packaging breakfast cereals. These popular products are enjoyable not only at the start of the day, but in snacks like bar cookies, too.

Makes 16 servings

1 cup peanut butter
4 tablespoons honey
3½ cups oven-toasted rice cereal
1 envelope unflavored gelatine
¼ cup cold milk
½ cup milk, heated to boiling
½ cup semisweet chocolate morsels
1 large egg
½ cup ice cubes (3 to 4)

1. Mix peanut butter and 2 tablespoons of the honey in medium bowl; stir in cereal. Press ½ of the mixture evenly in 8-inch square baking pan.

2. Sprinkle gelatine over cold milk in blender container; let stand until softened, about 5 minutes. Add hot milk; process at low speed until gelatine is dissolved, about 2 minutes.

3. Add remaining 2 tablespoons honey, the chocolate and egg; process at high speed until blended. With motor running, add ice cubes, 1 at a time; process at high speed until melted. Let stand until slightly thickened, about 5 minutes.

4. Transfer to baking pan; spread smooth. Press remaining cereal mixture in even layer on top of gelatine. Refrigerate until firm, several hours. To serve, cut into squares.

RUBY FRUIT COMPOTE

Dried fruits plump to perfection when simmered in a spiced blend of cranberry juice and port, lightly sweetened with honey.

Makes 8 to 10 servings

12 ounces pitted prunes (about 2 cups)
 8 ounces dried pear halves
1½ cups cranberry juice
1¼ cups port
 3 tablespoons honey
 2 sticks cinnamon (4 to 5 inches each)
 1 orange, cut in half, seeded, sliced

1. Combine prunes, pears, cranberry juice, 1 cup of the port, the honey and cinnamon sticks in 3-quart saucepan; heat to boiling. Reduce heat; barely simmer, stirring occasionally, 15 minutes.

2. Remove from heat; stir in orange. Let stand, covered, until cool. Gently stir in remaining ¼ cup port. Serve at room temperature or refrigerate until cold.

Ruby Fruit Compote

CHERRY-FILLED SUGAR COOKIES

Makes about 6 dozen

  1 cup margarine
1½ cups granulated sugar
  1 cup powdered sugar
  1 cup vegetable oil
  2 large eggs
  1 teaspoon vanilla
4¼ cups sifted all-purpose flour
  1 teaspoon salt
  1 teaspoon baking soda
  1 teaspoon cream of tartar
  1 can (21 ounces) tart cherry pie filling
  1 cup finely chopped nuts
 ¾ cup flaked coconut

1. Beat margarine, 1 cup of the granulated sugar and the powdered sugar in large mixer bowl until light and fluffy. Beat in oil, eggs and vanilla until blended.

2. Mix flour, salt, baking soda and cream of tartar in large bowl. Add flour mixture, ¼ at a time, to margarine mixture, mixing well after each addition. Refrigerate, covered, until cold, at least 1 hour.

3. For filling, combine pie filling, nuts, coconut and remaining ½ cup granulated sugar in medium bowl.

4. Roll out dough ⅛-inch thick on floured surface; cut out 2½-inch circles with cookie cutter. Place 1 teaspoon filling in center of each. Cookies can be left open-face; or, fold in half to enclose filling and pinch seams to seal.

5. Place cookies on greased baking sheets. Bake in preheated 350°F oven 8 to 10 minutes. Cool completely on wire racks.

ROSETTES

These crisp pastries are made on a special iron with a lacy pattern. When sprinkled lightly with powdered sugar, rosettes look like giant snowflakes which would indeed melt in your mouth.

Makes about 40 cookies

2 large eggs
1 tablespoon granulated sugar
¼ teaspoon salt
1 cup milk
1 cup sifted all-purpose flour
  Vegetable oil for frying
  Powdered sugar

1. Combine eggs, granulated sugar and salt in large mixer bowl; beat well. Add milk and flour; beat just until batter is smooth.

2. Heat 2 inches of oil in small heavy saucepan to 375°F. Place rosette iron in oil until very hot, about 5 minutes. Dip hot iron into batter to coat bottom and sides with thin layer; don't let batter go over top edge of iron or cookie will not release. Iron should be hot enough so that batter sets at once.

3. Dip batter-coated iron into hot oil; fry until cookie is golden, 20 to 30 seconds. Remove cookie from iron with fork; drain on paper toweling. Repeat until all batter has been used, heating iron in oil 2 to 3 seconds between cookies.

4. Cool cookies completely; sprinkle with powdered sugar. Store in airtight container.

Linzertorte

LINZERTORTE

This raspberry jam pie with its characteristic diamond-lattice top originated in Linz, Austria. The butter-rich pastry contains finely chopped nuts and fragrant spices.

Makes 8 to 10 servings

½ **pound butter or margarine, cold**
1 **cup all-purpose flour**
6 **ounces unblanched almonds, finely chopped**
½ **cup granulated sugar**
1 **teaspoon grated lemon rind**
1 **teaspoon ground cinnamon**
¼ **teaspoon ground cloves**
  Pinch salt
3 **large egg yolks**
1 **teaspoon vanilla**
1 **cup raspberry jam**
  Powdered sugar   *(Continued)*

1. Cut butter into flour in medium bowl until mixture resembles fine crumbs. Stir in almonds, granulated sugar, lemon rind, cinnamon, cloves and salt. Add egg yolks and vanilla; stir with fork until mixed. Knead in bowl until dough forms ball.

2. Refrigerate ¼ of the dough. Pat remaining dough in even layer on bottom and 1 inch up sides of ungreased 9-inch springform pan. Spread jam in even layer on bottom of crust.

3. Roll out remaining ¼ dough on floured surface into 9 × 4½-inch rectangle; cut lengthwise into 6 strips, ¾ inch wide.

4. Place 3 strips crosswise and evenly spaced on top of jam. Rotate pan 45° (⅛ turn). Place remaining 3 strips crosswise on top to form diamond-shaped lattice. Trim ends flush with side of pan; press lightly to seal.

5. Bake in preheated 350°F oven until pastry is crisp and light brown, 45 to 50 minutes. Cool in pan on wire rack 5 minutes. Remove side of pan; let cool completely. Sprinkle pastry with powdered sugar before serving.

Blueberry Cheese Tart

BLUEBERRY CHEESE TART

Makes 8 servings

1 package (8 ounces) cream cheese, room
    temperature
1 can (14 ounces) sweetened condensed milk
⅓ cup lemon juice
1 teaspoon vanilla
    Butter Cookie Tart Shell (recipe follows)
2 cups fresh or dry-pack frozen blueberries
⅓ cup blueberry jelly
    Whipped cream, blueberries and chocolate
    leaves for garnish

1. Beat cream cheese in large mixer bowl until smooth and
fluffy. Gradually add condensed milk, beating until blended;
beat in lemon juice and vanilla.

2. Spread cream cheese mixture in Butter Cookie Tart
Shell; refrigerate, covered, until filling is set, at least 3
hours.

3. Place blueberries on top of filling in single layer. Melt
jelly in small saucepan over medium heat; spoon over
blueberries to glaze. Refrigerate until ready to serve. Garnish with whipped cream, blueberries and chocolate
leaves. *(Continued)*

BUTTER COOKIE TART SHELL

1½ cups all-purpose flour
¼ cup sugar
¾ teaspoon grated orange rind
¼ teaspoon salt
⅔ cup butter, room temperature
2 large egg yolks
¾ teaspoon vanilla

1. Mix flour, sugar, orange rind and salt in medium bowl;
cut in butter until mixture resembles coarse crumbs. Stir in
egg yolks and vanilla; knead in bowl until smooth. Refrigerate, wrapped in plastic, at least 2 hours.

2. Roll out dough on lightly floured surface into 11-inch
circle; fit into 9 × 1-inch tart pan with removable bottom.
Line pastry with parchment paper; fill with pie weights.

3. Bake in preheated 400°F oven until pastry is set, about 10
minutes. Remove parchment and weights; continue baking
until pastry is golden, about 5 minutes longer. Cool completely on wire rack.

LEMON CHIFFON CAKE

First introduced in 1948, the chiffon cake made baking news. The secret ingredient is vegetable oil incorporated into a light, fluffy cake baked in a tube pan.

Makes 12 to 16 servings

2¼ cups sifted cake flour
1½ cups sugar
　1 tablespoon baking powder
　½ teaspoon salt
　6 large egg yolks
　½ cup corn oil
　½ cup water
　¼ cup lemon juice
　1 tablespoon grated lemon rind
　6 large egg whites, room temperature
　½ teaspoon cream of tartar
　　Lemon Glaze (recipe follows)
　　Finely slivered lemon rind for garnish

1. Sift flour, sugar, baking powder and salt into large mixer bowl. Add egg yolks, oil, water, lemon juice and grated lemon rind; beat at medium speed until smooth.

2. Beat egg whites and cream of tartar in clean large mixer bowl with clean beaters at high speed until stiff peaks form. Fold flour mixture into egg whites until blended. Pour into ungreased 10 × 4-inch straight-sided tube pan.

3. Bake in preheated 325°F oven until top springs back when lightly touched, 65 to 70 minutes. Invert pan immediately with center tube over funnel or bottle; cool the cake completely.

4. Loosen sides of cake with spatula; remove from pan. Spoon Lemon Glaze over top of cake; garnish with slivered lemon rind.

(Continued)

LEMON GLAZE

1 cup sifted powdered sugar
1 to 2 tablespoons lemon juice
½ teaspoon grated lemon rind

Mix sugar and enough of the lemon juice in small bowl to form glaze consistency; stir in lemon rind.

Makes about ½ cup

PEANUT BRITTLE CAKE

Golden flecks of crunchy candy dot a party make-ahead dessert to slice and serve with a flourish.

Makes 12 servings

　2 cups whipping cream
　2 tablespoons sugar
　1 teaspoon lemon extract
　1 baked sponge or angel food cake (10-inch diameter)
1½ cups crushed peanut brittle

1. Beat cream in large mixer bowl until stiff; fold in sugar and lemon extract.

2. Cut cake horizontally into 3 equal layers. Place bottom layer on serving plate; spread with 1 cup of the cream. Top with middle layer; spread with 1 cup of the cream. Cover with top layer.

3. Frost top and sides of cake with remaining cream. Press peanut brittle onto sides of cake; leave top plain. Refrigerate until ready to serve, at least 2 hours. Store leftover cake in refrigerator.

Lemon Chiffon Cake

BAKED CARAMEL CORN

Oven-easy does it with this crunchy treat. Middle America is corn country, and that includes some acres devoted to hybrid varieties which pop up big and fluffy.

Makes about 3 quarts

½ cup butter, room temperature
½ cup packed brown sugar
3 quarts unsalted popped popcorn
1 cup pecan halves or mixed nuts

1. Beat butter and sugar in large mixer bowl until light and fluffy. Add ⅓ of the popcorn at a time, mixing after each addition until evenly coated. Stir in nuts.

2. Spread mixture in large greased baking pan. Bake in preheated 350°F oven until crisp, about 8 minutes. Serve warm or cool to room temperature.

CARROT-APPLE CAKE

Makes 12 servings

1½ cups sugar
1 cup soybean oil
3 large eggs
2 teaspoons vanilla
2 cups shredded carrots
1 cup coarsely chopped pared apple
¾ cup golden raisins
¾ cup chopped pecans
2 cups all-purpose flour
2 teaspoons ground cinnamon
1 teaspoon baking powder
1 teaspoon baking soda
1 teaspoon salt
　Cream Cheese Frosting (recipe follows)
　Chopped pecans and carrot curls for garnish

(Continued)

Carrot-Apple Cake

1. Combine sugar, oil, eggs and vanilla in large mixer bowl; beat until smooth. Stir in shredded carrots, apple, raisins and ¾ cup pecans.

2. Mix flour, cinnamon, baking powder, baking soda and salt in medium bowl. Add flour mixture, ⅓ at a time, to carrot mixture, mixing well after each addition. Pour batter into 2 greased and floured 9-inch round cake pans, dividing evenly.

3. Bake in preheated 350°F oven until wooden pick inserted into center is withdrawn clean, 30 to 40 minutes. Cool in pans on wire racks 5 minutes. Remove from pans; cool completely on racks.

4. Place 1 cake layer on serving plate; spread with ½ of the Cream Cheese Frosting. Top with second cake layer; spread remaining frosting on top of cake. Garnish with pecans and carrot curls.

CREAM CHEESE FROSTING

1 package (3 ounces) cream cheese, room temperature
⅓ cup soybean-oil margarine
1 teaspoon vanilla
   Pinch salt
2 cups powdered sugar

Combine cream cheese, margarine, vanilla and salt in small mixer bowl; beat until light and fluffy. Gradually beat in sugar until smooth.

GINGERSNAPS

Enjoyment of home-baked ginger cookies is twofold: The spicy aroma that fills the kitchen while they bake is as tempting as the taste of the crisp goodies.

Makes about 4 dozen 2-inch cookies
1 cup packed brown sugar
¾ cup unsalted butter, room temperature
¼ teaspoon salt
1 large egg, room temperature
¼ cup light molasses
1 tablespoon ground ginger
2 teaspoons baking soda
1 teaspoon ground cinnamon
½ teaspoon ground cloves
2¼ cups all-purpose flour
⅓ to ½ cup granulated sugar

1. Beat brown sugar, butter and salt in large mixer bowl until light and fluffy. Beat in egg; gradually add molasses while beating at medium speed. Stir in ginger, baking soda, cinnamon and cloves. Add flour, ⅓ at a time, folding in with rubber spatula after each addition until flour is absorbed. (Dough will be soft and sticky.)

2. Divide dough into quarters; flatten each quarter on separate piece of plastic wrap; wrap securely. Refrigerate until cold, at least 1½ hours.

3. Working with ¼ of the dough at a time (leave remaining portions of dough in refrigerator), roll slightly rounded tablespoonfuls of dough between palms into balls. Roll balls in granulated sugar to coat generously. Place 4 inches apart on greased baking sheets.

4. Bake 2 sheets of cookies at a time in preheated 350°F oven until centers feel slightly firm, about 10 minutes. Cool cookies on baking sheets on wire racks 5 minutes. Remove cookies from baking sheets; cool completely on wire racks.

DOUBLE CHOCOLATE FUDGE

Makes 2¼ pounds

3 cups sugar
2 jars (7 ounces each) marshmallow cream
1 can (13 ounces) evaporated milk
½ cup butter or margarine
½ teaspoon salt
1 package (12 ounces) semisweet chocolate morsels
1 package (12 ounces) milk chocolate morsels

1. Combine sugar, marshmallow cream, evaporated milk, butter and salt in large saucepan; heat over medium heat, stirring constantly, to full boil. Boil, stirring constantly to prevent scorching, 5 minutes; remove from heat.

2. Pour 3½ cups of the mixture into medium bowl. Add semisweet chocolate; stir until chocolate is melted. Pour into aluminum-foil-lined 15 × 10 × 1-inch baking pan; refrigerate until top is crusty, 5 to 10 minutes.

3. Add milk chocolate to remaining hot mixture; stir until chocolate is melted. (If mixture has cooled too much, heat over low heat until chocolate melts.) Pour over semisweet chocolate layer in pan; refrigerate until firm, about 2 hours. Cut into 1-inch squares.

BLACK-BOTTOMED PRUNE & APPLE PIE

A unique two-fruit pie filled with ginger- and sherry-flavored prunes and apples.

Makes 8 to 10 servings
½ cup plus 1 tablespoon sugar
2 tablespoons all-purpose flour
¾ teaspoon ground ginger
¼ teaspoon salt
¾ cup sherry
2 tablespoons lemon juice
12 ounces pitted prunes (about 2 cups)
6 cups sliced pared tart apples
   Pastry dough for 1 double-crust 9-inch pie
1 large egg, beaten
   Sweetened whipped cream and ground nutmeg, if desired

1. Combine ½ cup of the sugar, the flour, ginger and salt in 3-quart saucepan; whisk in sherry and lemon juice until smooth. Cook and stir over medium heat until mixture thickens and bubbles for 1 minute.

2. Add prunes; cook and stir 1 minute. Remove prunes with slotted spoon, draining well.

3. Add apples to sherry mixture; cook and stir 2 minutes. Remove from heat; let cool.

4. Roll out ½ of the pastry dough on lightly floured surface into 12-inch circle; fit into 9-inch pie pan. Spread prunes evenly on bottom of pastry; top with apple mixture.

5. Roll out remaining pastry into 11-inch circle; cut several slits for steam vents. Place on top of pie. Trim edges; seal and flute. Brush top with egg; sprinkle with remaining 1 tablespoon sugar.

6. Bake in preheated 425°F oven 10 minutes; reduce oven setting to 375°F. Continue baking until crust is golden brown and apples are tender, 40 to 45 minutes. Cool on wire rack; serve warm or room temperature. Top with whipped cream and nutmeg.

CREAMY COCONUT PIE

Toast coconut by spreading a thin layer in a shallow pan and letting it bake in a 350°F oven for a few minutes until lightly browned.

Makes 6 to 8 servings

    1 package (3 ounces) cream cheese, room
        temperature
    1 tablespoon sugar
    ½ cup milk
    3½ cups frozen whipped topping, thawed
    1⅓ cups flaked coconut
    ½ teaspoon almond extract
    1 packaged graham cracker pie crust (6-ounce)
    Toasted coconut for garnish

1. Beat cream cheese in large mixer bowl until smooth and soft; beat in sugar. Gradually add milk, beating until smooth.

2. Fold in whipped topping, flaked coconut and almond extract; spoon into pie crust. Freeze 4 hours.

3. Let pie stand at room temperature to soften slightly before serving, 10 to 20 minutes. Garnish with toasted coconut.

RHUBARB CRUMBLE

Makes 4 to 6 servings

    1 cup all-purpose flour
    ½ cup packed brown sugar
    ½ cup butter or margarine, cold
    1 pound fresh rhubarb, cut into ½-inch slices
        (about 4 cups)
    ¾ cup granulated sugar
    2 teaspoons quick-cooking tapioca
    ½ teaspoon ground cinnamon
    ⅛ teaspoon ground nutmeg
    Whipped cream and ground nutmeg, if desired

(Continued)

1. Mix flour and brown sugar in medium bowl; cut in butter until mixture resembles coarse crumbs.

2. Combine rhubarb, granulated sugar, tapioca, cinnamon and ⅛ teaspoon nutmeg in 2-quart baking dish; mix well. Sprinkle evenly with flour mixture.

3. Bake in preheated 375°F oven until rhubarb is tender, sauce is bubbly, and topping is brown and crisp, about 35 minutes.

4. Serve warm or cold, topped with whipped cream, sprinkled with nutmeg.

BLACK FOREST CAKE

Makes 8 to 10 servings

    1 cup chopped drained maraschino cherries
    ¼ cup cherry brandy
    2 tablespoons light corn syrup
    3 chocolate cake layers (9-inch diameter)
    2 cups whipping cream, whipped
    Shaved chocolate and whole maraschino
        cherries for garnish

1. Combine chopped cherries, brandy and corn syrup in small bowl; stir to mix. Let stand, covered, 8 hours.

2. Drain cherries well, reserving brandy marinade. Brush top of each cake layer with reserved marinade.

3. For filling, mix chopped cherries and 1 cup of the whipped cream in medum bowl. Spread ½ of the filling on top of 1 cake layer on serving plate; top with second cake layer. Spread with remaining filling; cover with remaining cake layer.

4. Spread 2 cups of the remaining whipped cream on top and sides of cake to cover evenly. Press remaining 1 cup whipped cream through pastry bag fitted with plain tip in rosettes on top of cake. Press chocolate into sides of cake to cover; decorate top with whole cherries and chocolate.

Rhubarb Crumble

Chocolate Zucchini Cake

CHOCOLATE ZUCCHINI CAKE

Try grating zucchini to use like fresh apple in spicy quick-bread and cake batters. It adds moisture and a subtle flavor.

Makes 12 to 16 servings

2½ cups all-purpose flour
½ cup unsweetened cocoa powder
2½ teaspoons baking powder
1½ teaspoons baking soda
 1 teaspoon salt
 2 cups sugar
¾ cup butter or margarine, room temperature
 2 teaspoons ground cinnamon
¾ teaspoon ground nutmeg
 3 large eggs
 2 cups shredded unpared zucchini (about ½ pound)
 2 teaspoons vanilla
½ cup milk
 Cinnamon Cream Cheese Frosting (recipe follows)

1. Mix flour, cocoa powder, baking powder, baking soda, and salt in medium bowl.

2. Combine sugar, butter, cinnamon and nutmeg in large mixer bowl; beat until light and fluffy. Beat in eggs; stir in zucchini and vanilla. *(Continued)*

3. Add flour mixture, ⅓ at a time, alternating with milk, beating well after each addition. Pour batter into 2 greased and floured 9-inch round cake pans.

4. Bake in preheated 350°F oven until wooden pick inserted into center is withdrawn clean, about 30 minutes. Cool in pans on wire racks 5 minutes. Remove from pans; cool completely on racks.

5. Place 1 cake layer on serving plate; spread with ½ of the Cinnamon Cream Cheese Frosting. Top with second layer; spread top with remaining frosting.

CINNAMON CREAM CHEESE FROSTING

 1 package (3 ounces) cream cheese, room temperature
⅓ cup butter or margarine, room temperature
¾ teaspoon ground cinnamon
 4 cups powdered sugar
 1 teaspoon vanilla
1½ to 2 tablespoons milk

Combine cream cheese, butter and cinnamon in large mixer bowl; beat until light and fluffy. Gradually beat in powdered sugar until smooth; beat in vanilla. Gradually beat in milk until frosting is spreading consistency.

214

Rocky Peaks to Ranchos
THE GREAT WEST

This is trail country with wide open spaces, high mountains and homes on the range. Although the old routes are now paved highways to be traveled in vehicles equipped with heaters and air conditioning, the foods show strong traces of the people who traveled the trails at various times. There were Indians, Spaniards, fur trappers, miners, Mexicans, ranchers, homesteading families, religious groups and entrepreneurs of all nationalities. They lived off the land where they could, carried their own staples and planted what would grow in the land where they put down roots.

In this chapter, you'll find recipes that maintain some of the flavor of the Old West but are designed for today, when cooking and eating outdoors is usually done by choice, not by necessity. Beef Jerky, the dried meat which helped to sustain the Western pioneers, can be made in the oven. And you need not gather wild nuts and berries to prepare Trail Mixes to use as easy, delicious snacks.

Wonderful ways to roast and grill beef come from a region known for its livestock. You can serve Bronco Bustin' Steak with bourbon-laced Cowpuncher Spiked Sauce or enjoy Texas Blackeyes and Beef, flavored with chili powder. Barbecued Round-Up Roast is marinated and then cooked on a charcoal grill.

In the mountains, pastures also provide grazing areas for sheep. You can build an authentic Western meal around Tangy Braised Lamb Shanks, flavored with garlic, raisins and spices, or a stew called High Country Lamb and Bean Pot. Rivers and streams yield trout and other game fish. The recipe for Herb-Stuffed Trout is an angler's delight.

Many of the recipes in this region reflect the strong Mexican and Spanish heritage of the Southwest. You'll learn how to make Nachos, the popular, tasty appetizer of tortilla chips topped with cheese and hot chilies.

"Chile" and "chili" sound alike, but have different meanings. Chile is the Spanish name for pepper. Depending on the variety, chilies may be mild, hot or very hot. Shrimp in Fiery Garlic Butter will satisfy the most devoted fans of hot chile flavor. Use the milder green bell pepper in Mexican-inspired Chiles Rellenos, peppers stuffed with cheese.

The dish known as "chili" is usually a combination of beef and tomatoes—with or without beans—seasoned with chili powder or with one or more kinds of chile peppers. Almost as many versions of chili exist as cooks who make it. Sample the peppy "OK Corral" Beef Chili or, for variety, make a Chili Hero open-faced sandwich.

Delicious breads in the Western U.S. come in all shapes and sizes. Crisp and tasty Crusty Mexican Rolls are known locally as *bolillos*. Scrumptious Crumble-Top Orange Rolls have an attractive pattern of sweet streusel swirls or squares on top. The quick and easy recipes for Honey-Nut Wheat Bread and for Cornmeal Bread yield hearty loaves to accompany any meal. Tortillas—those versatile flat breads—can be baked with a savory meat filling, as in Enchiladas in Green Sauce or fried crisp into taco shells for Backyard Bean Tacos.

Not all food in this region, of course, is influenced by south-of-the-border cooking methods. The Sun Belt produces juicy oranges and grapefruit to use in a delightful Orange Salad with red onion and mint, or Grapefruit Vegetable Aspic, in which grapefruit juice flavors a combination of cabbage, carrots and bell peppers. Farther north, vegetable growers produce sweet onions that can be stuffed and baked as in Hash-Stuffed Onions. Idaho potatoes, topped with tasty mixtures, are Spectacular Spuds indeed!

There is no lack of desserts to satisfy a sweet tooth. For a delightfully smooth finish to a meal of spicy foods, serve a creamy Orange Coconut Flan or Burnt Strawberry Cream, a combination of rice, strawberries and cream topped with caramelized brown sugar. Cake lovers will dote on the moist Golden Apple-Mincemeat Cake or squares of an easy-to-make Honey Cake.

MINI BEEF TOSTADAS

Makes 4 dozen appetizers

1 pound ground beef
1 tablespoon instant minced onion
1 can (8 ounces) refried beans
1 can (4 ounces) chopped green chilies, if desired
½ cup bottled taco sauce
4 dozen round tortilla or corn chips
1 cup shredded Cheddar cheese

1. Cook and stir beef and onion in large skillet over medium heat until beef is no longer pink, about 10 minutes; drain and discard drippings.

2. Stir in beans, chilies and taco sauce; cook and stir until bubbly, about 4 minutes. Spoon about 1 heaping tablespoon of the beef mixture on top of each tortilla chip; sprinkle with cheese. Place on baking sheets.

3. Bake in preheated 375°F oven until cheese is melted, about 2 minutes.

To microwave: Crumble beef into 1-quart microwave-safe bowl; stir in onion. Microwave, covered, on HIGH, stirring once, 5 minutes; drain. Stir in beans, chilies and taco sauce; microwave, covered, on HIGH, stirring once, 4 minutes. Spoon about 1 heaping tablespoon of the beef mixture on top of each tortilla chip; sprinkle with cheese. Arrange 12 mini-tostadas on each of 4 microwave-safe plates. Microwave each plateful on HIGH 1 minute and 15 seconds.

Sparkling Grape Sangria

CREAM OF ZUCCHINI SOUP

Makes 4 servings

1½ cups chicken broth
2 large zucchini, sliced
½ cup chopped onion
½ teaspoon dried thyme, crumbled
⅛ teaspoon garlic powder
2 tablespoons butter
2 tablespoons all-purpose flour
½ teaspoon salt
⅛ teaspoon white pepper
1 cup milk
½ cup sour cream

1. Combine broth, zucchini, onion, thyme and garlic powder in medium saucepan. Heat to boiling; reduce heat. Simmer, covered, 10 minutes. Process vegetable mixture in blender until smooth.

2. In same saucepan, melt butter; stir in flour, salt and pepper until smooth; cook and stir over low heat 1 minute. Stir in milk; cook and stir over medium heat until mixture thickens and boils.

3. Stir in zucchini mixture; cook until hot. Serve with sour cream.

SPARKLING GRAPE SANGRIA

Makes 8 to 10 servings

1 cup green seedless or red grapes
1 bottle (750 mL) rosé or dry white wine, cold*
⅔ cup Grape Syrup, cold (recipe follows)
2 cups ice cubes
1 bottle (375 mL) dry champagne or club soda, cold
Lime and lemon slices

1. Rinse grapes; arrange in single layer in shallow baking pan. Place in freezer until frosty and partially frozen, 20 to 30 minutes.

2. Mix wine and Grape Syrup in large pitcher. Add ice cubes; stir well. Add champagne; stir gently. Gently drop in partially frozen grapes and the lime and lemon slices.

Note: For heavier flavor and darker color, substitute dry red wine.

GRAPE SYRUP

6 pounds green seedless or red grapes, rinsed, stemmed

1. Crush grapes in large heavy kettle; heat over medium-low heat until juice forms and bubbles. Reduce heat to low; simmer, uncovered, stirring occasionally, 1 hour.

2. Place large sieve over bowl. Spoon about ¼ of the grapes into sieve and press lightly with back of spoon to extract juice; discard pulp. Repeat until all grapes have been pressed.

3. Return grape juice to kettle; cook and stir over medium-low heat until thickened, 5 to 10 minutes. Cool completely; refrigerate, covered.

Makes about 1⅓ cups

Shrimp Cocktail

DILLED HAM DEVILED EGGS

Plunge hard-cooked eggs into cold water with ice cubes the moment the cooking time is up. This stops the cooking process and usually prevents the yolks from turning dark at the edges.

Makes 12 deviled eggs

  6 hard-cooked eggs
  3 tablespoons mayonnaise or salad dressing
  ¼ **teaspoon dried dill weed, crumbled**
1½ ounces cooked ham, finely chopped

1. Cut eggs lengthwise into halves; remove yolks. Mash yolks in small bowl. Mix in mayonnaise and dill until smooth. Stir in ham.

2. Fill each egg white half with about 1 tablespoon of the yolk mixture. Refrigerate 1 to 4 hours to blend flavors.

OLIVE PATÉ

Here's a spread both simple to prepare and sophisticated to savor with crisp crackers and crunchy vegetables.

Makes 1⅔ cups

1½ cups pitted California ripe olives
  1 cup shredded Monterey Jack cheese
  2 hard-cooked eggs, cut into quarters
  2 teaspoons brandy
1½ teaspoons dried basil
  ¾ **teaspoon dried tarragon**
  ¼ **teaspoon pepper**
  1 small clove garlic
    Minced parsley for garnish
    Assorted raw vegetables, French bread or
      crackers *(Continued)*

1. Combine all but 3 olives, the cheese, eggs, brandy, basil, tarragon, pepper and garlic in blender container; process until almost smooth.

2. Pack mixture into 2-cup crock or serving bowl. Refrigerate, covered, until ready to serve.

3. Slice remaining 3 olives; use to decorate top. Sprinkle with parsley; serve with raw vegetables, French bread or crackers.

SHRIMP COCKTAIL

Shrimp as a first course at a sit-down dinner deserve something special in the way of a cocktail sauce. Here's one that gets its hotness from mustard rather than peppers.

Makes 6 servings

  1 pound shrimp, shelled, deveined, tails intact
  1 can (16 ounces) whole-berry cranberry sauce
  ½ **cup catsup**
  ½ **cup grapefruit juice**
  2 green onions, sliced
  2 tablespoons chopped celery leaves
  1 tablespoon prepared mustard
    Lettuce leaves

1. Combine shrimp with enough water to cover in large saucepan; cook, covered, over high heat just until shrimp turn pink. Rinse under cold water to cool; drain well. Refrigerate, covered with plastic wrap, until ready to serve.

2. Combine remaining ingredients except lettuce in blender container; process until smooth. Refrigerate until cold.

3. To serve, place shrimp on lettuce leaves in individual serving dishes; serve with sauce.

TRAIL MIXES

Gorp, otherwise known as "good ole raisins and peanuts," is just the beginning of a variety of satisfying snacks for hikers and campers. You can add other dried fruits, chocolate bits or peanut butter chips, and even cereal, sunflower seeds or shredded coconut.

GORP

1 cup roasted peanuts
1 cup raisins

Mix peanuts and raisins in medium bowl.

Makes about 2 cups

CRUNCHY COMBO

1 cup roasted peanuts
1 cup raisins
1 package (6 ounces) semisweet chocolate
   morsels
1 cup dried apple pieces

Mix all ingredients in medium bowl.

Makes about 4 cups
(Continued)

MELLO MUNCH

1 cup roasted peanuts
1 cup raisins
1 cup miniature marshmallows
¼ cup dried apricots, cut into quarters

Mix all ingredients in medium bowl.

Makes about 3 cups

LIMA CLAM CHOWDER

Large dry lima beans are so compatible in flavor with clams that in a chowder containing both, you can get by with half the amount of clams.

Makes 4 servings

1½ cups canned or cooked dried large lima beans,
   undrained
   Water
2 tablespoons chopped onion
1 tablespoon butter
1 can (7 ounces) minced clams, undrained
1 teaspoon Worcestershire sauce
½ cup half-and-half
   Chopped parsley and paprika for garnish

(Continued)

Trail Mixes

1. Process limas with their liquid in blender until smooth; add enough water to measure 2 cups.

2. Saute onion in butter in large saucepan over medium heat until soft, about 4 minutes. Stir in lima puree, clams and Worcestershire sauce; heat to boiling. Reduce heat to low. Stir in half-and-half; cook and stir just until hot. Garnish with parsley and paprika.

MANHATTAN-STYLE VARIATION: Substitute ¾ cup diced fresh or canned tomatoes for the half-and-half; add ⅛ teaspoon dried thyme, crumbled. Cook and stir over low heat 5 minutes.

CARAWAY CHEESE STICKS

Makes 3 dozen

     1 cup all-purpose flour
     ¼ teaspoon salt
     ½ cup butter or margarine, cold
     ½ cup shredded sharp Cheddar cheese
     1 tablespoon caraway seeds
     1 teaspoon dry mustard
        Pinch paprika
        Pinch ground red pepper
        Dash hot red pepper sauce
     2 to 3 tablespoons cold milk, white wine or water
     ¼ cup grated Parmesan cheese

1. Mix flour and salt in medium bowl; cut in butter until mixture resembles fine crumbs. Add Cheddar cheese, caraway seeds, mustard, paprika, red pepper and pepper sauce; toss to mix well.

2. Sprinkle flour mixture with milk while stirring and tossing with fork until mixture cleans sides of bowl. Gather dough into ball; refrigerate, wrapped in plastic wrap, 2 hours.

3. Roll out dough ¼ inch thick on lightly floured surface; cut into 5 × ½-inch strips. Place strips on greased baking sheets; sprinkle with Parmesan cheese.

4. Bake in preheated 425°F oven until crisp and golden, 10 to 12 minutes.

NACHOS

Munching nachos used to be restricted to Mexico and the southwestern part of the U.S. Today they are everywhere.

Makes 6 dozen nachos

1½ cups canned refried beans
1½ cups shredded Monterey Jack cheese
1½ cups shredded mild Cheddar cheese
   6 dozen corn tortilla chips
   1 large tomato, seeded, chopped
   ½ cup thinly sliced pickled jalapeno chilies

1. Heat refried beans in small saucepan over medium heat until hot. Mix Jack and Cheddar cheeses in small bowl.

2. Spread 1 teaspoon of the beans on each tortilla chip. Arrange chips in single layer, with edges slightly overlapping, on 2 or 3 baking sheets or large ovenproof platters.

3. Sprinkle chips evenly with tomato and chilies; top with cheese mixture.

4. Bake in preheated 400°F oven until cheese is melted and bubbly, 5 to 8 minutes. Serve immediately.

Tex-Mex Mix

TEX-MEX MIX

There's nothing timid about this popcorn mixture spiced with chili powder and cumin. The melting cheese lends a pleasing flavor and texture contrast.

Makes 2 quarts

   2 quarts popcorn popped in vegetable oil
   2 teaspoons chili powder
   2 teaspoons paprika
   2 teaspoons ground cumin
   1 cup diced (¼-inch) Monterey Jack cheese

1. Keep popped corn warm in preheated 250°F oven.

2. Mix chili powder, paprika and cumin in small bowl. Sprinkle over popped corn; toss to mix evenly. Add cheese; mix well.

Gazpacho

GAZPACHO

Often called "salad in a soup bowl," this splendid pureed mixture of raw garden vegetables is served in chilled cups or bowls.

Makes 4 to 6 servings

    3 cups tomato juice
    1 small onion, cut into chunks
    1 small green bell pepper, cut into chunks
    1 small cucumber, pared, cut into chunks
    1 clove garlic
    2 tablespoons lemon juice
    1 tablespoon olive oil
    ¼ teaspoon liquid pepper sauce
    ¼ teaspoon Worcestershire sauce
    ¼ teaspoon salt
       Accompaniments: 1 cup each chopped
          cucumber, chopped green bell pepper,
          chopped green onions and croutons

1. Combine all ingredients except accompaniments in blender container; process until smooth. Refrigerate, covered, until cold, several hours.

2. Serve soup with accompaniments to be added to individual taste.

HOT 'N' SPICY HOT DOGS

Mixed pickling spices and crushed red peppers release their pungency to wieners submerged overnight in a vinegary marinade.

Makes 8 to 10 appetizer servings

    2 cups water
    1½ cups cider vinegar
    2 tablespoons mixed pickling spice
    2 tablespoons sugar
    1 teaspoon crushed red pepper
    1 pound hot dogs   *(Continued)*

1. Combine all ingredients except hot dogs in large saucepan; heat to boiling. Add hot dogs; heat to boiling again. Transfer to bowl.

2. Cover hot dogs with plate; top plate with weight to keep hot dogs immersed. Refrigerate overnight. Cut hot dogs into 2-inch lengths; serve with cocktail picks.

Note: Wieners may be reheated and served hot.

PEPPERED MUSHROOMS

Coarsely cracked black pepper and hot red pepper sauce give a fiery flavor to these cocktail-time tidbits.

Makes 12 appetizer servings

    1½ pounds small mushrooms
    ¼ cup butter or margarine
    1 small clove garlic, minced
    ⅓ cup Worcestershire sauce
    ½ teaspoon dried thyme, crumbled
    ¼ teaspoon hot red pepper sauce
    ¼ teaspoon cracked pepper

1. Saute mushrooms in butter in large skillet over medium heat 5 minutes. Add garlic; saute 5 minutes longer. Add Worcestershire sauce, thyme, red pepper sauce and cracked pepper; cook and stir 5 minutes.

2. Cover pan; cook until mushrooms are dark and glossy and liquid has almost evaporated, about 10 minutes longer. Serve hot or at room temperature with cocktail picks.

WESTERN HALIBUT CHEESE SOUP

"Simmer" is the important word when preparing this satisfying main-dish soup. The delicate-textured fish, the milk and the cheese all cook best below the boiling point.

Makes 6 to 8 servings

    ½ cup finely chopped onion
    ½ cup finely chopped green bell pepper
    ½ cup finely chopped celery
    ½ cup finely chopped carrot
    6 tablespoons butter or margarine
    2 pounds halibut, skinned, boned, cut into ¾-inch
       cubes
    3 cups chicken stock
    ¾ teaspoon salt
    ⅛ teaspoon white pepper
    2 cups milk
    3 tablespoons all-purpose flour
    2½ cups shredded sharp Cheddar cheese
    1 tablespoon minced parsley

1. Saute onion, green pepper, celery and carrot in 3 tablespoons of the butter in large saucepan over medium heat until soft, about 5 minutes. Stir in fish, stock, salt and white pepper; heat to boiling. Reduce heat; simmer, covered, 5 minutes. Stir in milk.

2. Mix flour with remaining 3 tablespoons butter until smooth; gradually stir into chowder. Cook and stir gently until thickened.

3. Add cheese; cook and stir over low heat just until cheese melts. Sprinkle with parsley.

HEARTY TURKEY CHICK PEA SOUP

Makes 4 to 6 servings

2 cans (10¾ ounces each) condensed chicken
   broth
3 cups water
¼ cup instant minced onion
2 tablespoons rice
1 tablespoon chili powder
1 can (20 ounces) chick peas, drained
2 cups diced cooked turkey or chicken
1 teaspoon lemon juice
   Salt and pepper to taste
½ ripe avocado, peeled, sliced, rubbed with lemon
   juice

1. Combine chicken broth, water, onion, rice and chili powder in medium saucepan. Heat over medium heat to boiling; reduce heat to low. Simmer, covered, stirring occasionally, 15 minutes.

2. Add chick peas, turkey and lemon juice to soup; simmer, covered, 5 minutes. Add salt and pepper.

3. Transfer soup to tureen or serving bowl; top with avocado slices.

THUMBPRINT MEATBALLS

Makes about 40 appetizers

1 pound ground beef
1 cup shredded Cheddar cheese
¼ cup dry bread crumbs
1 large egg, beaten
1 teaspoon chili powder
½ teaspoon salt
¼ teaspoon pepper
40 slices party rye bread, melba toast or snack
   crackers
   Butter
   Bottled chili sauce, barbecue sauce, taco sauce
   or horseradish sauce

1. Combine beef, cheese, bread crumbs, egg, chili powder, salt and pepper in large bowl; mix lightly but thoroughly. Shape into 1-inch balls; place in shallow baking pan. Press indentation in each meatball with thumb.

2. Bake in preheated 350°F oven until cooked through, 15 to 20 minutes.

3. Spread bread lightly with butter; top each piece with 1 meatball. Fill centers of meatballs with sauce; serve hot.

Hearty Turkey Chick Pea Soup

Tangy Braised Lamb Shanks

TANGY BRAISED LAMB SHANKS

Toast dried ancho chilies by placing them in a heavy skillet over medium heat, pressing them with a spatula and turning them occasionally until the color changes slightly. Remove from heat; when cool enough to handle, snip open lengthwise with scissors. Carefully pull out veins and seeds.

Makes 4 servings

2 dried ancho chilies, toasted, seeded, deveined*
1 cup boiling water
4 lamb shanks (about 1 pound each)
2 tablespoons lard or vegetable oil
2 medium white onions, cut lengthwise into
  ⅛-inch-thick slices
⅓ cup raisins
2 tablespoons packed brown sugar
3 cloves garlic, minced
¾ teaspoon dried oregano, crumbled
½ teaspoon ground cumin
1 can (28 ounces) whole peeled tomatoes,
  undrained, coarsely chopped
¾ cup beef stock
4 bay leaves
1 tablespoon cider vinegar
  Shredded romaine lettuce and pitted ripe olives
    for garnish
  Refried beans, if desired   *(Continued)*

1. Combine chilies with boiling water in small bowl; let soak 1 hour.

2. Combine chilies and ⅓ cup of the soaking liquid in blender container; process until smooth. Discard remaining soaking liquid.

3. Cook lamb shanks in lard in Dutch oven over medium heat, turning occasionally, until brown on all sides, about 20 minutes; remove to plate.

4. Remove and discard all but 2 tablespoons drippings from Dutch oven. Add onions; saute over medium heat until soft, about 4 minutes. Reduce heat to medium-low. Stir in raisins, sugar, garlic, oregano and cumin. Add chili puree; cook and stir 2 minutes.

5. Add tomatoes, stock and bay leaves; heat over high heat to boiling. Add lamb shanks; reduce heat to low. Simmer, covered, turning occasionally, until lamb is very tender, 2 to 2½ hours.

6. Remove lamb to serving plates; keep warm. Skim and discard fat from cooking sauce; stir in vinegar. Heat sauce over medium-high heat to boiling; cook, uncovered, stirring frequently, until sauce is thickened, about 10 minutes. Spoon sauce over lamb. Garnish with lettuce and olives; serve with refried beans.

***Note:** Wear rubber gloves when handling chilies and wash hands with warm soapy water. Avoid touching face or eyes.*

BARBECUED ROUND-UP ROAST

Makes 12 servings

1 beef round tip roast or beef chuck cross-rib
    roast (5 pounds)
1 cup strong black coffee
1 cup orange juice
1 cup chopped onion
1 tablespoon dried rosemary
1 tablespoon dried thyme
1 teaspoon pepper
    Parsley sprig for garnish
    Salt to taste

1. Place roast in shallow glass baking dish. Mix coffee, orange juice, onion, rosemary, thyme and pepper in medium bowl; pour over roast. Refrigerate, covered, turning occasionally, at least 6 hours, no longer than 48 hours.

2. Prepare charcoal grill for barbecuing. Move glowing coals with tongs to outside edges of grill. Place metal drip pan in center of grill. Push coals around sides of drip pan. Place grill rack 6 inches above drip pan.

3. Cook roast on grill over medium-hot coals, turning every 15 minutes and basting occasionally with marinade, 1½ to 2½ hours.

4. After 1½ hours, begin testing for doneness. Insert meat thermometer into center of roast and take a reading. Thermometer should register 135°F for rare, 155°F for medium, and 165°F for well done. (Internal temperature will rise 5°F upon standing after cooking.) If additional cooking is needed, remove thermometer and continue grilling, testing occasionally.

5. When roast is cooked to desired stage, remove from grill; let stand in warm place 15 minutes. To serve, garnish with parsley. Cut into thin slices; sprinkle with salt.

HIGH COUNTRY LAMB AND BEAN POT

Makes 8 servings

1 pound dried Great Northern beans
¼ pound bacon, diced
2 cups chopped onions
1 clove garlic, minced
5 cups beef or lamb stock
2 teaspoons salt
1 teaspoon pepper
1 teaspoon dried thyme, crumbled
1 bay leaf
3½ pounds lamb shoulder chops or lamb shoulder
    roast
2 tablespoons oil
1 can (16 ounces) tomato sauce
1 jar (22 ounces) sauerkraut, rinsed, drained
1 tablespoon sugar
1 can (16 ounces) sliced carrots, drained

1. Soak beans in large bowl of cold water overnight.

2. Saute bacon in Dutch oven over medium heat 2 minutes. Add onions and garlic; saute until soft, about 4 minutes.

3. Drain beans; add to Dutch oven. Stir in stock. Heat to boiling; skim and discard surface foam. Stir in salt, pepper, thyme and bay leaf; reduce heat. Simmer, partially covered, stirring occasionally, 1½ hours.

4. Remove lamb from bones; cut meat into 1-inch cubes. Cook lamb and bones in oil in large skillet over medium heat until brown on all sides, about 10 minutes.

5. Add lamb and bones to beans; stir in tomato sauce, sauerkraut and sugar. Simmer, partially covered, stirring occasionally, 1½ hours. Remove and discard bones and bay leaf. Stir in carrots; heat until hot.

Barbecued Round-Up Roast

STIR-FRY MEAL-IN-ONE

Tiny bits of crisp bacon impart a wonderful smoky flavor to all the good things in this easy supper main dish.
Makes 4 to 6 servings

    4 slices bacon, diced
 ½ cup chopped onion
    2 whole chicken breasts (about 12 ounces each),
       skinned, boned, cut into thin strips
    1 cup frozen peas, thawed
    3 cups cooked rice (cooked in chicken broth)
    1 can (4 ounces) sliced mushrooms, drained
 ¼ cup diced pimientos
    1 teaspoon salt
 ½ teaspoon seasoned pepper

1. Cook bacon and onion in large skillet over medium heat until onion is soft, about 4 minutes. Add chicken; stir-fry 5 minutes.

2. Add peas; stir-fry 1 minute. Stir in remaining ingredients; cook and stir until hot throughout.

BAKED BEEF BRISKET

Makes 10 to 12 servings

    1 boneless beef brisket (4 pounds)
    2 teaspoons salt
 ½ teaspoon pepper
    1 clove garlic, minced
    3 medium onions, thickly sliced
    1 cup hot water
    2 tablespoons cornstarch
    1 cup cold water

1. Place brisket, fat side up, in shallow roasting pan. Sprinkle with salt, pepper and garlic; top with onions.

2. Roast in preheated 350°F oven until onions turn brown, about 1 hour.

3. Add hot water to pan; cover tightly with aluminum foil. Reduce oven setting to 300°F; continue cooking until very tender, about 2 hours. Remove brisket and onions to heated platter; transfer pan juices to medium saucepan.

4. Mix cornstarch and cold water in small bowl; stir into pan juices. Cook, stirring constantly, over medium-high heat until thickened. Serve with brisket.

Stir-Fry Meal-in-One

Steak Imperial

STEAK IMPERIAL

Makes 6 servings

1½ pounds beef sirloin steak, cut into thin strips
½ cup dry red wine
¼ cup teriyaki marinade
2 tablespoons butter or margarine
1 can (10½ ounces) mushroom gravy
2 tablespoons red currant or other tart red jelly
1½ cups green bell pepper strips
2 tart apples, cored, sliced into rings
Salt and sugar to taste
3 cups hot cooked rice

1. Combine steak, wine and teriyaki marinade in large bowl; mix well. Let stand 20 minutes.

2. Drain steak, reserving marinade. Saute steak in butter in large skillet over high heat until brown, about 5 minutes. Stir in gravy, jelly and reserved marinade; heat to boiling.

3. Arrange peppers and apples on top of steak; sprinkle lightly with salt and sugar. Reduce heat; simmer, covered, 5 minutes. Serve over rice.

ENCHILADAS IN GREEN SAUCE

Makes 8 servings

2 medium onions, finely chopped
1 green bell pepper, finely chopped
1 clove garlic, minced
3 tablespoons vegetable oil
1¾ pounds ground beef chuck or round
1 cup dry red wine
2 tablespoons chicken stock
2 tablespoons chili powder

(Continued)

1 tablespoon crushed red pepper flakes
1½ teaspoons cumin seeds
2 bay leaves
16 flour tortillas (8-inch size)
Green Sauce (recipe follows)
½ pound sharp Cheddar cheese, shredded

1. Saute onions, green pepper and garlic in oil in large skillet over medium heat 6 minutes. Add meat, breaking up into small pieces.

2. Stir in wine, stock, chili powder, pepper flakes, cumin and bay leaves; heat to boiling. Reduce heat; simmer, covered, stirring occasionally, 30 minutes. Remove and discard bay leaves.

3. Dip each tortilla in Green Sauce to coat; fill with meat mixture, dividing evenly. Roll up tortillas; place seam side down in single layer in greased large baking dish. Spoon remaining Green Sauce evenly over enchiladas; sprinkle with cheese.

4. Bake in preheated 350°F oven until hot in center and bubbly around sides, about 30 minutes.

GREEN SAUCE

2 large tomatoes, peeled, cut into halves
1 large onion, cut into quarters
1 can (4 ounces) mild green chilies, drained, seeded
3 tablespoons vegetable oil
2 cups sour cream

1. Combine tomatoes, onion and chilies in blender container; process until smooth.

2. Heat oil in medium saucepan over medium heat until hot. Add vegetable puree; cook, stirring frequently, 10 to 15 minutes. Remove from heat; stir in sour cream.

Bronco Bustin' Steak

BRONCO BUSTIN' STEAK

Makes 8 to 12 servings

  4 **pounds beef top loin steaks (New York strip**
      steaks)
  4 **large cloves garlic, slivered**
1½ **teaspoons cracked black peppercorns**
     Lettuce leaves, tomato wedges and parsley
      sprigs for garnish

1. Sprinkle steaks with garlic and peppercorns pressing seasonings firmly into meat. Refrigerate, covered, at least 6 hours, no longer than 48 hours.

2. Grill steaks 4 inches from medium-hot coals for 4 to 5 minutes per side for rare or until desired doneness. Serve with lettuce, tomatoes and parsley.

HOT & SPICY BEEF BACK RIBS

Makes 8 to 10 servings

  7 **pounds beef back ribs**
 ¾ **cup water**
  1 **cup catsup**
  2 **tablespoons lemon juice**
  1 **teaspoon ground cinnamon**
  1 **teaspoon hot red pepper sauce**
 ½ **to 1 teaspoon crushed red pepper**

1. Place each slab of ribs, meat side down, in center of double-thick rectangle of heavy-duty aluminum foil. Sprinkle ¼ cup of the water over rib bones. To form packets, bring 2 opposite sides of foil together over top of ribs; fold edges over 3 or 4 times, leaving some air space; crease each fold tightly. Flatten foil at 1 open end; fold and crease *(Continued)*

to form triangle. Fold edge several times toward package, pressing tightly to seal. Repeat procedure at other open end.

2. Place packets on grill over low to medium-hot coals. Place cover on cooker; cook 1½ hours, turning packets every ½ hour.

3. Meanwhile, mix catsup, remaining ½ cup water, the lemon juice, cinnamon, pepper sauce and crushed red pepper in small saucepan; heat to boiling. Reduce heat; simmer 10 to 12 minutes.

4. Remove ribs from foil packets. Grill, uncovered, over medium-hot coals, turning and brushing with sauce occasionally, 30 to 40 minutes. Serve remaining sauce with ribs.

COWPUNCHER SPIKED SAUCE

Makes 1¼ cups

  2 **cloves garlic, finely chopped**
 ¼ **teaspoon pepper**
  2 **teaspoons vegetable oil**
  2 **teaspoons butter**
 ½ **cup bourbon**
  1 **cup beef stock**
 ¼ **cup Worcestershire sauce**
 ¼ **teaspoon salt**
    Dash hot red pepper sauce

1. Saute garlic and pepper in oil and butter in small saucepan over medium heat 1 minute. Carefully add bourbon; cook until reduced to about ¼ cup. If bourbon flames, cover pan with lid until flame is gone.

2. Stir in stock, Worcestershire sauce, salt and pepper sauce; heat to boiling. Reduce heat; simmer, uncovered, 10 minutes. Serve over grilled or broiled steak.

CHILI HERO

Green, white and red, the colors in the Mexican flag, show up prominently among garnishes for main dishes with a south-of-the-border accent. Avocados, sour cream and tomatoes do the honors on these big open-faced sandwiches, with shredded cheese and lettuce as additional choices.

Makes 4 servings

  2 **tablespoons water**
  2 **tablespoons instant minced onion**
  ½ **teaspoon instant minced garlic**
  2 **tablespoons vegetable oil**
  1 **pound ground beef**
  1 **can (16 ounces) tomatoes, undrained, chopped**
  2 **teaspoons chili powder**
  1 **teaspoon salt**
  ½ **teaspoon dried oregano, crumbled**
  ⅛ **teaspoon pepper**
  ¼ **cup sliced pitted ripe olives**
  1 **pound loaf Italian bread, about 12 inches long**

(Continued)

Sliced avocado
Diced tomato
Sour cream
Shredded lettuce
Shredded Cheddar cheese

1. Combine water, onion and garlic in small bowl; let stand 10 minutes.

2. Heat oil in large skillet over medium heat. Add rehydrated onion and garlic; saute 2 minutes. Add beef; cook and stir, breaking into small pieces, until brown, about 5 minutes. Drain and discard excess fat.

3. Add canned tomatoes, chili powder, salt, oregano and pepper to skillet; mix well. Heat to boiling; reduce heat. Simmer, uncovered, 10 minutes. Stir in olives; keep warm.

4. Heat bread in preheated 350°F oven until warmed through, about 10 minutes. Cut bread lengthwise in half; slightly hollow out centers.

5. Fill each bread boat with hot beef mixture; cut each boat crosswise into halves. Top with sliced avocado and diced tomato; serve with sour cream, lettuce, and cheese.

Chili Hero

SURPRISE BEEF SANDWICHES

Makes 4 servings

1 pound ground beef
¾ teaspoon dried mixed Italian herbs
1 teaspoon salt
⅛ teaspoon ground pepper
4 pieces mozzarella cheese, 2½ × ½ × ½ inches each
¼ cup catsup
4 pieces French bread 4 inches long, split horizontally
¼ cup chopped green bell pepper
¼ cup chopped onion

1. Combine ground beef, Italian herbs, salt and ground pepper in large bowl; mix lightly but thoroughly. Divide into 4 equal portions.

2. Thread 2 pieces of cheese lengthwise onto each of 2 long metal skewers. Press ¼ of the beef mixture firmly around each piece of cheese to cover completely.

3. Grill over medium-hot coals or broil, turning occasionally and brushing with catsup, until cooked through, 8 to 12 minutes. Serve on French bread; sprinkle with green pepper and onion.

CAMPERS' BREAKFAST

Here's a one-skillet meal cooked over the coals to satisfy big appetites sharpened by crisp mountain air.

Makes 4 servings

1 can (7 ounces) luncheon meat, cut into thin strips
1 cup chopped onion
¼ cup sliced celery
¼ cup vegetable oil
1 can (16 ounces) pork-and-beans in tomato sauce
1 can (16 ounces) plum tomatoes in tomato paste, undrained, chopped
1 teaspoon salt
¼ teaspoon ground red pepper
4 large eggs

1. Saute luncheon meat, onion and celery in oil in large skillet over medium heat until meat is brown, about 10 minutes. Remove and reserve about ⅓ of the meat strips.

2. Add pork-and-beans, tomatoes, salt and pepper to skillet; mix well. Make 4 indentations in bean mixture; carefully break 1 egg into each indentation. Scatter reserved meat strips around eggs.

3. Cook, covered, over low heat until egg whites are set, 4 to 6 minutes. Serve immediately.

Campers' Breakfast

"OK Corral" Beef Chili

"OK CORRAL" BEEF CHILI

Those lined up against beans cooked in chili contend that the flavor of chili gets better every time the fiery mixture is reheated, but the beans only get softer. They cook chili in big batches and eat it with rice or beans on the side.

Makes 8 to 12 servings

    6 dried ancho chilies*
3½ cups boiling water
    2 to 3 tablespoons vegetable oil
    3 pounds boneless beef chuck, cut into ½-inch
        cubes
    4 cloves garlic, minced
    3 bay leaves, crumbled
    2 to 3 tablespoons chili powder
        Salt to taste
    6 cups hot cooked rice

1. Remove and discard stems and seeds from chilies. Chop chilies coarsely; combine with boiling water in medium bowl. Let soak 30 minutes.

2. Heat oil in Dutch oven over medium heat. Add ½ the beef; cook until brown on all sides, about 5 minutes. Remove to plate. Repeat with remaining beef. Return all beef to pan.

3. Drain chilies, reserving liquid.

4. Add 2½ cups of the chili liquid to beef; stir in garlic and bay leaves. Heat to boiling; reduce heat to medium-low. Cook, partially covered, stirring occasionally, 1 hour.

5. Combine chilies, remaining soaking liquid and chili powder in blender container; process until smooth. Stir into beef mixture; add salt. Cook, stirring occasionally, over medium heat until beef is tender, about 30 minutes. Serve with rice.

Note: *Ancho chilies are sweet and fairly mild. They give the chili a rich dark color and a unique flavor. Wear rubber gloves when working with chilies and wash hands with warm soapy water. Avoid touching face or eyes.*

APPLE SAUSAGE PANCAKE

Here's a puffy baked pancake that's a breakfast of sausage, cereal, eggs and fruit in one pan. If your camp stove has an oven, this first meal of the day is great served outdoors.

Makes 4 servings

    1 package (8 ounces) breakfast sausage links
    1 cup milk
  ⅔ cup all-purpose flour
    2 large eggs
  ¼ cup crushed bran cereal (nuggets, flakes or
        squares)
    1 tablespoon sugar
  ½ teaspoon salt
    2 tablespoons vegetable oil
    1 to 1¼ cups sliced apples

1. Cook sausages in medium skillet over medium heat, turning occasionally, until golden, about 7 minutes; drain on paper toweling.

2. Measure 1 tablespoon sausage drippings; place in medium bowl. Add milk, flour, eggs, cereal, sugar and salt; beat until smooth.

3. Place oil in 10-inch skillet with oven-proof handle, or in 9-inch square baking pan; tilt skillet to coat bottom evenly. Pour batter into skillet; arrange sausages and apples on batter, spoke-fashion.

4. Bake in preheated 425°F oven until pancake is puffed and golden brown, about 40 minutes. Serve immediately.

Apple Sausage Pancake

Sausage and Beans Tampico

SAUSAGE AND BEANS TAMPICO

Apples work their subtle magic with smoked sausage and beans by mellowing the flavor and introducing nuggets of cooked fruit to the finished dish.

Makes 6 servings

12 ounces smoked country-style sausage, cut into 1-inch pieces
1 cup chopped yellow onion
3⅓ cups cooked or canned pinto or kidney beans, drained
1 cup tomato juice
1 teaspoon salt
1 teaspoon chili powder
¼ teaspoon garlic powder
¼ teaspoon pepper
2 cups pared, cored, thickly sliced apples
4 to 6 cups hot cooked rice
½ cup sour cream
Green onions, yellow chilies and corn chips, if desired

1. Saute sausage and yellow onion in large skillet over medium heat, 5 minutes. Stir in beans, tomato juice, salt, chili powder, garlic powder and pepper; simmer, uncovered, 10 minutes.

2. Stir in apples; cook, stirring occasionally, until most of the liquid has evaporated, about 10 minutes. Transfer to serving dish; serve with rice, sour cream, green onions, chilies and corn chips.

SOUTHWESTERN STRATA

Makes 6 servings

8 ounces bulk pork sausage
⅔ cup chopped onion
⅓ cup chopped green bell pepper
8 slices day-old white bread, cut into 1-inch cubes
1½ cups shredded American cheese
1 cup shredded Monterey Jack cheese
2 cups milk
1 cup mild salsa ranchero
4 large eggs, beaten

1. Combine sausage, onion and green pepper in medium skillet; cook and stir over medium heat until sausage is brown and finely crumbled, about 10 minutes. Drain and discard drippings.

2. Place half of the bread cubes in buttered 2-quart rectangular baking dish; sprinkle with ½ of the sausage mixture and ½ of the cheeses. Repeat layers once.

3. Mix milk, salsa and eggs in medium bowl; pour over mixture in baking dish. Cover tightly with plastic wrap; refrigerate several hours or overnight. Remove from refrigerator 1 hour before baking.

4. Bake, uncovered, in preheated 325°F oven until knife inserted into center is withdrawn clean, 50 to 55 minutes. Let stand 10 minutes before serving.

BEEF JERKY

Thin strip of dried meat called "jerky" fit as neatly into the rations of today's recreational backpacker as they did when being on the trail was a way of life.

Makes 8 to 12 servings

1 beef flank steak (about 1½ pounds)
Soy sauce
Garlic salt
Pepper

1. Trim all visible fat from beef. Place beef in freezer until partially frozen, about 1 hour.

2. Cut beef lengthwise, with the grain, into ⅛-inch-thick slices. Dip slices into soy sauce to coat. Arrange slices in single layer and close together on wire racks; place racks over baking pans.

3. Sprinkle beef lightly with garlic salt and pepper; turn slices over. Sprinkle second side with garlic salt and pepper.

4. Bake in preheated 140°F oven until beef is dried out and chewy, 8 to 10 hours. Beef should dry out, not cook. Store in tightly covered container.

Note: *Round steak can be substituted for flank steak.*

CHIPPED BEEF AND POTATO SKILLET

Makes 4 to 6 servings

1 package (3 ounces) smoked sliced beef
¼ cup butter
3 large potatoes, pared, cut into cubes (about 4 cups)
1 medium onion, chopped
1 can (13 ounces) evaporated milk
1 cup boiling water
½ teaspoon salt
Pinch pepper

(Continued)

1. Break beef into small pieces; saute in butter in large skillet over medium heat until edges begin to curl. Remove beef from skillet.

2. Add potatoes and onion to skillet; saute over low heat until most of the butter is absorbed and onion is soft, about 4 minutes.

3. Stir in milk and water; cook, uncovered, stirring occasionally, until potatoes are tender and sauce begins to thicken, 20 to 30 minutes. Add beef; cook and stir until hot, about 3 minutes longer. Stir in salt and pepper.

KABOBS WITH SESAME-LIME MARINADE

Makes 4 servings

¼ cup lime juice
2 tablespoons vegetable oil
2 tablespoons sesame seeds
1 tablespoon soy sauce
2 cloves garlic, minced
½ teaspoon liquid pepper sauce
1½ pounds beef top round, cut in 1½-inch cubes
2 medium zucchini, cut into 1-inch pieces
2 medium onions, parboiled, cut into 1¼-inch pieces
16 cherry tomatoes

1. Whisk lime juice, oil, sesame seeds, soy sauce, garlic and liquid pepper sauce in medium bowl. Add beef; mix well. Refrigerate, covered, stirring occasionally, at least 5 hours or overnight.

2. Drain beef, reserving marinade; thread beef on skewers. Thread vegetables on separate skewers, alternating pieces of zucchini, onion and tomato. Brush beef and vegetables with reserved marinade.

3. Grill over hot coals, 6 to 8 inches from heat; baste beef and vegetables frequently during grilling and turn skewers occasionally. Allow 15 to 20 minutes for beef and 10 to 12 minutes for vegetables.

Kabobs with Sesame-Lime Marinade

Stacked Cheese Enchiladas

HASH-BROWN CHICKEN BAKE

Convenient frozen hash-brown potatoes mixed with sharp Cheddar cheese, eggs and flour bake to a golden brown crispness atop seasoned chicken and vegetables.

Makes 10 to 12 servings

    2 whole broiler-fryer chickens (3 pounds each)
      Water
3½ teaspoons salt
    3 stalks celery, cut crosswise into ½-inch-thick
        slices
    2 large carrots, cut crosswise into ½-inch-thick
        slices
    1 medium onion, sliced
  ¾ cup plus ⅔ cup all-purpose flour
    2 packages (12 ounces each) frozen shredded
        hash-brown potatoes, thawed
    1 cup shredded sharp Cheddar cheese
  ¼ teaspoon pepper
    2 large eggs, lightly beaten
      Chopped parsley for garnish

1. Combine chickens, 6 cups water and 2 teaspoons of the salt in large kettle; heat over medium heat to simmering. Reduce heat; simmer, covered, until tender, 1 to 1½ hours.

2. Remove chickens to plate; let cool slightly. Remove and discard bones and skin; cut chicken into ½-inch pieces. Skim fat from chicken broth; measure broth. Add water if needed to make 4 cups.

3. Combine broth, celery, carrots and onion in large saucepan; simmer, covered, until tender, about 12 minutes.

4. Mix ¾ cup of the flour and 2 cups cold water in small bowl until smooth; gradually stir into vegetable-broth mixture. Cook, stirring constantly, over medium-low heat until mixture thickens and bubbles for 3 minutes. Stir in chicken.

(Continued)

Transfer mixure to two 13 × 9 × 2-inch baking dishes, dividing evenly.

5. Place potatoes in large bowl; separate with fork. Add cheese, remaining ⅔ cup flour, remaining 1½ teaspoons salt and the pepper; toss to mix. Stir in eggs. Spoon over chicken mixture, dividing evenly. Cover dishes with aluminum foil.

6. Bake in preheated 350°F oven 30 minutes. Sprinkle with parsley.

STACKED CHEESE ENCHILADAS

Makes 6 servings

    2 cans (15 ounces each) tomato sauce
  ¼ cup instant minced onion
    1 tablespoon chili powder
  ½ teaspoon salt
  ¼ teaspoon ground cumin
  ¼ teaspoon garlic powder
  12 corn tortillas
    8 ounces shredded Cheddar or Monterey Jack
        cheese

1. Combine tomato sauce, onion, chili powder, salt, cumin and garlic powder in medium saucepan; heat to boiling. Reduce heat; simmer, covered, 15 minutes.

2. Spread ¼ cup of the sauce in bottom of 9-inch square baking dish; top with 1 tortilla. Spread tortilla with 2 tablespoons of the sauce; sprinkle with 2 rounded tablespoons of the cheese. Repeat layering remaining tortillas with sauce and cheese.

3. Bake in preheated 350°F oven until hot, about 20 minutes; remove tortilla stack to serving plate.

4. Add sauce remaining in baking dish to remaining sauce in saucepan; heat until hot. Cut tortilla stack into wedges; serve with sauce.

TEXAS BLACKEYES AND BEEF

Makes 4 to 6 servings

  ½ pound (1 cup) dried blackeyes
      Water
    1 pound ground beef
1½ cups chopped onions
1½ cups sliced celery
1½ cups tomato puree
    1 to 2 tablespoons chili powder
    1 teaspoon salt
  ⅛ teaspoon pepper
  ⅛ teaspoon garlic powder

1. Soak beans in 6 cups cold water in large bowl at room temperature overnight.

2. Cook and stir beef in Dutch oven over medium heat until brown, about 10 minutes. Add onions and celery; cook and stir 3 minutes. Stir in tomato puree, chili powder, salt, pepper and garlic powder; stir in 1¼ cups water.

3. Drain and rinse beans; add to Dutch oven. Cook over low heat, stirring occasionally, until chili is thick and beans are tender, 1 to 2 hours; add water occasionally if mixture becomes too thick.

TURKEY TAMALE PIE

You might think of this casserole as a giant tamale in a baking dish. A yellow cornmeal mixture around the outside and a chili-seasoned turkey filling makes a tasty meal.

Makes 4 servings

> **Water**
> 1 **can (13¾ ounces) chicken broth**
> 1½ **teaspoons salt**
> 1½ **cups uncooked yellow cornmeal**
> 1 **cup cold water**
> 1 **cup chopped onion**
> 1 **teaspoon minced garlic**
> 1 **tablespoon vegetable oil**
> 1 **can (1 pound) stewed tomatoes, undrained**
> 1 **can (12 ounces) vacuum-packed whole-kernel corn**
> 1 **tablespoon chili powder**
> ½ **teaspoon dried oregano, crumbled**
> 2 **cups cubed cooked turkey**
> **Parsley sprig for garnish**

1. Add enough water to broth to measure 2½ cups; transfer to medium saucepan. Add ¾ teaspoon of the salt; heat over medium heat to simmering.

2. Mix 1¼ cups of the cornmeal with 1 cup cold water in small bowl; gradually stir into simmering broth. Cook and stir over medium heat until mixture thickens and boils. Reduce heat to very low; cook, covered, stirring occasionally, until very thick, about 10 minutes. Remove from heat; reserve.

3. Saute onion and garlic in oil in large skillet over medium heat until soft, about 5 minutes. Stir in tomatoes, corn, chili powder, oregano and remaining ¾ teaspoon salt. Heat to boiling; reduce heat and simmer 5 minutes.

(Continued)

4. Slowly stir remaining ¼ cup cornmeal into tomato mixture; cook until thickened, about 5 minutes. Stir in turkey; remove from heat.

5. Line 5½-cup shallow baking dish with the reserved cornmeal mixture, using all but 1 cup. Fill with turkey mixture. Pipe remaining 1 cup cornmeal mixture through pastry bag fitted with large star tip in ring on top of casserole.

6. Bake in preheated 350°F oven until hot throughout, 20 to 30 minutes. Garnish with parsley.

Note: *Recipe can be doubled to serve 8. Use a 2½-quart baking dish; reserve 1½ cups cooked cornmeal mixture for top edge and bake 30 to 40 minutes. Or, make double recipe in two 5½-cup baking dishes; bake one and freeze the other.*

TURKEY HASH

Spoon a dollop of leftover cranberry sauce atop each serving of this tasty hash made from leftover turkey and potatoes.

Makes 4 servings

> ¾ **cup diced cooked potato**
> 3 **tablespoons chopped onion**
> 2 **tablespoons chopped green bell pepper**
> 2 **tablespoons butter or margarine**
> 3 **cups diced cooked turkey**
> ⅓ **cup evaporated milk**
> 1½ **teaspoons Worcestershire sauce**
> ½ **teaspoon salt**
> ⅛ **teaspoon ground black pepper**

Saute potato, onion and green bell pepper in butter in large skillet over medium heat until light brown, about 5 minutes. Stir in remaining ingredients; cook over low heat, stirring frequently, until mixture is hot, about 10 minutes.

Turkey Tamale Pie

PAPRIKA LEMON CHICKEN

Makes 8 to 12 servings

⅔ cup lemon juice
⅔ cup water
½ cup catsup
3 tablespoons packed dark brown sugar
3 tablespoons paprika
3 tablespoons onion powder
1 tablespoon garlic powder
1 tablespoon cornstarch
3 teaspoons salt
1 teaspoon dry mustard
¾ teaspoon ground red pepper
¼ cup vegetable oil
6 pounds broiler-fryer chicken, cut into serving-size pieces
Lemon slices for garnish

1. Mix lemon juice, water, catsup, brown sugar, paprika, onion powder, garlic powder, cornstarch, 2 teaspoons of the salt, the mustard and red pepper in a small saucepan. Add oil; cook, stirring constantly, over medium heat until sauce thickens, about 3 minutes. Remove from heat.

2. Sprinkle chicken with remaining 1 teaspoon salt; place on rack in broiler pan. Broil 8 inches from heat source, turning and brushing with sauce frequently, until chicken is tender, about 30 minutes.

3. Transfer chicken to serving platter. Garnish with lemon slices.

SMOKED RAINBOW TROUT

Show off your catch by cooking them in the gentle, moist heat of a smoker. It's a relaxed, easy way to cook with gourmet results.

Makes 6 servings

2 cups cold water
2 tablespoons salt
6 rainbow trout, cleaned (about 12 ounces each)
½ cup vegetable oil
1 lemon, sliced
6 strips bacon

1. About 3 hours before serving, make brine by mixing water and salt in small bowl until salt dissolves. Pour brine over trout in shallow bowl or baking dish; refrigerate, covered, 30 minutes.

2. Start soaking 2 or 3 chunks of wood or handful of wood chips, unless smoker takes dry wood.

3. Fill fire pan almost full of charcoal briquettes and start fire. When coals turn grey, drain wood pieces; add them to coals. (For electric units: Unless the smoker takes dry wood, drain the wood pieces and put them in their special pan.)

4. Put water pan in place; fill about ⅔ full with hot water. Set cooking grill in place.

5. Drain trout; rinse under cold water. Drain; pat dry. Brush both sides of trout with oil; place lemon slices in body cavities. Cover each trout with bacon strip.

6. Arrange trout on cooking grill; add brine to water pan, if desired, or discard it. Cover smoke-cooker (plug in electric smoker). Smoke-cook until the trout is firm to the touch and flakes easily with fork, 2 to 3 hours.

STUFFED CHICKEN THIGHS

Makes 4 servings

½ cup finely chopped celery
½ cup finely chopped onion
3 tablespoons bacon drippings
2 tablespoons dry sherry
¼ teaspoon poultry seasoning
¼ teaspoon pepper
2 cups soft breadcrumbs
3 slices bacon, cooked, crumbled
8 chicken thighs, boned, skin intact
½ teaspoon garlic salt

1. Saute celery and onion in 2 tablespoons of the bacon drippings in medium skillet over medium heat until soft, about 4 minutes; remove from heat. Add sherry, poultry seasoning and ⅛ teaspoon of the pepper; mix well. Add breadcrumbs and bacon; mix well.

2. Place chicken thighs, skin side down, on flat surface. Spread each thigh with 2 tablespoons of the breadcrumb mixture; roll up and fasten with wooden picks.

3. Place thighs seam side down in single layer in shallow baking dish. Brush lightly with remaining 1 tablespoon bacon drippings; sprinkle with garlic salt and remaining ⅛ teaspoon pepper.

4. Bake in preheated 450°F oven 7 minutes. Reduce oven setting to 350°F; bake until chicken is golden and fork-tender, about 45 minutes longer.

WESTERN ROAST CHICKEN

Makes 4 servings

2 cups soft breadcrumbs
½ large orange, peeled, diced
¼ cup finely chopped celery
2 tablespoons chopped onion
2 tablespoons finely chopped green bell pepper
6 tablespoons hot water
2 tablespoons butter, melted
2 teaspoons soy sauce
½ teaspoon salt
¼ teaspoon ground ginger
1 whole fryer chicken (about 3½ pounds)
⅓ cup fresh orange juice
1 teaspoon grated orange rind
½ teaspoon sugar
⅓ cup vegetable oil

1. Combine breadcrumbs, orange, celery, onion and green pepper in medium bowl; toss to mix. Mix water, butter, 1 teaspoon of the soy sauce, ¼ teaspoon of the salt and the ginger in small bowl. Add to breadcrumb mixture; mix well.

2. Spoon stuffing into chicken, packing loosely; truss chicken. Place breast side up on rack in shallow roasting pan.

3. For basting sauce, mix orange juice, orange rind, remaining 1 teaspoon soy sauce, the sugar and remaining ¼ teaspoon salt in small bowl; whisk in oil until blended.

4. Brush chicken with basting sauce. Roast, uncovered, in preheated 350°F oven, basting occasionally, until leg feels tender when pressed and moves freely in socket, 1½ to 2 hours. Let stand 15 minutes before carving.

Stuffed Chicken Thighs

Mexican Fish Rolls

MEXICAN FISH ROLLS

Taco seasoning mix lends an agreeable spiciness to the crunchy coating for baked fish fillets.

Makes 6 servings

   1 package (3 ounces) cream cheese, room
       temperature
   2 tablespoons bottled onion salad dressing
3½ teaspoons taco seasoning mix
   2 tablespoons finely chopped onion
   2 tablespoons finely chopped celery
   6 fresh or thawed frozen farm-raised catfish
       fillets (6 to 8 inches long)
   1 teaspoon onion salt
  20 round buttery crackers, finely crushed
   2 tablespoons butter or margarine, melted
       Parsley sprigs, green onion brushes and lemon
       slice twists for garnish

1. Mix cream cheese, salad dressing and 1½ teaspoons of the taco seasoning mix in small bowl; stir in chopped onion and celery.

2. Sprinkle fish with onion salt; place ⅙ of the cream cheese mixture at 1 end of each fillet. Roll up fillets to enclose cream cheese mixture; secure with wooden picks.

3. Mix cracker crumbs and remaining 2 teaspoons taco seasoning mix in shallow bowl. Dip each fish roll in butter and roll in crumb mixture to coat completely. Place rolls in a well-greased 12 × 8 × 2-inch baking dish.

4. Bake in preheated 350°F oven until fish flakes with fork, about 30 minutes. Transfer to serving platter; garnish with parsley, green onions and lemon slices.

HERB-STUFFED TROUT

Makes 4 servings

   1 small onion, finely chopped
   5 tablespoons butter or margarine
   1 clove garlic, minced
1½ cups soft breadcrumbs
   ¼ cup minced parsley
   2 tablespoons lemon juice
   1 teaspoon fines herbes
   4 whole trout (10 to 12 ounces each)
       Salt
       Pepper
   ¼ teaspoon paprika
       Parsley sprigs for garnish
       Lemon wedges

1. Saute onion in 4 tablespoons of the butter in medium skillet over medium heat until soft, about 3 minutes. Stir in garlic; remove from heat. Add breadcrumbs, minced parsley, 1 tablespoon of the lemon juice and the fines herbes; toss to mix well.

2. Sprinkle trout inside and out with salt and pepper; brush with remaining 1 tablespoon lemon juice. Spoon breadcrumb mixture into body cavities, dividing evenly.

3. Place trout in single layer in greased shallow baking dish. Melt remaining 1 tablespoon butter; drizzle over trout. Cover dish loosely with aluminum foil.

4. Bake in preheated 400°F oven 8 minutes. Remove foil; continue baking just until trout are opaque in center, about 7 minutes longer. Remove trout to platter; sprinkle with paprika. Garnish with parsley sprigs; serve with lemon wedges.

CHICKEN AND PEACHES PIQUANT

Makes 6 servings

1 pound skinned boned chicken breasts
1 teaspoon seasoned salt
¼ teaspoon ground black pepper
1½ tablespoons vegetable oil
1 large onion, sliced
1 cup catsup
1 can (16 ounces) sliced peaches, drained, syrup reserved
2 tablespoons soy sauce
Water
1 large green bell pepper, diced (¾-inch)
3 cups hot cooked rice

1. Cut chicken into thin strips; sprinkle with salt and pepper. Saute in oil in large skillet over medium heat 2 minutes.

2. Add onion; saute until onion is crisp-tender, about 2 minutes.

3. Mix catsup, reserved peach syrup, the soy sauce and enough water to measure 2½ cups; add to skillet. Heat to boiling; reduce heat. Simmer, covered, 20 minutes.

4. Stir in green pepper and peaches. Simmer, covered, 10 minutes longer. Serve with rice.

SHRIMP IN FIERY GARLIC BUTTER

The name of this shrimp dish says it all. If you prefer a milder flavor, use fewer chilies and remove some or all of the seeds.

Makes 4 servings

½ cup butter
¼ cup vegetable oil
8 cloves garlic, finely chopped
1 to 3 dried de arbol chilies, coarsely crumbled*
1 tablespoon fresh lime juice
¼ teaspoon salt
1½ pounds medium shrimp, shelled, deveined, tails intact
Slivered green onion tops for garnish
Crusty French or Italian bread

1. Heat butter and oil in medium skillet over medium heat until butter is melted and foamy. Add garlic, chilies, lime juice and salt; cook and stir 1 minute. Remove from heat.

2. Spread shrimp in even layer in shallow 2-quart gratin pan or baking dish. Pour hot butter mixture over shrimp.

3. Bake shrimp in preheated 400°F oven, stirring once or twice, just until opaque throughout and sizzling hot, 10 to 12 minutes. (Do not overcook or shrimp will be dry and tough.) Garnish with green onions; serve immediately. Use bread to blot up butter sauce.

__Note:__ Any small hot red chilies can be substituted. Wear rubber gloves when handling chilies and wash hands with warm soapy water. Avoid touching face or eyes.

Chicken and Peaches Piquant

CRUNCHY CALICO SALAD

A vegetable salad as bright and colorful as the multi-hued prints in a piece of patchwork.

Makes 4 to 6 servings

  1 can (17 ounces) whole-kernel corn, drained
  2 cups finely chopped fresh spinach or romaine
      lettuce
  1 cup diced (¼ inch) carrot
  1 cup diced (¼ inch) seeded pared cucumber
  2 green onions, sliced
½ cup vegetable oil
¼ cup white wine vinegar
  1 tablespoon Dijon-style mustard
  1 teaspoon dried dill weed
⅛ teaspoon garlic powder
    Salt and pepper to taste
    Lettuce leaves
⅓ cup crumbled feta cheese

1. Combine corn, spinach, carrot, cucumber and green onions in large bowl. Whisk oil, vinegar, mustard, dill, garlic powder, salt and pepper in small bowl until blended. Pour dressing over vegetables; toss to mix well.

2. Transfer vegetable mixture to salad bowl lined with lettuce leaves. Top with cheese; serve immediately.

TEXAS-STYLE LOBSTER SALAD

You'd never guess that hard-cooked egg yolks are the basis for the special dressing with its bite of mustard and red pepper.

Makes 6 servings

  6 large hard-cooked eggs
½ cup vegetable oil
  1 tablespoon sugar
  1 teaspoon dry mustard
  1 teaspoon salt
¼ teaspoon ground red pepper
½ cup vinegar
  1 pound fresh or thawed frozen spiny lobster
      meat, cooked
1½ cups chopped celery
1½ cups chopped green onions
  2 tablespoons capers with liquid
    Salad greens

1. Mash egg yolks in small bowl until smooth; gradually stir in oil. Stir in sugar, mustard, salt and pepper; stir in vinegar.

2. Chop egg whites. Cut lobster meat into ½-inch cubes. Combine egg whites, lobster, celery, green onions and capers in large bowl; toss to mix. Add dressing; mix lightly. Serve on bed of salad greens.

Crunchy Calico Salad

Grapefruit Vegetable Aspic

GRAPEFRUIT VEGETABLE ASPIC

The lively flavor of grapefruit juice is the background for a colorful mixture of cabbage, garden peppers and carrot.

Makes 6 servings

 1 envelope unflavored gelatin
1¼ cups grapefruit juice
 ¼ cup sugar
 2 tablespoons lemon juice
 1 tablespoon cider vinegar
 3 to 4 drops hot red pepper sauce
1½ cups finely shredded red, green or Chinese
     cabbage or mixture of all 3
 ½ cup shredded carrot
 ¼ cup chopped red or green bell pepper
     Lettuce leaves
 ½ cup plain yogurt
 1 tablespoon finely chopped parsley

1. Sprinkle gelatin over grapefruit juice in medium saucepan; let stand 5 minutes to soften. Add sugar; cook and stir over medium heat until gelatin is dissolved.

2. Transfer gelatin mixture to large bowl; stir in lemon juice, vinegar and pepper sauce. Refrigerate, stirring occasionally, until syrupy.

3. Fold in cabbage, carrot and pepper; spoon into 6 oiled individual molds. Refrigerate until set, several hours.

4. To serve, unmold onto lettuce leaves; top with yogurt and sprinkle with parsley.

WINTER APPLE SALAD

A cooked dressing sets this apart from other apple salads. Slightly tart, very crisp eating apples are an especially good choice for the salad.

Makes 4 servings

 3 tablespoons sugar
 2 tablespoons all-purpose flour
 1 teaspoon salt
 1 teaspoon dry mustard
 ¼ teaspoon ground red pepper
 ¾ cup milk
 2 large egg yolks, lightly beaten
 ¼ cup cider vinegar
1½ teaspoons margarine
 ½ cup chopped celery
 ½ cup chopped pitted dates
 ½ cup raisins
 2 cups diced apples
 ½ cup chopped pecans

1. For dressing, mix sugar, flour, salt, mustard and pepper in top of double boiler; stir in milk and egg yolks until smooth.

2. Cook, stirring constantly, over hot, not boiling, water until thickened, about 10 minutes. Stir in vinegar and margarine; let cool completely.

3. Combine celery, dates, raisins and dressing in medium bowl; mix well. Refrigerate, covered, until serving time. Fold in apples and pecans just before serving.

Sweet Spanish Onion Pull-Aparts

SWEET SPANISH ONION PULL-APARTS

Makes 4 to 6 servings

2 or 3 large sweet Spanish onions
Vegetable oil for frying
Tempura batter mix

1. Cut onions crosswise into thin slices; separate slices into rings. Cut larger rings crosswise into halves.

2. Heat oil in deep-fat fryer to 375°F. Prepare tempura batter mix in large bowl according to package directions.

3. Add onion rings to batter; stir to coat well. Remove rings, letting excess batter drain off; stack rings in basket of deep-fat fryer.

4. Fry in oil until crisp and golden; drain well. Serve with forks to pull rings apart.

ONION-BUTTERED JULIENNE VEGETABLES

Makes 4 servings

2 cups julienne-cut carrots (2 × ⅛ × ⅛-inch)
1 cup julienne-cut celery (2 × ⅛ × ⅛-inch)
¼ cup Onion Butter (recipe follows)
1 cup julienne-cut zucchini (2 × ⅛ × ⅛-inch)

Saute carrots and celery in Onion Butter in large skillet over medium heat 3 minutes. Stir in zucchini; cook, covered, over low heat until vegetables are crisp-tender, about 3 minutes longer. *(Continued)*

ONION BUTTER

1 cup butter, room temperature
1 envelope onion soup mix

Beat butter in small mixer bowl until creamy; beat in soup mix. Refrigerate, covered.

Makes about 1¼ cups

SPINACH AND AVOCADO SALAD

Makes 6 servings

11 ounces fresh spinach, torn into bite-size pieces
3 avocados, pared, pitted, sliced
7 slices bacon, cooked, crumbled
1 cup sliced mushrooms
½ cup sliced green onions
2 tablespoons fresh lemon juice
1 large egg yolk
1 clove garlic, minced
½ teaspoon salt
¼ teaspoon sugar
⅛ teaspoon dry mustard
⅛ teaspoon pepper
6 tablespoons olive oil

1. Combine spinach, avocados, bacon, mushrooms and onions in large salad bowl; toss to mix well.

2. Whisk lemon juice and egg yolk in small bowl until smooth; whisk in garlic, salt, sugar, mustard and pepper. Gradually whisk in oil until blended.

3. Pour dressing over spinach mixture; toss to mix well.

BACKYARD BEAN TACOS

Makes 4 servings

1 cup chopped onion
½ cup chopped green bell pepper
2 tablespoons vegetable oil
1 can (16 ounces) red kidney beans, drained
½ cup plain yogurt
¼ cup chopped parsley
½ teaspoon liquid pepper sauce
¼ teaspoon ground cumin
4 taco shells
1 cup shredded lettuce
½ cup chopped tomato

1. Saute onion and green pepper in oil in large skillet over medium heat until soft, about 4 minutes. Stir in beans, yogurt, parsley, pepper sauce and cumin; heat over medium-low heat just until hot, 1 to 2 minutes.

2. Spoon bean mixture into taco shells; top with lettuce and tomato.

ORANGE SALAD

Makes 6 to 8 servings

2 tablespoons wine vinegar
2 tablespoons minced parsley
2 tablespoons minced fresh basil or 1 teaspoon dried basil
1 tablespoon minced fresh mint leaves
½ teaspoon salt
⅛ teaspoon pepper
6 tablespoons olive oil
6 oranges, peeled, sliced
2 medium red onions, cut into quarters, sliced
½ pound romaine lettuce leaves

1. Mix vinegar, parsley, basil, mint, salt and pepper in small bowl; gradually whisk in oil until blended.

2. Arrange oranges and onions on lettuce-lined salad plates. Drizzle with dressing.

DEEP-FRIED MEXICAN POTATO BALLS

Makes 6 servings

1½ cups water
4½ tablespoons butter or margarine
1 teaspoon salt
3 cups instant potato flakes
¾ cup milk
2 teaspoons olive oil
½ cup finely chopped onion
½ cup finely chopped green bell pepper
½ cup finely chopped ripe tomato
½ cup diced cooked ham
2 teaspoons chopped fresh coriander
1 clove garlic, minced
¼ teaspoon hot red pepper sauce
¼ teaspoon dried oregano, crumbled
2 large eggs, beaten
½ cup yellow cornmeal
   Vegetable oil for frying
   Shredded lettuce
   Tomato wedges for garnish

1. Combine water, butter and salt in large saucepan; heat to rolling boil. Remove from heat; stir in potato flakes and milk. Mix until smooth; refrigerate, covered, until cool enough to handle.

2. Meanwhile, heat olive oil in large skillet over medium heat until hot. Add onion, pepper, chopped tomato, ham, coriander, garlic, pepper sauce and oregano; saute until vegetables are tender and liquid has evaporated, about 4 minutes.

3. Measure ¼ cup mashed potatoes; flatten into ¼-inch-thick circle on waxed paper. Place 1 heaping tablespoon of the vegetable-ham mixture in center; press potato around filling to form ball. Repeat until all potato is used.

4. Dip potato balls in beaten egg; roll in cornmeal to coat evenly.

5. Heat 2 inches of oil in large saucepan or deep-fat fryer to 375°F. Fry 3 or 4 balls at a time until golden on all sides; drain on paper toweling. Serve on platter lined with lettuce; garnish with tomato wedges.

Backyard Bean Tacos

Ham-Filled Tomatoes

JICAMA SALAD

Jicama (with the J pronounced like an H) is a crisp root vegetable popular in Mexico and the Southwest. Jicama is generally peeled and served raw in appetizers and salads.

Makes 6 servings

   1 jicama (1¼ to 1½ pounds)*
   1 small cucumber, cut in half, seeded, thinly
       sliced
   ½ cup very thinly slivered mild red onion
   2 tablespoons fresh lime juice
   ½ teaspoon grated lime rind
   1 clove garlic, minced
   ¼ teaspoon salt
   ⅛ teaspoon crushed red pepper
   3 tablespoons vegetable oil
     Leaf lettuce

1. Pare jicama; cut lengthwise into 8 wedges; cut wedges crosswise into ⅛-inch-thick slices.

2. Combine jicama, cucumber and onion in large bowl; toss to mix.

3. Mix lime juice, lime rind, garlic, salt and pepper in small bowl. Gradually whisk in oil until blended. Pour over jicama mixture; toss to coat. Refrigerate, covered, 1 to 2 hours.

4. To serve, spoon into salad bowl lined with lettuce leaves.

Note: *If unavailable, substitute Jerusalem artichokes. Cut pared artichokes lengthwise into halves; cut halves crosswise into thin slices.*

ESCALLOPED CARROTS

Makes 6 servings

   10 medium carrots, pared, sliced
    1 medium onion, minced
    2 tablespoons butter or margarine
    3 tablespoons all-purpose flour
    ½ teaspoon salt
    ¼ teaspoon dry mustard
    ⅛ teaspoon pepper
    ⅛ teaspoon celery salt
    1 cup milk
    6 ounces Cheddar cheese, sliced
    3 tablespoons breadcrumbs

1. Cook carrots in boiling water in large saucepan until crisp-tender, about 6 minutes; drain, reserving ¼ cup of the liquid.

2. Saute onion in butter in medium saucepan over medium heat, 3 minutes. Stir in flour, salt, mustard, pepper and celery salt until smooth; gradually whisk in milk. Cook and stir until sauce thickens and bubbles for 1 minute. If sauce is too thick, add reserved carrot liquid.

3. Arrange ½ of the carrots in 1-quart casserole; top with ½ of the cheese. Repeat layers once; pour sauce over all. Sprinkle with breadcrumbs. Bake in preheated 350°F oven 25 minutes.

HAM-FILLED TOMATOES

To peel or not to peel salad tomatoes, that is the question. If your answer is yes, either plunge them into boiling water for a few seconds to loosen the skin, or insert a fork at the stem end and rotate slowly over the flame of a gas range.

Makes 4 servings

  ½ cup finely chopped cooked ham
  ½ cup drained canned crushed pineapple
  ¼ cup plus 2 tablespoons mayonnaise
  ¼ cup plus 1½ teaspoons chopped pecans
  ¼ cup finely chopped celery
   4 medium tomatoes
     Leaf lettuce

1. Combine ham, pineapple, ¼ cup of the mayonnaise, ¼ cup of the pecans and the celery in medium bowl; mix well.

2. Cut each tomato lengthwise into 6 wedges, leaving them attached at base. Spread wedges apart slightly; place on salad plates lined with lettuce.

3. Spoon ham mixture into tomatoes. Top each with dollop of remaining 2 tablespoons mayonnaise; sprinkle with remaining 1½ teaspoons pecans.

Jicama Salad

Crab-Baked Broccoli

CRAB-BAKED BROCCOLI

Versatile, colorful broccoli co-stars with tender crab meat in a glamorous luncheon or supper main dish.

Makes 6 servings

2 packages (10 ounces each) frozen broccoli
   spears
⅓ cup chopped hazelnuts or almonds
¼ cup margarine or butter
3 tablespoons all-purpose flour
½ teaspoon salt
⅛ teaspoon pepper
1½ cups milk
1 chicken bouillon cube, crushed
2 packages (6 ounces each) frozen king crab meat,
   thawed, drained
1 tablespoon lemon juice
2 tablespoons grated Parmesan cheese

1. Cook broccoli according to package directions; drain well. Arrange in oven-proof platter or shallow 2-quart baking dish; keep warm.

2. Cook hazelnuts in margarine in medium saucepan over medium heat until golden, 3 to 4 minutes; remove hazelnuts with slotted spoon.

3. Add flour, salt and pepper to margarine in saucepan; mix well. Add milk and bouillon cube; cook and stir until sauce thickens and bubbles for 1 minute. Fold in crab meat and lemon juice.

4. Spoon sauce over broccoli; sprinkle with hazelnuts and cheese. Bake in preheated 400°F oven until hot throughout, about 15 minutes.

CHILES RELLENOS

Makes 8 servings

4 tomatoes, peeled, chopped
1 small onion, chopped
1 chicken bouillon cube
½ teaspoon dried oregano, crumbled
½ teaspoon salt
⅛ teaspoon ground black pepper
8 small green bell peppers or 16 sweet finger
   peppers
½ pound Monterey Jack cheese, cut into 3 × ½ × ½-
   inch strips
3 large eggs, separated
6 tablespoons all-purpose flour
   Vegetable oil for frying
½ cup shredded sharp Cheddar cheese

1. Combine tomatoes, onion, bouillon cube, oregano, salt and ground pepper in large saucepan; mix well. Heat to boiling; reduce heat. Simmer, covered, stirring occasionally, 8 minutes. Remove from heat; keep warm, covered.

2. Cut slit lengthwise in side of each bell pepper; carefully remove seeds. Stuff peppers with Monterey Jack cheese, dividing evenly.

3. Beat egg whites in large mixer bowl until soft peaks form. Whisk egg yolks in small bowl until blended; add to egg whites. Sprinkle 3 tablespoons of the flour over egg mixture; fold together.

4. Heat 1 inch oil in large heavy skillet to 375°F. Dust peppers with remaining 3 tablespoons flour; dip in egg batter to coat evenly. Fry, turning occasionally, until golden on all sides; 4 to 6 minutes; drain on paper toweling.

5. Place peppers in shallow baking dish; spoon tomato sauce over peppers. Sprinkle with Cheddar cheese. Bake in preheated 350°F oven until the cheese is melted, 15 to 20 minutes.

FRONTIER HAZELNUT-VEGETABLE PIE

Toasting develops the full flavor of hazelnuts. It is easy to do. Spread shelled nuts in a shallow pan and roast in a 275°F oven for 20 to 30 minutes, until skin cracks. While still warm, rub nuts between hands to remove the skins.

Makes 6 servings

1 cup chopped fresh broccoli
1 cup thinly sliced fresh cauliflower
2 cups chopped fresh spinach
1 cup shredded Cheddar cheese
1 small onion, diced
½ green bell pepper, diced
1 cup coarsely chopped toasted hazelnuts
1½ cups milk
1 cup biscuit mix
4 large eggs, beaten
1 teaspoon garlic salt
½ teaspoon ground pepper
   Tomato wedges and parsley sprig for garnish

1. Cook broccoli in small saucepan of boiling water until crisp-tender, about 3 minutes; drain well. Repeat with cauliflower.

2. Combine broccoli, cauliflower, spinach, cheese, onion and green pepper in medium bowl; toss to mix. Spread in well-greased deep 10-inch pie plate; sprinkle with nuts.

3. Combine milk, biscuit mix, eggs, garlic salt and ground pepper in medium bowl; whisk until smooth. Pour over vegetables.

4. Bake in preheated 400°F oven until center is set, 35 to 40 minutes; let stand 5 minutes before cutting. Garnish with tomatoes and parsley.

CREAMY FRUIT MOLD

Makes 6 to 8 servings

1 can (15 ounces) mandarin oranges
   Water
1 envelope unflavored gelatin
½ cup sugar
½ cup orange juice
¼ cup lemon juice
2 large eggs, beaten
1 cup sour cream
1 package (3 ounces) cream cheese, room
   temperature
2 bananas, sliced
½ cup chopped pecans

1. Drain oranges, reserving syrup. Add enough water to syrup to equal ¾ cup liquid. Sprinkle gelatin over liquid; let stand 1 minute to soften.

2. Combine gelatin mixture, sugar, orange juice and lemon juice in medium saucepan; cook and stir over medium heat until gelatin is dissolved. Remove from heat.

3. Gradually whisk ½ of the hot gelatin mixture into eggs in small bowl; gradually whisk egg mixture into remaining gelatin mixture in pan. Cook, stirring constantly, over low heat until thickened, about 2 minutes; do not boil. Remove from heat.

4. Add sour cream and cream cheese to pan; whisk or beat with electric mixer until smooth. Refrigerate, stirring occasionally, until thick enough to mound slightly when dropped from spoon.

5. Fold oranges, bananas and pecans into gelatin mixture; pour into 5½-cup ring mold. Refrigerate, covered, until completely set, several hours. Unmold just before serving.

Frontier Hazelnut-Vegetable Pie

Taco Topping (left); Stir-Fry Topping (center); Cheesy Topping (right)

1. Saute onion in butter in large saucepan over medium heat until soft, about 3 minutes. Add rice; stir to coat with butter. Stir in stock; heat to boiling.

2. Add remaining ingredients; mix well. Simmer, covered, over low heat until rice is tender and liquid is absorbed, about 45 minutes.

SPECTACULAR SPUDS

Idaho has moved its russet potato into a national spotlight. An excellent baker, this spud with a meaty texture stars as an entree when topped with saucy meat and cheese mixtures.

TACO TOPPING

    1 pound ground beef
    1 envelope beefy onion soup mix or onion-
      mushroom soup mix
    1 can (8 ounces) tomato sauce
    1 can (4 ounces) chopped green chilies
    ½ cup water
    ¾ cup shredded Cheddar cheese
    4 hot baked potatoes, split
      Taco chips, crumbled
      Chopped tomatoes
      Shredded lettuce

1. Cook and stir beef in skillet over medium heat until brown, about 10 minutes; drain off fat.

2. Stir in soup mix, tomato sauce, green chilies and water. Heat to boiling; reduce heat. Simmer, stirring occasionally, 10 minutes.

3. Remove from heat; stir in cheese until melted. Spoon over potatoes; sprinkle with chips, tomatoes and lettuce.

Makes 4 servings

STIR-FRY TOPPING

    1 tablespoon vegetable oil
    1 pound boneless pork or chicken, cut into thin
      strips
    ½ pound broccoli, cut into ½-inch pieces
    1 can (8 ounces) water chestnuts, drained, sliced
    1 envelope golden onion soup mix
    1 cup water
    2 tablespoons soy sauce
    ½ teaspoon ground ginger
    4 hot baked potatoes, split

1. Heat oil in wok or large skillet over medium-high heat until hot. Add pork or chicken; stir-fry until light brown, about 3 minutes. Add broccoli and water chestnuts; stir-fry 2 minutes.

2. Mix soup mix, water, soy sauce and ginger in small bowl; stir into wok. Heat to boiling; continue cooking, stirring occasionally, until sauce is thickened, about 5 minutes. Spoon over potatoes.

Makes 4 servings

CHEESY TOPPING

    1 envelope golden mushroom soup mix
    1 cup milk
    ½ cup beer
    ¾ cup shredded Swiss cheese
    ¾ pound cooked ham, diced
    4 hot baked potatoes, split

1. Mix soup mix, milk and beer in medium saucepan. Heat to boiling; reduce heat. Simmer, stirring occasionally, 5 minutes.

2. Stir in cheese until melted. Stir in ham; cook until hot. Spoon over potatoes.

Makes 4 servings

CRUSTY MEXICAN ROLLS

Makes 10 rolls

  1 package (¼ ounce) active dry yeast
1⅓ cups warm water (105 to 115°F)
  1 tablespoon honey
  1 tablespoon lard or vegetable shortening,
     melted, cooled
1½ teaspoons salt
3¼ to 4 cups bread flour
  ¼ cup cold water
  1 teaspoon cornstarch

1. Mix yeast and warm water in large mixer bowl; let stand 5 minutes.

2. Stir honey, lard and salt into yeast mixture; add 2½ cups of the flour. Mix at low speed; then beat at medium speed until very elastic, about 5 minutes. Gradually stir in as much of the remaining flour as needed to make soft dough, ½ to 1 cup.

3. Knead dough on floured surface, adding as much remaining flour as needed to prevent sticking, until dough is smooth and elastic, 15 to 20 minutes. Place in greased bowl; turn dough over. Let rise, covered, in warm place until doubled, about 1 hour.

4. Punch down dough; knead briefly. Let rest 10 minutes. Divide dough into 10 equal pieces; roll each piece into ball.

5. Starting at center and working toward opposite ends, roll each ball on floured surface with palms of hands into oval tapered at both ends. Each piece should be about 5½ inches long and 2 inches wide at center. Place, evenly spaced, on 2 greased baking sheets; let rise, loosely covered, until almost doubled, about 25 minutes.

6. Mix cold water and cornstarch in small saucepan. Cook over high heat, stirring constantly, until mixture thickens and boils for 2 minutes. *(Continued)*

7. Brush risen rolls with warm cornstarch mixture. Slash each roll lengthwise with razor blade to ½ inch from each end, cutting about ½ inch deep.

8. Bake in preheated 375°F oven until rolls are golden brown and sound hollow when tapped, 30 to 35 minutes. Remove from baking sheets; cool on wire racks.

CHERRY-UP BISCUITS

Turn these easy-to-bake biscuits cherry side up the moment you take them out of the oven, and serve them piping hot.
Makes 12

1½ cups all-purpose flour
  1 tablespoon baking powder
1½ teaspoons granulated sugar
  ½ teaspoon salt
  ½ teaspoon cream of tartar
  ¼ cup solid vegetable shortening
  ½ cup milk
  ½ cup margarine, melted
  ⅓ cup packed brown sugar
  1 can (21 ounces) tart cherry pie filling

1. Sift flour, baking powder, granulated sugar, salt and cream of tartar into medium bowl; cut in shortening until mixture resembles coarse crumbs. Add milk all at once; stir until dough forms ball.

2. Knead dough a few times on lightly floured surface; roll out ½ inch thick. Cut out with 2½-inch biscuit cutter.

3. Put 1 teaspoon margarine, 1 teaspoon brown sugar and 1 heaping tablespoon pie filling in bottoms of 12 muffin tin cups. Place 1 biscuit in each cup; brush with margarine.

4. Bake in preheated 425°F oven until biscuits are golden brown, 12 to 15 minutes. Invert and unmold biscuits; serve warm.

Crusty Mexican Rolls

Cherry Buns (top and bottom); Cherry-Up Biscuits (left and right)

WALNUT SOUR CREAM COFFEE CAKE

Makes 12 servings

  1 cup sugar
½ cup butter or margarine
  1 teaspoon vanilla
  2 large eggs
  1 cup sour cream
1½ cups all-purpose flour
1½ teaspoons baking powder
  1 teaspoon baking soda
⅛ teaspoon salt
½ cup chopped walnuts

Topping
¾ cup walnut pieces
½ cup sugar
1½ teaspoons ground cinnamon

1. Combine sugar, butter and vanilla in large mixer bowl; beat until light and fluffy. Beat in eggs and sour cream until blended.

2. Mix flour, baking powder, baking soda and salt in medium bowl; gradually add to batter, mixing until smooth. Stir in nuts.

3. Mix topping ingredients in small bowl. Pour ½ of the batter into greased 10-inch tube pan; sprinkle with ½ of the topping. Repeat layers once.

4. Bake in preheated 350°F oven until wooden pick inserted into center is withdrawn clean, 45 to 50 minutes. Cool in pan on wire rack 15 minutes. Remove from pan; cool completely.

CHERRY BUNS

Makes 3 dozen

  2 cups milk, scalded
  1 cup solid vegetable shortening
⅔ cup sugar
  2 teaspoons salt
  2 packages (¼ ounce each) active dry yeast
½ cup warm water (105 to 115°F)
  2 large eggs
  8 to 9 cups all-purpose flour
  1 can (31 ounces) cherry pie filling
¼ cup butter or margarine, melted

1. Combine milk, shortening, sugar and salt in large bowl; stir until shortening is melted. Cool to lukewarm.

2. Sprinkle yeast over water in small bowl; stir to dissolve yeast. Let stand 5 minutes.

3. Stir yeast mixture into milk mixture; whisk in eggs. Gradually whisk in 3 cups of the flour; beat until smooth and elastic, about 5 minutes. Gradually stir in as much of the remaining flour as needed to make soft dough.

4. Knead on floured surface until smooth and elastic, 5 to 10 minutes. Place in greased bowl; turn dough over. Let rise, covered, until doubled, about 1½ hours.

5. Punch down dough; let stand, covered, 10 minutes. Roll out dough on floured surface to less than ½-inch thickness. Cut out dough with 2½-inch round cutter; place rounds 2 inches apart on greased baking sheets. Let rise, covered, until almost doubled, about 45 minutes.

6. Press deep depression in center of each bun; fill with pie filling. Bake in preheated 375°F oven 15 minutes. Brush buns with butter.

Sausage Oatmeal Bread

SAUSAGE OATMEAL BREAD

This hearty bread ring has sausage or bologna baked right in the middle. Store in the refrigerator any part of the ring not eaten fresh from the oven.

Makes 2 loaves

5½ cups all-purpose flour
1 cup plus 3 tablespoons quick-cooking oats
1 package (¼ ounce) quick-rising dry yeast
1 teaspoon salt
1 teaspoon seasoned salt
¼ teaspoon ground pepper
1¾ cups hot water (125°F)
3 tablespoons vegetable oil
2 large eggs
2½ pounds kielbasa, smoked sausage or ring bologna
¾ cup chopped onion
¾ cup chopped red and green bell pepper
½ teaspoon dry mustard
¼ teaspoon ground ginger
Prepared mustard

1. Combine 4½ cups of the flour, 1 cup of the oats, the yeast, salt, seasoned salt and ground pepper in large bowl; mix well. Add water, oil and 1 egg; mix well. Knead dough on floured surface, adding as much remaining flour as needed to prevent sticking, until smooth and elastic, 6 to 8 minutes.

2. Place dough in greased bowl; turn dough over. Let rise, covered, until doubled, about 30 minutes.

3. Meanwhile, pierce sausages at 1-inch intervals; score on 2 opposite sides, about ¾ inch apart and ⅜ inch deep. Roast sausage in pan in preheated 450°F oven 15 minutes; drain on paper toweling.

4. Blanch onion and bell pepper in saucepan of boiling water 30 seconds; drain well. Drain on paper toweling; mix with dry mustard and ginger in small bowl.

5. Punch down dough; divide into 4 equal pieces. Roll out each piece on floured surface into 18 × 5-inch strip; brush

(Continued)

each strip with some of the remaining egg, beaten. Press ¼ of the onion mixture down center of each strip.

6. Dust sausage with flour. Cover 1¼ pounds sausage by winding 2 strips of dough around it, as you would wind a bandage around a finger. Place in well-greased 6½-cup ring mold. Repeat with remaining 1¼ pounds sausage and 2 strips of dough.

7. Brush tops with beaten egg; sprinkle each with 1½ tablespoons of the remaining oats. Let rise 10 minutes. Bake in preheated 375°F oven until golden, about 40 minutes. Cool in pans on wire racks 10 minutes; remove from pans. Serve warm with prepared mustard.

HONEY-NUT WHEAT BREAD

Makes 2 loaves

1 cup milk
1 cup water
½ cup honey
¼ cup butter or margarine
3 cups whole wheat flour
3 to 4 cups all-purpose flour
2 packages (¼ ounce each) active dry yeast
1 tablespoon salt
2 teaspoons ground cinnamon
1 large egg
1 cup raisins
1 cup chopped walnuts

1. Combine milk, water, honey and butter in medium saucepan; heat to 110°F.

2. Mix 2 cups of the whole wheat flour, 1 cup of the all-purpose flour, the yeast, salt and cinnamon in large mixer bowl. Add warmed milk mixture; beat until thoroughly blended. Beat in egg.

3. Stir in raisins and nuts by hand. Gradually stir in remaining 1 cup whole wheat flour and enough of the all-purpose flour to form stiff dough.

4. Knead on floured surface until smooth and elastic, 8 to 10 minutes. Place in greased bowl; turn dough over. Let rise, covered, in warm place until doubled, about 1½ hours.

5. Punch down dough; divide in half. Shape into loaves; place in 2 greased 9 × 5-inch loaf pans. Let rise, covered, in warm place until doubled, 40 to 60 minutes.

6. Bake in preheated 350°F oven until tops are golden and bottoms sound hollow when tapped, 40 to 45 minutes. Remove from pans; cool on wire rack.

CRUMBLE-TOP ORANGE ROLLS

Makes 12 rolls

⅓ cup sugar
¼ cup lard or vegetable shortening
2 teaspoons grated orange rind
¾ teaspoon salt
1 cup milk, scalded
2 packages (¼ ounce each) active dry yeast
¼ cup warm water (105 to 115°F)
3 large eggs
5 to 5½ cups all-purpose flour
Orange Crumble Topping (recipe follows)

(Continued)

1. Add sugar, lard, orange rind and salt to hot milk; stir until lard is melted. Let cool to lukewarm, about 10 minutes.

2. Mix yeast and warm water in large mixer bowl; let stand 5 minutes.

3. Mix milk mixture and eggs into yeast mixture; add 3 cups of the flour. Mix at low speed; then beat at medium speed until smooth and elastic, about 5 minutes. Gradually stir in as much of the remaining flour as needed to make soft dough, about 1¾ cups.

4. Knead dough on floured surface, adding as much remaining flour as needed to prevent sticking, until dough is smooth and elastic, 10 to 15 minutes. Place in greased bowl; turn dough over. Let rise, covered, in warm place until doubled, 45 to 60 minutes.

5. Punch down dough; knead briefly. Divide into 12 equal pieces; roll each piece into ball. Place evenly spaced on 2 greased baking sheets.

6. For each roll, press about 1 tablespoon Orange Crumble Topping between hands into 3-inch circle and place on top of dough ball. Cut spiral or cross-hatch design in topping with tip of sharp knife.

7. Let rolls rise, loosely covered, in warm place until almost doubled, about 30 minutes.

8. Bake in preheated 375°F oven until rolls are light brown and sound hollow when tapped, 20 to 25 minutes. Remove from baking sheets; cool on wire racks.

ORANGE CRUMBLE TOPPING

¾ **cup all-purpose flour**
½ **cup sugar**
¾ **teaspoon ground cinnamon**
½ **teaspoon grated orange rind**
¼ **cup butter or margarine, cold**
1 **large egg yolk**
1 **teaspoon orange juice**

1. Mix flour, sugar, cinnamon and orange rind in medium bowl. Cut in butter until mixture resembles coarse crumbs.

2. Beat egg yolk and orange juice in small bowl; add to flour mixture, stirring with fork until blended.

PEPPERONI-STUFFED PIZZA BREAD

A springform pan has the same advantage for this hearty bread as for cheesecake or fancy desserts. After baking, it's easy to remove the side piece by unlatching and lifting it off the bottom.

Makes 4 to 6 servings

3 **cups all-purpose flour**
1 **package (¼ ounce) quick-rising dry yeast**
1 **teaspoon salt**
1 **cup hot water (125°F)**
2 **tablespoons vegetable oil**
6 **ounces thinly sliced pepperoni**
2½ **cups shredded mozzarella cheese**
2½ **cups prepared spaghetti sauce**
⅓ **cup chopped red and green bell pepper, if desired**
Red and green bell pepper rings for garnish

1. Mix flour, yeast and salt in large bowl; stir in water and oil until smooth. Knead on floured surface 1 minute; let dough rest 5 minutes.

2. Divide dough into 2 pieces, 1 slightly larger than the other. Place larger piece in well-greased 10-inch springform pan; pat out to cover bottom and at least 1½ inches up sides of pan.

3. Reserve ¼ of the pepperoni for topping. Arrange ½ of the remaining pepperoni, overlapping, to cover bottom of dough in pan. Sprinkle evenly with 2 cups of the cheese. Arrange remaining ½ of the pepperoni, overlapping, to cover cheese.

4. Pat out remaining piece of dough into 10-inch circle; place on top of pizza. Brush top and bottom edges of dough lightly with water; pinch to seal and make ½-inch-high rim around pizza. Cut 3 or 4 steam vents in top crust.

5. Bake in preheated 400°F oven until dough is golden and sounds hollow when tapped, about 40 minutes. Cool on wire rack 10 minutes; remove sides of pan.

6. Place pizza on baking sheet; top with spaghetti sauce, chopped bell pepper, the reserved pepperoni and remaining ½ cup cheese. Bake at 400°F until sauce is bubbly, about 8 minutes. Garnish with pepper rings.

Pepperoni-Stuffed Pizza Bread

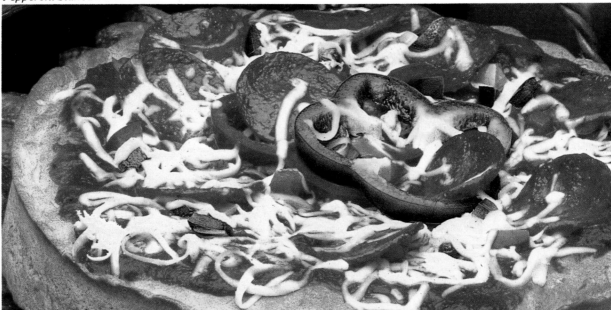

DATE-NUT MUFFINS

What a way to start off the day! Moist muffins chock full of dates and nuts. Quick and easy, too!

Makes 12 muffins

1 package (8 ounces) pitted dates, coarsely
   chopped
¾ cup boiling water
¼ cup corn oil
½ teaspoon vanilla
1 cup all-purpose flour
½ cup whole wheat flour
½ cup sugar
⅓ cup coarsely chopped walnuts
½ teaspoon baking soda

1. Combine dates, water, oil and vanilla in large bowl; stir to mix.

2. Mix flours, sugar, walnuts and baking soda in medium bowl. Add to date mixture; stir just until moistened. Spoon into 12 greased muffin tin cups.

3. Bake in preheated 375°F oven until tops are golden brown and firm to the touch, about 25 minutes. Immediately remove from pan; serve warm, or cool on wire rack.

Date-Nut Muffins

CORNMEAL BREAD

Two of the most important staples of the territory, cornmeal and wheat flour, come together in a round, yeast-bread loaf with a light corn flavor.

Makes 1 loaf

¼ cup yellow cornmeal
½ cup boiling water
⅓ cup warm water (105 to 115°F)
3 tablespoons packed brown sugar
1 package (¼ ounce) active dry yeast
⅓ cup instant nonfat dry milk solids
1 tablespoon butter or margarine, melted
1 teaspoon salt
2 to 2½ cups all-purpose flour
   Vegetable oil

1. Gradually stir cornmeal into boiling water in small bowl until smooth; let cool to 105 to 115°F.

2. Combine warm water, 1 tablespoon of the sugar and the yeast in large bowl; stir to dissolve yeast. Let stand until bubbly, about 5 minutes.

3. Add cornmeal mixture, remaining 2 tablespoons sugar, the milk solids, butter and salt to yeast mixture; beat well. Add 1 cup of the flour; beat well. Gradually stir in as much of the remaining flour as needed to make smooth soft dough.

4. Knead dough on floured surface until smooth and elastic, about 8 minutes; shape into ball. Place on greased baking sheet; flatten into 6-inch circle.

5. Brush dough with oil; let rise, covered, in warm place until doubled, about 1 hour.

6. Bake in preheated 375°F oven until top is golden and bottom sounds hollow when tapped, 25 to 30 minutes. Remove from baking sheet; cool on wire rack.

PEAR CHEESE MUFFINS

Makes 14 to 16 muffins

2 cups all-purpose flour
⅓ cup sugar
1 tablespoon baking powder
½ teaspoon salt
¼ teaspoon pumpkin pie spice
1 cup shredded Colby cheese
2 medium pears, pared, cored, cut into large
   pieces
1 cup milk
2 large eggs
¼ cup butter, melted

1. Mix flour, sugar, baking powder, salt and pumpkin pie spice in large bowl; stir in cheese.

2. Combine pears, milk, eggs and butter in blender container; process until pears are finely chopped.

3. Add pear mixture to flour mixture; stir just until moistened. Spoon into paper-lined muffin tin cups, filling ⅔ full.

4. Bake in preheated 425°F oven until wooden pick inserted into center is withdrawn clean, 20 to 25 minutes. Serve warm.

Cream Cheese Coffee Cake

CREAM CHEESE COFFEE CAKE

This scrumptious coffee cake owes its flaky texture to the Danish-pastry technique used in rolling and folding the butter into the dough.

Makes 2 coffee cakes

1½ cups butter, room temperature
4½ cups all-purpose flour
  2 packages (¼ ounce each) active dry yeast
  ¼ cup warm water (105 to 115°F)
  1 cup warm milk (105 to 115°F)
  1 large egg, lightly beaten
  3 tablespoons sugar
  ½ teaspoon salt
    Cream Cheese Filling (recipe follows)
    Powdered Sugar Glaze (recipe follows)
  ⅓ cup chopped pecans

1. Beat butter and ½ cup of the flour in small mixer bowl until smooth; refrigerate, covered, 45 minutes.

2. Sprinkle yeast over water in large bowl; stir to dissolve. Let stand 5 minutes.

3. Whisk milk, egg, sugar and salt into yeast mixture. Gradually whisk in 2 cups of the flour; beat until smooth and elastic, about 5 minutes. Gradually mix in remaining 2 cups flour.

4. Roll out dough on lightly floured board into 16-inch square.

5. Place cold butter-flour mixture on floured board; press into 16×8-inch rectangle. Place rectangle on ½ of dough; fold other ½ of dough over butter mixture to enclose. Pinch edges to seal.

6. Pound dough lightly with rolling pin into 16×12-inch rectangle; fold dough in thirds like a business letter. Refrigerate, covered, 30 minutes, or place in freezer 10 minutes.

7. Roll out dough into 16-inch square; fold in thirds. Roll out into 16-inch square. *(Continued)*

8. Spread Cream Cheese Filling evenly on ½ of dough, leaving ½ inch of edges uncovered. Fold other ½ of dough over filling to enclose; pinch edges to seal. Cut crosswise in half; pinch cut edges to seal.

9. Place each half in greased 9-inch round baking pan. Slash tops at ¾-inch intervals to allow filling to bubble out during baking. Let rise, covered, in warm place until almost doubled, 45 to 60 minutes.

10. Bake in preheated 375°F oven until dough is golden and sounds hollow when tapped, about 25 minutes. Cool slightly, then carefully remove from pans; cool on wire racks. Drizzle with Powdered Sugar Glaze; sprinkle with pecans.

CREAM CHEESE FILLING

  1 package (8 ounces) cream cheese, room temperature
2½ cups sifted powdered sugar
  ¼ cup sour cream
  1 large egg
  1 tablespoon lemon juice
  1 teaspoon grated lemon rind
  ¾ cup all-purpose flour
  ½ cup chopped pecans

1. Beat cream cheese and sugar in large mixer bowl until smooth. Add sour cream, egg, lemon juice and lemon rind; beat until smooth.

2. Add flour; mix well. Stir in pecans.

POWDERED SUGAR GLAZE

  2 cups sifted powdered sugar
  3 tablespoons milk
  ½ teaspoon vanilla

Mix all ingredients in small bowl until smooth.

Banana Loaf Cake

BANANA LOAF CAKE

Makes 1 loaf; 12 to 16 servings

1¾ cups all-purpose flour
2¼ teaspoons baking powder
¼ teaspoon salt
⅓ cup butter or margarine, room temperature
⅔ cup sugar
1½ teaspoons apple pie spice
2 large eggs
1 teaspoon vanilla
1 cup mashed ripe bananas

1. Mix flour, baking powder and salt in medium bowl.

2. Beat butter, sugar and apple pie spice in large mixer bowl until light and fluffy. Beat in eggs, 1 at a time; beat in vanilla.

3. Add flour mixture, ⅓ at a time, alternating with banana, mixing well after each addition. Pour into greased and floured 9×5×3-inch loaf pan.

4. Bake in preheated 350°F oven until wooden pick inserted into center is withdrawn clean, about 55 minutes. Cool in pan on wire rack 5 minutes. Remove from pan; cool completely on rack.

CHOCOLATE PEANUT BUTTER ICE CREAM

Whether you turn the crank on the freezer by hand or by electricity, homemade ice cream is irresistable.

Makes 2 quarts

6 squares (1 ounce each) semisweet chocolate
2 cups milk
1 cup sugar
½ cup smooth peanut butter
2 cups whipping cream
2 teaspoons vanilla
⅔ cup chopped peanut butter cups

1. Combine chocolate, milk and sugar in heavy 2-quart saucepan; cook, stirring frequently, over medium heat, until chocolate melts. Stir in peanut butter until smooth; let cool to lukewarm.

2. Stir in cream and vanilla; refrigerate until cold, about 1 hour.

3. Freeze in ice cream maker according to manufacturer's directions. Transfer ice cream to plastic freezer container; stir in peanut butter cups. Let ripen in freezer, covered, at least 3 hours before serving.

MARASCHINO CHERRY SPICE CAKE

Bright red maraschino cherries are more than just a pretty decoration. Cherries are also baked in the batter of a rich and handsome tube cake.

Makes 12 servings

1½ cups whole maraschino cherries, drained
  2 cups all-purpose flour
  2 teaspoons baking powder
  2 teaspoons ground cinnamon
  1 teaspoon baking soda
  ½ teaspoon salt
  ½ teaspoon ground allspice
  ½ teaspoon ground nutmeg
  ¼ teaspoon ground ginger
  1 cup solid-pack canned pumpkin
  ⅔ cup soured milk*
  1 cup granulated sugar
  ½ cup butter or margarine
  2 large eggs
    Powdered sugar

(Continued)

1. Pat cherries dry with paper toweling. Sift flour, baking powder, cinnamon, baking soda, salt, allspice, nutmeg and ginger together into medium bowl. Mix pumpkin and milk in small bowl.

2. Beat granulated sugar and butter in large mixer bowl until light and fluffy. Add eggs, one at a time, beating well after each addition. Add ⅓ of the flour mixture at a time, alternating with pumpkin mixture, beating well after each addition.

3. Pour ½ of the batter into greased 10-inch tube pan. Sprinkle evenly with 1 cup of the cherries; top with remaining batter.

4. Bake in preheated 350°F oven until wooden pick inserted in center is withdrawn clean, about 1 hour. Cool cake in pan on wire rack 10 minutes. Remove from pan; cool completely on rack.

5. Before serving, sprinkle cake with powdered sugar; decorate top with remaining ½ cup cherries.

Note: *To sour milk, place 2 teaspoons vinegar in measuring cup; add enough milk to measure ⅔ cup. Mix well; let stand 30 minutes.*

Maraschino Cherry Spice Cake

ORANGE COCONUT FLAN

Makes 8 servings

1 cup sweet orange marmalade
8 large eggs
2 cans (13 ounces each) evaporated milk
1 cup flaked or shredded coconut
2 teaspoons vanilla
⅛ teaspoon salt
2 medium oranges for garnish

1. Lightly oil sides of 1½-quart metal mold. Spread ½ cup of the marmalade in bottom of mold; place mold in larger baking pan

2. Combine remaining ½ cup marmalade and eggs in large bowl; whisk until blended. Stir in milk, coconut, vanilla and salt. Carefully ladle milk mixture into the mold, being careful not to disturb marmalade layer.

3. Pour hot water into baking pan to come halfway up sides of mold. Bake in preheated 325°F oven until knife inserted into custard 1 inch from edge is withdrawn clean, about 1 hour; center will still be slightly soft.

4. Remove mold from water bath; cool completely on wire rack. Refrigerate until cold.

5. Just before serving, peel and slice oranges; cut slices into halves. Unmold flan onto serving dish, letting syrup run down sides. Garnish with orange slices.

Note: Flan can be baked in 8 individual 6-ounce custard cups. Lightly oil each custard cup; spread 1 tablespoon marmalade in bottom of each cup. Prepare custard as in recipe. Reduce baking time to about 45 minutes.

CARAMEL ALMOND CAKE

Makes 9 servings

¾ cup sugar
2 large eggs
1¼ cups all-purpose flour
1¼ teaspoons baking powder
½ cup butter or margarine, melted
2 tablespoons milk
Caramel Almond Topping (recipe follows)

1. Beat sugar and eggs in large mixer bowl until thick and lemon-colored, about 5 minutes. Add flour and baking powder; beat until smooth. Add butter and milk; beat until blended. Pour into greased 9-inch square baking pan.

2. Bake in preheated 350°F oven until wooden pick inserted into center is withdrawn clean, about 35 minutes.

3. Remove cake from oven; spread top evenly with Caramel Almond Topping. Broil 6 inches from heat source until topping bubbles and begins to caramelize, 5 to 10 minutes. Cool on wire rack; serve warm or cool.

CARAMEL ALMOND TOPPING

1 cup packed brown sugar
½ cup sliced almonds
¼ cup butter or margarine
2 tablespoons all-purpose flour
2 tablespoons cream or milk

Combine all ingredients in medium saucepan. Cook over medium heat, stirring constantly, until butter melts and mixture boils.

Orange Coconut Flan

APPLE CRESCENTS

Makes 12 turnovers

1 tablespoon lemon juice
2 pounds apples, pared, cored, sliced
¾ cup sugar
1 tablespoon cornstarch
1 teaspoon ground cinnamon
Pastry dough for 2 double-crust 9-inch pies

1. Sprinkle lemon juice over apples in large bowl; toss to coat. Mix sugar, cornstarch and cinnamon in small bowl; sprinkle over apples and toss to coat evenly.

2. Roll out ¼ of the dough at a time on lightly floured surface; cut out three 7-inch circles from each ¼. Place ½ cup apple filling on bottom ½ of each circle; fold top ½ of circle over filling. Pinch edges to seal; crimp with fork.

3. Place crescents on lightly greased baking sheets; cut small steam vents in top of each. Bake in preheated 425°F oven until pastry is light brown, about 15 minutes. Serve warm, or cool on wire racks.

NUTTY RAISIN PIE

Aromatic spices and raisins join crunchy pecans in a luscious pie for special occasions.

Makes 8 servings

1 cup sugar
3 large eggs
1 cup coarsely chopped raisins
1 cup coarsely chopped pecans
1½ teaspoons cider vinegar
1 teaspoon vanilla
1 teaspoon ground cinnamon
½ teaspoon ground cloves
¼ teaspoon ground nutmeg
1 unbaked 9-inch pie shell
Whipped cream, if desired

1. Combine sugar and eggs in medium bowl; beat until blended. Stir in remaining ingredients except pie shell and whipped cream, mixing well. Pour into pie shell.

2. Bake in preheated 350°F oven until knife inserted 3 inches in from edges is withdrawn clean, about 45 minutes. Cool completely on wire rack; serve with whipped cream.

MEXICAN CHOCOLATE MOUSSE

Makes 4 servings

6 to 6½ ounces Mexican chocolate, coarsely chopped
1½ cups whipping cream
3 tablespoons golden rum, if desired
¾ teaspoon vanilla
Sliced almonds for garnish

1. Combine chocolate and 3 tablespoons of the cream in top of double boiler; heat over simmering water, stirring occasionally, until smooth. Gradually stir in rum; remove from water. Let cool at room temperature 15 minutes.

2. Combine remaining cream and the vanilla in small mixer bowl; beat until stiff. Fold into chocolate mixture until uniform in color.

3. Spoon mousse into 4 individual dessert dishes; refrigerate until firm, 2 to 3 hours. Garnish with almonds.

Fried Biscuit Puffs

FRIED BISCUIT PUFFS

Yeast-raised biscuit squares which puff up like pillows when deep-fried to a golden brown are among the Southwest's most popular desserts.

Makes 24 fritters; 8 servings

1 package (¼ ounce) active dry yeast
⅓ cup warm water (105 to 115°F)
¾ cup warm milk (105 to 115°F)
3 tablespoons solid vegetable shortening
3 cups all-purpose flour
½ teaspoon baking powder
½ teaspoon salt
1 cup apple jelly
3 tablespoons water
½ teaspoon ground cinnamon
Vegetable oil for frying

1. Sprinkle yeast over ⅓ cup warm water in large bowl; stir to dissolve yeast. Let stand 5 minutes.

2. Add milk and shortening to yeast; stir until shortening melts. Add 2½ cups of the flour, the baking powder and salt; mix well. Stir in as much of the remaining flour as needed to form stiff dough.

3. Knead dough on floured surface until smooth and elastic, 5 to 10 minutes. Cover dough with inverted bowl; let stand 10 minutes.

4. Meanwhile, combine jelly, 3 tablespoons water and cinnamon in small saucepan. Heat to boiling, stirring until smooth; keep warm over low heat.

5. Heat 2 inches of oil in large deep saucepan to 425°F.

6. Roll out dough on floured surface to 12 × 10-inch rectangle. Cut lengthwise into four 2½-inch-wide strips; cut strips crosswise at 2-inch intervals.

7. Slip 5 pieces, top side down, into oil. Fry, turning frequently, until golden, about 3 minutes. Drain on paper toweling. Repeat until all pieces have been fried. Drizzle with jelly mixture; serve warm.

Golden Apple-Mincemeat Cake

GOLDEN APPLE-MINCEMEAT CAKE

Makes 12 to 16 servings

   3 cups all-purpose flour
   4 teaspoons baking powder
   1 teaspoon ground allspice
   1 teaspoon ground cinnamon
   ½ teaspoon salt
   1½ cups vegetable oil
   1½ cups packed brown sugar
   2 cups grated pared Golden Delicious apples
   1 cup prepared mincemeat
   ½ cup chopped pecans
   1½ teaspoons vanilla
   3 large eggs
      Hard Sauce (recipe follows) or 1 to 2
         tablespoons powdered sugar

1. Mix flour, baking powder, allspice, cinnamon and salt in medium bowl.

2. Combine oil and brown sugar in large mixer bowl; beat
(Continued)

well. Add ½ the flour mixture; mix well. Stir in grated apple, mincemeat, pecans, and vanilla. Add remaining flour mixture; mix well.

3. Add eggs, one at a time, beating well after each addition. Transfer batter to greased 10-inch fluted tube pan.

4. Bake in preheated 350°F oven until wooden pick inserted in center is withdrawn clean, about 1 hour.

5. Cool cake in pan on wire rack 15 minutes; unmold cake. Serve slightly warm with Hard Sauce or cool completely on rack and sprinkle with powdered sugar.

HARD SAUCE

   ½ cup butter, softened
   1 cup powdered sugar
   1 tablespoon brandy

Beat butter in small mixer bowl until light and fluffy. Gradually beat in powdered sugar. Stir in brandy. Refrigerate, covered, 1 hour.

CHOCOLATE TORTILLA STACK

Flour tortillas are versatile enough to use in desserts. Here, they're spread with chocolate and covered with sour cream to make a handsome dessert.

Makes 8 to 10 servings

- **2 cups semisweet chocolate morsels (12 ounces)**
- **2 cups sour cream**
- **3 tablespoons powdered sugar**
- **1 teaspoon ground cinnamon**
- **½ teaspoon vanilla**
- **4 large flour tortillas**

1. Combine 1 cup of the chocolate morsels, 1 cup of the sour cream, 1 tablespoon of the powdered sugar and the cinnamon in top of double boiler. Heat and stir over simmering water until chocolate melts and mixture is smooth and thick, about 5 minutes. Remove from water; stir in vanilla. Let stand 5 minutes.

2. Place one tortilla on serving plate; spread evenly with ⅓ of the chocolate mixture. Repeat tortilla and chocolate layers 2 more times. Cover with inverted bowl; refrigerate until chocolate sets.

3. Top torte with fourth tortilla. Mix remaining 1 cup sour cream with remaining 2 tablespoons powdered sugar in small bowl; spread evenly on top and sides of torte. Refrigerate until sour cream sets, at least 2 hours.

4. Melt the remaining 1 cup chocolate morsels in top of double boiler over simmering water. Spread chocolate evenly on baking sheet lined with waxed paper to make circle ¼- to ⅛-inch thick. Refrigerate until slightly hardened, about 10 minutes.

5. Cut chocolate circle into 6 wedges. Slide spatula under each wedge to remove; arrange wedges on top of torte, spoke-fashion. Refrigerate until serving time.

HEAVENLY CHOCOLATE CHIFFON PIE

Unflavored gelatin is the unseen, untasted and unsung hero of chiffon pies. Unassisted it captures the air bubbles in the whipped egg whites and keeps them in suspension.

Makes 8 servings

- **1 envelope unflavored gelatin**
- **1 cup sugar**
- **½ cup unsweetened cocoa powder**
- **¼ teaspoon salt**
- **6 large eggs, separated**
- **1 cup milk**
- **1 teaspoon vanilla**
- **½ teaspoon cream of tartar**
- **1 baked 9-inch pie shell**
- **Whipped cream and chocolate curls for garnish**

1. Mix gelatin, ¼ cup of the sugar, the cocoa powder and salt in medium saucepan. Beat egg yolks and milk in medium bowl; stir into gelatin mixture. Cook over low heat, stirring constantly, until gelatin dissolves and mixture thickens slightly, about 5 minutes.

2. Remove pan from heat; stir in vanilla. Refrigerate, stirring occasionally, until mixture mounds slightly when dropped from spoon. Remove from refrigerator.

3. Beat egg whites and cream of tartar in large mixer bowl until soft peaks form; gradually beat in the remaining ¾ cup sugar. Beat until stiff peaks form.

4. Pour gelatin mixture over egg whites; fold in. Refrigerate, stirring occasionally, until mixture forms high mounds which do not flatten out when dropped from spoon.

5. Spoon gelatin mixture into pie shell. Refrigerate until filling is set, several hours or overnight. Garnish with whipped cream and chocolate curls.

Chocolate Tortilla Stack

BRANDY-SPIKED ICE CREAM

A sophisticated frozen dessert to spoon into footed sherbets or parfait glasses. It's delicious by itself, but outstanding when layered with either chocolate or coffee ice cream.

Makes 8 servings

¾ cup chopped pitted prunes (about ¼ pound)
3 tablespoons brandy
4 large egg yolks
1½ cups sugar
2 cups milk, scalded
1 pint coffee ice cream, if desired
1 pint chocolate ice cream, if desired
  Chocolate curls for garnish
8 whole pitted prunes for garnish

1. Combine chopped prunes and brandy in small bowl; let soak several hours or overnight.

2. Beat egg yolks in large mixer bowl until pale, 1 to 2 minutes; gradually beat in sugar. On medium speed, gradually beat in milk until blended; refrigerate until cold.

3. Stir prune mixture into milk mixture; transfer to metal pan or metal bowl. Freeze until slushy, 2 to 3 hours.

4. Beat with electric mixer until smooth; return to metal pan. Freeze until firm, 2 to 3 hours (ice cream will not harden completely). Serve with additional scoops of coffee and chocolate ice creams; garnish with chocolate curls and whole prunes.

FRESH RASPBERRY PIE

To prevent the edges of the pie from getting too brown, protect them with long narrow strips of aluminum foil before the fruit pie goes into the oven. Remove foil halfway through baking time.

Makes 8 servings

1 cup sugar
3 tablespoons cornstarch
4 cups fresh raspberries
  Pastry dough for 1 double-crust 9-inch pie
1 tablespoon corn oil margarine

1. Mix sugar and cornstarch in large bowl. Add raspberries; toss to coat well.

2. Roll out ½ of the pastry dough on lightly floured surface into 12-inch circle; ease into 9-inch pie plate.

3. Spoon raspberry mixture into pie shell; dot with margarine.

4. Roll out remaining pastry into 11-inch circle. Cut small hole in center of pastry; cut 4 steam vents. Place pastry on top of pie; trim pastry edges leaving ½-inch overhang. Fold edges under and pinch to seal; flute edge.

5. Bake in preheated 425°F oven until crust is brown and filling is bubbly, 35 to 45 minutes.*

Note: *Occasionally pie filling may bubble over. If desired, place pie plate on baking sheet or piece of aluminum foil to catch drippings.*

Fresh Raspberry Pie

Blueberry Cake Squares

BLUEBERRY CAKE SQUARES

A long-time favorite dessert that has never lost its appeal. Made with canned blueberries, its goodness is always in season.

Makes 6 to 8 servings

1 can (17 ounces) blueberries
1½ cups all-purpose flour
2 teaspoons baking powder
½ teaspoon salt
¾ cup sugar
⅓ cup vegetable shortening
1 large egg
1 teaspoon vanilla
⅓ cup milk
1 teaspoon grated lemon rind
Blueberry Sauce (recipe follows)
Whipped cream or ice cream

1. Drain blueberries well; reserve syrup for Blueberry Sauce.

2. Mix flour, baking powder and salt in small bowl.

3. Beat sugar and shortening in large mixer bowl until light and fluffy; beat in egg and vanilla. Add flour mixture, ½ at a
(Continued)

time, alternating with milk, beating well after each addition. Fold in blueberries and lemon rind.

4. Pour batter into greased 9-inch square cake pan. Bake in preheated 350°F oven until wooden pick inserted near center is withdrawn clean, 25 to 30 minutes.

5. Cool cake in pan on wire rack 10 to 15 minutes. Cut into squares; serve warm with Blueberry Sauce and whipped cream.

BLUEBERRY SAUCE

Reserved blueberry syrup
1 tablespoon plus 1 teaspoon cornstarch
1 tablespoon sugar
2 teaspoons grated lemon rind

1. Measure reserved blueberry syrup; add water if needed to make 1 cup.

2. Mix cornstarch, sugar and lemon rind in small saucepan; stir in 1 cup blueberry syrup.

3. Cook and stir over medium heat until mixture thickens and bubbles for 3 minutes; cool completely.

Makes about 1 cup

Burnt Strawberry Cream

BURNT STRAWBERRY CREAM

Makes 8 servings

    3 cups cooked rice
    3 cups milk
⅓ cup granulated sugar
¼ teaspoon salt
    2 packages (3 ounces each) cream cheese, diced,
        room temperature
1½ teaspoons vanilla
    1 cup whipping cream
    1 package (16 ounces) frozen whole strawberries,
        thawed, drained, cut into halves
⅓ cup packed brown sugar
        Whipped cream and strawberry slices for
        garnish

1. Combine rice, milk, granulated sugar and salt in large saucepan; cook over medium heat, stirring frequently, until thick and creamy, about 30 minutes. Remove from heat.

2. Add cream cheese and vanilla; stir until cheese is melted. Transfer to large bowl; refrigerate, covered, until cold.

3. Beat 1 cup cream in small mixer bowl until stiff; fold into rice mixture. Refrigerate until cold.

4. Arrange halved strawberries in bottom of 12 × 7½ × 2-inch flameproof baking dish. Spoon rice mixture evenly over berries; spread top smooth. Press brown sugar through sieve to form even layer on top of rice mixture.

5. Broil 6 inches from preheated broiler just until sugar caramelizes, 1 to 2 minutes. Watch carefully so sugar does not burn. Let cool until sugar hardens, about 1 minute. Serve immediately or refrigerate 1 hour.

6. Spoon into footed glasses or dessert dishes; garnish with whipped cream and strawberry slices.

FRUIT-NUT NUGGETS

There's just enough cookie dough to hold these chewy, delicious mounds of chopped apricots, dates and nuts together.

Makes about 6 dozen

1½ cups dried apricots, coarsely chopped
1½ cups Brazil nuts, coarsely chopped
1¼ cups pitted dates, coarsely chopped
    1 cup blanched almonds, coarsely chopped
½ cup pecans or walnuts, coarsely chopped
    1 cup plus 2 tablespoons all-purpose flour
¾ cup packed brown sugar
½ cup butter, room temperature
    2 large eggs
    1 teaspoon dry sherry
½ teaspoon baking powder
½ teaspoon baking soda
½ teaspoon ground cinnamon
¼ teaspoon salt

1. Combine apricots, Brazil nuts, dates, almonds and pecans in large bowl. Sprinkle with 2 tablespoons flour; toss to coat fruit and nuts with flour.

2. Beat sugar and butter in large mixer bowl until very light and fluffy. Add eggs and sherry; beat 5 minutes.

3. Mix remaining 1 cup flour, the baking powder, baking soda, cinnamon and salt in medium bowl. Add to butter mixture; stir until smooth. Stir in fruit-nut mixture. Drop by heaping teaspoonfuls onto greased baking sheets.

4. Bake 2 sheets of cookies at a time in preheated 350°F oven until cookies are firm and edges are light brown, 10 to 12 minutes. Remove cookies from baking sheets; cool completely on wire racks.

SQUASH PEANUT PIE

Makes 6 to 8 servings

1 unbaked 9-inch pie shell
6 tablespoons butter or margarine, room temperature
½ cup plus 2 tablespoons packed light brown sugar
1½ teaspoons pumpkin pie spice
2 large eggs, lightly beaten
¼ cup sour cream
1 cup cooked mashed winter squash
1¾ cups milk
1½ teaspoons vanilla
¼ teaspoon salt
1 cup chopped unsalted peanuts
Whipped cream and ground nutmeg for garnish

1. Pierce pie shell all over with fork. Bake in preheated 400°F oven for 10 minutes; cool on wire rack.

2. Beat 4 tablespoons of the butter, ½ cup of the sugar and the pumpkin pie spice in large mixer bowl until blended. Beat in eggs and sour cream. Beat in squash; stir in milk, vanilla and salt. Pour into pie shell. Bake at 400°F 15 minutes.

3. Meanwhile, melt remaining 2 tablespoons butter in small saucepan; stir in remaining 2 tablespoons sugar. Cook and

(Continued)

stir over low heat until sugar is dissolved. Remove from heat; stir in peanuts.

4. Spoon peanut mixture on top of pie filling; reduce oven setting to 325°F. Continue baking pie until knife inserted into center is withdrawn clean, about 40 minutes; cool completely on wire rack. Garnish with whipped cream sprinkled with nutmeg.

PEACHES BUTTERSCOTCH

Makes 8 servings

½ cup packed brown sugar
2 tablespoons water
2 tablespoons butter
4 fresh peaches, peeled, cut into halves, pitted
1 pint peach, vanilla or butter pecan ice cream

1. Combine sugar, water and butter in medium skillet; heat and stir over medium heat until sugar melts.

2. Place peaches cut sides down in butterscotch mixture; simmer gently, basting occasionally, until peaches just begin to soften.

3. Remove peaches with slotted spoon; place in individual serving dishes, cut sides up. Top each with scoop of ice cream; drizzle with butterscotch sauce. Serve immediately.

Squash Peanut Pie

OLD-FASHIONED PEANUT BARS

Makes 2 dozen

½ cup butter, room temperature
1 cup packed light brown sugar
1 large egg
1 teaspoon vanilla
1 teaspoon rum extract
1 cup crushed graham crackers
1 cup all-purpose flour
2 teaspoons baking powder
½ teaspoon salt
1 cup milk
1 cup chopped peanuts
½ cup raisins
Peanut Velvet Frosting (recipe follows)

1. Beat butter in large mixer bowl until light and fluffy. Add brown sugar; beat until light and fluffy. Beat in egg, vanilla and rum extract; fold in graham cracker crumbs.

2. Sift flour, baking powder and salt onto plate. Add ⅓ of the flour mixture at a time to butter mixture, alternating with milk, mixing well after each addition. Stir in peanuts and raisins.

3. Spread batter in greased 13 × 9 × 2-inch baking pan. Bake in preheated 350°F oven until wooden pick inserted into center is withdrawn clean, 35 to 40 minutes. Cool completely in pan on wire rack.

4. Spread top with Peanut Velvet Frosting; cut into 24 bars.

(Continued)

PEANUT VELVET FROSTING

¼ cup butter, room temperature
2 cups sifted powdered sugar
3 tablespoons milk
1 teaspoon vanilla
¼ teaspoon salt
½ cup creamy peanut butter

Heat butter in medium saucepan over low heat until golden. Gradually beat in sugar, alternating with milk, until smooth. Stir in vanilla and salt. Add peanut butter; mix well.

PECAN SHORTBREAD COOKIES

Polvorones is the Mexican name for these rich cookies delicately flavored with vanilla, ground cinnamon and a few finely crushed anise seeds.

Makes about 3 dozen

1 cup sugar
½ cup butter or margarine, room temperature
½ cup lard or solid vegetable shortening, room temperature
1 large egg yolk
1 teaspoon vanilla
2¼ cups all-purpose flour
¾ teaspoon ground cinnamon
¼ teaspoon anise seeds, finely crushed
Pinch salt
½ cup finely chopped pecans

(Continued)

Old-Fashioned Peanut Bars

1. Combine ¾ cup of the sugar, the butter and lard in large mixer bowl; beat until light and fluffy. Add egg yolk and vanilla; beat until smooth.

2. Mix flour, cinnamon, anise seeds and salt in medium bowl. Add flour mixture, ¼ at a time, to butter mixture, stirring to blend well after each addition. Stir in pecans.

3. Roll dough between palms into 1-inch balls; roll balls in remaining ¼ cup sugar to coat. Place 3 inches apart on ungreased baking sheets. Press balls with bottom of glass to flatten into ⅜-inch-thick circles, dipping glass into sugar each time to prevent sticking.

4. Bake in preheated 350°F oven 10 minutes. Reduce oven setting to 300°F; continue baking until cookies are light brown, 12 to 15 minutes longer. Cool on baking sheets on wire racks, 3 minutes. Remove from baking sheets; cool completely on racks.

Oatmeal Raisin Cookies

HONEY CAKE

Honey adds to the moistness and keeping qualities of this dark and spicy cake. The color of honey is generally a good guide to its flavor. Light honeys tend to be mild; amber honeys more intense.

Makes 6 servings

  2 cups all-purpose flour
  ½ teaspoon baking powder
  ½ teaspoon baking soda
  ½ teaspoon salt
  ¼ teaspoon ground nutmeg
  ¼ teaspoon ground cinnamon
  ¾ cup honey
  ½ cup packed brown sugar
  ½ cup warm brewed coffee
  ¼ cup vegetable oil
  2 large eggs
  1 tablespoon grated orange rind
  ¼ teaspoon orange extract
  ½ cup raisins, coarsely chopped

1. Mix flour, baking powder, baking soda, salt, nutmeg and cinnamon in medium bowl.

2. Combine honey, sugar, coffee, oil, eggs, orange rind, and orange extract in large mixer bowl; beat well. Add flour mixture; beat until blended. Stir in raisins.

3. Pour into greased and floured 9-inch square baking pan. Bake in preheated 375°F oven until wooden pick inserted into center is withdrawn clean, about 45 minutes.

CHERRY COBBLER

Makes 8 servings

  1 can (30 ounces) tart cherry pie filling
  1 cup apple juice
  1 teaspoon almond extract
  1 cup all-purpose flour
  2 tablespoons sugar
  1½ teaspoons baking powder
  ½ teaspoon salt
  ⅓ cup solid vegetable shortening
  1 large egg, beaten
  3 tablespoons half-and-half or milk
  Whipping cream or ice cream, if desired

(Continued)

1. Combine pie filling, apple juice and almond extract in large bowl; mix well. Pour into ungreased 8×8×2-inch baking dish.

2. Mix flour, sugar, baking powder and salt in medium bowl; cut in shortening until mixture resembles coarse crumbs. Add egg and half-and-half; stir until moistened. Drop dough by 8 spoonfuls onto cherry mixture.

3. Bake in preheated 375°F oven until topping is golden brown, 25 to 30 minutes. Serve warm with cream.

OATMEAL RAISIN COOKIES

Makes about 3 dozen

  1 cup all-purpose flour
  1½ teaspoons baking powder
  ¼ teaspoon salt
  ¾ cup corn oil
  ⅓ cup granulated sugar
  ⅓ cup packed light brown sugar
  1 large egg
  1 teaspoon vanilla
  1½ cups quick-cooking oats
  ⅔ cup raisins

1. Mix flour, baking powder and salt in small bowl.

2. Combine oil, granulated and brown sugars, egg and vanilla in large mixer bowl; beat on medium speed until sugar is dissolved and mixture is thick and smooth. Reduce speed to low; add flour mixture. Beat until blended. With spoon, stir in oats and raisins.

3. Drop batter by tablespoonfuls, 2 inches apart, onto greased baking sheets. Bake in preheated 375°F oven until light brown, 10 to 12 minutes. Cool slightly on baking sheets; remove from sheets. Cool completely on wire racks; store in tightly covered container.

Seascapes to Fertile Valleys
OUR PACIFIC COASTS

Cooking throughout the Pacific Coast region—which includes Alaska and Hawaii—is like an equation in which the whole is greater than the sum of its parts. In terms of the cooking here, the "factors" that make up this equation are: the tremendous abundance of regionally grown fruits and vegetables plus an almost greater amount of imported foods, a remarkable variety of fresh fish and shellfish, substantial Oriental and Latino communities with their distinctive culinary traditions, and the cooking heritage of the original groups who migrated to and settled the various parts of this region. The Pacific Coast is where "back east" meets "far east," where island fruits mingle with mainland ingredients. Taken together, all these elements add up to an exciting, inventive, and unique style of cooking.

Among the fruits and vegetables that flourish in California are artichokes, asparagus, avocados, blueberries, garlic, lettuce, raspberries, strawberries and tomatoes, to name just a few. Apples and pears are found in Washington and Oregon. Northern California and central Washington enjoy the perfect climate for growing grapes, and California is, of course, the center of the American wine industry. In the Manatuska valley, north of Anchorage, Alaska, a short summer that features more than 20 hours of sunlight a day is responsible for 70-pound cabbages and for carrots and radishes that weigh several pounds each. All kinds of nuts grow along the Pacific Coast, from almonds to walnuts. And, of course, the ocean itself has proved a bountiful source of all manner of seafood.

It was, perhaps, along the Pacific Coast that salads became substantial main dishes. You'll find Steak Salad with Sherry Vinaigrette, Marinated Monterey Salad, Chinese Chicken Salad, Taco Salad and Empress of the East Salad—dishes that mix meat or fish with a combination of fresh vegetables.

The fresh fruit of the region are used in salads as well. There's an unusual Frozen Blue Cheese Dressing designed for a brimming bowl of fresh fruit. Or you may wish to try a refreshing Apple Salad with Curry Dressing or a wonderful Harvest Pear Salad.

Lemons and limes are also much in evidence in Pacific Coast cooking. You'll find a luscious Lemon Sour Pie, tangy Chicken with Lime Butter and a fiery Lime-Garlic Broiled Shrimp.

In the spring and early summer, the apricots and strawberries you see in your local supermarket come from California. In this chapter, you'll find a number of delicious ways to use them—Apricot Streusel Pie, Fresh Strawberry Mousse, Strawberry Sponge Shortcake and Strawberry Rice Pudding.

The many kinds of nuts grown in this region find their way into a number of recipes from appetizers (Pistachio-Stuffed Mushrooms) to dessert (Almond Bavarian). Hazelnuts enliven a turkey casserole in Northwest Hazelnut Turkey Bake, and walnuts enhance Pear Nut Bread and Best Ever Walnut Pie.

Those who live near the Pacific Coast make good use of the ocean's bounty. Summertime Cioppino, for example, is a hearty mix of fish and shellfish that's a meal in itself. Your guests may enjoy either the Smoked Oyster Hors d'Oeuvres or the Seviche as an appetizer. Alaska has one of the largest fishing grounds in the world. Salmon, considered by many the king of fish, are plentiful there, and in the Curried Salmon and Rice, Broiled Salmon with Garlic Mayonnaise and the Foil-Baked Salmon recipes you'll find three fine ways to use it. Alaskan waters are also the source of king crabs, and two excellent recipes—Crab Louis and King Crab Celery Victor—are offered here.

The Japanese and Chinese residents of our mainland and island Pacific Coast areas have made great contributions to American cooking. Stir-frying and steaming—both Oriental techniques—are now widely used by cooks everywhere. Among the Chinese-oriented recipes included in this chapter are Chicken-Broccoli Stir Fry, Sanddabs Oriental, Pork and Crab Pot Stickers and Beef Strips Oriental, while a shrimp and vegetable Tempura and Teriyaki Steak with Onions are Japanese-inspired.

Our island state, Hawaii, adds a tropical dimension to Pacific cooking. Island fruits, such as pineapples and mangoes, are used in Pineapple Kiwi Fruit Salad and Snapper with Opakapaka-Mango Sauce. Macadamia nuts—unique to the Hawaiian islands—were never better than in Coconut Macadamia Pie.

Many classic dishes from around the world find new homes here. Sole Veronique, for example, could have been created with California seedless grapes and Napa valley Chardonnay in mind. You'll find French cassoulet and Spanish paella adapted to local ingredients in the California Cassoulet and California Paella recipes.

HASH-STUFFED ONIONS

Spanish onions grown in the Northwestern U.S. are so sweet and mild they make excellent containers for meat mixtures like corned beef hash or, possibly, vegetables like new green peas.

Makes 6 servings

6 medium sweet Spanish onions (6 to 8 ounces each)
2 cans (15 ounces each) corned beef hash
⅓ cup chopped green bell pepper
1 can (15 ounces) tomato sauce
3 to 4 drops hot red pepper sauce
2 tablespoons grated Parmesan cheese
Chopped parsley for garnish

1. Place onions in 1 inch water in large kettle; heat to boiling. Reduce heat; simmer, covered, just until tender, 10 to 15 minutes. Drain well.

2. Cut ½-inch slice from tops of onions; scoop out centers, leaving ½-inch shells.

3. Chop enough onion trimmings to measure ⅓ cup; reserve remaining onion trimmings for other use.

4. Mix hash and green pepper in medium bowl; spoon into onion shells. Place in shallow baking dish.

5. Mix reserved ⅓ cup chopped onion, tomato sauce and red pepper sauce in medium bowl; pour into baking dish. Sprinkle onions with cheese.

6. Bake in preheated 350°F oven, basting occasionally with sauce if desired, until heated through, 20 to 30 minutes. Sprinkle with parsley.

PEPPY CREAMED CORN

Makes 4 to 6 servings

3⅓ cups fresh corn kernels (about 6 small ears)
1 cup whipping cream
1 cup milk
2 to 3 teaspoons sugar
1 teaspoon salt
⅛ teaspoon ground red pepper
2 tablespooons butter, melted
2 tablespoons all-purpose flour

1. Combine corn, cream, milk, sugar, salt and pepper in medium saucepan; stir to mix. Heat to boiling; reduce heat. Simmer, uncovered, stirring occasionally, 5 minutes.

2. Mix butter and flour in small bowl until smooth; gradually whisk into corn mixture. Cook and stir over low heat until sauce thickens and bubbles for 1 minute.

RICE WITH RAISINS AND PINE NUTS

Makes 6 to 8 servings

½ cup finely chopped onion
2 tablespoons butter or margarine
2 cups long-grain rice
1 quart chicken stock or water
½ cup raisins
½ cup pine nuts
2 tablespoons lemon juice
1 teaspoon salt
⅛ teaspoon saffron

(Continued)

Hash-Stuffed Onions

SEVICHE

West Coast ingredients including sea scallops, avocado, bits of ripe tomato and a citrus marinade make up this popular appetizer.

Makes 8 appetizer servings

    1 pound fresh scallops
    5 tablespoons fresh lemon juice
    2 tablespoons fresh lime juice
    2 tablespoons virgin olive oil
  1½ tablespoons chopped fresh coriander or parsley
    ¼ teaspoon dried oregano, crumbled
    1 to 2 teaspoons finely chopped seeded fresh hot
       green chile*
    ½ teaspoon minced garlic
    ½ plus ⅛ teaspoon salt
    ¼ teaspoon freshly ground pepper
    2 ripe medium avocados
    1 cup diced seeded peeled fresh tomato
       Boston lettuce   *(Continued)*

1. Rinse and drain scallops; pat dry with paper toweling. Cut into ½-inch cubes.

2. Whisk 4 tablespoons of the lemon juice, the lime juice and oil in medium bowl until blended. Whisk in coriander, oregano, chile, garlic, ½ teaspoon of the salt and the ground pepper. Add scallops; toss to coat well. Refrigerate, covered, tossing occasionally, at least 4 hours or up to 12 hours.

3. Drain scallops, reserving marinade. Stir remaining 1 tablespoon lemon juice and ⅛ teaspoon salt into marinade.

4. Pare and pit avocados; cut into ½-inch cubes. Add to marinade; toss to coat well. Remove avocado from marinade with slotted spoon.

5. Combine scallops, avocado and tomato in medium bowl; toss gently. Serve on individual plates lined with lettuce.

Note: *Wear rubber gloves when handling chilies and wash hands with warm soapy water. Avoid touching face or eyes.*

Seviche

Summertime Cioppino

SUMMERTIME CIOPPINO

Portuguese fishermen combined chunks of fish and shell-fish in a steaming broth laced with wine for their lunch. This dish is still popular on the Pacific coast.

Makes 6 servings

1 can (16 ounces) tomatoes, undrained, chopped
½ cup water
½ cup dry red wine
1 envelope onion-mushroom soup mix
1 teaspoon dried rubbed sage
1 bay leaf
6 fresh hard-shell clams
1 pound haddock or halibut fillets, cut into 1½-inch pieces
½ pound scallops
½ pound medium shrimp, shelled, deveined, tails intact
⅛ teaspoon pepper

1. Combine tomatoes, water, wine, soup mix, sage and bay leaf in large saucepan; heat to boiling. Reduce heat; simmer, covered, stirring occasionally, 15 minutes.

2. Add clams; simmer, covered, 3 minutes longer. Add remaining ingredients; simmer, covered, stirring occasionally until clam shells open and seafood is opaque throughout, about 15 minutes longer. Discard any clams that do not open.

HOT TOMATO APPETIZERS

Makes 36 appetizers

2 sheets frozen puff pastry
2 medium onions, thinly slivered
1 large clove garlic, minced
2 tablespoons butter or margarine
1 teaspoon dried basil, crumbled
1 teaspoon dried oregano, crumbled
¾ teaspoon liquid pepper sauce
1 can (14 ounces) whole tomatoes, drained, chopped
¾ cup grated Parmesan cheese

1. Thaw pastry at room temperature 20 minutes; gently unfold. Roll out each sheet on floured surface into 9 × 7½-inch rectangle. Cut each rectangle into 18 pieces, 2½ × 1½ inches each. Bake pastry pieces on ungreased baking sheets in preheated 350°F oven until light brown but slightly underdone, about 12 minutes. Cool on wire rack.

2. Saute onions and garlic in butter in medium skillet over medium heat 3 minutes. Stir in basil, oregano and pepper sauce; cook 2 minutes longer. Stir in tomatoes; cook, stirring occasionally, until mixture thickens, about 15 minutes. Let cool to room temperature.

3. Lightly press center of each pastry to make a well. Spoon 1½ teaspoons of tomato mixture into each well; sprinkle with 1 teaspoon of the cheese. Bake at 350°F until cheese melts and pastries are hot, about 15 minutes.

GUACAMOLE

There's an easy way to tell if an avocado is ripe enough to mash nicely for guacamole. Hold the avocado between your hands and press gently. If the fruit yields with the light pressure, it is ready to use. If it is still firm, let it stand at room temperature a day or two and test again.

Makes about 2 cups

4 tablespoons finely chopped white onion
1½ tablespoons coarsely chopped fresh coriander
1 or 2 fresh serrano or jalapeno chilies, seeded, finely chopped*
¼ teaspoon chopped garlic, if desired
2 large soft-ripe avocados
1 medium very ripe tomato, peeled, seeded, chopped
1 to 2 teaspoons fresh lime juice
½ teaspoon salt
Corn Tortilla Chips (recipe follows)

1. Combine 2 tablespoons of the onion, 1 tablespoon of the coriander, the chilies and garlic in large mortar with rough surface. Grind with pestle until almost smooth. (Mixture can be processed in blender, if necessary, but it will become more watery than desired.)

2. Cut avocados lengthwise into halves; remove and discard pits. Scoop avocado flesh out of shells; add to chili mixture. Mash roughly, leaving avocado slightly chunky.

3. Add tomato, lime juice, salt and the remaining 2 tablespoons onion and ½ tablespoon coriander; mix well. Transfer to serving bowl. Guacamole is best served immediately, but can be refrigerated, covered, up to 4 hours. Serve with Corn Tortilla Chips.

*Note: Wear rubber gloves when working with chilies and wash hands with warm soapy water. Avoid touching face or eyes.

CORN TORTILLA CHIPS

12 corn tortillas (6-inch), preferably day-old
Lard or vegetable oil
½ to 1 teaspoon salt

1. If tortillas are fresh, let stand, uncovered, in single layer on wire rack 1 to 2 hours to dry slightly. Stack tortillas; cut through stack into 6 or 8 equal wedges.

2. Melt enough lard in deep, large skillet for ½-inch depth. Heat to 375°F.

3. Add as many tortilla wedges to skillet as will fit in single layer. Fry, turning occasionally, until crisp, about 1 minute. Remove with slotted spoon; drain on paper toweling. Repeat until all chips have been fried. Sprinkle with salt.

Makes 6 or 8 dozen chips

CHILI VARIATION: When all chips have been fried, pour off lard remaining in skillet. Sprinkle chips evenly with salt and 1 to 2 teaspoons chili powder. Return chips to skillet; cook over low heat, stirring constantly but gently, until chili powder is fragrant, 45 seconds to 1 minute. (Do not let chili powder burn.) Let cool slightly.

Note: Tortilla chips are best eaten fresh, but can be stored, tightly covered, in cool place 2 or 3 days. Reheat in 350°F oven a few minutes before serving.

Guacamole with Corn Tortilla Chips

SAN FRANCISCO MINESTRONE

Ladle out big bowls of thick Italian vegetable soup and pass the freshly grated Parmesan or Romano cheese to sprinkle generously on top.

Makes 6 to 8 servings

¼ pound salt pork or slab bacon, finely diced
1 medium onion, chopped
1 clove garlic, minced
5 cups water
1 cup beef stock
1 cup dried large lima beans
1 teaspoon salt
2 cups sliced celery
1 carrot, sliced
1 turnip, cut in half, sliced
½ bay leaf
¼ teaspoon dried basil
1½ cups canned stewed tomatoes, undrained
2 cups shredded cabbage
1 cup chopped spinach
¼ cup rice
Grated Parmesan or Romano cheese

1. Cook salt pork, onion and garlic in medium skillet over medium heat until light brown, 6 to 8 minutes.

2. Combine salt pork mixture, water, stock, beans and salt in Dutch oven; heat to boiling. Stir in celery, carrot, turnip, bay leaf and basil; heat to boiling. Reduce heat; simmer 1½ hours.

3. Stir in tomatoes, cabbage, spinach and rice; cook until rice is tender, about 30 minutes. Ladle into individual bowls; sprinkle with cheese.

SMOKED OYSTER HORS D'OEUVRES

Makes 20 appetizers

20 whole pitted prunes
20 medium-size smoked oysters (about 3½-ounce can), drained*
10 slices lean bacon, cut crosswise into halves

1. Stuff each prune with 1 oyster. Wrap each with ½ bacon slice; secure with wooden pick.

2. Broil, turning once, until bacon is crisp, 4 to 5 minutes. Remove picks; serve hot.

*Note: Whole toasted almonds can be substituted for the oysters.

MR. McGREGOR'S GARDEN DIP

Makes about 1⅓ cups

1 package (3 ounces) cream cheese, room temperature
1 cup small-curd cottage cheese
1 small onion, minced
1 tablespoon lemon juice
1 teaspoon prepared horseradish
1 teaspoon celery salt
½ teaspoon instant vegetable bouillon granules
¼ teaspoon dry mustard

Beat cream cheese in small mixer bowl until smooth; beat in cottage cheese. Add remaining ingredients; mix well. Refrigerate, covered, at least 1 hour to blend flavors.

COLD YOGURT SOUP

A splendid cool soup for that light, refreshing lunch on days when the temperature really soars.

Makes 4 servings

1 cup chopped cooked chicken
1 teaspoon lemon juice
¾ teaspoon minced fresh dill or ¼ teaspoon dried dill weed
½ teaspoon salt
⅛ teaspoon garlic powder
  Pinch white pepper
2 cups plain yogurt
1 small cucumber, seeded, diced
⅓ cup chopped celery
3 tablespoons sliced green onion
  Fresh dill sprigs for garnish

1. Combine chicken, lemon juice, minced dill, salt, garlic powder and pepper in small bowl; toss lightly. Refrigerate, covered, 30 minutes.

2. Stir yogurt in medium bowl with fork until smooth; stir in chicken mixture, cucumber, celery and onion. Serve cold, garnished with dill sprigs.

FRESH TOMATO SOUP

Fresh coriander has three different names depending on where you live and shop. Perhaps you know this green, feathery-leaved herb as cilantro or Chinese parsley.

Makes 6 servings

1 medium onion, chopped
1 clove garlic, minced
1 tablespoon vegetable oil
4 cups chopped fresh tomatoes
1 cup chicken broth
1 tablespoon chopped fresh coriander or parsley
½ teaspoon salt
⅛ teaspoon pepper
⅓ cup grated Parmesan cheese

1. Saute onion and garlic in oil in large saucepan over medium heat until onion is soft, about 4 minutes. Add tomatoes, broth, coriander, salt and pepper. Heat to boiling; reduce heat. Simmer, covered, 15 minutes.

2. Transfer tomato mixture to blender container; process until smooth. Return soup to saucepan; heat until hot.

3. Ladle soup into serving bowls; sprinkle with cheese.

Cold Yogurt Soup

Pistachio-Stuffed Mushrooms

STUFFED GRAPE LEAVES

You could use leaves from home-grown grape vines, but it is more practical to buy them in jars. The purchased leaves are uniform in size and picked from the varieties of grapes known to have leaves that make tender eating.

Makes about 10 dozen

    1 cup chopped yellow onion
    1 cup olive oil
1½ pounds cooked lamb, beef or chicken, finely
        chopped
    3 cups cooked rice
2½ cups sliced green onion
    ½ cup chopped parsley
    ½ cup lemon juice
    3 tablespoons chopped pine nuts or cashews
    2 tablespoons dried dill weed
    1 tablespoon dried mint
    1 tablespoon dried oregano
    2 to 3 teaspoons salt
    1 teaspoon freshly ground black pepper
    2 jars (8 to 9 ounces each) grapevine leaves
    1 cup parsley stems
1½ cups beef broth
    1 cup tomato juice

1. Saute yellow onion in ½ cup of the oil in medium skillet over medium heat until soft, about 4 minutes. Combine onion mixture, meat, rice, green onion, chopped parsley, ¼ cup of the lemon juice, the nuts, dill, mint, oregano, salt and pepper in large bowl; mix well.

2. Rinse grape leaves well to remove brine; drain very well. Spread leaves out, shiny sides down, veined sides up. Place about 1 tablespoon of the meat mixture in center of each

(Continued)

leaf. Fold stem end over filling; fold sides over filling and roll up tightly.

3. Spread parsley stems in bottom of Dutch oven. Arrange stuffed grape leaves snugly in layers on top of stems. Drizzle remaining ½ cup oil and ¼ cup lemon juice over leaves. Pour broth and tomato juice into Dutch oven.

4. Heat to boiling; reduce heat. Simmer, covered, until all liquid has been absorbed, 35 to 40 minutes.

PISTACHIO-STUFFED MUSHROOMS

Makes 20 appetizers

20 medium mushrooms
    3 tablespoons minced onion
    ¼ cup butter or margarine
    ½ cup breadcrumbs from day-old bread
    ¼ cup chopped shelled natural pistachios
    2 tablespoons chopped parsley
    ¼ teaspoon dried marjoram, crumbled
    ¼ teaspoon salt
        Pinch pepper
    3 tablespoons butter or margarine, melted

1. Remove stems from mushrooms; finely chop stems. Saute stems and onion in ¼ cup butter in medium skillet over medium heat until soft, about 4 minutes; remove from heat.

2. Add breadcrumbs, pistachios, parsley, marjoram, salt and pepper to skillet; mix well. Spoon into mushroom caps.

3. Place mushrooms on baking sheet; drizzle with 3 tablespoons melted butter. Bake in preheated 350°F oven until hot, 5 to 8 minutes.

Chicken-Broccoli Stir Fry

CHICKEN-BROCCOLI STIR FRY

Whole wheat croutons bring a delightful crunchiness to ginger-seasoned chicken and vegetables.

Makes 8 servings

  8 chicken thighs, boned
  ¼ teaspoon ground ginger
  ¼ teaspoon pepper
  1 bunch fresh broccoli
  3 tablespoons peanut oil
  1 cup diagonally sliced green onions
  ¾ cup plus 2 tablespoons chicken broth
  1 teaspoon salt
  ½ teaspoon sugar
  1 tablespoon cornstarch
  ¼ cup grated Parmesan cheese
  Whole Wheat Croutons (recipe follows)

1. Cut chicken into bite-size pieces; sprinkle with ginger and pepper. Cut broccoli flowerets into 1-inch pieces; cut stems crosswise into thin slices.

2. Heat oil in wok or large skillet over high heat until hot. Add chicken; stir-fry until brown, about 3 minutes. Add broccoli and green onions; stir-fry 3 minutes longer.

3. Quickly mix ¾ cup of the broth, the salt and sugar in small bowl; add to wok. Reduce heat to medium-high; cook, covered, 2 minutes.

4. Mix cornstarch and remaining 2 tablespoons broth in small bowl until smooth. Add to wok; cook and stir for 1 minute.

5. Transfer to serving dish; sprinkle with cheese and Whole Wheat Croutons. Serve immediately.

(Continued)

WHOLE WHEAT CROUTONS

  4 slices whole wheat bread, cut into 1-inch cubes
  2 tablespoons butter, melted
  ½ teaspoon garlic salt

1. Combine all ingredients in medium bowl; toss to mix well.

2. Spread bread cubes in large shallow baking pan. Bake in preheated 300°F oven until crisp, about 20 minutes.

Makes about 1½ cups

PEPPERED RIB ROAST

Since a roast continues to cook after it comes out of the cooker, you'll want to remove it when the thermometer reads 120 to 125°F to serve it rare.

Makes 12 servings

  1 standing beef rib roast (6 pounds)
  Pepper
  Tomato wedges for garnish

1. Prepare hot charcoal for grilling in covered grill; arrange coals around drip pan according to manufacturer's directions.

2. Sprinkle roast all over with pepper. Place on grill rack; cover grill. Grill-roast over medium-hot coals until instant-registering thermometer inserted into thickest part of meat not touching bone registers 120 to 125°F for rare, about 1 hour, or 130 to 140°F for medium-rare, about 1 hour and 15 minutes.

3. Let roast stand 15 minutes before carving. Garnish with tomatoes.

SUMMERTIME BOUNTY PIE

A hamburger crust baked in a pie pan holds your choice of cooked carrots, broccoli, summer squash, and other good things from the garden.

Makes 6 servings

1½ **pounds ground beef**
  2 **cups soft breadcrumbs**
  1 **cup sour cream**
  1 **large egg**
  1 **envelope onion or beefy-onion soup mix**
½ **teaspoon dried thyme or basil, crumbled**
  1 **tablespoon all-purpose flour**
1½ **cups shredded Cheddar cheese**
3½ **cups assorted hot cooked vegetables, such as broccoli, peas, tomatoes, chopped red and green bell pepper and sliced carrots, zucchini and yellow squash**
  1 **tablespoon chopped parsley**

1. Combine beef, breadcrumbs, sour cream, egg, soup mix and thyme in large bowl; mix well.

2. Sprinkle flour evenly in 9-inch pie pan. Press beef mixture in pan to cover bottom and extend ¾ inch above sides of pan.

3. Bake in preheated 350°F oven 45 minutes; drain off fat.

4. Sprinkle ½ of the cheese in bottom of beef shell. Fill with vegetables; sprinkle with parsley and remaining cheese. Bake until cheese is melted, about 15 minutes longer.

CASHEW HAM & CHICKEN WITH VEGETABLES

Makes 6 to 8 servings

  1 **ham steak (1 pound), trimmed, cut into 1-inch cubes**
  1 **pound skinless boneless chicken breasts, cut into 1-inch cubes**
  2 **tablespoons vegetable oil**
  1 **package (10 ounces) frozen green beans, thawed**
1½ **cups diagonally sliced celery**
  1 **can (8 ounces) water chestnuts, drained, sliced**
  1 **red bell pepper, cut into 1-inch pieces**
  1 **green bell pepper, cut into 1-inch pieces**
  1 **can (4 ounces) sliced mushrooms, drained**
  1 **onion, sliced**
  1 **cup chicken stock**
  1 **tablespoon cornstarch**
¼ **cup roasted cashews, coarsely chopped**

1. Saute ham and chicken in oil in large skillet over medium heat until light brown and cooked through, 6 to 8 minutes. Remove to plate.

2. Combine all vegetables and ¾ cup of the stock in skillet; heat to boiling. Reduce heat; simmer, covered, stirring occasionally, 5 minutes.

3. Mix cornstarch and remaining ¼ cup stock in small bowl; stir into skillet. Cook and stir over low heat until mixture thickens and bubbles for 3 minutes.

4. Stir in ham and chicken; cook and stir just until heated through. Sprinkle with cashews before serving.

Summertime Bounty Pie

BEEF STRIPS ORIENTAL

Round steak and colorful vegetables, braised tender in a soy-seasoned sauce, will appeal to the entire family.

Makes 6 to 8 servings

  2 pounds beef round steak, 1 inch thick, partially frozen
  2 tablespoons vegetable oil
    Water
  ⅓ cup soy sauce
  2 teaspoons sugar
  1 clove garlic, minced
  ¼ teaspoon ground black pepper
  3 carrots
  2 green bell peppers, cut into 1-inch pieces
  8 green onions, cut into 1½-inch lengths
  ½ pound mushrooms, cut into halves
  1 can (8 ounces) water chestnuts, cut into halves
  2 tablespoons cornstarch
    Hot cooked rice

1. Cut beef into ⅛-inch-thick slices; cut slices into 3- to 4-inch lengths. Cook beef in oil in large skillet over medium heat until brown, 3 to 4 minutes.

2. Pour drippings into measuring cup; add enough water to make 1 cup. Add to skillet; stir in soy sauce, sugar, garlic and ground pepper. Cook, covered, over low heat, for 45 minutes.

(Continued)

3. Using vegetable parer, cut carrots lengthwise into thin slices; cut slices crosswise into halves. Add carrots, green peppers, onions, mushrooms and water chestnuts to skillet; mix well. Cook, covered, until beef and vegetables are tender, about 10 minutes longer.

4. Mix ¼ cup water and the cornstarch in small bowl until smooth; stir into skillet. Cook and stir until sauce thickens and bubbles for 3 minutes. Serve over rice.

PEPPER AND OLIVE STEAK

Since green bell peppers turn red and sweet when they are ripe, both peppers are mild-flavored as well as colorful in this attractive steak topper.

Makes 4 to 6 servings

  1 beef flank steak (1½ pounds)
  1 onion, chopped
  1 green bell pepper, chopped
  1 red bell pepper, chopped
  2 cloves garlic, finely chopped
  2 tablespoons vegetable oil
  ½ cup beef broth
  1 jar (6 ounces) pimiento-stuffed olives, drained, chopped
  1½ teaspoons dried oregano, crumbled
  ¼ teaspoon ground black pepper

(Continued)

Beef Strips Oriental

1. Broil steak in preheated broiler 3 inches from heat source until desired doneness, about 6 minutes per side for rare.

2. Meanwhile, saute onion, green and red bell peppers and garlic in oil in large skillet over medium heat until onion is tender, about 4 minutes. Stir in remaining ingredients; simmer, covered, until peppers are tender, about 5 minutes.

3. Cut steak across the grain into thin slices; top with vegetable mixture.

TERIYAKI STEAK WITH ONIONS

Sliced sweet onion not only brings its own flavor to the steak accompaniment but also takes on Oriental spiciness from wine, soy sauce and grated ginger root.

Makes 4 to 6 servings

  ½ cup soy sauce
  ¼ cup dry white wine
  2 tablespoons packed brown sugar
  1 teaspoon grated fresh ginger root
  2 cloves garlic, minced
  1 beef flank steak (1½ pounds)
  1 large sweet onion, sliced
  1 tablespoon butter or margarine

1. Mix soy sauce, wine, sugar, ginger root and garlic in small bowl.

2. Place steak in heavy-duty plastic bag; add soy sauce mixture, turning steak to coat. Close bag securely; refrigerate 6 to 8 hours, turning at least once.

3. Remove steak from marinade, reserving marinade. Grill steak over medium-hot coals or broil in preheated broiler until desired doneness, about 6 minutes per side for rare.

4. Meanwhile, saute onion in butter in medium skillet over medium heat until soft, about 5 minutes. Stir in ¼ cup of the reserved marinade; cook and stir 4 minutes.

5. Cut steak diagonally across the grain into thin slices; serve with onion.

SMOKE-COOKED DUCKLING

Duckling prepared in a smoke cooker develops a deep brown, crispy skin. Plan to surround it with fresh tropical fruits such as pineapple, bananas, or papayas.

Makes 3 to 4 servings

  1 duckling (about 5 pounds)
  1 cup bottled teriyaki sauce
  2 tablespoons molasses or dark corn syrup
  ½ to 1 teaspoon dry mustard
  ½ to 1 teaspoon garlic powder
    Pineapple chunks and zucchini slices for
      garnish

1. Place duckling in large glass bowl or heavy-duty plastic bag. Mix remaining ingredients except garnish in small bowl; pour over duckling, being sure marinade coats inside as well as outside of bird. Cover bowl or close bag securely. Refrigerate overnight or at least several hours, turning duckling in marinade occasionally. *(Continued)*

2. About 7 hours before serving, remove duckling from refrigerator. Start soaking 2 or 3 chunks of wood or handful of wood chips, unless smoker takes dry wood.

3. Fill fire pan full of charcoal briquettes and start fire. When coals turn grey, drain wood pieces; add them to coals. (For electric units: Unless smoker takes dry wood, drain wood pieces and put them in their special pan.)

4. Put water pan in place; fill almost full with hot water. Set cooking grill in place.

5. Place duckling in center of cooking grill. Pierce skin in several places with two-tined fork, so fat can drain off. Pour marinade over duckling and into water pan. Cover smoke-cooker. (Plug in electric smoker.) Smoke-cook until duck leg moves easily in socket, about 6 hours. Check water pan after 4 hours and add 1 quart hot water if needed. Serve duckling garnished with pineapple and zucchini.

TORTILLA LASAGNE

Mexican and Italian heritages meet to create this family-style layered casserole made with tortillas and taco seasonings, plus both mozzarella and Cheddar cheeses.

Makes 4 to 6 servings

  1 pound ground beef
  ½ cup chopped onion
  ½ cup chopped green bell pepper
  ½ package (1¼-ounce size) taco seasoning mix
  1 can (8 ounces) tomato sauce
  1 can (6 ounces) tomato paste
  ½ cup sliced pitted ripe olives
  ¼ cup water
  1 cup shredded mozzarella cheese
  1 cup shredded Cheddar cheese
  4 flour or corn tortillas (7- to 8-inch diameter)
  2 cups coarsely crumbled corn chips
  1 cup sour cream

1. Cook and stir beef, onion and green bell pepper in large skillet over medium heat until beef is no longer pink, about 10 minutes; drain and discard drippings. Stir in taco seasoning mix.

2. Add tomato sauce, tomato paste, olives and water; cook, uncovered, stirring occasionally, until mixture is thick and bubbly, about 10 minutes.

3. Mix mozzarella and Cheddar cheeses in small bowl. Place 2 tortillas in bottom of 12 × 7-inch baking dish; top with ½ of the meat mixture, then with ½ of the cheese mixture and ½ of the corn chips. Repeat layers once.

4. Bake in preheated 350°F oven until hot throughout and bubbly around edges, 25 to 30 minutes. Let stand 10 minutes before serving. Cut into squares; top each serving with sour cream.

To microwave: Crumble beef into 2-quart microwave-safe casserole; stir in onion and green pepper. Microwave, covered, on HIGH, stirring once, 4 to 5 minutes; drain. Stir in seasoning mix, tomato sauce, tomato paste, olives and water. Microwave, uncovered, on HIGH, stirring once, until thick and bubbly, about 5 minutes. Layer tortillas, meat mixture, cheeses and chips in microwave-safe baking dish as in Step 3, omitting top layers of cheese and corn chips. Microwave, uncovered, on MEDIUM (50% power) 5 minutes. Rotate dish ¼ turn; microwave 5 to 8 minutes longer. Sprinkle with remaining cheese and corn chips; let stand 5 minutes before serving. Serve with sour cream.

Lamb Kabobs

CALIFORNIA CASSOULET

A West Coast derivative of a famous casserole that gets its name from the earthenware pot used for baking the original bean and pork main dish.

Makes 16 servings

1 pork loin roast (3 to 4 pounds)
4 to 6 cups cooked or canned large lima beans, drained
2 cups water
2 medium onions, sliced
2 cloves garlic, minced
1 teaspoon salt
2 carrots, cut into 1-inch lengths
½ pound Italian sausage, skinned, sliced
½ green bell pepper, cut into strips
1 can (8 ounces) stewed tomatoes, undrained
1 can (8 ounces) pearl onions, drained
1 cup dry red wine
1 cup seedless green grapes for garnish

1. Roast pork in roasting pan in preheated 375°F oven 30 minutes.

2. Combine pork, beans, water, onions, garlic and salt in large Dutch oven. Heat to boiling; reduce heat. Simmer, covered, 2 hours.

3. Add carrots to Dutch oven; continue cooking until meat is tender. Remove from heat. Remove pork to plate; let stand until cool enough to handle. Drain bean mixture, reserving 1 cup of the liquid.

4. Remove bones and fat from pork; cut pork into small pieces. Combine bean mixture, pork, 1 cup reserved liquid
(Continued)

and the remaining ingredients except grapes in Dutch oven; mix well.

5. Transfer mixture to greased 3-quart baking dish.* Bake, covered, in preheated 350°F oven 1½ hours. Garnish with grapes.

*Note: Recipe can be made ahead to this point; refrigerate, covered, up to 24 hours. Recipe can also be made in 2 smaller baking dishes; freeze 1 for later use. Increase baking time if recipe has been refrigerated or frozen.

LAMB KABOBS

Fresh green grapes are a key ingredient in this tempting sweet and spicy marinade and basting sauce for tender cubes of lamb.

Makes 4 servings

½ cup seedless green grapes
1 tablespoon red wine vinegar
1 tablespoon catsup
1½ teaspoons honey
1½ teaspoons vegetable oil
1 teaspoon minced garlic
½ teaspoon prepared mustard
¼ teaspoon paprika
1½ pounds lean boneless lamb for broiling, cut into 1-inch cubes
Curried Pilaf (recipe follows) or 4 cups hot cooked rice

1. Combine grapes, vinegar, catsup, honey, oil, garlic, mustard and paprika in blender container; process until smooth.
(Continued)

2. Mix grape marinade and lamb in glass bowl; refrigerate, covered, stirring occasionally, 2 to 3 hours.

3. Thread lamb on skewers, reserving marinade. Broil 8 inches from heat source, turning and brushing with reserved marinade frequently, until tender and brown, 10 to 12 minutes. Watch carefully to prevent rich marinade from burning; add small amount of water to bottom of pan if necessary to prevent drippings from burning.

4. Serve lamb on bed of Curried Pilaf; pass any remaining marinade separately.

CURRIED PILAF

½ cup chopped onion
2 tablespoons butter
1 teaspoon curry powder
1 cup long-grain rice
1 can (10¾ ounces) condensed chicken broth
1 can (8 ounces) stewed tomatoes, undrained
1 cup seedless green grapes
2 tablespoons chopped parsley

1. Saute onion in butter in medium saucepan until soft, about 4 minutes. Stir in curry powder; saute 10 seconds. Stir in rice to coat with butter.

2. Add broth to pan; heat to boiling. Cover pan; reduce heat to low. Simmer 10 minutes. Add tomatoes without stirring; simmer, covered, 10 minutes longer.

3. Add grapes and parsley to pan; stir lightly with fork. Simmer, covered, 5 minutes longer.

Makes 4 servings

LEG OF LAMB WITH TANGERINE SAUCE

Boneless leg-of-lamb roasts make carving as easy as slicing across the grain of the meat with a sharp knife.

Makes 15 to 20 servings

1 boned rolled leg of lamb (5 to 7 pounds)
2 cloves garlic, cut into slivers
1 teaspoon dried rosemary, crumbled
1½ cups tangerine juice
½ cup orange-flavored liqueur
½ cup apricot jam
2 tablespoons cornstarch
½ teaspoon dried mint, if desired
¼ teaspoon ground ginger
Salt and pepper to taste
Parsley sprigs, zucchini and yellow summer squash for garnish

1. Place lamb, fat side up, in shallow roasting pan. Cut deep slits in lamb; insert garlic slivers and rosemary into slits. Insert meat thermometer into thickest part of lamb.

2. Roast in preheated 325°F oven until thermometer registers 140°F for rare, 2 to 3 hours, or 150 to 155°F for medium, 3 to 4 hours. Let stand, loosely covered, 15 to 20 minutes before carving.

3. Meanwhile, combine remaining ingredients except garnish in medium saucepan; cook and stir over medium heat until sauce thickens and bubbles for 3 minutes. Garnish lamb with parsley, zucchini and yellow squash; serve with sauce.

Leg of Lamb with Tangerine Sauce

PORK AND CRAB POT STICKERS

The whimsical name is somewhat misleading because every effort is made to see that they neither stick to each other nor to the pan at any stage of cooking.

Makes about 28

1 package (3 ounces) cream cheese, room
   temperature
1 cup finely chopped cooked pork tenderloin
   (about ½ of 1 tenderloin)
1 can (6 ounces) crab meat, drained, flaked
¼ cup finely chopped onion
2 tablespoons finely chopped water chestnuts
2 teaspoons soy sauce
¼ teaspoon salt
⅛ teaspoon pepper
   About 28 round dumpling skins (about 3½-inch
   diameter)*
4 to 6 tablespoons vegetable oil
   Chinese mustard
   Soy sauce

1. Beat cream cheese in medium bowl until smooth. Add pork, crab, onion, water chestnuts, 2 teaspoons soy sauce, the salt and pepper; mix well.

2. Work with 1 dumpling skin at a time, keeping remaining skins covered with dry cloth. Place about 1 tablespoon filling off-center on 1 skin. Fold skin in half to enclose filling; moisten edges and pinch to seal. Stand dumpling with pinched edge facing up; press gently to flatten bottom. Cover with dry cloth. Repeat until all filling is used.

(Continued)

3. Heat 2 tablespoons of the oil in each of 2 large heavy skillets over medium heat until hot. Carefully place ½ of the dumplings in single layer in each skillet; do not let dumplings touch. Cook over medium heat until bottoms are brown, about 1 minute. Carefully add ½ cup water to each skillet. Reduce heat; simmer, covered, 10 minutes.

4. Uncover skillets; cook until water evaporates, 3 to 5 minutes. Add more oil if necessary to prevent sticking; cook, uncovered, 1 minute longer. Serve with mustard and soy sauce.

Note: *If round dumpling skins are not available, use thin square wonton skins; cut into rounds with 3½-inch cutter. Cooked dumplings can be kept warm in preheated 250°F oven up to 30 minutes before serving.*

ORIENTAL PORK DUMPLINGS

Makes about 36

1 cup finely chopped cooked pork tenderloin
   (about ½ of 1 tenderloin)
⅓ cup finely chopped Chinese cabbage
⅓ cup finely chopped celery
¼ cup finely chopped green onion
4 to 6 tablespoons plus 1 teaspoon vegetable oil
1 tablespoon soy sauce
1 tablespoon dry sherry
1½ teaspoons cornstarch
   About 36 round dumpling skins (about 3½-inch
   diameter)*
   Chinese mustard
   Soy sauce   *(Continued)*

Pork and Crab Pot Stickers (left); Oriental Pork Dumplings (right)

1. Combine pork, cabbage, celery and green onion in medium bowl; mix well. Mix 1 teaspoon of the oil, 1 tablespoon soy sauce and the sherry in small bowl; stir in cornstarch until smooth. Pour over pork mixture; toss to coat. Refrigerate, covered, 30 minutes.

2. Work with 1 dumpling skin at a time, keeping remaining skins covered with dry cloth. Moisten edges of skin with water; lay skin in palm of hand. Place about 2 teaspoons filling in center of skin. Cup palm to bring sides of skin up around filling; skin will begin to fold and pleat. Squeeze gently from below while pushing down on filling with spatula; squeeze pleats to seal. Flatten bottom slightly. Repeat until all filling is used.

3. Heat 2 tablespoons of the oil in each of 2 large heavy skillets over medium heat until hot. Carefully place ½ of the dumplings in single layer in each skillet; do not let dumplings touch. Cook over medium heat until bottoms are brown, about 1 minute. Carefully add ½ cup water to each skillet. Reduce heat; simmer, covered, 10 minutes.

4. Uncover skillets; cook until water evaporates, 3 to 5 minutes. Add more oil if necessary to prevent sticking; cook, uncovered, 1 minute longer. Serve with mustard and soy sauce.

Note: If round dumpling skins are not available, use thin square wonton skins; cut into rounds with 3½-inch cutter. Cooked dumplings can be kept warm in preheated 250°F oven up to 30 minutes before serving.

Glazed Ham Kabobs

GLAZED HAM KABOBS

Brush some of the basting sauce on the pears as soon as they are threaded on the skewer. This prevents the fruit from turning dark if not cooked immediately.

Makes 6 servings

  1 tablespoon cornstarch
  ½ cup chicken broth
  1 can (8 ounces) sliced pineapple, drained, syrup reserved
  ⅔ cup apricot preserves
  2 teaspoons lemon juice
  1 teaspoon prepared mustard
  ¼ teaspoon ground cinnamon
  ¼ teaspoon ground cloves
  ⅛ teaspoon salt
  3 medium pears
  1½ pounds fully-cooked ham, cut into 1¼-inch cubes
  2 green bell peppers, cut into 1-inch squares
  3 cups hot cooked rice

1. Mix cornstarch with broth in medium saucepan until smooth; stir in reserved pineapple syrup, the preserves, lemon juice, mustard, cinnamon, cloves and salt. Cook and stir over medium heat until sauce thickens and bubbles for 3 minutes. Remove from heat; keep warm.

2. Cut 3 of the pineapple slices into quarters; reserve remaining pineapple for other use. Core pears; cut each into 8 equal pieces. Using 12 metal skewers, thread pineapple, pears, ham and peppers onto skewers, dividing evenly.

3. Brush with sauce. Broil in preheated broiler 5 inches from heat source, turning and basting frequently with sauce, until hot and richly glazed, about 10 minutes. Serve with rice and remaining sauce.

VEAL PICCATA

Makes 4 to 6 servings

  1½ pounds veal scallops, cut ¼ inch thick
  8 tablespoons unsalted butter, room temperature
  1 cup all-purpose flour
  3 large eggs, beaten
  ½ cup veal or chicken stock
  1 tablespoon fresh lemon juice
  ½ teaspoon salt
  ⅛ teaspoon pepper
  1 tablespoon drained capers
  1 tablespoon chopped parsley
  Lemon slices for garnish

1. Pound veal between sheets of waxed paper with flat side of meat mallet until very thin.

2. Heat 4 tablespoons of the butter in large skillet over medium heat until foam subsides. Meanwhile, prepare as many pieces of veal as will fit in single layer in skillet without crowding.

3. Dip veal in flour to coat both sides; shake off excess. Dip in egg to coat both sides; let excess drain off. Saute veal in butter over medium heat, turning once, until brown, about 2 minutes per side. Remove to plate; keep warm. Repeat until all veal has been cooked.

4. Add stock, lemon juice, salt and pepper to skillet; cook and stir over high heat until reduced to coating consistency, 1 to 2 minutes. Reduce heat to low; stir in capers and parsley. Whisk in remaining butter, 1 tablespoon at a time, until smooth and blended. Pour sauce over veal; garnish with lemon slices.

Wine-Roasted Chicken with Rice Dressing

WINE-ROASTED CHICKEN WITH RICE DRESSING

Let the variety of California table wines inspire you to experiment with them in chicken recipes. What fun to try to detect the subtle flavor of a chablis, a chenin blanc or a Riesling.

Makes 4 servings

- 1 cup rice
- 2 tablespoons rendered chicken fat, butter or margarine
- 1 pound chicken gizzards, ground or minced
- 1 cup chopped onion
- ½ cup chopped celery
- 1 tablespoon chopped fresh chives
- 1½ cups chicken broth
- 2 teaspoons salt
- ¾ teaspoon pepper
- 2 tablespoons dry white wine
- 1 teaspoon paprika
- ¼ teaspoon dried rosemary
- 1 broiler-fryer chicken (about 3 pounds), cut into quarters
- Frosted red and green grapes for garnish

1. Cook rice in chicken fat in large skillet over medium heat until golden, about 6 minutes. Add gizzards, onion, celery and chives; saute until the gizzards are brown, about 3 minutes.

2. Add broth, 1 teaspoon of the salt and ½ teaspoon of the pepper; heat to boiling. Stir; reduce heat. Simmer, covered, 20 minutes.

3. Meanwhile, mix wine, paprika, rosemary, the remaining 1
(Continued)

teaspoon salt and the remaining ¼ teaspoon pepper in small bowl. Brush chicken with ½ of the wine mixture.

4. Place chicken, skin side up, in 13 × 9 × 2-inch baking pan. Bake, uncovered, in preheated 425°F oven 20 minutes.

5. Remove chicken from pan. Spoon rice mixture into pan; rearrange chicken on top of rice. Brush with remaining wine mixture; cover pan.

6. Reduce oven setting to 375°F. Bake until chicken is cooked through, about 30 minutes longer. Arrange chicken on top of rice on platter; garnish with grapes.

BLUSHING CHICKEN

Red currant jelly adds a rosy hue to the pan juices, which turn a delicious pink when the sour cream is added.
Makes 8 servings

- 4 broiler-fryer chicken breasts, split
- ½ cup butter or margarine
- ½ cup dry white wine
- 1½ cups red currant jelly
- 1 cup sour cream

1. Cook chicken in butter in large skillet over medium heat, turning once, until brown, about 4 minutes per side.

2. Add wine to skillet; cook, covered, over low heat 15 minutes. Add jelly to skillet; mix well. Continue cooking, turning chicken over and basting frequently, until tender, 15 to 20 minutes longer.

3. Remove chicken to platter; keep warm. Stir sour cream into skillet; cook and stir over very low heat until hot. Do not boil. Pour sauce over chicken.

CHICKEN WITH LIME BUTTER

Makes 6 servings

3 chicken breasts (1 pound each), split, skinned, boned
½ teaspoon salt
½ teaspoon pepper
⅓ cup vegetable oil
   Juice of 1 lime
8 tablespoons butter, room temperature
1 teaspoon minced fresh chives
¾ teaspoon chopped fresh dill or ¼ teaspoon dried dill weed
   Fresh dill sprigs for garnish

1. Sprinkle chicken with salt and pepper. Cook in oil in large skillet over medium heat until light brown, about 3 minutes per side.

2. Reduce heat to low; cook, covered, until tender, about 10 minutes. Remove chicken to plate; keep warm, covered.

3. Drain and discard oil from skillet. Add lime juice; cook over low heat until juice begins to bubble, about 1 minute.

4. Whisk in butter, 1 tablespoon at a time, until butter becomes opaque and forms a thickened sauce. Remove from heat.

5. Stir in chives and chopped dill; spoon sauce over chicken. Garnish with dill sprigs; serve immediately.

NORTHWEST HAZELNUT TURKEY BAKE

Makes 4 servings

1 cup coarsely chopped hazelnuts
½ green bell pepper, diced
2 tablespoons butter
1 can (10¾ ounces) condensed cream of celery soup
½ cup milk
2 cups diced cooked turkey
1 tablespoon chopped pimiento
½ teaspoon salt
8 ounces egg noodles, cooked
   Chopped parsley for garnish

1. Saute hazelnuts and green bell pepper in butter in medium skillet over medium heat until nuts are golden and pepper is tender, about 5 minutes.

2. Mix soup and milk in large bowl until smooth; stir in turkey, pimiento, salt and ¾ of the hazelnut mixture. Add noodles; mix well.

3. Transfer noodle mixture to greased 2-quart baking dish; sprinkle with remaining hazelnut mixture. Bake in preheated 350°F oven until hot throughout, 20 to 30 minutes. Garnish with parsley.

Chicken with Lime Butter

BAKED LOBSTER TAILS

Lettuce makes a novel but practical wrap for cooking lobster tails. The water in the lettuce steams the tender lobster.

Makes 4 to 6 servings

4 to 6 fresh or thawed frozen lobster tails
    (½ pound each)
8 to 12 lettuce leaves
⅔ cup margarine or butter, melted
½ teaspoon salt
¼ to ½ teaspoon garlic powder
    Paprika
    Parsley sprigs for garnish
    Lemon wedges

1. Fan-cut lobster tails by cutting off undershell, leaving tail fan and upper shell intact; place tails, shell side down, on baking sheet. Rinse and drain lettuce; do not pat dry.

2. Mix ⅓ cup of the margarine, the salt and garlic powder in small bowl; brush on lobster meat. Sprinkle lobster with paprika; cover tails completely with damp lettuce leaves.

3. Bake in preheated 400°F oven until lobster meat is opaque throughout, 15 to 20 minutes. Discard lettuce leaves; garnish with parsley. Serve with remaining margarine and lemon wedges.

LIME-GARLIC BROILED SHRIMP

Makes 6 servings

3 cloves garlic, minced
½ cup butter or margarine
2 tablespoons fresh lime juice
½ teaspoon salt
    Dash freshly ground pepper
2 pounds shrimp, shelled, deveined
2 tablespoons chopped parsley

(Continued)

1. Saute garlic in butter in small skillet over medium heat until tender but not brown, about 1 minute. Remove from heat; stir in lime juice, salt and pepper.

2. Arrange shrimp in single layer in 15 × 10 × 1-inch baking pan. Pour butter sauce over shrimp.

3. Broil in preheated broiler, 4 inches from heat source, until shrimp are opaque throughout, about 8 minutes. Sprinkle with parsley; serve immediately.

SANDDABS ORIENTAL

Smallest fish of the sole family, sanddabs make a tasty catch for sport and commercial fishermen. These delicate flatfish are unique to the Pacific and cook quickly in a Chinese or improvised steamer.

Makes 6 servings

3 pounds fresh or thawed frozen dressed
    sanddabs or sole fillets
1 tablespoon grated fresh ginger root
2 teaspoons salt
4 whole green onions
1 quart boiling water
⅓ cup peanut or vegetable oil, heated
⅓ cup soy sauce
    Slivered green onions

1. Arrange fish on heat-proof platter; sprinkle with ginger and salt. Top with whole green onions. Place platter on rack in steamer; add boiling water to steamer.

2. Steam, covered, over medium-low heat until the fish is opaque throughout, 5 to 10 minutes. Remove platter from steamer. Discard cooked onions; drain water from platter.

3. Mix oil and soy sauce in small bowl; pour over fish. Garnish with slivered green onions.

Baked Lobster Tails

Tempura

TEMPURA

Makes 4 servings

- **1 pound jumbo shrimp, shelled, deveined, tails intact**
- **2 small green bell peppers**
- **6 fresh shiitake mushrooms or 8 cultivated white mushrooms**
- **1 large carrot**
- **1 small mild red onion**
- **¼ pound fresh green beans, trimmed**
- **1 cup dashi***
- **¼ cup soy sauce**
- **2½ tablespoons sake**
- **1½ teaspoons sugar**
- **5 cups vegetable oil**
- **1 cup ice water**
- **1 large egg yolk**
- **1 cup plus 1 tablespoon all-purpose flour**
- **1 tablespoon cornstarch**
- **¼ cup grated daikon (Japanese white radish)**
- **2 teaspoons grated fresh ginger root**

1. Make 4 or 5 deep cuts crosswise in underside of each shrimp to prevent curling. Cut green bell peppers lengthwise into 6 equal pieces; cut pieces crosswise into halves. Remove and discard mushroom stems; cut caps into halves or, if large, into quarters.

2. Cut carrot crosswise into 2-inch lengths; cut each piece lengthwise into ⅛-inch-thick slices. Cut onion crosswise into ⅜-inch-thick slices; separate into rings. Pat shrimp and all vegetables thoroughly dry.   *(Continued)*

3. Mix dashi, soy sauce, sake and sugar in small saucepan; heat over medium heat to simmering. Remove from heat; keep warm.

4. Heat wok over high heat 30 seconds. Add oil; heat to 350°F. Adjust heat to maintain temperature.

5. Beat ice water and egg yolk in medium bowl. Add 1 cup of the flour and the cornstarch all at once; stir briefly with fork just to combine. Batter will be lumpy; do not overmix.

6. Working quickly, dip and fry foods according to following directions. Serve individual foods as they are cooked, or keep warm on rack in preheated 250°F oven for a short time. Tempura is served with the dashi mixture for dipping, to which daikon and ginger are added according to individual taste.

7. Dip shrimp into batter to coat; shake off excess. Fry 4 shrimp at a time, turning once, until batter is crisp and golden and shrimp are cooked through, 2 to 3 minutes. Remove with slotted spoon; drain on paper toweling. If batter seems too thin, stir in remaining 1 tablespoon flour.

8. Dip and fry 5 or 6 carrot slices at a time, about 2 minutes. Fry 6 green beans at a time, about 2 minutes. Fry 4 mushroom pieces at a time, 1 to 2 minutes. Fry 4 or 5 onion rings at a time, about 1 minute. Fry 5 or 6 green pepper pieces at a time, about 45 seconds.

*Note: *Dashi is a stock made from flakes of dried bonito fish. Instant dried dashi granules can be purchased in small packets or glass jars (similar to instant bouillon granules); all that is required is to add boiling water.*

Curried Salmon and Rice

CURRIED SALMON AND RICE

Curry powder seasons this dish that started in India, went round the world with the British, and finds a welcome wherever fresh, canned or smoked salmon is available.

Makes 4 main-dish servings

¼ cup thinly sliced green onions
¼ cup finely chopped green bell peppers
¼ cup finely chopped celery
2 tablespoons vegetable oil
1 to 2 tablespoons curry powder
3 cups cooked long-grain rice
1 pound cooked salmon, skinned, boned, flaked,
   or 1 can (15½ ounces) salmon, drained,
   skinned, flaked
2 hard-cooked eggs, cut into wedges
   Parsley sprigs for garnish
   Mustard Mayonnaise (recipe follows)

1. Saute onions, green pepper and celery in oil in small skillet over medium heat 2 minutes; stir in curry powder.

2. Combine rice and onion mixture in medium bowl; mix well. Spoon onto platter.

3. Arrange salmon on top of rice; arrange eggs at ends of platter. Garnish with parsley; serve with Mustard Mayonnaise.

MUSTARD MAYONNAISE

1 cup mayonnaise
1 tablespoon Dijon-style mustard
   Salt and pepper to taste

Mix all ingredients in small bowl.

Makes about 1 cup

HANGTOWN FRY

There's many a story about this dish from California's gold rush days when fresh eggs and Puget Sound oysters were scarce. In one story, a prisoner in the Hangtown jail requested fried eggs and oysters for his last meal. It took so long to ship them in that he escaped before they arrived.

Makes 6 servings

3 slices bacon, cut in 1-inch pieces
8 large eggs
¼ cup water
½ teaspoon salt
   Pinch pepper
½ cup dry bread or cracker crumbs
⅓ cup all-purpose flour
1 can (12 ounces) fresh or thawed frozen medium
   Pacific oysters, drained
¼ cup milk
2 tablespoons melted margarine or vegetable oil
2 teaspoons minced parsley
   Lemon wedges

1. Cook bacon in 10-inch skillet over medium heat until crisp; drain on paper toweling, reserving drippings.

2. Combine eggs, water, salt and pepper in medium bowl; beat slightly.

3. Mix breadcrumbs and flour in shallow bowl. Dip oysters in milk, then roll in breadcrumb mixture to coat evenly. Fry in margarine and bacon drippings over medium heat, turning once, until light brown, 2 to 3 minutes.

4. Sprinkle bacon over oysters; pour egg mixture over oysters. Cook over low heat, gently lifting edge of omelet with spatula to allow uncooked egg to flow to bottom of pan, just until eggs are set. Sprinkle with parsley; serve immediately with lemon wedges.

SOLE VERONIQUE

Makes 4 to 6 servings

2 pounds fresh or thawed frozen Dover sole
    fillets or other fish fillets
2 tablespoons lemon juice
1 teaspoon salt
1 cup dry white wine
1 cup green seedless grapes
¼ teaspoon fines herbes*
3 tablespoons margarine or butter
2 tablespoons all-purpose flour

1. Cut fish into serving-size pieces; sprinkle with lemon juice and salt. Arrange in well-greased 10-inch skillet in 1 or 2 layers.

2. Combine wine, grapes and fines herbes; pour over fish. Heat to simmering. Poach, covered, over low heat until fish flakes with fork, about 5 minutes.

3. Carefully remove fish from skillet; drain on paper toweling, then place on flameproof platter. Strain poaching liquid, reserving grapes.

4. Melt margarine in small saucepan. Stir in flour until smooth; cook and stir over medium heat until bubbly. Gradually whisk in poaching liquid until smooth. Cook and stir until sauce thickens and bubbles for 1 minute. If sauce is too thick, thin with small amount of additional wine or water.

5. Spoon sauce evenly over fish. Broil in preheated broiler, 4 inches from heat source, just until sauce is golden. Arrange reserved grapes around fish; serve immediately.

Note: A mixture of equal parts chives, parsley and tarragon can be substituted for fines herbes.

FOIL-BAKED SALMON

Makes 6 servings

2 tablespoons butter or margarine
2 medium onions, chopped
1 large green bell pepper, chopped
1 large tomato, seeded, diced
1 cup sliced mushrooms
2 tablespoons chopped parsley
2 tablespoons butter, finely diced
1 whole dressed salmon (4 to 6 pounds)
½ teaspoon salt
¼ teaspoon ground black pepper
3 slices bacon
    Parsley sprigs for garnish
    Lemon wedges

1. Line large baking dish with heavy-duty aluminum foil; spread foil with 2 tablespoons butter.

2. Mix onions, green bell pepper, tomato, mushrooms, chopped parsley and diced butter in medium bowl.

3. Place salmon in foil. Sprinkle body cavity with salt and ground pepper; fill with onion mixture. Secure opening with wooden picks. Top salmon with bacon; enclose in foil, sealing well.

4. Bake in preheated 450°F oven until salmon is opaque, 30 to 40 minutes. Carefully remove salmon from foil; place on serving platter. Remove skin from top of salmon. Garnish with parsley sprigs; serve with lemon wedges.

BROILED SALMON WITH GARLIC MAYONNAISE

Each clove of garlic has a thin skin to be removed before mincing. Place garlic on waxed paper and lay the flat side of a wide knife over it. Press down on the knife with the heel of the hand until garlic skin splits and peels off easily.

Makes 4 to 6 servings

2 large egg yolks, room temperature
4 large cloves garlic
1 teaspoon dry mustard
¼ teaspoon salt
¼ teaspoon white pepper
1 cup olive oil
1½ tablespoons fresh lemon juice, room
    temperature
4 to 6 salmon steaks (1 inch thick)
2 tablespoons butter, melted
    Lemon wedges
    Parsley sprigs for garnish

1. For mayonnaise, combine egg yolks, garlic, mustard, salt and pepper in blender container; process at medium speed until smooth.

2. With motor running at medium speed, add ½ of the oil in slow steady stream. Stop motor; scrape down sides of container. With motor running, add lemon juice; add remaining oil in slow steady stream. Stop motor and scrape down sides of container occasionally as sauce thickens.

3. Place salmon on preheated oiled broiler pan; brush with butter. Broil in preheated broiler, 2 to 3 inches from heat source, turning once, just until opaque throughout, 3 to 5 minutes per side. Serve with garlic mayonnaise and lemon wedges; garnish with parsley.

Broiled Salmon with Garlic Mayonnaise

CALIFORNIA PAELLA

A delectable assortment of shellfish, fish and chicken join saffron rice and vegetables in a stunning main dish transplanted from Spain.

Makes 6 servings

    6 cups chicken stock
    1 cup chopped onion
    2 large cloves garlic, finely chopped
    3 to 4 tablespoons olive oil
    2 cups long-grain rice
1½ cups Riesling wine
    2 tablespoons lemon juice
    1 teaspoon paprika
    1 teaspoon salt
    ¼ teaspoon saffron
    ¼ teaspoon ground black pepper
    1 bay leaf
    1 pound red snapper fillets, cut into 1½-inch pieces
    3 tomatoes, peeled, seeded, chopped
    6 fresh artichoke hearts, cooked, or 1 package (9 ounces) frozen artichoke hearts, thawed
    6 mussels, scrubbed, debearded
    6 hard-shell clams, scrubbed
    6 cooked chicken drumsticks
    6 large prawns, shelled, deveined, tails intact
    1 cup fresh or frozen peas
    1 red bell pepper, cut into strips
    Lemon wedges

1. Cook stock, uncovered, in medium saucepan over medium heat until reduced to 3 cups.   *(Continued)*

Snapper with Opakapaka-Mango Sauce

2. Saute onion and garlic in oil in 14-inch paella pan, shallow casserole or oven-proof skillet over medium heat until soft, about 3 minutes. Stir in rice; saute until translucent.

3. Add reduced stock, the wine, lemon juice, paprika, salt, saffron, ground pepper and bay leaf; mix well. Heat to boiling; reduce heat. Simmer, covered, 15 minutes.

4. Uncover pan; toss contents to fluff. Check doneness of rice; add a little water if needed. Stir in snapper, tomatoes and artichokes. Top with mussels, clams, chicken and prawns, pushing them partially into rice; place mussels and clams hinged side down. Sprinkle with peas and red pepper.

5. Bake, tightly covered, in preheated 350°F oven until rice is firm-tender and shellfish have opened, 20 to 30 minutes; discard unopened shells. Serve with lemon wedges.

SNAPPER WITH OPAKAPAKA-MANGO SAUCE

Take a lesson from Hawaiian cooks by including slices of mango or other tropical fruits in fish and meat dishes for mainland meals.

Makes 4 servings

1½ pounds red snapper fillets, skinned, boned, cut into 2-inch squares
  1 tablespoon lemon juice
  1 teaspoon salt
  ½ teaspoon white pepper
  ¼ cup butter
  ½ mango, pared, thinly sliced
    Rice Ring (recipe follows)
  ½ cup dry white wine
  1 cup whipping cream
  1 teaspoon chopped parsley

1. Sprinkle fish with lemon juice, salt and pepper. Saute in butter in large skillet over medium-high heat just until fish is opaque throughout, 3 to 5 minutes. Stir in mango; remove from heat.

2. Unmold Rice Ring onto serving dish. Remove fish and mango from skillet with slotted spoon; place in center of rice. Keep warm.

3. Add wine to skillet; cook over high heat until reduced by half. Stir in cream; cook until sauce is thickened and reduced, 3 to 5 minutes. Spoon sauce over fish and mango; sprinkle with parsley.

RICE RING

  ½ cup diced onion
  3 tablespoons vegetable oil
  1 cup long-grain rice
  2 cups chicken broth
  1 teaspoon salt
  ¼ teaspoon pepper

1. Saute onion in oil in oven-proof medium saucepan over medium heat 3 minutes. Stir in rice; saute 3 minutes longer. Stir in broth, salt and pepper; heat to boiling.

2. Cover pan tightly. Bake in preheated 400°F oven until rice is tender and liquid has been absorbed, about 45 minutes.

3. Pack rice into well-greased 4-cup ring mold. Keep warm, loosely covered, in 180°F oven until serving time.

Red Snapper Veracruz

RED SNAPPER VERACRUZ

When Californians borrow recipes from their Mexican neighbors, dishes like this enticing red snapper with onions and olives reach a whole new group of enthusiasts.

Makes 6 servings

  6 red snapper fillets (8 to 10 ounces each)
  ¼ teaspoon salt
  ⅛ teaspoon pepper
  ⅓ cup all-purpose flour
  3 cloves garlic, sliced
  ¼ cup olive oil
  2 medium white onions, slivered
  1½ pounds fresh plum tomatoes, peeled, seeded,
      finely chopped
  ½ cup tomato juice
  ¼ cup fresh lime juice
  ¼ cup sliced pimiento-stuffed olives
  1 or 2 pickled jalapeno chilies, seeded, finely
      chopped
  1 tablespoon drained capers
  1 bay leaf
  3 pounds cooked small red-skinned potatoes, cut
      into halves
  Chopped fresh coriander   *(Continued)*

1. Sprinkle fish with salt and pepper. Dip in flour to coat both sides; shake off excess.

2. Saute garlic in oil in 12-inch skillet over medium heat until golden, 2 to 3 minutes. Remove garlic with slotted spoon; discard.

3. Add as many fillets to skillet as will fit in single layer without crowding. Cook over medium heat, turning once, until light brown, about 2 minutes per side; remove to plate. Repeat with remaining fillets.

4. Add onions to skillet; saute over medium heat until soft, about 4 minutes. Stir in tomatoes, tomato juice, lime juice, olives, chilies, capers and bay leaf. Heat over high heat to boiling; reduce heat to low. Simmer, covered, 15 minutes.

5. Add any juices which have collected from fish on plate to skillet. Cook sauce, uncovered, over medium-high heat, stirring frequently, until thickened, 2 to 3 minutes. Remove and discard bay leaf.

6. Add fish to skillet. Spoon sauce over fish; reduce heat to low. Simmer, covered, just until fish is opaque throughout, 3 to 5 minutes. Serve immediately with potatoes; sprinkle with coriander.

Steak Salad with Sherry Vinaigrette

STEAK SALAD WITH SHERRY VINAIGRETTE

Score the flank steak by making diamond-shaped cuts diagonally on both sides of the meat. This will give the marinade more surface on which to work.

Makes 4 servings

   3 tablespoons white wine vinegar
   3 tablespoons dry sherry
   1 clove garlic, finely chopped
   ¼ teaspoon salt
   ⅛ teaspoon white pepper
   1 pound beef flank steak
   ¼ cup vegetable oil
   6 cups mixed salad greens (such as watercress,
       romaine, butter or red leaf lettuce)
   2 ounces blue cheese, crumbled
   ¼ cup sliced green onions

1. Mix vinegar, sherry, garlic, salt and pepper in small bowl; pour over steak in glass dish. Refrigerate, covered, turning occasionally, several hours or overnight.

2. Remove steak from marinade; reserve marinade. Broil steak 3 inches from heat source, 6 minutes per side for rare or until desired doneness. Let stand 10 minutes.

3. Whisk oil into reserved marinade until blended. Divide salad greens evenly among 4 plates.

4. Cut steak across the grain into thin slices; arrange steak and cheese on top of salad greens. Sprinkle with onions; serve with dressing.

APPLE SALAD WITH CURRY DRESSING

Frozen juice concentrate carries the good flavor of apples right into the salad dressing, where it picks up the pleasant spiciness of curry.

Makes 6 servings

   2 medium apples
   1 tablespoon lemon juice
   6 cups mixed salad greens in bite-size pieces
   1 cup diced (½-inch) Cheddar cheese
   ½ cup chopped celery
   ½ cup raisins
       Curry Dressing (recipe follows)

1. Core and chop apples; toss with lemon juice in large bowl. Add salad greens, cheese, celery and raisins; toss to mix. Refrigerate, covered, until serving time.

2. Just before serving, add Curry Dressing to taste; toss lightly.

CURRY DRESSING

   ⅔ cup vegetable oil
   ⅓ cup white wine vinegar
   3 tablespoons frozen apple juice concentrate,
       thawed
   1 tablespoon sugar
   ½ teaspoon celery salt
   ½ teaspoon curry powder

Combine all ingredients in jar with tight-fitting lid; shake vigorously until blended.

Makes about 1¼ cups

CHINESE CHICKEN SALAD

Here's an easy combination marinade and salad dressing with Oriental accents of soy sauce and sesame seeds.

Makes 6 servings

Sesame Seed Dressing (recipe follows)
4 cups cooked chicken cut in strips
¼ fresh pineapple, cored, sliced, or 1½ cups
    drained canned pineapple chunks
1 cup sliced celery
1 cup pitted ripe olives
1 cup red and green bell pepper strips
Lettuce leaves
Green onion flowers for garnish

1. Combine Sesame Seed Dressing and chicken in medium bowl. Refrigerate, covered, stirring occasionally, 1 to 2 hours.

2. Remove chicken from dressing with slotted spoon. Arrange chicken, pineapple, celery, olives and pepper on bed of lettuce. Garnish with onion flowers; serve with remaining dressing.

SESAME SEED DRESSING

⅓ cup rice vinegar
⅓ cup sugar
2 tablespoons finely chopped green onion
1½ teaspoons dry mustard
1½ teaspoons soy sauce
1 cup vegetable oil
1 tablespoon toasted sesame seeds

Mix vinegar, sugar, onion, mustard and soy sauce in medium bowl; gradually whisk in oil until blended. Stir in sesame seeds.

TACO SALAD

Makes 4 to 6 servings

1 pound ground beef
1 cup chopped onion
1 pound processed cheese food, diced
1 large tomato, chopped
2 to 4 ounces canned chopped green chilies,
    drained
1 medium head iceberg lettuce, torn into bite-size
    pieces
1 avocado, pared, pitted, chopped
1 cup canned kidney beans, drained
1 small green bell pepper, chopped
½ cup sliced pitted ripe olives
¼ cup sliced green onions
1 bag (7 to 8 ounces) corn chips, coarsely
    crumbled

1. Cook and stir beef and onion in large skillet over medium heat until beef is no longer pink, about 10 minutes; drain and discard drippings.

2. Add cheese to skillet; mix well. Cook and stir over medium-low heat until cheese is melted, about 5 minutes. Stir in tomato and chilies; cook and stir 1 minute.

3. Combine lettuce, avocado, beans, green pepper, olives and green onions in large bowl; toss to mix well. Divide evenly among salad plates; sprinkle with corn chips. Top with hot beef mixture.

To microwave: Crumble beef into 2-quart microwave-safe casserole; stir in onion. Microwave, covered, on HIGH, stirring once, 4 to 5 minutes; drain. Stir in cheese; microwave, covered, on HIGH, stirring once, until cheese is melted, 3 to 4 minutes. Stir in tomato and chilies; microwave on HIGH 30 seconds. Assemble salad as directed in Step 3.

Chinese Chicken Salad

CANTALOUPE WEDGES WITH HONEY DRESSING

Makes 4 servings

1 cantaloupe, cut into quarters, seeded
1 cup fresh blueberries or sliced strawberries or bananas
½ cup large-curd cottage cheese
1 tablespoon honey
1 tablespoon fresh orange juice
1 teaspoon grated orange rind
½ cup chopped pecans

1. Place cantaloupe quarters on platter. Spoon ¼ cup of the fruit into center of each quarter.

2. Combine cottage cheese, honey, orange juice and orange rind in blender container; process until smooth. Stir in pecans; spoon over fruit.

HEARTS OF PALM SALAD

Makes 8 servings

1 small head iceberg lettuce, shredded
4 large tomatoes, sliced
1 can (14 ounces) hearts of palm, drained, sliced
6 tablespoons olive oil
¼ cup lemon juice
2 teaspoons sugar
1 teaspoon salt
½ teaspoon ground cumin
¼ teaspoon ground turmeric
⅛ teaspoon pepper

1. Arrange lettuce on 8 salad plates; top with tomatoes and hearts of palm.

2. Whisk remaining ingredients in small bowl until blended; pour over salads and serve.

King Crab Celery Victor

ARTICHOKE BOTTOMS AND SPINACH

To get to the "bottom" of an artichoke, remove all leaves, choke and stem. With a sharp knife, trim the base into a cup, and simmer in boiling salted water until fork-tender.

Makes 8 servings

½ pound large mushrooms
6 tablespoons butter
1 tablespoon all-purpose flour
½ cup milk
3 bunches spinach, cooked, chopped, drained well
⅛ teaspoon garlic powder
8 artichoke bottoms, cooked, drained
1 cup sour cream
1 cup mayonnaise
¼ cup lemon juice

1. Remove stems from 8 of the mushrooms. Chop stems and remaining mushrooms. Saute the 8 mushroom caps in 2 tablespoons of the butter in medium skillet over medium heat until tender, about 4 minutes. Remove caps to plate; reserve.

2. Add 2 tablespoons of the butter and the chopped mushrooms to skillet; saute until dry, about 5 minutes.

3. Melt the remaining 2 tablespoons butter in large saucepan over medium heat. Stir in flour until smooth; cook and stir 1 minute. Whisk in milk; cook and stir until sauce thickens and bubbles for 1 minute. Stir in spinach, chopped mushrooms and garlic powder.

4. Place artichoke bottoms in single layer in baking dish; top with spinach mixture, dividing evenly.

5. Mix sour cream, mayonnaise and lemon juice in medium saucepan; heat over low heat just until warm. Spoon over spinach; top with reserved mushroom caps.

6. Bake in preheated 375°F oven until hot throughout, about 15 minutes.

KING CRAB CELERY VICTOR

Alaskan king crabs are the big ones, sometimes measuring six feet across and known for their succulent white meat.

Makes 6 servings

2 packages (6 ounces each) fresh, pasteurized or thawed frozen king crab meat or other crab meat
2 celery hearts
2 chicken bouillon cubes
3 cups boiling water
1 cup bottled French dressing
Romaine and Boston lettuce
Green seedless grapes and orange segments
Mint sprig for garnish

1. Drain crab meat; cut into 1-inch pieces. Cut celery hearts lengthwise into thirds; cut crosswise into 5-inch lengths.

2. Dissolve bouillon cubes in boiling water in 10-inch skillet; add celery. Simmer, covered, until celery is crisp-tender, about 10 minutes. Let celery cool completely in bouillon.

3. Drain celery; mix with French dressing in shallow bowl. Refrigerate, covered, at least 2 hours.

4. To serve, drain celery; arrange with crab meat and remaining ingredients in serving bowl.

West Coast Stuffed Eggplant

WEST COAST STUFFED EGGPLANT

Makes 4 to 6 servings

1 medium oval eggplant
4 tablespoons plus 1 teaspoon olive oil
2 large ripe tomatoes, peeled, chopped
1 large onion, chopped
2 cloves garlic, minced
4 tablespoons chopped parsley
    Salt and freshly ground pepper to taste
    Cherry tomatoes for garnish

1. Cut eggplant lengthwise in half; score cut sides with knife. Place, cut side down, in large saucepan or Dutch oven; add 2 inches water and 1 teaspoon of the oil. Heat to boiling; reduce heat to medium. Steam, covered, until flesh softens, 10 to 20 minutes. *(Continued)*

2. Drain eggplant; let stand until cool enough to handle. Remove as much eggplant pulp as possible from each half, without piercing skin; dice eggplant pulp.

3. Saute diced eggplant, chopped tomatoes, onion and garlic in 2 tablespoons of the oil in large skillet over medium heat 3 minutes; remove from heat. Stir in 2 tablespoons of the parsley and the salt and pepper.

4. Brush 12 × 9-inch baking dish with 1 tablespoon of the oil. Spoon tomato-eggplant mixture into eggplant skins; place in baking dish. Drizzle stuffed eggplants with remaining 1 tablespoon oil.

5. Bake in preheated 325°F oven until hot throughout, about 30 minutes. Serve hot or at room temperature. Sprinkle with remaining 2 tablespoons parsley just before serving; garnish with cherry tomatoes.

Empress of the East Salad

EMPRESS OF THE EAST SALAD

Chinese cabbage or long cabbage looks more like celery than its round American cousin. The head is oval with light green fringed leaves on white stalks. Bok choy, sometimes called Chinese cabbage, has even longer stalks and dark green leaves.

Makes 6 to 8 servings

 3 cups chopped Chinese cabbage
 ¼ pound spinach, torn into bite-size pieces
 2 cups chopped curly endive
 1 cup diced (1-inch) Swiss cheese
 ¼ cup milk
 1 tablespoon toasted sesame seeds
 2 medium white turnips, pared, cut in julienne
   strips
   Cherry tomatoes
   Ginger Dressing (recipe follows)

1. Toss cabbage, spinach and endive in large bowl; arrange in bed in large shallow salad bowl.

2. Dip cheese in milk, then in sesame seeds to coat. Arrange cheese, turnips and cherry tomatoes on greens. Serve with Ginger Dressing.

GINGER DRESSING

 2 tablespoons all-purpose flour
 2 tablespoons packed light brown sugar
 1 teaspoon salt
 1 teaspoon ground ginger
   Pinch ground red pepper
 1 cup milk
 1 large egg, beaten
 ¼ cup white wine vinegar
 1 teaspoon butter
 1 cup sour cream   *(Continued)*

1. Mix flour, sugar, salt, ginger and pepper in medium saucepan. Mix milk and egg in small bowl; gradually stir into flour mixture.

2. Cook, stirring constantly, over medium heat, until thick; cook and stir 1 minute longer. Remove from heat. Gradually stir in vinegar, then butter; let cool.

3. Fold sour cream into cooled dressing.

Makes about 2 cups

FROZEN BLUE CHEESE DRESSING

Luscious cubes of frozen salad dressing not only give a fresh fruit platter a new and different look, but also make it easy for guests to serve themselves.

Makes 4 to 6 servings

 1 package (3 ounces) cream cheese, room
   temperature
 4 ounces blue cheese
 ⅓ cup mayonnaise
 1 tablespoon lemon juice
 ½ teaspoon salt
 3 stalks celery, minced
 1 cup whipping cream
 4 to 6 cups mixed fresh fruits
 1 small pineapple, cut lengthwise into quarters,
   cored, if desired

1. Beat cream cheese in small mixer bowl until smooth. Add blue cheese, mayonnaise, lemon juice and salt; beat until blended. Stir in celery.

2. Beat cream in small mixer bowl until soft peaks form; fold into cheese mixture. Spread in ¾-inch-thick layer in metal pan; freeze until firm.

3. Just before serving, cut cheese mixture into cubes. Spoon mixed fruits over pineapple quarters on platter; sprinkle with cheese cubes.

GLAZED POTATOES AND CARROTS

Lemon and honey add sparkle and fresh flavor to a couple of vegetable regulars on the family dinner table.

Makes 4 servings

   2 medium potatoes, pared, cut into 1-inch pieces
   4 carrots, cut into 1-inch lengths
   2 tablespoons butter
   2 tablespoons honey
   1 tablespoon fresh lemon juice
   1 tablespoon chopped parsley
   ¼ teaspoon salt
     Pinch pepper

1. Cook potatoes and carrots in large saucepan of boiling water until fork-tender, 8 to 12 minutes; drain well.

2. Combine potatoes, carrots, butter, honey and lemon juice in saucepan; cook, stirring frequently, over medium-low heat until vegetables are glazed, about 5 minutes. Stir in parsley, salt and pepper.

To microwave: Place potatoes in center of 1½-quart microwave-safe casserole; arrange carrots around edge. Add butter, honey and lemon juice. Microwave, covered, on HIGH 5 minutes. Rotate dish ¼ turn; microwave 5 minutes longer. Let stand, covered, 5 minutes. Stir in parsley, salt and pepper.

ASPARAGUS IN SOUR CREAM

Makes 6 to 8 servings

   1 cup sour cream
   ¼ cup mayonnaise
     Juice of 1 lemon
   ¼ cup breadcrumbs
   2 tablespoons butter or margarine, melted
   2 pounds asparagus, cooked, drained
   1 teaspoon paprika

1. Mix sour cream, mayonnaise and lemon juice in small saucepan; heat over medium-low heat just until hot. Mix breadcrumbs and butter in small bowl.

2. Place asparagus in shallow 1½-quart casserole; pour sour cream sauce over asparagus. Sprinkle with buttered breadcrumbs and paprika. Bake in preheated 325°F oven until bubbly, about 20 minutes.

PINEAPPLE KIWI FRUIT SALAD

Peel off the fuzzy brown skin of the kiwi fruit to reveal a pale green flesh easily cut crosswise into bulls-eye slices. New Zealanders changed its name from Chinese gooseberry before introducing it to West Coast markets and across the country.

Makes 4 servings

   ½ cup orange juice
   ½ cup water
   ¼ cup sugar
   ½ teaspoon ground cinnamon
   1 tablespoon lime juice
   ½ small pineapple, pared, cored
   1 pint strawberries, sliced
   2 bananas, sliced
   1 kiwi fruit, pared, sliced
   ¼ cup toasted pine nuts or slivered almonds

(Continued)

1. Heat orange juice, water, sugar and cinnamon in small saucepan to boiling; reduce heat. Simmer, uncovered, 5 minutes. Let cool 10 minutes; stir in lime juice.

2. Cut pineapple lengthwise into 3 wedges; cut wedges crosswise into slices. Combine pineapple, strawberries, bananas and kiwi in large bowl; toss lightly to mix.

3. Pour warm syrup over fruit; stir gently. Refrigerate, covered, until cold. To serve, spoon fruit mixture into individual bowls; sprinkle with nuts.

HARVEST PEAR SALAD

Pears taste wonderful with garden vegetables in an attractive salad arrangement with herbed oil and vinegar.

Makes 2 servings

   ½ to 1 zucchini, sliced
   2 tablespoons white wine vinegar
   ½ teaspoon dried marjoram, crumbled
   ¼ teaspoon salt
   ¼ teaspoon dry mustard
   ⅛ teaspoon pepper
   2 tablespoons olive oil or vegetable oil
   1 Bartlett pear, cored, sliced
   2 teaspoons lemon juice
   1 small tomato, cut into wedges
   2 or 3 thin slices red onion, separated into rings
     Lettuce

1. Add zucchini to small saucepan of boiling water; cook over high heat until water returns to boiling. Rinse under cold water; drain well.

2. For dressing, mix vinegar, marjoram, salt, mustard and pepper in small bowl; whisk in oil until blended.

3. Dip pear into lemon juice. Arrange pear, tomato, zucchini and onion rings on 2 lettuce-lined salad plates and drizzle with dressing. Serve immediately or refrigerate, covered, up to 2 hours.

Harvest Pear Salad

MARINATED MONTEREY SALAD

A composed salad makes an eye-catching alternative to the tossed salad bowl. Place each kind of vegetable in a separate group to show it off!

Makes 4 servings

½ cup white wine vinegar
1 tablespoon chopped parsley
2 teaspoons minced fresh chives
1 teaspoon dried basil, crumbled
½ teaspoon dry mustard
¼ teaspoon pepper
⅛ teaspoon garlic powder
¾ cup vegetable oil
1 can (16 ounces) unsalted cut green beans, drained
½ small head iceberg lettuce
1 can (6½ ounces) water-packed tuna, drained
1 medium potato, pared, cooked, sliced
1 tomato, cut into thin wedges
1 hard-cooked egg, cut into wedges
2 tablespoons chopped red onion
Parsley sprig for garnish

1. For dressing, mix vinegar, parsley, chives, basil, mustard, pepper and garlic powder in small bowl. Gradually whisk in oil until blended.

2. Toss beans with 2 tablespoons of the dressing in medium bowl. Refrigerate, covered, stirring occasionally, 2 hours.

3. Just before serving, tear lettuce into bite-size pieces; place in shallow serving bowl. Mound tuna in center of lettuce; surround with beans. Arrange potato, tomato, egg and onion around beans. Garnish with parsley sprig; serve with remaining dressing.

CRAB LOUIS

This long-time favorite salad was created by the chef at the Olympic Club in Seattle. It gained national attention because of Enrico Caruso's fondness for it during his 1904 tour.

Makes 4 servings

1½ quarts shredded salad greens
Lettuce leaves
1 pound fresh or thawed frozen Dungeness crab meat or other crab meat
1 cup mayonnaise
¼ cup chili sauce
2 tablespoons finely chopped green bell pepper
2 tablespoons finely chopped onion
2 tablespoons finely chopped parsley
⅛ teaspoon ground red pepper
¼ cup whipping cream, whipped
½ pound fresh or thawed frozen Dungeness or king or other crab legs
2 large hard-cooked eggs, cut into quarters
2 tomatoes, cut into quarters
Ripe olives and parsley sprigs for garnish
Lemon wedges

1. Place salad greens on salad plates or in large shallow bowl lined with lettuce leaves. Mound body crab meat on top of greens.

2. Mix mayonnaise, chili sauce, green bell pepper, onion, chopped parsley and ground pepper in small bowl; fold in whipped cream. Spoon over crab meat.

3. Arrange crab legs, eggs and tomatoes around the crab meat. Garnish with olives and parsley sprigs; serve with lemon wedges.

Marinated Monterey Salad

Beef and Potato Salad

BEEF AND POTATO SALAD

Leave the skins on the potatoes when you cook and slice them. You'll serve more vitamins and minerals to your family and also add color and texture to the salad.

Makes 4 servings

  1 pound boneless beef round steak
  ½ pound broccoli
  ¼ cup red wine vinegar
  1 tablespoon Dijon-style mustard
  1 tablespoon chopped fresh basil or 1 teaspoon
      dried basil, crumbled
  2 cloves garlic, finely chopped
  ¾ teaspoon salt
  ½ teaspoon chopped fresh marjoram or ⅛
      teaspoon dried marjoram, crumbled
  ¼ teaspoon white pepper
  ¼ cup vegetable oil
  2 medium red-skinned potatoes, cooked, cut into
      quarters, thinly sliced
  1 cup sliced celery
  ½ cup diced red onion

1. Broil steak in preheated broiler 3 inches from heat source, turning once, to desired doneness, 6 to 7 minutes per side for rare. Let stand 20 minutes.

2. Cut broccoli flowerets into 1-inch pieces; cut stems into thin slices. Cook in large saucepan of boiling water 3 minutes. Rinse under cold running water; drain well.

3. Cut steak across grain into thin slices; cut slices into 1-inch pieces.

4. Combine vinegar, mustard, basil, garlic, salt, marjoram and pepper in large bowl; gradually whisk in oil until blended. Add steak; mix well. Let stand 30 minutes.

5. Add broccoli and remaining ingredients to steak mixture; toss to mix well. Refrigerate, covered, at least 2 hours or up to 5 hours before serving.

MOLDED CHICKEN AND VEGETABLES

Make this colorful, well-seasoned chicken salad first, and then blend in the gelatin and chicken broth.

Makes 8 servings

  6 broiler-fryer chicken thighs
  2 cups water
  1 small yellow onion, sliced
  1 stalk celery, cut in half
  1 cup mayonnaise
  2 tomatoes, peeled, seeded, chopped
  1 green bell pepper, diced
  1 cucumber, pared, seeded, chopped
  2 tablespoons finely chopped green onion
  1 teaspoon salt
  1 teaspoon lemon-pepper seasoning
  1 envelope unflavored gelatin
  ¼ cup cold water
    Lettuce leaves

1. Combine chicken, 2 cups water, yellow onion and celery in large saucepan. Heat to boiling; reduce heat. Simmer, covered, until chicken is very tender, 30 to 45 minutes.

2. Remove chicken to plate. Strain and reserve 1 cup of the chicken broth. When cool enough to handle, skin and debone chicken; cut chicken into ½-inch pieces.

3. Combine chicken, mayonnaise, tomatoes, green bell pepper, cucumber, green onion, salt and lemon-pepper in large bowl; mix well. Refrigerate, covered, until cold.

4. Sprinkle gelatin over cold water in small bowl; let stand 1 minute to soften. Heat reserved 1 cup broth to boiling; add to gelatin. Stir until gelatin is dissolved. Refrigerate, stirring frequently, until mixture is as thick as unbeaten egg white.

5. Add gelatin mixture to chicken mixture; stir gently to mix well. Pour into 2-quart mold or 8 individual molds. Refrigerate until set, several hours. To serve, unmold onto lettuce-lined plate.

PEAR NUT BREAD

Stir up a loaf of delicately spiced fruit bread made from juicy Bartlett pears picked and packed in the Northwest.

Makes 1 loaf

  1 can (16 ounces) Bartlett pear halves
2½ cups all-purpose flour
  ½ cup granulated sugar
  3 teaspoons baking powder
  1 teaspoon salt
  ⅛ teaspoon ground nutmeg
  ¼ cup vegetable oil
  1 large egg, beaten
  2 teaspoons grated orange rind
  ½ cup chopped walnuts
  1 cup sifted powdered sugar
  1 to 2 tablespoons orange juice

1. Drain pears, reserving syrup; reserve 1 pear half for topping. Process remaining pear halves in blender until smooth; transfer to 1-cup measure. Add as much of the reserved pear syrup as needed to make 1 cup. Reserve remaining syrup for other use.

2. Mix flour, granulated sugar, baking powder, salt and nutmeg in large bowl. Mix pear puree, oil, egg and orange rind in medium bowl. Add to flour mixture; stir just until moistened. Fold in walnuts; batter will be stiff.

3. Spoon batter into greased 8½ × 4½ × 2¾-inch loaf pan. Cut reserved pear half into 6 slices; arrange crosswise in a row on top of batter.

4. Bake in preheated 350°F oven until wooden pick inserted near center is withdrawn clean, 50 to 55 minutes. Cool in pan on wire rack 5 minutes.   *(Continued)*

5. Mix powdered sugar and as much of the orange juice as needed to make thin glaze consistency in small bowl until smooth. Remove bread from pan; spoon glaze on top of bread. Cool completely on rack. Wrap bread in aluminum foil; let stand overnight before slicing.

MIXED GRAIN BANANA MUFFINS

Fully ripe bananas give the best results in muffins and quick breads. They are the ones with a deep yellow peel flecked with brown.

Makes 16 to 18 muffins

  ½ cup butter or margarine, room temperature
  ½ cup packed light brown sugar
  2 large eggs
1½ cups mashed ripe bananas (4 to 5 medium)
  ¼ cup milk
  1 cup whole wheat flour
  1 cup quick-cooking oats
  1 teaspoon baking soda
  ½ teaspoon salt
  ½ cup chopped peanuts

1. Beat butter and sugar in large mixer bowl until light and fluffy. Add eggs, 1 at a time, beating well after each addition. Beat in bananas and milk.

2. Mix flour, oats, baking soda and salt in medium bowl; add all at once to banana mixture. Stir with spoon just until moistened; stir in peanuts.

3. Spoon batter into 16 to 18 greased muffin cups, filling ⅔ full. Bake in preheated 375°F oven until wooden pick inserted into center is withdrawn clean, 20 to 25 minutes. Cool in cups on wire rack 3 minutes. Remove from cups; serve warm, or cool completely on racks.

Pear Nut Bread

Blueberry Rice Hot Cakes

SOUR DOUGH RYE BREAD

The name "sour dough" comes from the Alaskan Yukon, but the fame for crusty bread with a unique tang belongs to San Francisco.

Makes 2 loaves

    2 packages (¼ ounces each) active dry yeast
    2 cups warm water (105 to 115°F)
    1 tablespoon sugar
    1 cup rye flour
    1 cup Sour Dough Starter (recipe follows)
    ½ cup plus 1 tablespoon white cornmeal
 1½ tablespoons caraway seeds
    1 tablespoon salt
    1 tablespoon dill weed, if desired
    1 tablespoon dry onion flakes, if desired
    4 to 6 cups bread flour
    1 large egg white
    1 teaspoon water

1. Sprinkle yeast over warm water in large bowl; stir to dissolve. Stir in sugar; let stand 10 minutes.

2. Whisk in rye flour, Sour Dough Starter and ½ cup of the cornmeal until smooth. Stir in caraway seeds, salt, dill and onion flakes. Add as much bread flour as needed, 1 cup at a time, to form stiff dough; mix well after each addition.

3. Knead dough on floured surface until firm, smooth and elastic, about 10 minutes. Divide in half; shape into 2 oval loaves.

4. Sprinkle 2 lightly greased baking sheets with the remaining 1 tablespoon cornmeal; place loaves on cornmeal. Let rise, covered, in warm place until doubled, about 1 hour.

5. Cut 4 shallow slits, 2 to 3 inches long, along sides of each loaf to prevent surface from rupturing. Lightly beat egg white and water in small bowl; brush over loaves.

6. Bake in preheated 450°F oven until bottoms sound hollow when tapped, 20 to 30 minutes. Cool completely on wire racks.

SOUR DOUGH STARTER

    2 cups all-purpose flour
    2 cups warm water
    1 tablespoon sugar

(Continued)

Mix all ingredients thoroughly in large bowl; let stand, covered, in warm place until mixture becomes bubbly and develops sour aroma, 2 to 5 days. Stir down; starter is ready to use. Refrigerate unused portion, loosely covered, several weeks.

BLUEBERRY RICE HOT CAKES

A little leftover cooked rice couldn't find a tastier use than in these fruit-studded buttermilk pancakes.

Makes 1 dozen 4-inch pancakes

    1 cup all-purpose flour
    ¼ cup sugar
    ½ teaspoon salt
    ½ teaspoon baking soda
 1½ cups buttermilk
    1 cup cooked long-grain rice, cold
    2 large eggs, separated
    2 tablespoons butter, melted
    1 teaspoon vanilla
    ¾ cup blueberries
    2 tablespoons vegetable oil
    Walnut-Honey Butter (recipe follows)

1. Mix flour, sugar, salt and baking soda in large bowl. Mix buttermilk, rice, egg yolks, butter and vanilla in medium bowl. Add to flour mixture; stir to mix.

2. Beat egg whites in small mixer bowl until stiff but not dry; fold into batter. Fold in blueberries.

3. Heat oil in 12-inch skillet over medium heat until hot. Using ¼ cup batter for each pancake, cook over medium heat until light brown, 2 to 3 minutes per side. Serve with Walnut-Honey Butter.

WALNUT-HONEY BUTTER

    ½ cup butter, room temperature
    ½ cup honey
    ¼ cup finely chopped walnuts
    ¼ teaspoon vanilla

Combine all ingredients in small mixer bowl; beat until light and fluffy.

Makes about 1¼ cups

Coconut Macadamia Pie

COCONUT MACADAMIA PIE

Most of the world's supply of macadamia nuts comes from the Hawaiian Islands. No wonder quantities stay limited; it can take as long as 18 years for a new grove to produce.

Makes 8 servings

⅓ cup large fresh coconut shreds*
¾ cup toasted whole macadamia nuts
 3 large egg yolks, room temperature
⅔ cup granulated sugar
¼ cup plus 1 tablespoon cornstarch
  Pinch salt
2½ cups half-and-half
½ cup finely grated fresh coconut*
 1 teaspoon vanilla
 1 tablespoon unflavored gelatin
2½ tablespoons cold water
 2 large egg whites, room temperature
 1 baked 9-inch pie shell
1½ cups sweetened whipped cream

1. Toast coconut shreds in small baking pan in preheated 350°F oven until golden, about 4 minutes.

2. Rub macadamia nuts in clean towel to remove salt. Reserve 8 whole nuts for garnish; chop remaining nuts.

(Continued)

3. Beat egg yolks in small mixer bowl until light and fluffy. Mix granulated sugar, cornstarch and salt in large heavy saucepan; gradually stir in half-and-half. Cook, stirring constantly, over medium heat until mixture simmers; remove from heat. Gradually stir ½ cup of the hot mixture into egg yolks; gradually stir egg yolk mixture into remaining hot mixture in pan. Cook, stirring constantly, over very low heat until thickened, about 6 minutes; do not boil. Remove from heat; stir in finely grated coconut and vanilla. Transfer custard to large bowl.

4. Sprinkle gelatin over cold water in small saucepan; let stand 1 minute to soften. Cook and stir over low heat just until gelatin is dissolved. Stir into custard. Refrigerate, stirring occasionally, until as thick as unbeaten egg white, about 30 minutes.

5. Beat egg whites in clean small mixer bowl until stiff but not dry. Fold ½ of the egg whites into custard. Fold in chopped nuts. Fold in remaining egg whites. Pour into baked pie shell, mounding filling in center. Refrigerate until set, at least 2 hours. Top with sweetened whipped cream and reserved nuts; sprinkle toasted coconut shreds around edge of pie.

Note: *To shell fresh coconut, puncture eyes with ice pick or nail and hammer. Drain and discard coconut liquid. Bake coconut in preheated 375°F oven 12 to 15 minutes. Crack shell open with hammer. Remove coconut meat from shell; pare brown skin from coconut meat.*

STRAWBERRY SPONGE SHORTCAKE

Makes 6 to 8 servings

2 large eggs
⅓ cup sugar
⅛ teaspoon salt
⅓ cup all-purpose flour
¼ cup cornstarch
1 cup whipping cream, whipped
Strawberry Filling (recipe follows)
Whole strawberries for garnish

1. Grease and flour bottom of 8-inch round cake pan.

2. Beat eggs in large mixer bowl until fluffy. Gradually beat in sugar and salt; beat until mixture is doubled in volume and mounds slightly when dropped from spoon.

3. Mix flour and cornstarch in small bowl. Sift over egg mixture; fold in. Pour into prepared pan.

4. Bake in preheated 350°F oven until top springs back when lightly touched, about 25 minutes. Cool in pan on wire rack 5 minutes. Remove from pan; cool completely on rack.

5. Cut cake horizontally in half with serrated knife. Place 1 layer on serving plate, cut side up; spread with 1 cup of the whipped cream. Top with 1 cup of the Strawberry Filling; cover with remaining cake layer. Spread remaining 1 cup Strawberry Filling on top of cake. Press remaining whipped cream through pastry bag fitted with star tip in rosettes on top of cake. Garnish with strawberries.

STRAWBERRY FILLING

¼ cup sugar
1 tablespoon cornstarch
½ cup water
½ cup crushed fresh strawberries
1½ cups sliced strawberries

1. Mix sugar and cornstarch in small saucepan; stir in water until smooth. Add crushed strawberries.

2. Cook, stirring constantly, over medium heat until mixture thickens and bubbles for 3 minutes. Stir in sliced strawberries; cool completely.

Makes about 2 cups

EGGNOG PRUNE CAKE

Serve this egg-rich pound cake, fragrantly spiced with nutmeg and containing marvelous bits of rum-soaked prunes throughout, at your next lunch.

Makes 12 to 14 servings

12 ounces pitted prunes (about 2 cups), cut into quarters
¼ cup Jamaica rum or orange juice
2¼ cups all-purpose flour
1¼ cups granulated sugar
1 cup butter or margarine, room temperature
¼ cup sour cream
2½ teaspoons ground nutmeg
1 teaspoon baking powder
½ teaspoon salt
5 large eggs
1 cup chopped walnuts
Powdered sugar

(Continued)

Whole pitted prunes, colored candy sprinkles and red and green candied cherries for garnish
Nutmeg Cream (recipe follows)
Sliced almonds and colored sugar, if desired

1. Toss quartered prunes with rum in small bowl; let stand 15 minutes. Drain, reserving rum.

2. Combine 2 cups of the flour, the granulated sugar, butter, sour cream, nutmeg, baking powder, salt and reserved rum in large mixer bowl. Beat on medium speed until smooth, about 3 minutes; mixture will be thick. Add eggs, 1 at a time, beating 1 minute after each addition.

3. Toss drained prunes with remaining ¼ cup flour in small bowl; fold prunes and walnuts into batter. Transfer batter to greased and floured 10-inch tube pan.

4. Bake in preheated 325°F oven until top is brown and springy to the touch, about 1 hour and 10 minutes. Cool cake in pan on wire rack 15 minutes. Remove from pan; cool completely on rack.*

5. Dust cake with powdered sugar. For garnish, roll whole prunes in candy sprinkles to coat; top each with 1 candied cherry. Arrange prunes on top of cake. Serve with Nutmeg Cream sprinkled with almonds and colored sugar.

*Note: Cake can be frozen, wrapped tightly, up to 1 month.

NUTMEG CREAM

1 cup whipping cream
2 tablespoons powdered sugar
1 teaspoon ground nutmeg
½ cup sour cream

Beat cream in small bowl until soft peaks form. Beat in sugar and nutmeg; fold in sour cream. Refrigerate, covered.

Makes about 2½ cups

Eggnog Prune Cake

CHOCOLATE WHISKY FONDUE

Makes 4 servings

    1 cup sugar
    ½ cup cold water
    3 ounces semisweet chocolate, chopped
    3 ounces unsweetened chocolate, chopped
    ¼ cup butter
    2 tablespoons whipping cream
    ¼ cup Scotch whisky
      Pound or angel food cake, cut into 1-inch cubes
      Fresh hulled strawberries and fresh pineapple
        chunks

1. Combine sugar and water in small heavy saucepan; heat over low heat to simmering. Simmer, covered, 5 minutes; remove from heat. Let cool, uncovered, to lukewarm.

2. Combine semisweet and unsweetened chocolates, butter and cream in top of double boiler; cook and stir over hot water until melted and smooth. Remove from water.

3. Add sugar syrup to chocolate mixture in thin stream while stirring with whisk until smooth. Reserve at room temperature until serving time.

4. To serve, reheat chocolate mixture in top of double boiler over hot water just until hot; stir in Scotch. Transfer mixture to warm fondue pot or serving dish. Serve with cake and fruit for dipping. Fondue will thicken as it cools.

Fresh Strawberry Mousse

FRESH STRAWBERRY MOUSSE

The topping for this berries-and-cream dessert is like a strawberry daiquiri with sliced berries added.

Makes 8 servings

    2 pints strawberries, hulled, sliced
    ¾ cup sugar
    2 envelopes unflavored gelatin
    ½ cup water
    1 teaspoon almond extract, if desired
    1 cup whipping cream
    ¼ cup rum

1. Place 2 cups of the strawberries in blender container; process until smooth. Transfer to medium bowl.

2. Mix ½ cup of the sugar and the gelatin in small saucepan; stir in water. Let stand 1 minute. Heat, stirring constantly, over low heat until gelatin dissolves, 2 to 3 minutes.

3. Add gelatin mixture and almond extract to strawberry puree; mix well. Refrigerate, covered, until mixture mounds slightly when dropped from spoon, about 1 hour.

4. Beat cream in small mixer bowl until stiff; fold into gelatin mixture. Pour into 1-quart mold; refrigerate, covered, until firm, about 3 hours.

5. Meanwhile, mix remaining strawberries, remaining ¼ cup sugar and the rum in medium bowl; let stand 1 hour.

6. Process 1 cup of the strawberries and rum in blender until smooth; mix with remaining strawberries and rum.

7. To serve, dip mold quickly into hot water; invert and unmold onto serving dish. Serve with strawberry-rum sauce.

CHERRY AMARETTO CREAM

Amaretto is an almond-flavored liqueur often chosen to complement cherries in sophisticated desserts.

Makes 10 to 12 servings

    2 envelopes unflavored gelatin
    1 cup cold water
    1 can (30 ounces) tart cherry pie filling
    ¼ cup sugar
    2 tablespoons lemon juice
    ¼ teaspoon salt
    ¼ teaspoon almond extract
    2 cups heavy cream, whipped
    2 tablespoons amaretto

1. Sprinkle gelatin over cold water in small saucepan; let stand 1 minute to soften. Cook and stir over low heat until gelatin is dissolved.

2. Finely chop 2 cups of the pie filling; place in large bowl. Stir in gelatin mixture, sugar, lemon juice, salt and almond extract. Refrigerate, stirring occasionally, until mixture thickens enough to mound when dropped from spoon.

3. Fold whipped cream into gelatin mixture; pour into 2-quart mold. Refrigerate until set, several hours.

4. Meanwhile, combine amaretto and the remaining pie filling in medium saucepan; cook over low heat until warm. Let cool to room temperature.

5. To serve, unmold dessert onto serving plate; top with cherry-amaretto sauce.

Apricot Streusel Pie

APRICOT STREUSEL PIE

Be sure to bake at least one pie when fresh apricots are in season. You'll love the buttery topping and hint of orange with the luscious fruit.

Makes 8 servings

   Flaky Pastry (recipe follows)
4½ cups fresh pitted apricot halves
 2 tablespoons fresh lemon juice
 4 tablespoons granulated sugar
 2 large eggs
 2 large egg yolks
 ½ cup packed brown sugar
 ½ cup sour cream
 1 tablespoon cornstarch
 ½ teaspoon vanilla
 ¼ teaspoon grated orange rind
 ⅓ cup plus 2 tablespoons all-purpose flour
 3 tablespoons butter, room temperature

1. Roll out Flaky Pastry on lightly floured surface into 12-inch circle. Fold circle in half; ease and unfold into 9-inch pie pan. Trim edges, leaving ½-inch overhang; fold overhang under itself. Press edges with tines of fork to seal and decorate. Pierce bottom and sides of pie shell in several places with fork.

2. Line pie shell with parchment paper; fill with pie weights or dry beans. Bake in preheated 425°F oven 10 minutes; remove paper and weights. Continue baking until bottom is set but not golden, about 5 minutes longer; cool on wire rack.
(Continued)

3. Toss apricots with lemon juice and 1 tablespoon of the granulated sugar in large bowl. Let stand 15 minutes.

4. Meanwhile, lightly whisk eggs and egg yolks in medium bowl. Stir in brown sugar, sour cream, cornstarch, vanilla and orange rind.

5. For streusel topping, mix flour, butter and remaining 3 tablespoons granulated sugar in small bowl with fingertips until crumbly.

6. Drain apricots; pat very dry with paper toweling. Cover bottom of pie shell with a layer of apricots, cut sides up; top with remaining apricot halves, cut sides down. Spoon egg mixture over apricots; sprinkle evenly with streusel mixture.

7. Bake in preheated 425°F oven 12 minutes. Reduce oven setting to 375°F. Continue baking until filling is bubbly, about 35 minutes longer. Cool completely on wire rack.

FLAKY PASTRY

1½ cups all-purpose flour
 1 teaspoon sugar
 ¼ teaspoon salt
 8 tablespoons unsalted butter, cold
 3 to 4 tablespoons ice water

Mix flour, sugar and salt in medium bowl. Cut in butter until particles the size of small peas form. Gradually add water, stirring and tossing with fork until particles are evenly moistened and just cling together when squeezed. Refrigerate, wrapped in plastic, 1 hour.

Mandarin Chocolate Souffle

MANDARIN CHOCOLATE SOUFFLE

Makes 4 to 6 servings

　Butter and granulated sugar for dish
　3 ounces semisweet chocolate, chopped
　1 tablespoon unsalted butter
　4 large egg yolks
　¼ cup granulated sugar
　2 tablespoons all-purpose flour
　½ cup milk, scalded
1½ teaspoons grated orange rind
　3 to 4 tablespoons orange-flavored liqueur
　6 large egg whites, room temperature
　Powdered sugar, if desired
　Custard Sauce (recipe follows) or sweetened
　　whipped cream

1. Wrap double-thick band of aluminum foil around 6- or 7-cup souffle dish to form collar extending 2 inches above rim of dish. Fasten collar with string. Butter inside of dish and collar; sprinkle with granulated sugar.

2. Melt chocolate and 1 tablespoon butter in top of double boiler over hot water.

3. Whisk egg yolks in heavy 2-quart saucepan. Cook over very low heat, whisking constantly and gradually beating in ¼ cup granulated sugar. Continue cooking and whisking until mixture turns pale yellow and sugar partially dissolves. Add flour; whisk until well blended, 1 to 2 minutes.

4. Remove saucepan from heat; slowly whisk in hot milk. Cook over low heat, whisking constantly, until mixture thickens to consistency of light pudding. Transfer to large bowl.

5. Stir chocolate mixture and orange rind into yolk mixture. Cover surface with lightly buttered plastic wrap; let stand until souffle is ready to be baked, several hours at room temperature. *(Continued)*

6. Just before baking, stir liqueur into chocolate mixture. Beat egg whites in large mixer bowl until stiff but not dry. Fold 1 cup of the whites into chocolate mixture; fold in remaining whites. Pour mixture into souffle dish; smooth top.

7. Place dish in lower third of preheated 400°F oven; immediately reduce oven setting to 375°F. Bake until top is puffed and center is set, 30 to 35 minutes.

8. Carefully remove and discard foil collar. Dust top of souffle with powdered sugar; serve immediately with Custard Sauce.

CUSTARD SAUCE

　7 large egg yolks
　1 cup milk
　1 cup half-and-half
　½ cup sugar
1¼ teaspoons vanilla
　Brandy or cognac, if desired

1. Whisk egg yolks and ½ cup of the milk in 1½-quart heavy saucepan until mixed.

2. Mix remaining ½ cup milk, the half-and-half and sugar in second 1½-quart saucepan. Heat over low heat, stirring once or twice, to simmering.

3. Gradually whisk hot milk mixture into egg-yolk mixture. Cook, stirring constantly, over low heat, until sauce thickens to consistency of unbeaten whipping cream, 5 to 10 minutes. Remove from heat.

4. Strain sauce into medium bowl. Cool to lukewarm; sauce will thicken slightly. Stir in vanilla and brandy to taste. Refrigerate, covered, until cold, about 4 hours.

LEMON SOUR PIE

Makes 6 to 8 servings

1¼ cups sugar
⅓ cup cornstarch
¼ teaspoon salt
1¾ cups water
4 large egg yolks
1 tablespoon butter or margarine
¼ cup lemon juice
2 teaspoons grated lemon rind
3 drops yellow food coloring, if desired
½ cup sour cream
1 packaged graham cracker crumb crust (6-ounce)

1. Mix sugar, cornstarch and salt in medium saucepan. Beat water and egg yolks in small bowl; stir into saucepan. Cook, stirring constantly, over medium heat until thick and bubbling; cook and stir over low heat 1 minute. Remove from heat.

2. Add butter to saucepan; stir until melted. Stir in lemon juice, lemon rind and food coloring. Add sour cream; stir until smooth. Pour into crust. Refrigerate until firm, 2 to 3 hours.

STRAWBERRY RICE PUDDING

Makes 6 servings

1 cup quick-cooking rice
1 cup water
¼ teaspoon salt
1 teaspoon grated orange rind
2 cups milk
1 package (3¾ ounces) instant vanilla pudding mix
1 pint strawberries

1. Combine rice, water and salt in small saucepan. Heat to boiling; remove from heat. Stir in orange rind; let stand, covered, until completely cool.

2. Pour milk into medium bowl. Add pudding mix; beat with electric mixer on low speed until thickened, about 2 minutes. Fold in cooled rice mixture; refrigerate, covered, until firm, at least 15 minutes.

3. Reserve 6 whole berries for garnish; hull remaining berries and cut into halves. Arrange halved berries and pudding mixture in alternating layers in parfait or individual dessert glasses.* Garnish with reserved whole strawberries.

Note: Berries and pudding can be mixed together, if desired.

ALMOND BAVARIAN

Makes 8 servings

½ cup sugar
1 envelope unflavored gelatin
⅛ teaspoon salt
2 large eggs, separated
1¼ cups milk
½ teaspoon almond extract
1 cup whipping cream
Apricot Sauce (recipe follows)
Toasted slivered almonds

(Continued)

1. Mix ¼ cup of the sugar, the gelatin and salt in small saucepan. Whisk egg yolks and milk in small bowl until blended. Stir into gelatin mixture; let stand 1 minute.

2. Cook and stir gelatin mixture over low heat until gelatin is dissolved. Transfer to large bowl; stir in almond extract. Refrigerate, stirring occasionally, until mixture mounds slightly when dropped from spoon.

3. Beat egg whites in small mixer bowl until soft peaks form; gradually beat in remaining ¼ cup sugar until stiff peaks form. Fold into gelatin mixture. Beat cream in small mixer bowl until stiff; fold into gelatin mixture.

4. Spoon into eight 6-ounce molds. Refrigerate until set, several hours. To serve, unmold into serving bowls. Spoon Apricot Sauce over bavarians; sprinkle with almonds.

APRICOT SAUCE

1½ cups apricot nectar
½ cup sugar
½ cup dried apricots, cut into quarters
1 teaspoon fresh lemon juice

Combine all ingredients in medium saucepan; mix well. Heat to boiling; reduce heat. Simmer, covered, until apricots are soft, 20 to 25 minutes. Refrigerate, covered, until cold. *Makes about 2 cups*

BEST EVER WALNUT PIE

Makes 8 servings

1½ cups dark corn syrup
1½ cups packed brown sugar
4 large eggs, lightly beaten
2 teaspoons vanilla
½ teaspoon salt
2 cups walnut pieces
1 unbaked 9-inch pie shell

1. Combine corn syrup, sugar, eggs, vanilla and salt in large bowl; stir briskly until blended; do not beat. Stir in nuts; pour into pie shell.

2. Bake in preheated 400°F oven 10 minutes. Reduce oven setting to 350°F; bake just until edges of filling are set and center trembles slightly, about 40 minutes longer. Cool completely on wire rack.

Almond Bavarian

ACKNOWLEDGMENTS

The Editors of CONSUMER GUIDE® wish to thank the
organizations and companies listed below for their
generous contributions of recipes for use in this book.

Alaska Seafood Marketing Institute
Almond Board of California
American Dairy Association
American Egg Board
American Lamb Council
The American National CowBelles, Inc.
American Soybean Association
The American Spice Trade Association
The Association for Dressings and Sauces
Best Foods (Mazola Corn Oil and Argo/Kingsford's Corn Starch)
Borden Inc.
California Beef Council
The California Dry Bean Advisory Board
California Olive Industry
California Pistachio Commission
California Prune Board
California Turkey Industry Board
Castle & Cooke Foods
Catfish Farmers of America
Chesebrough-Pond's Inc.
Chilean Winter Fruit Association
Chocolate Manufacturers Association of the U.S.A.
CocoRibe Coconut Rum
Cranberry Institute
Del Monte Corporation
Denmark Cheese Association Inc.
Dixie Crystals Sugar
Evaporated Milk Association
Florida Celery Committee
Florida Department of Citrus
Florida Department of Natural Resources
Florida Fruit & Vegetable Association
Florida Strawberry Growers Association
Florida Tomato Exchange
Fresh Garlic Association
Grower's Peanut Food Promotions
Halibut Association of North America
Idaho-Oregon Onion Promotion Committee
International Banana Association
International Olive Oil Council
Iowa Beef Industry Council
Keebler Company
Thomas J. Lipton, Inc.
Louisiana Sweet Potato Commission

Massachusetts Division of Marine Fisheries
The McIlhenny Company
The Michigan Bean Commission
Michigan Blueberry Growers Association
Minnesota Wild Rice Council
Mirassou Sales Co.
National Broiler Council
National Cherry Foundation
National Frozen Food Association, Inc.
The National Hot Dog & Sausage Council
National Kraut Packers Association
National Live Stock and Meat Board
National Marine Fisheries Service
National Pasta Association
National Peach Council
National Pecan Marketing Council
National Pork Producers Council
National Red Cherry Institute
National Turkey Federation
New Zealand Lamb Company, Inc.
North American Blueberry Council
Ocean Spray Cranberries, Inc.
Ohio Sea Grant Program
Oklahoma Peanut Commission
Oregon Filbert Commission
Oregon Fruit Products Company
Oregon Potato Commission
Pacific Bartlett Growers, Inc.
Pacific Coast Canned Pear Service
Peanut Advisory Board
Pepperidge Farm, Inc.
The Popcorn Institute
Rice Council of America
Rice Growers Association of California
The J. M. Smucker Company
South African Rock Lobster Service Corporation
B. F. Trappey's Sons, Inc.
United Fresh Fruit and Vegetable Association
Vermont Maple Industry Council
Walnut Marketing Board
Washington Apple Commission
Washington Fryer Commission
Western Growers Association
Western New York Apple Growers Association, Inc.

PICTURE CREDITS

The Editors of CONSUMER GUIDE® wish to thank the
organizations, companies and individuals listed below for
their generous contributions of photos for use in this book.

Alaska Seafood Marketing Institute, page 178
Almond Board of California, pages 51, 58, 63, 203
American Egg Board, page 40
American Home Foods, page 214 (middle left)
American Lamb Council, page 279
American Soybean Association, pages 156, 210
The American Spice Trade Association, pages 60, 61, 74, 77, 88, 94, 124, 135, 145, 164, 191, 201, 205 (bottom left), 213, 221, 227, 232, 254, 263
Orville Andrews, page 266 (bottom right)
Argo/Kingsford's Corn Starch, page 260
Borden Inc., page 6 (bottom right)
California Beef Council, pages 101, 169, 223, 226, 229 (top left), 290, 297
California Olive Industry, pages 46, 291
California Pistachio Commission, page 273
California Prune Board, pages 45, 206, 301
California Turkey Industry Board, page 233
Castle & Cooke Foods, page 64
Catfish Farmers of America, pages 89, 236, 266 (top right)
Chesebrough-Pond's Inc., page 24
Chilean Winter Fruit Association, pages 216, 278
CocoRibe Coconut Rum, page 137, Back Cover (bottom right)
Carl Corey, Chicago, IL, pages 48, 67, 158, 177, 193, 199, 249
State of Connecticut Department of Economic Development, pages 5 (top left), 6 (top left and middle right)
Del Monte Corporation, pages 159, 238, 296
Dixie Crystals Sugar, pages 142, 259
Carol Eastman, page 152 (top right)
Florida Department of Citrus, pages 73, 81, 139
Florida Department of Commerce, Division of Tourism, page 4 (bottom left and middle right)
Florida Department of Natural Resources, pages 79, 86, 121
Florida Fruit & Vegetable Association, page 126
Florida Strawberry Growers Association, page 302
Florida Tomato Exchange, page 109
Fresh Garlic Association, page 287
Georgia Department of Industry and Trade, page 70 (top left)
Grower's Peanut Food Promotions, pages 141, 148, 218
Idaho-Oregon Onion Promotion Committee, pages 171, 240, 246
Illinois Department of Commerce and Community Affairs, page 152 (bottom left)
State of Indiana Department of Commerce, pages 4 (top right and bottom right), 152 (bottom right)
International Olive Oil Council, pages 108, 293
Thomas J. Lipton, Inc., pages 9, 20, 22, 25, 82, 84, 91, 103, 144, 163, 205 (top right), 247, 269, 275
Louisiana Sweet Potato Commission, pages 107, 125
Debra Lovelien, page 214 (top left)
Maryland Department of Economic & Community Development, Office of Seafood Marketing, page 70 (middle left)
Massachusetts Division of Marine Fisheries, pages 12, 32, 34

Mazola Corn Oil, pages 13, 209, 252, 265
The McIlhenny Company, pages 110, 220, 231, 241, 266 (middle left)
The Michigan Bean Commission, pages 127, 228
Michigan Blueberry Growers Association, pages 200, 208, Back Cover (bottom left)
Jeff Mintz, page 152 (top left)
Missouri Division of Tourism, page 5 (top right)
National Broiler Council, pages 106, 180, 184, 235, 274, 283
National Cherry Foundation, pages 53, 136, 255
The National Hot Dog & Sausage Council, pages 10, 14, 98, 175, 229 (bottom right), 250, 251
National Kraut Packers Association, page 183
National Live Stock and Meat Board, pages 15, 276, 294, 305
National Marine Fisheries Service, pages 35, 75, 83, 85, 87, 92, 93, 122, 244, 284, 292
National Pasta Association, pages 33, 36, 176
National Peach Council, pages 115, 116
National Pecan Marketing Council, pages 37, 56, 72, 119, 131, 133, 138, 147, 179, 242, 253
National Pork Producers Council, pages 18, 95, 167, 170, 280
New York State Department of Commerce, pages 4 (top left and middle left), 6 (bottom left)
North American Blueberry Council, pages 57, 62
Ocean Spray Cranberries, Inc., pages 69, 182, 217, 239
Oklahoma Peanut Commission, pages 59, 78, 151, 197, 264
Oregon Department of Transportation, Travel Information Section, page 266 (top left)
Oregon Filbert Commission, page 245
Oregon Fruit Products Company, page 261
Pacific Bartlett Growers, Inc., page 295
Pacific Coast Canned Pear Service, page 298, Back Cover (middle left)
Peanut Advisory Board (1985), pages 102, 113
The Popcorn Institute, pages 149, 219
Rice Council of America, pages 143, 168, 224, 225, 230, 237, 262, 281, 282, Back Cover (top left)
Rice Growers Association of California, pages 41, 286, 288, 299
Robert K. Seyfried, pages 4 (center), 214 (bottom left)
The J. M. Smucker Company, pages 256, 257
South Carolina Department of Parks, Recreation & Tourism, page 4 (lower left)
Cliff K. Swanson, page 266 (bottom left)
Texas Division of Tourism, pages 70 (top right), 214 (bottom right)
United Fresh Fruit and Vegetable Association, pages 39, 112, 114
State of Vermont, Agency of Development and Community Affairs, Vermont Travel Division, page 6 (top right)
Washington Apple Commission, page 258
State of West Virginia, Governor's Office of Economic and Community Development, page 70 (bottom left)
Wisconsin Division of Tourism, page 152 (middle left)
Wyoming Travel Commission, page 214 (top right)

INDEX

Sister. "Don't you dare look at it!"

She shut it again. But his fingers were still in it.

"Ouch!" he said.

"And that's not all. I don't want a boyfriend. But if I did, it wouldn't be you!"

"But—" said Herbert.

"So march yourself down the stairs!"

"But—" said Herbert.

"And out the door!"

Herbert went slowly down the stairs.

Sister watched to be sure he left. But he didn't leave.